N

Governmental Policy and International Education

Governmental Policy and International Education

Edited by STEWART FRASER

A symposium held at the
International Center
George Peabody College for Teachers
Nashville, Tennessee
October 22–24, 1964

> *sponsored by*
> *Phi Delta Kappa*
> *National Association for*
> *Foreign Student Affairs*
> *Comparative Education Society*

JOHN WILEY & SONS, INC.   *New York · London · Sydney*

Library of Congress Catalog Card Number: 65-26845
Printed in the United States of America

Dedicated to the memory of
ADLAI E. STEVENSON
Statesman and International Educator

Preface

The United States is recognized today as a country with one of the largest populations of foreign students, scholars, and researchers to be found in her institutions of higher learning. In terms, however, of total educational involvement and as a percentage of the total student population, those from overseas represent only a modest proportion. This is quickly discernible when a comparison is made with many Western European countries. In terms, however, of educational aid to various countries, especially many in the so-called developing areas of Asia, Africa, and Latin America, the overseas educational concerns of the United States are significant by any international standard.

The traditional interest of countries such as Britain, France, and Germany in offering higher educational facilities for overseas students is well known. More recently, the growth of foreign student populations in countries as educationally divergent as Australia, Argentina, and the Soviet Union has become a significant and interesting factor in international education.

An important theme of the conference papers presented in this compilation has been the interest, involvement, and at times, perhaps, the lack of governmental interest in international education.

The concern, for the most part, of each of the contributors has centered on their interpretation of the involvement of governmental agencies and their role vis-à-vis nongovernmental agencies in developing international educational and cultural relations with other countries. Some of the contributors, however, have chosen to explore the historical, political, and anthropological approaches to interpreting the cross-cultural effects of education. Other of the contributors have related the role of specific educational institutions to their function in the field of comparative and international education and, indirectly, their influence on governmental interest, policy, and action. The studies in this collection, while oriented generally toward an analysis of governmental policies, cannot be considered as a comprehensive account of contemporary activity. In fact there is a bias clearly discernible in the emphasis on two areas of concentration, namely, the effort of the United States as a relatively recent leader in international education and the growing activities of international communism as an even more recent and major phenomenon in international educational relations.

The studies on the United States are illustrated, for example, by the leadership role of an academic institution in relating the study of comparative education to an understanding of governmental interest in education as a changing force in society. This is well presented in a review of the activities of the Comparative Education Center at the University of Chicago. A perusal of the interests of the Center and the activities of its staff and graduate students illustrates the need for basic research and governmental planning in expanding educational facilities throughout the world. The historical development of the National Association for Foreign Student Affairs, a leading professional association for those working in international education, is also amply discussed. The Association has pioneered the careful scrutiny and study of United States involvement in international education and now plays a major role in adjudicating between university, private, and governmental agencies in their programs for foreign students in the United States. It has recently been concerned with investigating the cultural background of its foreign student clientele, and its efforts in guidance and counseling are now being emulated in other countries with large overseas student populations.

The increasing interest in the traffic of foreign students by the Soviet Union in recent years is illustrated by a review of the growth recorded during the past decade. The study of the role in international education of various European Communist countries is complemented by an analysis of the interest by Communist China in extending its worldwide political influences through intercultural exchanges.

Area studies in this compilation on Canada, France, Germany, Japan, and the United States are illustrative of different levels of involvement by governments in international education. The North American studies are interestingly contrasted to two from Western Europe. The paper on Japan is of a different order. It is an exploratory study linking an economic and historical analysis of educational development with some of the related or causal factors attributable to cross-cultural effects of international education.

The collection of papers has appended to it an extensive and partly annotated bibliography on the conference theme of *governmental and international policy* in educational exchange. This bibliography is included as an aid to developing further studies in the field of "foreign student affairs" and should assist in supplementing the collection of conference papers.

The expansion of international facilities for the interchange of ideas, scholars, and students during the last two decades has been startling and diffusive. Yet the mere increase in travel facilities and the greater availability of international scholarships do not lead automatically to an increased state of good will between countries. The greater understanding of a neighbor's viewpoint, unfortunately, does not guarantee the betterment of international relations. The long history of international education shows clear evidence that alien and subversive, as well as progressive and welcome, ideas are the price that governments may have to pay in facilitating a sojourn abroad of their best young students. The direct interest and greater involvement of governments in educational relations with other countries is likewise no automatic guarantee that beneficial results will obtain to any of the participating parties. The growth, however, of fellowships and greater opportunities for the interchange of students has been generally encouraged by most countries, especially the predominantly so-called recipient countries in Asia, Africa, and Latin America.

That there have been difficulties in governmental exchange programs in countries with diverse backgrounds such as Australia, Britain, France, Germany, the United States, and the Soviet Union does not obviate the fact that greater and more extensive governmental-sponsored educational exchanges are becoming available for overseas study. The manipulation of foreign student exchanges for chauvinistic and nationalistic ends by various countries is an accepted fact in international education. Some countries piously deny such involvement, while others appear to be indifferent to criticism on this point. Some countries, however, proudly emphasize their interest in indoctrinating as well as educating foreign students so that they may become cultural and political infiltrators on their return home. Other nations show evidence of a multiplicity of motives—some of which are internally conflicting and some of which may vary from year to year and from one government agency to another.

The symposium papers presented here reflect a series of generally disparate views on certain of the various problems and successes of governments in international education. They represent a survey of some of the work being accomplished in the extensive field of cross-cultural educational exchange. They will highlight current research and suggest further work which needs to be undertaken before a comprehensive survey can be undertaken in the comparative and international role that governments play in encouraging and/or controlling their educational and cultural relations with other countries.

STEWART FRASER

Peabody International Center
Nashville, Tennessee
August, 1965

Acknowledgments

I am personally indebted to many persons who were involved in the research and presentation of papers at this conference. Their scholarly contributions are gratefully acknowledged.

The late United States Ambassador to the United Nations, the Honorable Adlai Stevenson, graciously opened our Conference on *Governmental Policy and International Education* at Peabody College and later spoke in the War Memorial Building in Nashville on behalf of the United Nations Association of Tennessee. Ambassador Stevenson's speech for the Association, on the occasion of the nineteenth anniversary of the founding of the United Nations, is included with the conference papers in recognition of his long-standing interest in international education. Appreciation is recorded of the kindness of Mrs. Arville Wheeler and Mr. Joseph Sills, of the United Nations Association of Tennessee, in facilitating Mr. Stevenson's visit to Nashville.

Kind acknowledgment is made to President Felix Robb, of Peabody College, for personally encouraging and assisting in the conference arrangements. President Robb's long-standing interest in the welfare of overseas students in the United States and international education is well known and was fully manifest during the symposium.

The assistance in planning and participation by faculty of the various institutions of higher learning in Nashville was most encouraging, and the interest of representatives from Fisk University, Scarritt College, Tennessee Agricultural and Industrial State University, and Vanderbilt University is duly acknowledged. Particular reference is made to the assistance of the conference committee composed of Mr. James Bass, American Airlines, Nashville; Dr. Ina Corinne Brown, Scarritt College;

Dr. Lyman Burbank, Vanderbilt University; Dr. Nelson Fuson, Fisk University; Dr. Edgar Gumbert, Georgia State College; Dr. Almonte Howell, University of North Carolina; Mr. Nelson Nee, University of Tennessee; Dr. Franklin Parker, University of Oklahoma; John Seigenthaler, *The Nashville Tennessean;* Edwin Shea, Nashville Area Chamber of Commerce; and Dr. Malcolm Williams, Tennessee Agricultural and Industrial State University.

I must acknowledge also the considerable help of the Commission on International Relations in Education of *Phi Delta Kappa,* the *Comparative Education Society,* the Research Committee of the *National Association for Foreign Student Affairs,* and especially Peabody College *Psi Campus Chapter* of *Phi Delta Kappa,* whose interest in the proceedings of the conference insured its success.

The generous support of the following community sponsors in Nashville is also most gratefully acknowledged: *American Airlines, International Travel, Nashville Area Chamber of Commerce, The Nashville Tennessean,* and *Trans World Airlines.*

In addition to the various contributors of research papers I have been assisted extensively in the compilation of a suitable bibliography by Franklin Parker, University of Oklahoma, and his associates: Jack C. Willers, University of Illinois; Paul A. McWilliams, University of Connecticut; Richard R. Renner, University of Florida; Josef Mestenhauser, University of Minnesota; and A. Stan Rescoe, George Peabody College for Teachers.

To Mrs. Margaret Walker and Mr. Joseph Sakas, of the Peabody International Center, must go my grateful thanks for seeing the conference program and research papers through their various stages of production. Their untiring secretarial and administrative assistance in producing a viable manuscript from the conference proceedings is greatly appreciated.

Participants in the Conference on Governmental Policy and International Education

DONALD K. ADAMS is Associate Professor of Education and Director of the Center for Development Education, Syracuse University. He holds the doctorate from the University of Connecticut and is a member of the board of directors, Comparative Education Society. He was one of the consultants in the Teacher Education program in Korea of George Peabody College with the International Cooperation Administration, 1957–1958. His latest publication, as co-author, is *Patterns of Education in Contemporary Societies*, 1964.

C. ARNOLD ANDERSON is Professor of Education and Sociology, Director of the Comparative Education Center, The University of Chicago, and a member of the consultant panel, UNESCO International Institute for Educational Planning. He was Fulbright Professor of Sociology at the University of Uppsala in 1955–1956. Dr. Anderson is joint author of *Education, Economy, and Society*, 1961.

HAROLD R. W. BENJAMIN is Emeritus Professor of Education, George Peabody College for Teachers. He holds the doctorate in comparative education from Stanford University. Among his many prominent positions in the field of international education can be listed Dean, College of Education, University of Colorado and University of Maryland; member UNESCO Constitutional Convention, London, 1945; and Director, Division of International Education, United States Office of Education, 1945–1947. Among his many publications can be found his recent *Higher Education in the American Republics*, 1964.

ROBERT M. BJORK is Chairman of the Economics and Sociology Department at George Peabody College for Teachers. He holds the doctorate from

Syracuse University and has taught at the University of Colorado and Syracuse University. He served as Assistant Director of the Seminar in American Studies, Salzburg, Austria.

WILLIAM W. BRICKMAN is Professor of Educational History and Comparative Education at the University of Pennsylvania. He holds the doctorate from New York University and is editor of *School and Society,* a member of the Advisory Committee of East European Exchanges of the Institute of International Education, and a member of the Council of the International Association for the Advancement of Educational Research. Among his many recent publications can be listed his *John Dewey's Impressions of Soviet Russia and the Revolutionary World Mexico-China-Turkey 1929,* 1946.

INA CORINNE BROWN is Professor of Anthropology, Scarritt College, Nashville University Center, Tennessee. She holds the doctorate in Anthropology from the University of Chicago and has served as visiting professor at Peabody College, Fisk University, Vanderbilt University, and the Nashville School of Social Work. She has held the position of Senior Specialist in Social Studies, United States Office of Education, and has written extensively in her field of anthropology; one of her latest works is *Understanding Other Cultures,* 1963.

OLIVER J. CALDWELL is Acting Associate Commissioner and Director Division of International Education in the Office of Education, United States Department of Health, Education, and Welfare. He was born in Foochow, China, where he received his early education, and is a graduate of Oberlin College, Oberlin, Ohio. He has done graduate work and field studies in the United States and China. He has traveled extensively and serves as educational consultant to various United States government agencies and educational institutions and organizations. In addition, he is a regular contributor to professional journals on international education and Far Eastern affairs.

THEODORE HSI-EN CHEN is Professor and Chairman of the Department of Asian Studies and Director of the Asian-Slavic Studies Center, University of Southern California, holding the doctorate from that institution. His special interests lie in Communist education with emphasis on contemporary China. He has written extensively for journals and encyclopaedias and is the author of *Thought Reform of the Chinese Intellectual,* 1960, and *Teacher Training in Communist China,* 1960.

JAMES M. DAVIS is Vice President for Foreign Student Programs of the Institute of International Education, New York. He holds the doctorate from Teachers College, Columbia University, and was, until recently, Director of the International Center and Associate Professor of Higher Education at the University of Michigan. He is a past president of the National Association for

Foreign Student Affairs and past chairman of the Commission on International Relations in Education of Phi Delta Kappa. He has written extensively for journals on foreign student affairs and international education.

STEWART E. FRASER is the Director of the International Center and Professor of Comparative and International Education, George Peabody College for Teachers. A native of Melbourne, Australia, he holds graduate degrees from Melbourne, Oxford, and Stanford Universities and the doctorate from the University of Colorado. He has written various articles in international education and recent books include *Jullien's Plan for Comparative Education 1816–1817,* 1964, and *Chinese Communist Education: Records of the First Decade,* 1965.

RENÉ GOLDMAN is in the process of completing his doctorate at Columbia University and is a member of the Asian Studies Department, University of British Columbia. He was born in Luxembourg, received his early education in French and Polish schools, and was a foreign student at Peking University, China, 1953–1958. He has contributed to an anthology of ancient Chinese folknovels translated into French for UNESCO. He took his M.A. at Columbia University with the assistance of a Ford Foundation Fellowship and has written several articles for journals including the *China Quarterly.*

JOSEPH KATZ is Professor of Education at the University of British Columbia, Vancouver, Canada. He is the chairman of the Commission of International Relations in Education of Phi Delta Kappa, past president of the Comparative Education Society, and author of many books and articles. Recent publications include symposia *Canadian Education Today,* 1956, and *Elementary Education in Canada,* 1961.

M. ROBERT KLINGER is Acting Director of the International Center, University of Michigan, and holds the doctorate from that institution. He is president of the National Association for Foreign Students Affairs and has served in various capacities in respect to international and foreign student affairs. He is a regular contributor to the *NAFSA Newsletter* and has written articles for the *Personnel and Guidance Journal.*

JOSEF A. MESTENHAUSER is Assistant Professor and Assistant Director of the Office of the Adviser to Foreign Students, University of Minnesota, and holds the doctorate from that institution. He is a member of the Board of Directors, National Association for Foreign Student Affairs and has served as educational specialist attached to the United States Consulate General in Hong Kong. Dr. Mestenhauser was, for a short term, consultant to the Fulbright Commission, serving as Fulbright lecturer in Korea and the Philippines. He has written several articles for journals including the *Journal of College and Student Personnel.*

WIEGAND PABSCH was Deputy Chief of the Cultural Section and is now Second Secretary of the Embassy of the Federal Republic of Germany, Washington, D.C. He holds the degree of Doctor in Law, and has been Assistant Teacher of Penal Law at the University of Bonn, Germany, and served in the capacity of Assistant Judge in Bonn, Germany. Prior to his present appointment, Dr. Pabsch served as Attaché, German Embassy in Ankara, Turkey, and in the Minister's Bureau of the Foreign Office, Bonn, Germany.

FRANKLIN PARKER of the University of Oklahoma at Norman holds the doctorate from George Peabody College for Teachers. He has served on the Phi Delta Kappa Commission on International Relations in Education; was Vice President and is now Secretary of the Comparative Education Society. His book, *African Development and Education in Southern Rhodesia,* 1960, and a chapter on "Africa" in *New Nations Around the Globe,* 1965, are based on African field studies. He is a contributor to *The Year Book of Education* and regularly writes "Recent Events in World Education" for the *Comparative Education Review.*

JACQUES POUJOL is Deputy Cultural Counselor of the French Embassy, New York. He holds the doctorate from the University of Paris and was Professor of French at the University of Southern California during the years 1949–1961. He has contributed many articles on French literature and history which were published in France and the United States and is currently editor of *Education in France,* a quarterly review published by the French Cultural Services.

ADLAI STEVENSON was the late United States Ambassador to the United Nations from 1961 to 1965. He was a graduate of Princeton University and of Northwestern University Law School. He served as assistant to the Secretary of the Navy, 1941–1944, and as assistant to the Secretary of State in 1945. Mr. Stevenson was elected governor of Illinois in 1948 and was the Democratic presidential candidate in 1952 and 1956. Among his extensive writings can be found his *Friends and Enemies: What I Learned in Russia,* 1959.

Contents

Part I

*General Survey and
Background Studies*

CHAPTER 1

The United Nations and International Relations: A Speech Commemorating the United Nations Nineteenth Anniversary

ADLAI E. STEVENSON

It hardly seems possible that in a period of less than twenty-four hours, last October, two of the greatest governments on earth changed hands, and another on-rushing power, Red China, exploded its first atom bomb. The transition in Great Britain, of course, was democratic and orderly, but it generated new problems, new adjustments, new policies. England is such a close ally, however, that we can contemplate almost any change there with equanimity. But what of Russia and its new leadership? What of Communist China and its new bomb?

The first official statements from both countries have been nonbelligerent, but the rest of the world is wisely taking a calm attitude of wait-and-see. And one big reason the rest of the world is not more anxious over these sudden developments is the stabilizing influence of the United States and the United Nations—separately and in combination. It takes explosive events like those of last October to make us realize and appreciate that the United States and the United Nations are to the rest of the world what a modern stabilizer is to a great ship. Almost imperceptibly, over the last two decades, the world has come to expect and depend on the steady, poised, sober, reliable, bipartisan foreign policy of America to keep the ship of international state from capsizing where crises have generated storms and heavy seas.

The United States has not *always* met this test—but *nearly* always—

under both Democratic and Republican leadership. It has acted on its own when it had to, but more often it has acted through the United Nations. The recent eruptions in Russia and China are not our only immediate concerns. We are presently struggling to maintain order in Cyprus, in Malaysia, in Viet Nam, in Laos, in the Congo, in the Middle East, just to name some of the hot spots, and in one way or another the United Nations is deeply involved in all of these efforts.

The United Nations has not been uniformly successful in keeping the peace, but it is keeping it better than it has ever been kept before. That is why millions of people all over the world hold meetings during October to celebrate the birthday of the United Nations. This year marks the 19th anniversary of the beginning of the United Nations and also the end of the Second World War. It was in the bloody twilight of the last war and then under the shadow of an atomic cloud that the nations agreed in 1945 to organize a system of world order in which war would be banned and disputes would be settled by peaceful means. That is the event we commemorate each October—the signature of the Charter of the United Nations. And here I remind you that the Charter is based on the universal ideas and principles that underlie our own founding documents:

Faith in the fundamental human rights, in the dignity and worth of the individual;

Justice and respect for the obligations . . . of international law . . . social progress and better life in larger freedom.

These words and ideas from the Preamble of the Charter were familiar to Americans before the Charter was written. Thus did the events of 1776 and 1787 of the new American Republic find a global echo in the events of 1945. The question was whether man would subordinate his old quarrels to peaceful settlement and his new power for destruction to international control. The answer to the second part of the question turned out to be *no*. But, to our everlasting credit, it must be recalled that the United States, sole possessor of the revolutionary atomic weapon, sought seriously to place all aspects of atomic power in the safe hands of an international authority committed to its peaceful use.

Alas, there was no room in the Communist ideology of class struggle for such peaceful collaboration among nations. There was no room in Stalin's plans of world conquest for such an accommodation. There was no room in the Soviet Union for the international inspectors which were a necessary part of the plan. Stalin opted for the closed society, for empire and for a nuclear arms race. The Second World War was not a year into history before a gigantic struggle was under way that came to be known as the cold war. The cold war and the United Nations raised contradictory visions of the realities and prospects for life on this earth. One vision was of total and permanent hostility between conflicting social systems until the world is transformed in the image of one side or the other. This view was committed to a black-and-white version of human affairs, to dogmatic solutions to human problems, and to doctrinaire answers to human questions. This view allowed for no diversity in social organization or economic system or even of cultural values. It denied the possibility of accommodation, and had no interest in negotiation. It was a fundamentalist, apocalyptic view; it dominated the conduct of world affairs and the thinking of many people about those affairs.

Ten short years ago, many of our people were hypnotized by the vision of a world split into halves, permanently organized around two super powers, locked in ongoing struggle for world dominion. At the two opposing poles of power, scientists searched frantically for ways to deliver the new-found H-bomb, to carry the nuclear arms race another spiral.

Professional demonologists spoke and wrote darkly of a secret master plan for communist world conquest, of the unifying force of communist ideology . . . on the dread powers of communist propaganda . . . of the deadly techniques of infiltration, subversion, and brainwashing . . . of the superhuman cunning of professional "masters of conflict" sitting in the Kremlin, manipulating their moves on a global chessboard with wicked precision as they knocked off one country after another as a warm-up for gobbling whole continents.

And somehow the impression gained currency that the United States and its friends were in headlong retreat before the invincible and irreversible tide of communist conquest. This was the so-called bipolar world, the frozen world of cold war, structured by rigid military alliances, overshadowed by the thermonuclear arms race. And, for a period, this *was* the essential reality.

Yet throughout these tense and dangerous times the United States had an alternative view of the world. It was a more peaceful, a more hopeful view and a much more realistic one at that. The United States Government has worked hard and long, through thick and thin, to move the world out of the sterile stalemate of cold war, out of the straitjacket of nuclear confrontation into a more flexible, more dynamic, more negotiable state of affairs in which we can safely probe for areas of common interest and warily work for a consensus on survival. And thus toward our chosen alternative to a third world war, a world safe for diversity.

Let me pause to note that there are those in our land who oppose this goal. They remind me that a famous humorist once said the trouble with the world is that there are too many foreigners in it.

Now when I speak of United States foreign policy I do not mean Democratic foreign policy or Republican foreign policy but genuine, bottled-in-bond *American* foreign policy. I mean a foreign policy worked out painfully over twenty years by both Republican and Democratic Presidents, a policy broadly based on the approval of a majority of the American people, and tested in the fiery trials of what may well prove to be the most dangerous and hopeful period in the history of mankind. This policy cannot be named for any one man, not Roosevelt or Truman or Marshall or Vandenberg or Stimson, or Acheson or Eisenhower or Dulles or Kennedy or Johnson or Rusk. Postwar United States foreign policy has emerged from the work of these men and many more. It is bona fide American foreign policy of, by, and for the whole nation. That policy has paid important dividends.

This world is a somewhat safer and saner planet than it was a few years back. I speak only relatively, of course. Yet, we *do* have a treaty banning all but underground nuclear tests ending the pollution of the atmosphere and bringing the runaway thermonuclear death dance under the first semblance of control.

We *do* have a direct open line between Washington and Moscow to reduce the danger of war by mistake or miscalculation.

We *do* have a joint undertaking not to orbit weapons of mass destruction in outer space.

We *have* taken mutual steps to cut back on the rate of production of fissionable materials for nuclear weapons.

And at last we seem to have a tacit understanding that it makes no sense to go on forever piling up unneeded nuclear weapons. Meanwhile the exclusive bipolar structure of world power and world influence is clearly a thing of the past. The illusion of a monolithic communist empire under the thumb of Moscow has been shattered. Old dreams of world conquest are fading in the face of harsh reality. And old visions of world conformity, to *anyone's* pattern, are yielding to the hardy persistence of nationalism, independence, and diversity. All in all it begins to look a good deal more like our kind of world —colorful, diverse, pluralistic, more viable, more negotiable, more intent on survival.

And how, let us ask on the nineteenth birthday of the United Nations, did the United Nations fit into all of this? I should say it fitted in, in three major ways.

First, the view of the world that has been pursued by the United States through successive national administrations for the past decade and a half is essentially the view of the world projected in the United Nations Charter. We are on all fours with all nations who want the kind of world projected in the Charter and, with a few important exceptions, that means just about everybody.

Second, the United Nations has been largely instrumental in developing a system of peaceful settlement of international disputes, and it has been more successful than many seem to realize.

On at least twenty occasions since the end of the Second World War, armed hostilities between states have started and then stopped without ultimatums, without declarations of war, without organized large-scale fighting, or armistice negotiations or victories or defeats for anybody. On at least twenty other occasions, there has been violence in one country of a kind that, in another day, almost surely would have led to outside intervention and international war. All these have been halted or contained by "cease-fires" sometimes at the call of regional organizations but usually with the help of an appeal or mediation or a peacekeeping force provided by the United Nations.

And, third, the United Nations has succeeded in building a substantial community of world organizations which is doing more and more of the world's urgent business on a cooperative basis and at a near-universal level.

This has not come about by international agreement on grandiose ideas for world reform; it has happened, step-by-step, because there is no other way to conduct important business in a world in which science and technology have made nation-states interdependent whether they like it or not. We simply cannot explore space without international allocation of radio frequencies.

We cannot fly aircraft around the globe without international safety and navigation standards.

We cannot develop a world weather-reporting system without a world organization to do it, nor control the spread of communicable disease without international action, nor do any of thousands of things that need doing today without doing them through international organizations, agreements, and regulations.

All these things and many more are now being done through international institutions, including international assistance for economic and social progress for the new and impoverished nations.

And still more of the world's business will be done at a world level in the next decade and even more in the next, for such are the requirements of scientific discovery and technological change that world organization is a plain and practical necessity of our times. So we have moved more rapidly than many know toward a system of peaceful settlement as a potential alternative to the war systems for dealing with disputes among nations.

At the very heart of our system lies this capacity for accommodation, the ability to see where the common interest overrides conflicting interests: this and the practice of tolerance. If the great compromises had failed in Philadelphia nearly two centuries ago, if conciliation and consensus had eluded the best efforts of the Founding Fathers, if common interests had not triumphed over mutual differences, if tolerance had been smothered in hostility, then the American revolution would have been no more than another colonial revolt; no more than an exchange of distant rulers for local rulers and the start of a new chapter in the history of wars between states.

This is the great overriding question in world affairs today. Will a firm consensus be reached on a common interest in mutual survival? The answer is, "Not yet."

Indeed, there are those in our own society today who refuse to face the question on the grounds that the answer is preordained and that the answer is *no*.

They believe that all virtue is on one side and all sin on the other, and that one or the other must perish.

They believe that negotiation is wicked, and accommodation would be fatal.

They believe that the road to peace is paved all the way with raw power and nothing else.

So they would go another way.

They would turn away from the view of the world which this country has held for the last two decades. They would turn from the path toward peaceful settlement of international disputes, and the path toward world community which we have traveled so far within the United Nations. They would, instead, cancel treaties, withdraw from accommodation, abandon cooperation, refuse to negotiate, remove the brake from the arms race, get on with more nuclear testing, develop outer space for military purpose, pile super-bomb upon "overkill," staking everything conspicuously on power without discernible purpose.

Where would we go from there? Having chosen hostility as a way of life and stalemate as the national posture, what next? Those who peddle these doctrines would, they say, proceed by a process of ultimatum and intimidation to dismantle the societies that displease us. And they assure us that the rest of the world would roll over and play dead.

We know that proud nations, like proud people, react to hostility with hostility and reply to ultimatum with defiance. We know that once two great powers have the capacity to destroy each other, even once, then national security for both sides lies not in further accumulation of power but in the limitation of power. We know that once the issue is outright survival, then a consensus on survival is the first requirement of existence.

Finally, we know we cannot travel this road alone, not in the second half of the twentieth century, in the second decade of atomic power, in the eighth year of the age of space. But, being realists, we know that the road is uphill all the way. And let me say in passing that by realism I do not mean the absence of ideals but the art of being effective in the real world.

In the real world peace is not easy. Resolution of conflict is not simple. There is no easy way to accommodation, no short-cut to world order or stability, or growth. This is an untidy, undisciplined, contentious world, and we might just as well face it.

We might as well face, too, the fact that on its nineteenth birthday the United Nations had plenty of trouble on its platter. The United Nations has met problems and lived through crises from the day it was born. Indeed I once pointed out that the United Nations was built for trouble and thrives on it. It may very well be that all of us owe our lives today to the fact that the United Nations was there to pour water on a score of small blazes that could have led to that searing fireball which is partner to the mushroom cloud. But it is not enough now to thank our stars for all that, or simply to assert we are "for" the United Nations and want to "strengthen" it in some undefined way. For one thing the United Nations is faced with the challenges of an administrative character. Its peacekeeping machinery is not as strong or as reliable or as flexible as it should be.

Its far-flung programs of economic and social cooperation, after a decade or so of rapid growth, need improved budgeting, programming and coordination; its search for professional and technical personnel is up against diminishing sources of qualified people. These are not trivial matters, for they have to do with the effective capacity of the United Nations to operate in practice, but at least they are subject to administrative solution.

This is not the case with another group of essentially political problems that arises from contradictory principles and contradictory attitudes on the part of the members. We have, on the one hand, the almost sacred proposition that every member has one vote and each vote weighs the same on the scales of decision—a proposition which no member is likely to yield in principle. On the other hand, we have the plain fact of great disparity in the strength and influence, the contributions and responsibility for results among the members. Then, we have the rules and procedures that make the difference between order and chaos in the work of an organization. But we also have feelings and passions that are no less real because they conflict with orderly procedure and the integrity of the rules. On the one hand, we have extensive and unprecedented programs for cooperative assistance between the most developed and the less developed members. On the other hand, we have the bitter frustrations of the impoverished peoples whose patience is worn thin and who view the wide and growing gap between the rich and poor as an intolerable injustice. We have a Charter which commits its members to promote human rights, and we have too many members who violate the human rights of their poor citizens.

So the house of peace is teeming with contradictions with potentially serious political consequences.

How could it be otherwise?

We know that contradictions exist side-by-side in national life, in professional life, and indeed within our individual selves. The physical scientists know that contradictions exist side-by-side within nature.

Yet for some reason we seem to have trouble adjusting to the notion that contradictions also exist side-by-side in world affairs. Well, we had better, all of us, adjust to that reality. Realism tells us that the future of the United Nations will be no bed of roses.

But I have faith that on its twentieth anniversary the United Nations will be at least a bit better than on its nineteenth.

This planet is too small for a big nation to go it alone.

This world is too dangerous for a powerful nation to be primitive.

Our times are too late to leave the path to peace.

And man, for all his sins, deserves something better than an endless prospect of mindless hostility, monotonous arrogance, and monstrous weapons.

CHAPTER 2

Criteria for Judging the Worth of an International Educational Program

HAROLD R. W. BENJAMIN

In a certain sense, perhaps I am like the imaginative hobo who sat with a relatively unimaginative comrade on a bank overlooking the freight yard. This was in the good old days when a tramp could ordinarily get a hand-out in the morning and then find an empty boxcar going in his direction. But on this morning the good old days had temporarily disappeared. Unfriendly housewives had slammed doors in the faces of these two bums. Freight trains going east were all loaded, going west were sealed tight, and it appeared that these poor men, weak with hunger, would have to ride the blinds on an express train.

In these circumstances, the imaginative tramp spoke. "I wish I had a coconut cream pie as big around as one of them switch-engine drive wheels," he said dreamily.

The unimaginative tramp listened, greed welling in his throat.

"I wish," continued the imaginative bum, "that I had a deep-dish apple pie as big as that there water tank."

His unimaginative colleague swallowed convulsively but said nothing.

"I wish," said the dreamer, "that I had a great big juicy pumkin pie as fur across and as deep as that there doggone freight depot."

The unimaginative hobo could stand the recital no longer. "If you had a pie that big, you'd give me a piece of it, wouldn't you?" he asked.

"No," snarled the imaginative tramp. "If you want pie, damn you, wish for it yourself."

11

Here, then, is a pie I have dreamed up which may be called *Some Criteria for Evaluation of International Education Programs.*

I use the term international education program to include every organized activity which attempts to pass educational practices and concepts from one country to another. We want criteria that will be valid when applied to Horace Mann's collection of what he called "beneficial hints, for our warning or our imitation, from Germany, France, Holland, and parts of Great Britain, and Ireland." [1] We want the same criteria to be applicable to the most recent educational phases of the programs of the Agency for International Development. We want to be able to apply these criteria to all the international commerce in educational ideas, procedures, and institutions between these two extremes, from the United States Army sergeants teaching in Cuba after the Spanish-American War, to the League of Nations' Educational Mission to China in 1931; from Calvin E. Stowe's 1837 report to the governor and Legislature of Ohio on *Elementary-Public Instruction in Europe* to the most recent education missions of UNESCO.

First, we need to examine the purposes of education in a country to which educational ideas and practices are being exported. Suppose there are main purposes to which the would-be exporters do not and perhaps cannot subscribe. For example, here is a country which seeks to use education to keep an oligarchical dictatorship in power. It wants a school system to train the lower classes for efficient service to the dictatorship and make them content in that station of life in which it pleases the dictatorship to hold them.

It can be stated at once that the exportation to such a country of ideas seeking to change these educational purposes has built-in guarantees of failure. Of course, the importing country ordinarily will welcome the transaction since it brings prestige and sometimes actual money, especially when it comes from the United States. Educators in the country will often say earnestly that they agree with the purposes of education in the exporting country. As soon as the real purpose of keeping the oligarchy in power and the lower classes in their proper places is really threatened, however, all horses are suddenly of a different color.

Perhaps the most common way of avoiding this issue is for the exporters to come into the country with their wares and work to improve educational instruments, programs, and institutions without bothering the sensitive areas in which purposes reside. Thus we have had magnificent efforts to improve higher educational facilities in Indonesia, to establish basic educational programs in Haiti, to upgrade teacher education in Peru, and to develop effective secondary education in Bolivia, with results that are painful to contemplate.

Sometimes, nevertheless, the exporters try to meet head-on this problem of elevating the purposes of education. They set up an administrative and supervisory complex in the national capital which is, in effect, a second ministry of education. The usual effect is to split the country's educational leaders and their political supporters into warring camps. After the next revolution, whether from right or left, imported educational concerns of any kind are likely to get trampled in the rush for political insurance with the new regime.

The first criterion of a program of international trade in education, therefore, may be stated as follows:

The educational purposes of any country must be the products of the people's own wants in that country. The one best way to help the people improve their educational purposes is by helping to educate their leaders. Examples of profound changes in national educational purposes, from the Danish cultural renaissance in the last quarter of the nineteenth century to the school reforms of the Mexican Revolution in the second quarter of the twentieth century, show very clearly that this is the part of educational change that must be homegrown. No conceivable amount of foreign educational advice or other aid would have been likely to improve the educational purposes of Nikolai Grundtvig, Christen Kold, Moises Saenz, and Raul Ramirez. Foreign aid, even in the supposedly cheap form of advice, would have handicapped if not ruined any one of these men's efforts to re-state and re-vitalize their countries' educational purposes.

The importing agency, therefore, will find that it has more important work to do than trying to persuade a people to change their fundamental educational purposes to fit a foreign pattern. This is emphatically a job for their own people.

What would be the effect on United States' enterprises of educational aid to other countries if this criterion were generally followed? The first result would be a considerable reduction in the number of countries aided by the United States. A second result would be an intensification of aid to countries which are solving their problems of purpose. The latter countries can be aided without the political and cultural handicaps imposed by an outside agency trying to mess with their educational purposes.

The second criterion is applied to a country's importation of educational facilities and institutions. Does the country's educational purpose require changes in its programs? Can the exporting agency provide skills and technical knowledge that will help produce such changes? Do the importing country's leaders, supported by substantial elements of its population, request this help for educational reasons as contrasted, for example, to reasons of prestige or monetary aid? A negative answer to any of these questions simplifies at once the decision concerning how much and what kind of aid should be given by an outside agency.

I shall not multiply examples of how this criterion operates in various situations, but I cannot resist remembering and mentioning the earnest request from an outstanding South Korean secondary-school administrator in 1954 for aid in setting up core-curriculum programs in his war-devastated country. Many schools had been destroyed, and of those which remained standing a large number were still occupied as barracks and administrative offices by the South Korean Army. Those which were used for school purposes were unheated with broken windows in the dead of winter and were shockingly overcrowded. A room designed to hold a maximum of forty would have ninety or one hundred pupils packed into it in sardine-like rows. Books were almost nonexistent; teachers were scarce, untrained, and so underpaid as to be almost working for nothing but public esteem.

Of all the changes required in the country's educational program, the adoption of the core-curriculum would have appeared to merit a rather low priority. There was certainly also a question, moreover, as to whether the education teams of the United Nations' Korean Reconstruction Agency possessed the requisite skills and technical knowledge to help the Korean secondary schools set up the core-curriculum. Why, then, was it requested? The answer, I think, is simple. The core-curriculum would give prestige. In the face of problems that appeared at the time insoluble, here was a short cut. The teachers and pupils were hungry and cold and frustrated. With a core-curriculum they could at least starve, freeze, and despair in hightoned manner.

Of course, the request for the core-curriculum did not have general support among the country's educational leaders, much less among the general population. Yet where did it originate? I will give you one guess, and I know you'll hit the mark the first time. There was a core-curriculum expert from the United States of America who had been in a previous educational aid enterprise in the country, an expert in persuasion as well as in the core-curriculum.

The third criterion for evaluating the exchange of educational ideas and practices is concerned with the importing country's teaching personnel. Are the teachers and administrators of the country's instructional programs skilled enough to carry out the country's educational purposes? If so, they need no outside aid. If they need additional skills, how can they best acquire them? Are the political and cultural leaders of the country willing to have their educational personnel get those skills from an outside agency? If so, the method of furnishing the skills becomes very important.

This problem of upgrading personnel is best solved when attacked cooperatively by the aided country and the outside agency. Generally speaking, professional training in the aided country is superior to that secured in other countries. It is also more economical of time, effort, and money. It helps develop pride in local institutions instead of an attitude of superiority nurtured in foreign parts. It provides field experiences in situations like those in which the trainee will eventually work.

Here, therefore, is my sketch of these three main criteria for helping us determine the direction and rate of international trade in education. There are inadequate and imperfect systems of education all over the world. Certainly we have many of them in the United States, and we have limited resources for improving them. We have to be prudent and practical in exporting and importing educational aid. There are obviously boundaries which must be set in our attempts to move all the world ahead in education.

In this paper I have suggested criteria for determining those boundaries under the three main headings of purpose, program, and personnel. The potentially most fruitful of these areas for international trade in education is personnel.

NOTE

1. Horace Mann, *Seventh Annual Report, 1844,* 4th ed. (London: Simpkin, Marshall, and Co., 1857), p. 3.

Historical Development of Governmental Interest in International Higher Education

WILLIAM W. BRICKMAN

There can be no doubt of the popularity of international education at the present time. Virtually everyone loves to travel abroad, and there are many candidates for foreign teaching and administrative posts under UNESCO, United States' governmental, or other auspices. Every educator pays tribute to education's role in international relations and world peace. It is no exaggeration to claim that all college and university personnel are anxious to help the foreign students in their midst.

What is by far less certain is the extent to which educators and scholars of various preparations and persuasions are prepared to exert themselves to study international education from its roots and origins. Not many, thus far, have shown a disposition to learn how to read the languages which open wide sources of information and data shedding light on the development, current status, controversies, complexities, and problems of international education.

The historical and comparative dimensions of this theme have not been studied with any degree of depth. The research has dealt, in the main, with the psychological and sociological aspects of student exchange, the problems of linguistic and academic adjustment. All this is helpful, but the historical and comparative perspectives must also receive due recognition in any program of research in international education.

To facilitate somewhat the historical presentation, it might be desirable to define briefly the key terms. By *government* is meant any system of political administration of an identifiable national unit of

17

territory. *Interest* connotes general intention, policy, or activity, or any combination of these elements. *International higher education* refers to the transfer of media and individuals concerned with advanced and professional learning. This term comprises professor and student interchange, international learned organizations and congresses, educational and cultural aid to other countries, intervisitation by scholars and educated persons, exchange and translation of learned writings, and so forth.

It is obvious that a satisfactory historical analysis of such a topic would represent a tall order within the limitations of a conference paper or even a longer chapter in the conference proceedings. Many a scholar might even tend to be skeptical toward such a venture. Nevertheless, some effort should be made to write along these lines, if only to get others to extend or to correct this introductory account.

A form of international technical aid is described in the Bible. During the tenth century B.C., King Solomon made a request of King Hiram of Tyre for skills and materials for the construction of the Holy Temple in Jerusalem. One specialist in metals, Hiram, of Tyrian-Jewish lineage, is credited in the Bible [1] with having been responsible for the ornamentation of the structure. While this example is not exactly within the realm of higher education in the formal, academic sense, it is nonetheless an instance of cultural aid and cooperation across national frontiers.

Centuries later, there is a more extensive type of international higher education. Emperor Asoka the Great of India, who reigned from 273 B.C. to 232 B.C., undertook ambitious programs of spreading Buddhist teachings by means of missionaries. Called by historians the St. Paul or the Constantine of Buddhism, Asoka sent out missionaries all over West Asia, East Europe, and North Africa. As stated in his Rock Edict Number 13, "everywhere men follow His Sacred Majesty's instruction in the Law of Piety." [2] In fact, "Even where the envoys of His Sacred Majesty do not penetrate, there too men hearing His Most Sacred Majesty's ordinance based on the Law of Piety and his instruction in that Law, practise and will practise the Law." [3] Asoka, himself a conqueror, rejected war and, like Alexander the Great, began to preach Buddhism, not only for its own sake but also for the attainment of peace among nations. The "only true conquest," he maintained in his Rock Edict devoted to his missionary activity, is "the conquest won by piety." In place of arms, he urges "patience and gentleness."

Even if some doubt might be expressed as to the geographical breadth of the penetration claimed by Asoka, it is clear that Buddhist thought was transmitted through his efforts and those of others at later periods. But Asoka must be regarded as a prime mover. During his reign, the University of Taxila (Takshashila) attained considerable eminence, mainly because of its faculty. Perhaps the most striking requirement was for students to travel abroad following their graduation.[4] Very likely, they were also fired with the zeal to propagate Buddhism. Taxila, it should be noted, was one of the oldest international universities in that it attracted students from Asia Minor. No less a personage than Alexander the Great had been attracted to this institution to meet its teachers.

Small wonder, then, that the Taxila students had excellent equipment for their educational task. The missions of Asoka were justifiably regarded as "among the greatest civilizing forces of the Far East." [5] Through the application of his own interest and power, Asoka was enabled to organize "the most comprehensive scheme of religious missionary enterprise recorded in the history of the world." [6] This campaign resulted not merely in immediate success in India and Ceylon, but after a time in the Far East, Central Asia, and Southeast as well. And while Buddhism did not penetrate into some Asiatic countries for centuries after the death of Asoka, "the diffusion of the religion in them was due to the impetus given by the great Buddhist emperor of India, who transformed the creed of a local Indian sect into a world-religion. . . ." [7] The inclusion of Asoka among such outstanding rulers as Charlemagne and Alfred the Great [8] is hardly an exaggeration.

In a neighboring culture, that of ancient Persia, it is possible to trace another instance of governmental influence on international educational relations. The University of Jundishapur (Gundisapur), owing to inspiration by King Noshirwan the Just (531–579), became "the greatest intellectual center of the time; there Greek, Jewish, Christian, Hindu, and Persian ideas could be compared, exchanged, and eventually syncretized." [9] It was at Jundishapur that the Byzantine scientists, philosophers, and craftsmen found a haven after they had been expelled from Constantinople during the antipagan campaign of Emperor Justinian.[10] Doubtless, it was the policy of Noshirwan that encouraged them to carry on their cultural and educational work, as well as to influence Persian thought. Sykes says that "at this period, Persia was the central mart for the exchange of ideas between the East and the West." [11] This was brought about, it is reasonable to infer, by the contrasting policies of two governments—the repressive one of Byzantium and the permissive one of Persia.

Still in the Western Asiatic area, one notes the 'Abbasid dynasty's policy in Bagdad. Caliph 'Abdallāh al-Ma'mūn (813–833), who had a Persian mother and a Persian wife, procured Greek manuscripts from Byzantium and set about having them translated. In 830, he established the Bayt al-hikma (House of Wisdom), an institution combining the functions of an academy of science, library, and observatory. Modeling his institute on the Museum in Alexandria, al-Ma'mūn commissioned Arabic translations of Greek and Latin works. In the words of Sarton, ". . . Arabic science was the fruit of the Semitic genius fertilized by the Iranian genius. . . . Within a couple of centuries (*c.* 750–950), the Islamic rulers, using their polyglot subjects, most of them Christians and Jews, caused the best of Greek knowledge to become available in the Arabic language." [12] This pattern of interreligious, intercultural, and one can confidently say international cooperation was a worthy product of enlightened governmental policy, not only in the Middle East, but proved in later centuries to be profitable also in Moslem Spain and elsewhere. The Islamic success in keeping science alive resulted, in time, in the reintroduction of Greek science and philosophy into Europe, once more with the cooperation of Christian and Jewish translators and learned men. It is also noteworthy that some European rulers, Frederick II Hohenstaufen in the thirteenth century, for example, followed the pluralistic tradition of the Persian and Islamic rulers.

Let us now, briefly, turn our attention to the Far East. The emperors of the T'ang Dynasty (620–907) generally fostered international educational relations. This was the main period in Chinese history when intellectual relations were maintained at a high level with India. It was during the first century of this dynasty that the influential pilgrims, Hiuen Tsang (Yuan Chwang) and I'Tsing, spent close to three decades studying Buddhism at its source before returning to their native land. China was also receptive to Buddhist Indian missionaries. But the Chinese rulers did not restrict their people to the doctrines of Buddhism; they also welcomed Nestorian Christianity, Manichaeanism, Mazdaism (Zoroastrianism), and Islam. In the ninth century, the foreign systems of belief, except Buddhism, were persecuted in a reversal of imperial policy. For the most part, however, "the T'ang Court welcomed foreigners, took a deep interest in alien customs and religions, and extended a friendly welcome to priests and travellers from western regions. . . . Secure in their isolation, and confident of their power to repel invasions, the T'ang emperors did not fear foreign intercourse as a menace to the state, while the spirit of intellectual curiosity and tolerance which marked this age encouraged a sympathetic attitude to religious and artistic ideas of foreign origin." [13]

In the western capital of the T'ang Dynasty, the city of Ch'ang An, there was evidence that it was "frequented by men of the most diverse races, from Siberian tradesmen to the jungle peoples of southern India, Greeks, Arabs, Persians and Japanese." [14]

The second T'ang monarch, Emperor T'ai Tsung (627–650), extended his contacts virtually all over Asia. [15] According to the official new T'ang History, he founded in 639 the Ch'ung Wen Kuan ("Honoring Literature Institute") at his Eastern Palace in Ch'ang An for instruction in the classics. "From all quarters barbarian peoples [e.g., Koreans] . . . one after another sent students to enter the schools until the number reached over 8,000." [16] This figure, which seems to include both Chinese, and foreign students, is substantiated by the Old T'ang History, a rather controversial publication, which also adds: "Confucian learning like this had never been seen in former times." [17]

During the reign of a concubine of T'ai Tsung, Empress Wu Hou (684–705), all education, national and international, seems to have been neglected, but the reaccession of Emperor Chung Tsung once more revived the fortunes of education. Almost at once he promulgated an edict opening the national institutions of higher learning, including the Law School, "to students from foreign peoples on the western and eastern borders—students from Japan being among those mentioned." [18] Very likely, these were also students from Korea and Tibet.

The Japanese Empire profited considerably from its cultural and educational relations with China of the T'ang Dynasty. "Japan, indeed, was then almost a new land, hardly known in the Han period, but now sending embassies to China, and enthusiastically borrowing the culture and political organisation of the T'ang Empire." [19] But the Japanese were also impressed by the higher educational system of China. The rector of the Imperial University (Daigaku no kanii), Kiyogimi Sugawara (770–842), an outstanding scholar, adopted the methods of Chinese university administration in his institution. Likewise, his son, Koreyoshi Sugawara (812–880), a professor of literature who succeeded his father as rector, continued to borrow educational ideas from China. [20]

Fitzgerald contrasts the attitude of the Chinese emperors with those of the Mongol conquerors from Genghis Khan (1222) onward. He grants that the Mongol monarchs continued the Chinese imperial "policy" toward foreigners since the Han Dynasty. However, he insists, somewhat by way of minor contradiction, that, "whereas the Chinese Emperors tolerated foreign religions out of indifference, and employed foreigners for their skill in strange arts and crafts, the Mongols used aliens out of policy, fearing to give authority to the natives of the land." [21] All the same, it does not seem to be stretching the point too far to claim that about 1,500 years of cultural relations with foreign persons do constitute a governmental policy in favor of international exchange.

It would be appropriate, once the Mongol conquest has been mentioned, to call attention to another indication of Chinese governmental interest with reference to international educational relations. When Niccolò and Maffeo Polo, jewel merchants from Venice and the first Europeans to reach the court of Kublai Khan in 1266, arrived they were most warmly received by the Great Khan of China. After learning all he could from them about Europe, he commissioned them to bring to the Pope letters requesting one hundred scholarly missionaries to teach his Tatars and to carry on disputations with representatives of other faiths. After some delay, the recently crowned Pope Gregory X sent two Dominican friars as a token mission. En route they turned back, and the Polos went on accompanied by Niccolò's son Marco, arriving at Kublai Khan's summer palace at Xanadu. At the very least, "the sojourn of the Polos in China opens a new era in European knowledge of the Far East." [22] Marco Polo's account of his trip fascinated many persons in the West. "European readers of Marco Polo admired the tolerance of the Great Khan, who employed Christians, and Moslems, Buddhists and Taoists, and men of all nations according to their capacity, regardless of race and creed." [23] Even if the ambitious scheme of the Great Khan was not realized, it is obvious that, whatever the basic reason behind the unusual request to Rome, the Chinese power had some concern for international educational contacts.

Let us now turn to the historical development of government policy and interest in international education as manifested in intra-European relations, as well as in cultural connections with other continents. Perhaps the most likely place to begin would be the Hellenistic period. It was Alexander the Great who brought about the transition from Hellenic to Hellenistic culture, during the fourth century B.C., as a result of his conquests in Asia and Africa. According to Diodorus, Alexander's will provided for a kind of Rhodes Scholarship.[24] His founding of the city of Alexandria proved to be a signal achievement in the history of culture and education, both domestic and international. Alexandria became ". . . one of the greatest centers of cultural exchange and diffusion, and this . . . brought forth far-reaching consequences in the intellectual development of both sides of the world, the East and the West." [25] The Ptolemaic Dynasty did much to advance the influence of Alexandria as an international intellectual center. Even if Cleopatra did not appear to contribute to an equal degree to the development of international educational relations, she at least practiced some sort of internationalism.[26]

Elsewhere in the Hellenistic world, too, there were stirrings in international education. Athens, in particular, began to attract students from various countries to its higher educational institutions. As Athens became increasingly a university town, "Foreign potentates . . . vied with one another in endowing her with beautiful buildings, while students of all ages and nationalities thronged her streets and drew inspiration from her associations." [27] One might assume that the foreign monarchs contributed students as well as buildings, so that the University of Athens "became the school not of Greece only, but the world." [28]

The early Roman emperors made their contributions to international education. Although Emperor Augustus expelled foreigners from Rome, he excepted foreign physicians and teachers because they served the public welfare. Emperor Hadrian, in the following century, organized the Athenaeum in Rome as a locale of learning in which Greek and Roman philosophers and poets showed their wares. First Hadrian, then Antoninus Pius, and later Marcus Aurelius endowed chairs at the University of Athens. Among the encouraging acts by Hadrian was his waiving the requirement of Roman citizenship for the head of the University. But by the fourth century A.D., however, governmental authorities began to issue regulations and increased their interference in higher education, possibly because of the personal disputes among the professors.[29]

One of these quarrels turned out to be a windfall for one of the participants, Prohaeresius of Armenia, the brilliant professor of rhetoric at the fourth-century University of Athens. After suffering exile because of the jealousy of his colleagues, he managed to make an impression upon royalty. According to his student, Eunapius, Prohaeresius "had so won over [Emperor Flavius Julius] Constans that he sat at his table along with those whom he most honoured." [30] Constans, who was the youngest son of Emperor Constantine the Great, named Prohaeresius as his intellectual ambassador to "the Gallic provinces" and later to Rome. As an exchange Professor, Prohaeresius may often have spoken above the heads of his students in the Transalpine territories, but he seemed to please everyone. The "Gallic" people expressed admiration for his character and physique. As for Emperor Constans, his motives in sending a scholar to Gaul may not have been those of science for the sake of science. According to Eunapius, the emperor "was ambitious to show them what great men he ruled over." [31] This objective was fully realized, not merely in provincial Gaul, but also in cosmopolitan Rome, where the inhabitants erected in honor of the peregrinating professor "a bronze statue life size with this inscription: 'Rome the Queen of cities to the King of Eloquence.' " [32] Libanius testifies that Athens likewise honored Prohaeresius. In the ancient world, the case history of Prohaeresius is an instructive example of success in a governmental program of exchange of academic personnel.

We find still another instance of governmental activity in exchange during the late Roman empire. A decree, dated 370, by the Emperors Valentinian, Valens, and Gratian handed down to Olybrius, Prefect of Rome, specifies controls over students and punishments for the delinquent. "But to those who carefully devote their attention to their studies, permission is given to remain at Rome until the twentieth year of their age; but, after this time, he who shall have neglected to withdraw voluntarily shall be sent back to his country by the care of the prefect even though his education be unfinished. But for fear that these measures should be taken in a perfunctory way, your high Sincerity is to instruct the Office of Censuales to take a note every month of the names of the students, whence they come, and which ones ought to be sent back to Africa or to other provinces because of the time of their sojourn, those only being accepted who are attached to the offices of corporations. Similar notes will be addressed every year to the archives of our Mansuetudo [Clemency], in order that we may be able to know the merits and aptitudes of each, and judge how and when they will be serviceable to us." [33] It is evident that the government took a particular interest in the selection, guidance, deportment, and achievements of the overseas students not so much because it was convinced of the basic values of student interchange, but because it was concerned with choosing the best for the imperial service. In later centuries, too, as in the age of Peter the Great in Russia, this was the fundamental motivation for international educational exchange.

Earlier in this essay mention was made of the international cultural activities of the Byzantine government. There is a great deal more to the full account, but time and space limitations make it advisable to defer a more detailed treatment for another occasion. But it is tempting to call attention to the summing up of Byzantine policy by the renowned Byzantinist, Charles Diehl. According to him, "the crudest, simplest, and most direct way of influencing foreign nations was by means of money. Money was always regarded by Byzantine diplomats as being an irresistible argument, and was used indiscriminately and sometimes unwisely. . . ." [34] This approach has something of a contemporary ring about it, but it is difficult to conceive of financial aid to underdeveloped nations of the ancient world without some imperial policy of cultural interchange and impact. On one occasion at least there was a reverse influence. The closing by Emperor Zeno in 489 of the school at Edessa, the center of Nestorianism, and its consequent transfer to Nisibis under Persian rule is an example of the negative attitude on the part of one ruler and the positive attitude of another combining into an international educational transfer.[35]

We come now to the Middle Ages of Western Europe. During this period, the European university, essentially an international institution of higher learning, came into existence. While universities or *studia generalia* were founded at various times by masters, it was not until the thirteenth century that governmental authority took an active hand in the establishment of these higher schools. Two outstanding examples are the founding of the University of Naples by Emperor Frederick II Hohenstaufen in 1224 and that of the University of the Pontifical Court by Pope Innocent IV in 1244 or 1245.[36] Thus, the imperial and papal powers supported and promoted international educational exchange. Even more, the governmental practice of conferring upon universities the power to grant the *ius ubique docendi* (right of teaching anywhere in Christendom) indicated the wider extent of imperial and papal influence in the international dissemination of education. So important was this privilege that the older universities—Bologna and Paris—which had not been founded by pope or emperor, were happy to be invested in 1291–1292 with the power to administer the *ius ubique docendi* by Pope Nicholas IV. The outstanding exceptions, Oxford and Padua, apparently felt sufficiently secure that they did not apply for official recognition of their degrees.[37]

It is interesting to note that the papal conferment upon the University of Paris of the right to grant degrees resulted in the gain of special prestige by the possessors. Thus, a student with a license was considered a *Doctor universalis ecclesiae* and could teach or preach anywhere. He was not only a doctor of the church in Paris, but also everywhere ("doctor non solum Parisiensis ecclesiae, sed etiam universalis").[38]

The mass exodus of masters and students from the University of Paris in 1229 prompted a "pressing invitation" by King Henry III of England, who saw an opportunity of expanding higher education in his realm. Many academic people took advantage of the offer and "reinforced the rising universities of Oxford and Cambridge." [39]

Sovereigns in Western Europe commissioned translators, during the tenth and subsequent centuries, for the advancement of learning without regard to frontiers. Among these were Emperor Otto the Great, various Norman kings, and especially Emperor Frederick II Hohenstaufen. Frederick was the patron of Michael Scot, the Scottish scholar, who translated and supervised translations from Greek and Arabic works. These translations exercised an impact on such minds as Roger Bacon and Albertus Magnus.[40]

The grasp of the significance of languages in missionary, cultural, and commercial activities led to special provisions for study and to the endowment of centers of translation. In 1248, Pope Innocent IV ordered that ten boys who knew Arabic and other Oriental languages well should be trained in theology at the University of Paris so as to be qualified as missionaries in the East.[41] King Alfonso X the Wise of Castile issued in 1254 a charter of privilege for a *studium generale* at Seville to encourage Arabic studies, primarily to bring about the conversion of the Saracens to Christianity. At the same time, however, he encouraged translations from the Arabic in order to benefit from the Arabs' science.[42] The Spanish scholar, Ramón Lull, undertaking propaganda in Paris (1298–1299) for the study of the Arabic, Tatar, and Greek languages, emphasized the missionary motive as the basic value. He predicted that such a program of studies will result in "the greatest exaltation and extension" of Christianity and that from the University of Paris "will come light to all peoples, and thou wilt offer testimony to the truth, and masters and disciples will flock to thee, and all shall hear all sciences from thee." [43] An important outcome of Lull's campaign was the statute promulgated in 1312 at the Council of Vienne under the leadership of Pope Clement V. This decree ordered provisions for instruction in and translation from Hebrew, Greek, Arabic, and Aramaic at the Universities of Rome, Paris, Oxford, Bologna, and Salamanca. The objective was for those trained in such languages to "spread the faith salubriously to infidel nations." [44]

Once more, space and time limitations make necessary mere mention of other events illustrating governmental policy and practice in international education. It would be proper to discuss the colleges of translators or trilingual colleges, such as the College of San Ildefonso established by Cardinal Francisco Ximénes de Cisneros, in accordance with the bull by Pope Alexander VI in 1499, at the University of Alcalá.[45] It is tempting to analyze the college of translators at Toledo where "Englishmen, Italians, Frenchmen, and Germans worked side by side with Jews and christianized Arabs, under the encouragement and stimulus of two learned Archbishops . . . Raymond of Toledo and Rodriguez Ximenes." [46] One would like more details on the Abbaye de Royaumont, established by Blanche of Castile in 1235, where scholars from various countries taught history and literature in two-week sessions in the summer.[47] Also of great interest is the appeal by Pope Innocent III in 1205 to the professors and students of the University of Paris to aid Baldwin, the new Latin emperor of Constantinople, in "the reform of the study of letters there," and his promise that they would receive "besides temporal riches and honors, the rewards of eternal glory." [48] In these events, one might see the germ of such modern ideas as the Peace Corps. It is clear that the medieval period of European history was characterized by many efforts by governmental powers in the area of international educational relations.

The idea of Greek translation projects continued with even greater vigor during the Renaissance. Brief mention has been made of the work of Cardinal Ximénes at the turn of the sixteenth century. The collection of classical manuscripts founded by Pope Nicholas V (1447–1455) has been used by scholars from all parts of the world to this day. He also became the patron of a translation project in which outstanding Greek scholars, such as Cardinal Bessarion, Theodoros Gaza, and Georgios Trapezuntius (George of Trebizond), rendered Plato and Aristotle into Latin.[49]

The Reformation and the Counter-Reformation of the sixteenth century furnished several examples of governmental encouragement of international education. One might be cited at this time. Matteo Ricci, the Italian Jesuit missionary, taught science, mathematics, and finally religion to Chinese scholars and government officials in the late sixteenth century. In 1601, the respect he had won obtained for him permission to live and preach in Peking, a house, and a stipend from the government treasury.[50]

From the seventeenth century on, it became customary for monarchs to charter and support academies of scientific men. By the very nature of science, such academies were generally international in membership and activity. The Royal Society of London, chartered by King Charles II in 1662, "freely admitted Men of different Religions, Countries, and Professions of Life . . . for they openly profess, not to lay the Foundation as English, Scotch, Irish, Popish or Protestant Philosophy but a Philosophy of Mankind." [51]

Also of international significance was the Académie Royale des Sciences, organized in 1667 in Paris by Jean-Baptiste Colbert with funds from the treasury of King Louis XIV. In 1700, with a charter granted by Elector Frederick I of Prussia, Gottfried Wilhelm von Leibniz established the Berlin Academy of Sciences, along the lines of the English and French academies. The Academy of Sciences founded by Tsar Peter the Great in 1725 in St. Petersburg was manned largely by German scientists and scholars.

An interesting, unique international plan was projected and almost started in 1667 by Frederick William, the Great Elector of Brandenburg when he approved the "Foundation of the New Brandenburg University of the Nations, Sciences, and Arts" ("Fundatio Novae Brandenburgicae Gentium, Scientiarum et Artium"). Devised by the Swedish Baron Bengt Skytte, this plan had been previously offered to King Charles II of England, but ignored, possibly because of the king's preoccupation with the founding of the Royal Society of London. The project involved an educational and research institute for scholars, scientists, artists, and men of letters from many nations. This City of the Wise ("Sophopolis") was to consist of libraries, laboratories, a museum, a printing press with foreign type faces, and other facilities. There was to be academic freedom for all, and the only restriction was against proselytization for one's faith. The Great Elector was all set to supply funds and a location at Tangermünde on the Elbe when he gave up the project in response from pressure by the Swedish government, to whom Skytte was now *persona non grata*.[52]

At this point, it becomes appropriate to refer to the policies of the Russian tsars with regard to international education. From the time of Tsar Boris Godunov (1598–1602), the rulers of Russia sought the aid of foreign specialists in technology and scholarship. Boris sent many young men to study in France, England, and Germany, and offered substantial rewards to the foreign scientists and scholars who came to Russia. Tsar Michael Romanov (1613–1645) continued this policy and sent young Russians to Cambridge University, but these did not return to benefit their homeland. The major effort at international educational relations was made by Tsar Peter the Great (1689–1725), who not only sent students abroad and attracted foreign specialists, but also went himself to Germany, Holland, and England to learn foreign technology at first hand. One result of the trip was the opening of the School of Mathematics and Navigation in 1701 in Moscow, very likely on the pattern of the Royal Mathematical School of Christ's Hospital, which Peter visited while in England.[53] It is noteworthy that, Peter profiting by the experience of his predecessors, prescribed rules which ensured the return to Russia by those whom he had sent to study in foreign countries.

The University of Moscow, founded by Michael V. Lomonosov in 1755, received the active support of Empress Elizabeth, who also made possible the import of German professors to staff the institution.

Catherine the Great (1762–1796), an admirer of French philosophy, invited Denis Diderot to be her consultant on the establishment of an educational system in Russia. Diderot did present a program in 1770, a "Plan d'une Université pour la Russie," but it proved to be too advanced for a country which was as yet underdeveloped in educational matters. After trying the German-French Baron Friedrich Melchior von Grimm, she turned to Fedor Jankovitch de Mirievo, a Serbo-Croatian educator with experience in Austria and Hungary. Catherine appointed Jankovitch de Mirievo special adviser to the Commission for the Establishment of Schools and he helped introduce school practices and to supervise the preparation of textbooks based on Austrian models.[54]

It is also interesting to note that the government of Poland, shortly before the disappearance of this country from the map, called upon the famous philosopher-educator Jean-Jacques Rousseau to help plan its educational system. Rousseau prepared a program, published posthumously as "Considérations sur le gouvernement de Pologne" (1782), but, for obvious reasons, it could have no impact.

In the New World, during the Colonial period and during the early years of the infant republic of the United States, there was some skeptical sentiment toward the benefits of a foreign education. Thus, when the Common Council of Philadelphia made a donation to Benjamin Franklin's Academy in 1750, it stated its hope that, with this school now available, no young person would be "under necessity for going abroad" for an education, "Whereby not only considerable Expense be saved to the Country, but a stricter Eye may be had over their morals by their Friends and Relations." [55]

Benjamin Waterhouse, future professor at the Harvard Medical School, wrote to Franklin in 1780 from the University of Leyden, where he was a student, that he hoped that Americans "will in time be convinced that it is not so necessary for a man to come to Europe to learn to cure diseases of his nextdoor neighbor as they imagine. . . ." [56] Thomas Jefferson, more than once, mentioned objections to foreign education. In a letter from Paris to J. B. Bannister, Jr., October 15, 1785, the future President conceded that medical students might go to Europe, but insisted that all others could pursue their studies at home without much loss. He crystallized his attitude in the observation that "an American, coming to Europe for education, loses in his knowledge, in his morals, in his health, and in his habits," [57] as well as in his ability to adjust himself to his fellow Americans. "The consequences of foreign education are alarming to me, as an American. I sin, therefore, through zeal, whenever I enter on the subject." [58] A similar expression occurs in Jefferson's letter, August 10, 1787, to his nephew, Peter Carr: "There is no place where your pursuit of knowledge will be so little obstructed by foreign objects, as in your own country, nor any, wherein the virtues of the heart will be less exposed to be weakened." [59]

But Jefferson seemed to think better of foreign educational institutions than one might suspect from the sentiments just quoted. Writing to Governor Wilson C. Nicholas of Virginia, November 22, 1794, he described the Universities of Edinburgh and Geneva as " 'the two eyes of Europe' " [60] and endeavored to persuade the Virginia legislature to transplant the University of Geneva to its soil, possibly as a state-financed institution of higher education. Jefferson tried to persuade President George Washington in a letter, February 23, 1795, that, should the University of Geneva be brought over to the United States, it would satisfy the needs of Americans for advanced learning. However, Washington appeared to be a staunch nationalist. In his reply, March 15, 1795, he repeated what he had written on November 27, 1794, to John Adams, namely, that the refoundation of the University of Geneva as a unit on American soil might be harmful, "for by so doing they retain the language, habits, and principles, good and bad, which they bring with them." [61]

A letter written by Washington to Governor or Robert Brooke of Virginia on March 16, 1795, further revealed his opposition to study in Europe. The President was convinced that "a serious danger is encountered by sending abroad among other political systems those who have not well learned the value of their own"; accordingly, "It is with indescribable regret that I have seen the youth of the United States migrating to foreign countries in order to acquire the higher branches of erudition and to obtain a knowledge of the sciences." [62] Instead of study abroad, Washington urged the establishment of a national university.

It is all too easy to ascribe nationalist feelings to the early governmental and intellectual leaders in the United States. However, it is more proper to say that they did not oppose foreign study *per se*, but rather by the immature. Thus, Noah Webster's opposition was directed at young people between the ages of twelve and twenty, who would be exposed to subversive political ideas and moral corruption. His insistence that *"men should travel, and not boys"* [63] is an indication of his fear for the adolescent age only.

Jefferson himself tended to treat foreign educational ideas and institutions with greater respect as the eighteenth century approached its close. In Herbert Baxter Adams' judgment, by this time "Jefferson's educational ideals were now thoroughly European." [64] He was in frequent touch with European thinkers on educational problems. No sooner did Pierre Samuel DuPont de Nemours arrive from France in January, 1800, when Jefferson prevailed upon him to devise a plan for a national system of education and a national university. The program of the eminent French economist-philosopher, completed on June 15, 1800 and published later that year, proved to be too ambitious for the new nation. [65] Clearly, then, Jefferson did not disdain drawing upon the ideas and experience of foreign origin. After he left the presidency, at the time he was laying the foundation of the University of Virginia, he imported professors from Britain and Germany. [66]

On the state level, there was active opposition by some legislatures to foreign study by young persons. The charter of the University of Georgia, granted on January 27, 1785, maintained that "sending them abroad to other countries for their education . . . is too humiliating an acknowledgment of the ignorance or inferiority of our own [principles of religion, morality, and education] and will always be the cause of so great foreign attachments, that upon principles of policy is not admissible." [67] On February 7, 1785, the Georgia legislature put teeth into this opinion. Under the law, young persons under sixteen who studied in a foreign country were to be "considered and treated as aliens" [68] and to be ineligible for public or military office for a period of at least three years, depending upon the length of time abroad. Later that year, on December 1, the Virginia House of Delegates passed a resolution in support of a national university as against study in a foreign university. Such study, in the opinion of the Virginia legislators, ". . . exposes them [the young persons] to the danger of imbibing political prejudices disadvantageous to their own republican forms of government, and ought therefore be rendered unnecessary and avoided." [69]

But this apparently xenophobic attitude did not last very long in the United States. The year 1815 marked the beginning of the great trek by young Americans to German universities. The enrollment of George Ticknor and Edward Everett, great scholars of the future, at the University of Göttingen was a long-delayed sequel to a visit to this institution by Benjamin Franklin in 1766; to the correspondence carried on by the Rev. William Bentley of Salem and President Ezra Stiles of Yale with Christoph Daniel Ebeling of Hamburg, a graduate of Göttingen; and to the translation in 1814 of Madame de Staël's "De l'Allemagne," with its emphasis on German culture and particularly the University of Göttingen. [70] It is noteworthy that Edward

Everett was also active in government as governor of Massachusetts, secretary of state, and U.S. Senator, and in diplomacy. Also of interest is that Franklin, who was long engaged in government service and diplomacy, was the recipient of actual and honorary memberships in learned societies, and honorary degrees, in Scotland, Germany, Holland, France, Italy, Spain, England, and Russia.[71] It is not unlikely that the involvement of men with foreign intellectual interest and experience, such as Franklin and Everett, in governmental affairs had some positive effect on the official attitude toward international educational relations.

A great deal of ground has been covered in this essay from ancient times until the beginning of the nineteenth century. From this time onward, there is a proliferation of governmental activity in the field of international higher education. To do justice to all of these interesting and significant activities would require a modest volume. With time and space at a premium, it is only possible to outline the major lines of development.

During the nineteenth century, the history of governmental participation in international higher education may be classified according to the categories of official reports on foreign school systems, educational missions from abroad to aid the awakening countries, educational missions from a developing ceuntry to learn from the established nations, and official programs of information on education in different countries. These do not exhaust by any means all the categories, but they will suffice to give meaning to the developments in the nineteenth century.

Let us begin with the reports. Perhaps the most influential international report of modern times was the one on German education written for the French government by the philosopher Victor Cousin (1792–1867) in 1831.[72] This was speedily translated into other languages [73] and was read and acted upon on both sides of the Atlantic. Cousin, who was to serve for eight months as Minister of Public Instruction, also wrote for his government an interesting report on education in Holland.[74] Like its predecessor, this report was translated with little delay and was studied carefully in other countries.[75] Thus, the French government contributed to a great extent to the educational enlightenment and reform movements of other countries.

In the United States, the legislature of Ohio commissioned the Rev. Calvin Ellis Stowe, professor at the Lane Theological Seminary in Cincinnati, to make a study of European schools and to prepare a report. The resultant document,[76] a comparative analysis of Ohio and German schools, received considerable attention. The Ohio legislature published 10,000 copies for domestic use, while the legislatures of Massachusetts, Michigan, North Carolina, Pennsylvania, and Virginia reprinted Stowe's report for study by their schoolmen and citizens. A report along the lines of Stowe's, and drawing upon it to some extent, was submitted by the Rev. Benjamin M. Smith in 1839 to Governor David Campbell of Virginia.[77]

The great educational scholar-statesman, Henry Barnard, after assuming in 1839 the post of secretary of the State Board of Commissioners for Common Schools in Connecticut, published a report on his observations of education in Europe which he had made in a private capacity during 1835–1836. This document, plus additional material, was reprinted 25 years later in book form.[78]

Without doubt, the most provocative official report in the United States was the Seventh Annual Report [79] issued in 1844 by Horace Mann, secretary of the Board of Education of Massachusetts. This famous document summed up the observations and analysis of the schools visited by Mann during the previous year in Great Britain, Belgium, Holland, France, and the German areas. Students of the history of American education are well acquainted with the unfavorable reaction to this report by the Boston schoolmasters. It is also noteworthy that Mann, in turn, inspired the writing of official reports by two outstanding South American educational officials, Domingo Faustino Sarmiento of Argentina and José Pedro Varela of Uruguay. On the European side, a good example of governmental activity was the commissioning by the Newcastle and Taunton Commissions in England of Matthew Arnold, Her Majesty's Inspector in the Education Department, to study education in France, Holland, Germany, Switzerland, and Italy.[80] Whatever the influence of these reports, it is significant that they helped establish Matthew Arnold as a significant contributor to the infant field of comparative education. Again, interest by governments led to the exchange of information and to the subsequent initiation of educational reforms.

One of the characteristics of the nineteenth century was the emergence of some new nations and the entrance of others into the mainstream of international education and culture. One underdeveloped country, Persia, made an effort to modernize itself through educational contacts with the more advanced nations. In 1858, Shah Nasir-ud-Din sent forty-two students to European institutions of higher learning in order to become competent in medicine, engineering, political science, and other fields. When these men returned with the proper qualifications, they received appointments in suitable posts, with one returnee being chosen as Minister of Public Instruction.[81]

Apparently the Persian government felt that it had received much value from this practice, since it continued to send students during the following century to Belgium, England, France, Germany, Switzerland, and the United States.[82] The successful experience of Persia may possibly have served as an example to other countries which were concerned with the great leap forward into modern times.

The propaganda campaign by Yung Wing (B.A., Yale, 1854) in Chinese governmental circles to have young Chinese, like himself, obtain a higher education in the United States, bore fruit in 1871, when the Imperial Government approved his program of educating 120 young men. These students, twelve to fourteen years old, came to the United States, at the rate of thirty a year, from 1872 to 1875, and were to remain for fifteen years to complete their higher education. The plan provided for Chinese teachers "to keep up their knowledge of Chinese while in the United States" [83] and to keep them *au courant* with their native culture. Nevertheless, Chinese government officials became suspicious, not without some basis, that the young men were being attracted to the alien ideologies of Christianity and republicanism. The charges that young Chinese were becoming Christians were sufficient to bring about the termination of the Chinese Educational Mission in 1881. Nonetheless, China did benefit, since the "returned students" pioneered in engineering, railroad construction, and other technical fields. One returnee, Tong Shao-yi, interestingly enough, became Prime Minister of the Chinese Republic some decades later.

Along with the brief history of the Chinese Educational Mission to the United States, we should consider the outcomes of the Boxer Rebellion of 1900 as an instance of intergovernmental cooperation in cultural and educational activities. After the first shock of the defeat, the Chinese government began sending large numbers of young men to study in Japan; with as many as 15,000 Chinese in Japanese universities in 1907. The reason for this "huge exodus" was, in the main, the campaign by the viceroy of Hupeh and Hunan provinces, Chang Chih-tung, an educational reformer who preferred that the Chinese study in Japan because it was geographically accessible and economical, and because the Chinese and the Japanese shared a cultural heritage and customs.[84]

When the United States government showed a disposition to aid China after the Boxer Rebellion, the Chinese government began to consider the possibility of utilizing the American educational resources for its young people. President Theodore Roosevelt, in his message to Congress on December 3, 1907, pledged the help of the United

States to enable China to become a modern country. "One way of doing this is by promoting the coming of Chinese students to this country and making it attractive to them to take courses at our universities and higher education institutions." [85] As a result, Congress passed a resolution in 1908 to remit a portion of the Boxer Indemnity which China was supposed to pay to the United States. The sum involved, about $12 million, was to be used by the Chinese Imperial Government to send students to American institutions, mainly to study engineering, architecture, science, business, agriculture, and, to a lesser extent, law, political science, and education. [86] A portion of this fund was applied to the establishment in 1911 of Tsing Hua College in Peking to select and prepare students for their study abroad. Eventually, Congress passed, on May 21, 1924, an act of remission of the entire fund, and the China Foundation for the Promotion of Education and Culture was set up as the administering agency of the fund. It is also significant that Great Britain, in 1922, remitted a portion of its Boxer Indemnity fund so that Chinese could study at British universities, but no "indemnity students" were selected until 1933. [87]

The Boxer program of international higher education must have been a boon to China. Such famous men as V. K. Wellington Koo, the diplomat, and Y. C. James Yen, the leader in adult literacy education, studied at Columbia and Yale, respectively. A study of the 960 biographies in the "Who's Who in China" for the year 1931 revealed that 521 individuals had studied in foreign countries, and of these, 206 received their education in the United States. [88] Quantitatively, it is noteworthy that the China Foundation for the Promotion of Education and Culture was able to pay, prior to the Communist revolution of 1949, for many educational projects in China and America, including the study by more than 3,000 Chinese in American higher institutions. [89]

The Japanese government's experience in international higher education is also worthwhile tracing. The first indication of the official desire to learn from other countries was the fifth article of the Charter Oath of Five Articles sworn by the Emperor on April 6, 1868, the year of the Meiji Restoration: "Knowledge shall be sought throughout the world, so that the welfare of the Empire may be promoted." [90] A few years later, acting upon the advice of the Rev. Guido Verbeck, a missionary of the Dutch Reformed Church in America, the Japanese Imperial Government sent an educational mission to European countries and to the United States to study foreign technology and to recruit technical specialists to work in Japan. This mission, headed by Prince Tomomi Iwakura, Minister of Foreign Affairs, was abroad during 1871–1873. The letter of credentials from the Emperor which Prince Iwakura presented to President U. S. Grant made the following point: "It is our purpose to select from the various institutions prevailing among enlightened nations such as are best suited to our present condition, and adopt them, in gradual reforms and improvements of our policy and customs, so as to be upon an equality with them." [91] Students of the subsequent history of Japan are familiar with the extent to which this objective was realized in later decades.

Out of the Iwakura Mission resulted another tendency in governmental interest in international higher education during the nineteenth century. One of its major appointees was Professor David Murray of Rutgers University, a mathematician, as National Superintendent of Schools and Colleges and as Adviser to the Japanese Ministry of Education. From 1873 to 1879, Murray succeeded in introducing various reforms into the Japanese educational system. Together with Fujimaro Tanaka, Vice-Minister of Education, Murray visited in 1876 the Philadelphia Centennial Exposition, where the Japanese official took note of the educational exhibits of various countries. [92]

Another important contribution by the Iwakura Mission was the invitation to President William Smith Clark of the Massachusetts Agricultural College (now the University of Massachusetts) to establish the Sapporo Agricultural College (now Hokkaido University). The members of the Mission had become intensely interested in the technical-military training program of the American land-grant college and determined to make use of its experience in meeting the educational needs of the Japanese people. Clark served only for eight months from the summer of 1876, but he managed to introduce the scientific approach to agricultural education, military training, and Christian education. That the short period of service did not mean a limited influence was evident from the long recollection by the Japanese of Clark and his final words of advice, "Boys, be ambitious!" As Anderson testifies, "This simple admonition struck a responsive chord among Japanese youth and became one of the mottoes of the schoolboys throughout the nation, remembered and quoted to this day." [93] Again, the foresight by the Japanese educational mission paid long-term dividends.

We can close the nineteenth-century period in international higher educational cooperation on a governmental basis by discussing briefly the official programs of cooperation and information concerning education and culture. Perhaps the earliest instance, in the United States at least, was the joint resolution by Congress in 1840 to establish a system of exchange of publications between the Library of Congress and the leading libraries of other countries. The first secretary of the Smithsonian Institution, Joseph Henry, organized a system of international exchange of scientific publications. In 1867, the Smithsonian Institution was given the responsibility of exchanging government documents for those of foreign governments, with the latter to be sent to the Library of Congress. At the Brussels convention in 1886, several governments established agencies to exchange official documents and unofficial publications of a scientific and literary nature.[94]

The United States Bureau of Education, established in 1867 with Henry Barnard as Commissioner, began to disseminate not only information on education in the United States, but also concerning developments in other countries. In the first annual report of the commissioner, dated 1868, there appeared essays on "Female Education at Home and Abroad" and "Secondary Schools in Prussia." Subsequently, descriptive and comparative articles on foreign educational systems and problems were published frequently, so that the entire collection of reports could have been said to "cover the whole field of contemporary educational thought, and constitute in themselves a library of education." [95] The Bureau of Education produced literature on comparative and foreign descriptive education on a scale hitherto unknown. As mentioned previously, governments produced works of international educational significance, such as those by Victor Cousin, Horace Mann, Calvin E. Stowe, and Matthew Arnold. But it remained for the reports of the Bureau (now Office) of Education to contribute on a systematic basis to international educational enlightenment. First Henry Barnard, then General John Eaton, and later William Torrey Harris became internationally known for their efforts at bringing to the attention of the world the educational developments in the various countries. In fact, in the late nineteenth century, the Bureau of Education was often praised in European educational circles as the model agency for the collection and dissemination of educational information. A Dutch pioneer in the international exchange of educational information, Herman Molkenboer, proposed in 1885 an international agency modeled upon the Bureau of Education.[96] Finally, the Education Department of England established in 1893 an Office of Special Inquiries and Reports, with Michael Sadler as director, again following the example of the Bureau of Education.[97] The reports on foreign education produced under Sadler's direction have been justly hailed by specialists in comparative education.

The twentieth century saw the rapid growth of a variety of governmental programs in international educational relations. The developments become so numerous, in this era of shrinking distances and more

rapid means of communications, that only a special study can do
justice to the widespread activities by the many national governments,
on a two-way or a multiple basis. To all this must be added the official
educational cooperation with the League of Nations, the Pan American Union, the Organization of American States, other intergovernmental bodies, and most strikingly with UNESCO. Since it is not
feasible, within the bounds of a limited essay such as this one, to offer a thorough account, the best that can be done under the circumstances is to record the highlights in more or less the same categories
as in the analysis of the nineteenth century.

At the beginning of the twentieth century, Major General Leonard
Wood, the United States military commander of the occupied territory
of Cuba, took advantage of the offer by Harvard University to train
without cost over 1,200 Cubans as teachers during the summer of 1900.
This was "a valuable experience and . . . it helped Cuba meet its
immediate and pressing need for teachers." [98] General Wood left Cuba
in 1902, but not before he drew up a contract with the New Paltz, N.Y.,
State Normal School to train sixty Cuban teachers, but the sovereign
Cuban government failed to ratify this contract.

The services of American scholars were in demand in various countries to aid in various educational projects. James Mark Baldwin,
professor of psychology at the Johns Hopkins University, helped the
Mexican government, during 1909–1913, as an education adviser to
the movement for school reform and in the founding of a new national
university and the Escuela de Altos Estudios.[99] Just about this period,
the Peruvian government enjoyed the services of Harry Erwin Bard
and Albert A. Giesecke in the reorganization of its school system. Bard
was the director general of the Ministry of Education of Peru, while
Giesecke received an appointment as the rector of the University of
Cuzco.[100]

Many more examples might be cited of the use by governments of
foreign specialists to help on all levels of educational service. It will
suffice to mention a few well-known individuals. John Dewey, professor of philosophy at Columbia University, was invited by the Chinese government to deliver lectures at its universities and to confer
with its educators, and the American educator fulfilled his obligations
in a manner conducive to a lasting influence.[101] In 1924, Dewey was
invited by the Ministry of Education in Turkey to report on its school
system.[102] A third official invitation, from the government of Mexico,
came to Dewey in 1926. Here, as in China and Turkey, Dr. Dewey's
advice on education made a notable impression on the school system.[103]

In at least one instance, a government issued a call for a commission of foreign educators to study its educational system and to recommend improvements, as when the Educational Inquiry Commission, consisting of a group of American educators, was invited by the government of Iraq. Under the chairmanship of Paul Monroe, director of the Institute of International Education, Teachers College, Columbia University, the Commission included Professor William C. Bagley of Teachers College and Professor Edgar W. Knight of the University of North Carolina. The report of the Commission,[104] which was presented in 1932 to the Iraqi government, resulted in the establishment two years later of the Rural Teachers College.[105] It is especially worthy of note that a British educator who prepared a later report on compulsory education in Iraq found the comments and observations of the Monroe Commission "as valid in 1950 as they were in 1932." [106]

On an intergovernmental level, the United States, beginning with the Economic Cooperation Administration, set up by the Foreign Assistance Act of 1948, provided various forms of aid, including personnel, toward the rehabilitation and reconstruction of educational systems and universities in Europe. President Harry S. Truman's Point Four Program, the Mutual Security Administration, and the Foreign Operations Administration carried on this function under different agency nomenclature and on a wider geographical basis. The International Cooperation Administration, established in 1955 as a semiautonomous unit in the Department of State, carried on the functions of these agencies.[107] Most recently, the Agency for International Development, created by the Foreign Assistance Act of 1961, took over the educational and other functions which accumulated in the period after the Second World War.[108]

One of the most conspicuous developments in international higher education was the increase in the migration of students and scholars to foreign countries, as well as student and faculty interchange on an international basis. To some extent, this was a matter of individual choice or an arrangement involving private organizations, such as the Institute of International Education and the Deutsche Akademische Austauschdienst. Also contributing to the growth of student and faculty exchange were the individual governments and UNESCO and other intergovernmental bodies.

Mention has already been made of the application of the Boxer Indemnity Fund toward the instruction of Chinese in the United States and Great Britain. The British Council has given, since 1937, more than 5,000 scholarships, most of them to postgraduate students "from many parts of the world." [109] The exchanges involving the United States and many other countries under the Fulbright, Smith-Mundt, and Fulbright-Hays Acts, are very familiar. Under the provisions of the Fulbright-Hays Act,[110] "each year, nearly 8,000 persons representing over 130 countries and territories are exchanged to teach, study, lecture, and engage in research or in other educational and cultural activities. . . ."[111] Finally, the Peace Corps, established by Congress on September 22, 1961, proved to be of educational aid to many countries. "Volunteers who can teach—all subjects at all levels—are those most requested by developing nations," announces an official brochure.[112] The numerous teachers working under the Peace Corps administration must also be considered as part of the international educational exchange program of the United States government. It is of interest, in addition, that the Peace Corps of the United States has served as a model for the German Development Service of the government of the Federal Republic of Germany. The first group of German "Peace Corps" volunteers left for Tanganyika in August, 1964.

Another aspect of governmental activity in international higher education during the twentieth century is the development of the cultural relations program by various nations. In view of the already excessive length of this essay, only the basic facts will be mentioned. By way of a definition, "the cultural relations of a people are its efforts toward mutual acquaintance and the mutual understanding that such acquaintance brings."[113] The scope of a program of cultural relations may be quite broad and all-embracing, as in the case of the United States Information and Educational Exchange Act of 1948: "an information service to disseminate abroad information about the United States, its people, and policies . . . an educational exchange service to cooperate with other nations in—(a) the interchange of persons, knowledge, and skills; (b) the rendering of technical and other services; (c) the interchange of developments in the field of education, the arts, and sciences."[114] Since most of these activities have already been discussed, we can devote our attention to the governmental organizations stressing information programs. In 1925, the U.S.S.R. government founded the All-Union Society for Cultural Relations with Foreign Countries (VOKS in the Russian abbreviation) in order to publicize in foreign countries the Soviet way of life, society, and culture. The Prussian Ministry of Science, Art, and Public Education founded in 1929 the Deutsche Pädagogische Ausslandsstelle to furnish information concerning educational exchanges with other countries. In the United States, we might mention the various agencies established by the Department of State: Division of Cultural Relations (1938), the Interdepartmental Committee on Cooperation with the American Republics (1938), the United States Information Agency (1953), the Bureau of Educational and Cultural Affairs (1959), and the U.S. Advisory Commission on International and Cultural Affairs (1962).[115] The last form of governmental interest in international higher education is the special university for foreign students. The Patrice Lumumba University of the Friendship of the Peoples, opened in Moscow in the fall of 1960, was designed by the Soviet government for the instruction of students from Asia, Africa, and Latin America.[116] A similar institution was founded by the government of Czechoslovakia a year later under the name of the University of November 17 in Prague.

The foregoing pages represent an overview of a significant, interesting subject that deserves comprehensive treatment on the basis of documentary materials in various languages. The scope of such a study might be broadened to include the cultural relations which are a by-product of government-sponsored trade, diplomacy, and war.

Whatever information is obtainable on the history of government participation in international higher educational relations, it is important to keep in mind the basic needs for any lasting impact of the nations on each other. These are: purpose, program, and personnel. When these requirements are met satisfactorily, there is a good chance for the development of successful international relations in culture and education.

NOTES

1. I Kings 7:13–45; II Chronicles 4:11–22.
2. Text in Vincent A. Smith, *Asoka: The Buddhist Emperor of India,* 2nd ed. (Delhi: Chand, 1957), p. 175.
3. *Ibid.*
4. Cf. William W. Brickman, "Introduction to the History of International Relations in Higher Education," mimeographed, o.p. (New York: School of Education, New York University, 1960), p. 45.
5. T. Walter Wallbank, *India* (New York: Holt, 1948), p. 12.
6. Smith, *op. cit.,* p. 46.
7. *Ibid.*
8. Fritz Kern, *Asóka: Kaiser und Missionar* (Bern: Francke, 1956), p. 107.
9. George Sarton, *Introduction to the History of Science,* Vol. I (Washington: Carnegie Institution, 1927), p. 435.
10. Hans-Wilhelm Haussig, *Kulturgeschichte von Byzanz* (Stuttgart: Kröner, 1959), p. 262.
11. Percy Sykes, *A History of Persia,* Vol. I (London: Macmillan, 1930), p. 459.

12. George Sarton, "Islamic Science," in T. Cuyler Young, editor, *Near Eastern Culture and Society* (Princeton: Princeton University Press, 1951), pp. 87–88.

13. C. P. Fitzgerald, *China: A Short Cultural History*, rev. ed. (London: Cresset, 1950), p. 325.

14. *Ibid.*

15. G. F. Hudson, *Europe and China* (London: Edward Arnold, 1931), p. 129.

16. Quoted in Howard S. Galt, *A History of Chinese Educational Institutions*, Vol. I (London: Arthur Probsthain, 1951), p. 328.

17. Quoted in *ibid.*, p. 328.

18. *Ibid.*, p. 333.

19. Fitzgerald, *loc. cit.*

20. George Sarton, *Introduction to the History of Science, op. cit.*, p. 582.

21. Fitzgerald, *op. cit.*, p. 437.

22. Hudson, *op. cit.*, p. 150. On the Polos in China, see *ibid.*, pp. 148–151, 164; Eileen Power, "The Opening of Land Routes to Cathay," in Arthur P. Newton, editor, *Travel and Travellers of the Middle Ages* (New York: Knopf, 1950), pp. 132–138; and Margaret T. Hodgen, *Early Anthropology in the Sixteenth and Seventeenth Centuries* (Philadelphia: University of Pennsylvania Press, 1964), pp. 89–90; and Raymond Dawson, "Western Conceptions of Chinese Civilization," in *The Legacy of China* (Oxford: Clarendon, 1964), pp. 4–6.

23. Fitzgerald, *loc. cit.*

24. Diodorus Siculus, *Historical Library* (Bibliotheke Historike), Vol. XVIII, p. 4.

25. George Sarton, *Introduction to the History of Science, op. cit.*, p. 124.

26. Cf., John P. Mahaffy, *The Silver Age of the Greek World* (Chicago: University of Chicago Press, 1906), p. 197.

27. John W. H. Walden, *The Universities of Ancient Greece* (New York: Scribner, 1909), p. 52.

28. W. W. Capes, *University Life in Ancient Athens* (London: Longmans, Green, 1877), p. 3.

29. See Clarence A. Forbes, "Ancient Universities and Student Life," *Classical Journal*, Vol. XXVIII (March 1933), pp. 414, 420, 421; Frederick Eby and Charles F. Arrowood, *The History and Philosophy of Education: Ancient and Medieval* (New York: Prentice-Hall, 1940), pp. 498–501; and Brickman, *op. cit.*, p. 54.

30. Philostratus and Eunapius, *The Lives of the Sophists*, translated by Wilmer Cave Wright (London: Heinemann, 1922), p. 507.

31. *Ibid.*

32. *Ibid.*, p. 508.

33. Codex Theodosianus, Book XIV, t. 9, 1. 1, as translated in Percival R. Cole, *Later Roman Education in Ausonius, Capella and the Theodosian Code* (New York: Teachers College, Columbia University, 1909), p. 31.

34. Charles Diehl, *Byzance: Grandeur et décadence* (Paris: Flammarion,

1930), p. 55; Charles Diehl, *Byzantium: Greatness and Decline* (New Brunswick: Rutgers University Press, 1957), p. 55.

35. Eby and Arrowood, *op. cit.*, p. 615.

36. Hastings Rashdall, *The Universities of Europe in the Middle Ages,* new edition edited by F. M. Powicke and A. B. Emden, Vol. I (London: Oxford University Press, 1936), p. 8.

37. *Ibid.*, p. 10.

38. Quoted in Heinrich Denifle, *Die Entstehung der Universitäten des Mittelalters bis 1400* (Berlin: Weidmann, 1887), p. 773, note.

39. Rashdall, *op. cit.*, p. 336.

40. Mehdi Nakosteen, *History of Islamic Origins of Western Education, A.D. 800–1350* (Boulder: University of Colorado Press, 1964), p. 185. See also Rashdall, *op. cit.*, pp. 358, 360–361, notes.

41. Lynn Thorndike, *University Records and Life in the Middle Ages* (New York: Columbia University Press, 1944), p. 125.

42. Rashdall, *op. cit.*, Vol. II, pp. 64, 90–91; Nakosteen, *op. cit.*, pp. 292–293.

43. Document in Thorndike, *op. cit.*, p. 127.

44. Document in *ibid.*, p. 150.

45. Rashdall, *op. cit.*, Vol. II, pp. 70, note, 106.

46. Maurice De Wulf, *Philosophy and Civilization in the Middle Ages* (Princeton: Princeton University Press, 1922), p. 80.

47. Brickman, *op. cit.*, p. 64.

48. Document in Thorndike, *op. cit.*, p. 25.

49. John E. Sandys, *A History of Classical Scholarship,* Vol. II (New York: Hafner, 1958), pp. 65–66.

50. Hudson, *Europe and China, op. cit.*, p. 299.

51. Thomas Sprat, *The History of the Royal Society of London* (London, 1772), p. 43.

52. Brickman, *op. cit.*, pp. 90–96.

53. William W. Brickman, "The Development of Education in Tsarist Russia," in George Z. F. Bereday, William W. Brickman, and Gerald H. Read, editors, *The Changing Soviet School* (Boston: Houghton Mifflin, 1960), pp. 25–27, 30.

54. *Ibid.*, pp. 32–34.

55. Minutes of the Common Council of Philadelphia, July 31, 1750, as quoted in Francis N. Thorpe, *Benjamin Franklin and the University of Pennsylvania.* Circular of Information, No. 2, U.S. Bureau of Education (Washington: Government Printing Office, 1892), p. 245. For the original text, see *Minutes of the Common Council, 1704–1776* (Philadelphia, 1817), pp. 529–530.

56. Quoted in Brooke Hindle, *The Pursuit of Science in Revolutionary America: 1735–1789* (Chapel Hill: University of North Carolina Press, 1956), p. 289.

57. Document in Saul K. Padover, editor, *The Complete Jefferson* (New York: Tudor, 1943), p. 1056.

58. *Ibid.*, pp. 1056–1057.

59. Document in *ibid.*, p. 1060.

60. Quoted in Roy J. Honeywell, *The Educational Work of Thomas Jefferson* (Cambridge: Harvard University Press, 1931), p. 59.

61. Document in Edgar W. Knight, editor, *A Documentary History of Education in the South before 1860,* Vol. II (Chapel Hill: University of North Carolina Press, 1950), p. 86.

62. Document in *ibid.*, p. 6.

63. Noah Webster, Jun., *A Collection of Essays and Fugitive Writings on Moral, Historical, Political and Literary Subjects* (Boston: Thomas and Andrews, 1790), p. 35. This statement is in an essay, "On the Education of Youth in America," which was originally published in the *American Magazine* (May 1788).

64. Herbert B. Adams, *Thomas Jefferson and the University of Virginia,* Circular of Information, no. 1, 1888, U.S. Bureau of Education (Washington: Government Printing Office, 1888), p. 45.

65. *Ibid.*, pp. 49–51.

66. *Ibid.*, pp. 110–111.

67. Document in Knight, *op. cit.*, Vol. III, 1952, pp. 5–6.

68. Document in *ibid.*, Vol. II, 1950, p. 4.

69. Document in *ibid.*, p. 6.

70. Henry A. Pochmann, *German Culture in America: Philosophical and Cultural Influences, 1600–1900* (Madison: University of Wisconsin Press, 1957), pp. 45, 51–57. On Ticknor and Everett at Göttingen, see Orie W. Long, *Literary Pioneers: Early American Explorers of European Culture* (Cambridge: Harvard University Press, 1935), pp. 3–76.

71. Thomas Woody, "A Sketch of Franklin's Life," in *Educational Views of Benjamin Franklin* (New York: McGraw-Hill, 1931), pp. 30–31.

72. Victor Cousin, *Rapport sur l'état de l'instruction publique dans quelques pays de l'Allemagne et particulièrement en Prusse* (Paris, 1831).

73. ———, *State of Public Instruction in Prussia* (London: Wilson, 1834).

74. ———, *De l'instruction publique en Hollande* (Paris, 1837).

75. ———, *On the State of Education in Holland* (London: Murray, 1838).

76. Calvin E. Stowe, *Report on Elementary Public Instruction in Europe* (Boston: Dutton and Wentworth, 1837).

77. "Rev. Benjamin M. Smith's Report on the Primary School System of Prussia, January 15, 1839," in Knight, *A Documentary History of Education in the South before 1860, op. cit.,* Vol. II, pp. 412–460.

78. Henry Barnard, *National Education in Europe* (Hartford: Case, Tiffany, 1854).

79. Horace Mann, *Seventh Annual Report of the Secretary of the Board* (Boston: Dutton and Wentworth, 1844).

80. Matthew Arnold, *The Popular Education of France with Notices to That of Holland and Switzerland* (London: Longmans, 1861); *Schools and Universities on the Continent* (London: Macmillan, 1868); *Higher Schools and Universities of Germany* (London: Macmillan, 1874).

81. Issa K. Sadiq, *Modern Persia and Her Educational System* (New York: Bureau of Publications, Teachers College, Columbia University, 1931), p. 18.

82. *Ibid.*, pp. 78–79.

83. Yung Wing, *My Life in China and America* (New York: Holt, 1909), p. 173.

84. Wen-Han Kiang, *The Chinese Student Movement* (New York: King's Crown Press, 1948), p. 16.

85. "Remission of a Portion of the Chinese Indemnity: Message from the President of the United States . . . ," 60th Congress, 2nd Session, House Doc. No. 1275 (1909), p. 6 as quoted in Guy S. Métraux, *Exchange of Persons: The Evolution of Cross-Cultural Education* (New York: Social Science Research Council, 1952), p. 21.

86. Métraux, *op. cit.*, p. 20, note; I. L. Kandel, *United States Activities in International Cultural Relations* (Washington: American Council on Education, 1945), p. 81.

87. Kiang, *op. cit.*, pp. 150–151.

88. *A Survey of Chinese Students in American Colleges and Universities in the Past One Hundred Years* (New York: China Institute in America, 1954), p. 21.

89. *Government Programs in International Education (A Survey and Handbook)*, 85th Congress, 2nd Session, House Report No. 2712 (Washington: U.S. Government Printing Office, 1959), p. 29.

90. Quoted in G. B. Sansom, *The Western World and Japan* (New York: Knopf, 1950), p. 318.

91. Kengi Hamada, *Prince Ito* (Tokyo: Sansaido, 1936), pp. 65–66, as quoted in Ronald S. Anderson, *Japan: Three Epochs of Modern Education*, Bulletin 1959, No. 11, U.S. Office of Education (Washington: U.S. Government Printing Office, 1959), p. 5.

92. On Murray's educational activities and influence in Japan, see Merle Curti and Kendall Birr, *Prelude to Point Four: American Technical Missions Overseas, 1838–1938* (Madison: University of Wisconsin Press, 1954), pp. 57–62; Robert S. Schwantes, *Japanese and Americans: A Century of Cultural Relations* (New York: Harper, 1955), pp. 130–133; and Anderson, *op. cit.*, pp. 6–7.

93. Anderson, *op. cit.*, p. 8.

94. *Government Programs in International Education (A Survey and Handbook)*, *op. cit.*, p. 33.

95. Will S. Monroe, *Bibliography of Education* (New York: Appleton, 1897), p. 175.

96. P. Rosselló, *Les précurseurs du Bureau International d'Education* (Geneva: Bureau International d'Education, 1943), pp. 47, 51.

97. W. H. G. Armytage, *Four Hundred Years of English Education* (Cambridge: University Press, 1964), p. 195; Franz Hilker, *Vergleichende Pädagogik* (Munich: Hueber, 1962), p. 47.

98. Curti and Birr, *op. cit.*, p. 90; Charles A. Thomson and Walter H. C.

Laves, *Cultural Relations and U. S. Foreign Policy* (Bloomington: Indiana University Press, 1963), p. 29.

99. Curti and Birr, *op. cit.*, pp. 196–197.

100. *Ibid.*, p. 200.

101. William W. Brickman, editor, *John Dewey's Impressions of Soviet Russia and the Revolutionary World: Mexico–China–Turkey, 1929* (New York: Bureau of Publications, Teachers College, Columbia University, 1964), p. 11.

102. *Ibid.*, pp. 12–15.

103. *Ibid.*, p. 16.

104. Paul Monroe et al., *Report of the Educational Inquiry Commission* (Baghdad: Government Press, 1932).

105. Roderic D. Matthews and Matta Akrawi, *Education in Arab Countries of the Near East* (Washington: American Council on Education, 1949), p. 184.

106. Victor Clark, *Compulsory Education in Iraq* (Paris: UNESCO, 1951), p. 19. Cf. p. 20.

107. *Government Programs in International Education (A Survey and Handbook)*, *op. cit.*, p. 38.

108. *The AID Program* (Washington: Agency for International Development, 1964), p. 5.

109. *Annual Report, 1962–1963* (London: British Council, [1963]), p. 38.

110. 87th Congress, Public Law 256, *Mutual Educational and Cultural Exchange Act of 1961.*

111. *1965–66 Teacher Exchange Opportunities,* U.S. Office of Education OE–14047–66 (Washington: U.S. Government Printing Office, 1964), p. 1.

112. *Peace Corps Facts* (Washington: Peace Corps, n.d.), p. 2. See also *Peace Corps: 2nd Annual Report* (Washington: Peace Corps, n.d.).

113. Ruth E. McMurry and Muna Lee, *The Cultural Approach: Another Way in International Relations* (Chapel Hill: University of North Carolina Press, 1947), p. 1.

114. 80th Congress, Public Law 802, 1948, p. 1.

115. See McMurry and Lee, *op. cit.*; Charles A. H. Thomson, *Overseas Information Services of the United States* (Washington: Brookings Institution, 1948); Thomson and Laves, *op. cit.*; and Francis J. Colligan, *Twenty Years After: Two Decades of Government-Sponsored Cultural Relations,* Department of State Publication 6689 (Washington: U.S. Government Printing Office, 1958).

116. Seymour M. Rosen, *The Peoples' Friendship University in the U.S.S.R.* (Washington: U.S. Office of Education, 1962).

CHAPTER 4

The Cultural Background of International Education

INA CORINNE BROWN

In dealing with the cultural factors in international education there are, in any particular situation, at least three variables involved: the motives, objectives, and perceptions of the receiving country, those of the sending country, and those of the individual students concerned. None of these variables can be precisely defined and the various terms are used here only in a common-sense fashion. When we add to these considerations the variations in culture patterns within some countries, the variations from one country to another, and the fact that in the United States alone in the academic year 1963–1964 there were something like seventy-five thousand foreign students from more than one hundred and fifty countries,[1] the problems involved in making any sort of valid generalizations about the subject of this paper become formidable. In the light of these difficulties I shall limit discussion for the most part to the United States as a receiving country, and I shall give most of the attention to those things that, from a cultural aspect, are most relevant to the general problem of international understanding.

While we should not lose sight of the fact that the main purpose of international education is education and that this purpose is worthy in and of itself, there is no escaping the fact that, whatever the avowed motive of the United States in encouraging students from other countries to come here, there are certain expectations beyond the strictly academic ones.

We find ourselves in a world that within this century has taken on certain characteristics that were not present in an earlier day. It is, of

47

course, a shrinking world in which the human voice can be heard around the globe; events occurring in one hemisphere can be relayed by television through space stations to the other hemisphere; and astronauts can circle the globe in a matter of minutes. But this shrinking of the world means that the individual's real world has expanded to the same degree. Human beings even in the most out of the way places must now see themselves in a world context. When we add to these facts our economic interdependence and the destructive power at man's disposal, some sort of international understanding and accord are seen as the price of survival.

Nor should we underestimate the role of the student in such understanding. The student has been an important means of cultural exchange throughout history. Today, with new nations coming on to the world stage in rapid succession, with the economic underdevelopment of many of these countries, and with the almost total lack of an educated leadership in some of them, the direction taken by any particular country in the future may well depend on where its students go for an education and the kinds of experiences they have in the host country.

There is, of course, no such thing as *the* foreign student if we imply by that term that all foreign students are alike in all ways. It is true that foreign students do have some things in common that set them apart from the student who is studying in his home country. In addition to the problems of adjustment that all students face, the foreign students, whatever their age, sex, status, or home country, do face certain adjustments growing out of the fact that they encounter a different culture in a different national setting. Frequently, if not usually, they must use a second language and adjust to a different educational pattern including an unfamiliar relationship between professor and student. All foreign students find themselves perceived in new ways, and whereas at home they could, and usually did, take their culture for granted they find that when abroad their own culture patterns are regarded with curiosity, if not considered peculiar or downright unnatural. In short, the major factor setting all foreign students apart is the fact of cultural difference and the ramifications of this fact.

It would, of course, be equally mistaken to assume that all foreign students are in other ways alike. The students represent an infinite variety of nationalities, cultures, and specific backgrounds, and they come to this country with various purposes and expectations. The students from modern industrially developed areas such as western Europe, Britain, Canada, and Australia come with experiences and attitudes regarding their own countries and the United States, that may differ markedly from the experiences and attitudes of students with non-European backgrounds or who come from the less developed areas of the world. Students from particular areas such as South Asia, Southeast Asia, Africa, or Latin America may each have some things in common with other students from the same area, but the culture and political background may differ from country to country within each area. There are thus likely to be differences in the way these students perceive the United States, and they have different perceptions of the way the people of the United States view their respective countries.

Perhaps at this point we should distinguish between problems of communication and problems of perception. Problems of communication are sometimes purely linguistic or semantic. The student may be simply deficient in his knowledge of English so that he has difficulty in understanding or in making himself understood. Or particular words or expressions may have different shades of meaning or different overtones to peoples of different countries. There are such differences in English as used in Britain, Canada, Australia, and the United States. An example of different meanings given to the same expression was reported during the visit of Nikita Khrushchev to the United States. On one occasion Mr. Khrushchev referred to an incident of Russian triumph with the remark, "Only our faces were red." His hearers were puzzled until someone explained that in Russia a "red face" implied health and vigor, not embarrassment.

Differences in perception are more profound though they too may have a linguistic base. Linguistic differences are often much more than a difference in vocabulary. The linguistic structure itself tends to structure perception and to establish the categories into which one's experience is organized. In any case, both language and culture affect the way in which objects, actions, and events are perceived. The foreign student, like the rest of us, perceives his own as well as other cultures, through a particular enculturative screen. Or, as it has been expressed in another way, "Facts do not speak for themselves; they are always cross-examined and given meaning in accordance with the assumptions of the examiner." [2] And the assumptions of the examiner are affected by the fact that each culture has its own way of organizing experience. As a member of a given society the individual learns what has been called the grammar of his culture in the same way that he learns the grammar of his language. Both types of grammar are then taken for granted and become a part of one's thinking.

It would be difficult to overestimate the significance of these differences in perception. There is a Chinese proverb to the effect that two-thirds of what a man sees depends on what is behind his eyes, not in front of them. Sidney Hook expresses the same idea by saying, "The world we live in is an interpreted world," [3] and Julian Huxley reminds us that in the long run our actions are related to our overall pictures, our map of reality. Our perceptions, he points out, are not snapshot pictures of reality projected into our minds but quite elaborate mental constructions based on a mass of assumptions derived from what we have learned from experience. If the maps of reality are distorted or incorrectly perceived the individual's behavior may not be consistent with the actual realities.[4]

We are, of course, aware of individual differences of perception within our own culture. Even within a given community we may see things differently because, in part at least, of variations in our experiences and in the different positions from which we view reality. Old and young, parent and child, teacher and pupil, employer and employee, urbanite and rural dweller, rich and poor, northerner and southerner, white and Negro may all represent different positions from which certain aspects of reality are viewed, and diverse sets of experiences that affect the perception of particular circumstances and events.[5]

If these differences in perception exist among persons who have essentially the same cultural background of language, religion, history, and general experience, it becomes all the more remarkable that peoples whose experiences have been almost totally different can understand one another at all.

Furthermore, there is a selective factor in our perceptions so that particular experiences we have had or particular circumstances in a given situation may not only color what we see but may determine in some measure what we actually see at all. Again, we know that this selective factor operates within our own culture. A smartly dressed young woman leading a dog will likely be perceived differently by a fashion conscious woman, an elderly grandfather, a young bachelor, and a small boy. Each will "notice" certain things about the scene and "not notice" certain other things that may attract the attention of one or another of the other viewers. The foreign student in our midst is likely to be keenly conscious of certain aspects of our culture that do not engage the conscious attention of most of us.

Foreign students may also do what many of the rest of us do—perceive their own ideal culture while being very much aware of the real culture of others. Sometimes, of course, these perceptions present a very confused image bearing little resemblance to reality. I have known foreign students who perceived their own culture in ideal terms and whose perception of American culture was a blurred pattern of race prejudice, universal wealth, and luxurious living.

There are many other factors that enter into the varied perceptions of foreign students—factors that make it risky to generalize even about students from the same country. For one thing, there often are very great cultural variations within national units. There are today many political units that are made up of peoples who vary in race, national origin, language, religion, and culture. In many areas there are rural and urban differences as well as economic or class differences. All too often we have acted as if all Chinese, all Africans, or all Latin Americans were alike.

It is important, also, that previous experiences with other nations be taken into account. Students from countries that have been under colonial rule are likely to have their perceptions of the West colored by that fact. Persons from newly independent nations may be expected to perceive and react to certain of our patterns in ways that may differ from those of persons whose home countries have long been on a basis of equality with the West. Students who have been subjected to color discrimination or whose countries have been in subjection to white rulers may perceive and react to our racial patterns in ways that are different from those of persons who have never been on the receiving end of discrimination.

We must also take into account the rapidly changing cultural situation particularly in the underdeveloped countries. Anthropologists who once wrote freely in what is called the ethnological present—that is, as if earlier practices were still the rule—now find it more expedient to use the ethnological past [6] when describing current practices that might be considered "backward." Almost any area of the world now has some people who are, or who consider themselves to be, *evolués, assimilados,* or "intellectuals" by virtue of their having acquired a degree of formal education, facility in a European language, or a degree of familiarity with Western ways. There are, in fact, some countries in which students of culture find themselves more acceptable when labeled sociologists rather than anthropologists because to the sensitive local élite the term anthropologist is associated with an interest in "primitive" culture.

It is also well to take into account the fact that in the present world changes may come with such overwhelming force or suddenness that a society may be unable to maintain its equilibrium. Sometimes the shock may come from the outside as when a previously isolated island community was occupied by Western soldiers during the Second World War. Sometimes it is a problem of peoples of no political experience being forced to adjust to changing circumstances beyond their comprehension as in the Congo when people of many different tribal backgrounds and loyalties found themselves confronted with the problem of living together as an independent nation. There are other peoples today who are trying to introduce modern technology into a preindustrial culture—a sort of putting new wine into old wineskins. There is scarcely a non-Western country today that does not have in some form this imbalance of old and new—an imbalance that varies in particulars from one country to another but which in each case must be reckoned with if we are to make progress toward international understanding.

A common assumption underlying most programs involving exchange of persons is that the contact will in itself promote international understanding and good will. While such understanding and good will do often result from contact, particularly if the contact is prolonged and the circumstances favorable, the notion that if we would just get to know one another we would be friends and everything would be all right is as dangerous as it is sentimental. We have before us all too many instances of people who know one another very well but who are at one another's throats. In fact, in most of the trouble spots in the world today the conflict is not between strangers but between peoples who have long occupied the same or adjacent territories. They are frequently of the same race, often speak the same language, and may practice the same religion. In East and West Germany, in North and South Korea, in North and South Viet Nam, and in numerous other places the conflict is between peoples who are basically alike and who have had every opportunity to know one another. Some of the world's bitterest conflicts have been in the form of civil wars in which brother and brother, or father and son often found themselves on opposing sides.

We may say then, that while getting to know one another can, and often does, promote understanding and good will it by no means insures such results. Therefore, merely sending our students abroad or bringing students from other countries here are practices that may be considered useful preludes to understanding but are not in themselves any guarantee that international understanding or good will will be furthered. Such contact under some circumstances could have the opposite effect. The student or other visitor may very well be disillusioned or embittered by what he finds or by the treatment he receives. This is a particular risk in the case of a student whose race or color sets him apart.

Persons who work with students from other cultures generally have not been unmindful of the culture shock and disillusionment that foreign students may experience—whether it is our own students going abroad or students from other countries coming here. Government and private agencies of various kinds have sought to cushion the shock and prepare the students for more realistically facing and constructively responding to the new experiences. Many agencies have set up orientation programs of various kinds. Whether such programs are effective seems to be open to question. To the extent that the programs are primarily informational and of the do-this–don't-do-that variety it is unlikely that they will go very far toward preventing culture shock or increasing understanding. It is not possible to anticipate all the problems that may arise and even if one has been told what to expect, or what to do in a given situation, understanding and insight do not necessarily follow. The basic weakness of many of the so-called area orientation programs is that they are often simply informational and even the information may be a bits and pieces affair that does nothing to give the student a theoretical framework within which he can organize what he sees, hears, and experiences into a meaningful whole.

Various studies suggest that students who stay in the United States long enough do often, if not usually, get some idea of how to interpret and evaluate what they see and hear, and that they do develop at least some degree of objectivity about their own as well as their host country. In the interest of international understanding as well as in the interest of the student's personal welfare and growth it is desirable that this process be speeded up and made more effective. Many students do come expecting the impossible; many go through a period of disillusionment; and many do not stay long enough to come to an understanding of their host country. And no matter how brief or how long the student's period of study he faces readjustment to his own culture on his return, and inevitably he is expected to interpret the United States to his own people when he returns home.

Can the American college and university do anything to aid in, or to speed up, the development of objectivity and thus of insight and understanding on the part of the foreign student? There are various programs designed to do this—such as having students visit or for a time live in American homes, and there are the orientation programs of various kinds. Although I do not know to what extent there already exist programs particularly designed to give foreign students a theoretical understanding of the nature of culture and of their own enculturation, my own experience in teaching students from other cultures suggests that such programs could have great value. Most of the students who come to this country are mature people, many are graduate students, and many of them are themselves experienced teachers or professional workers of various kinds. They are therefore capable of studying their own situation and, at least to some extent, are able to evaluate their own experience in the light of a general knowledge of the nature of culture and its role in human behavior.

The key to understanding any culture lies primarily in two things: an understanding of the nature of culture, that is, what it is and what it does, and a knowledge of the variety of ways in which human behavior has been institutionalized. The foreign student in the United States, or his American counterpart abroad, should not have to find out by trial and error that human beings perceive the world about them in different ways, and that their perceptions depend at least in part upon their socialization in different cultures. Nor should it be left to chance whether the student comes to the realization that all societies face the same basic human problems of meeting physical needs, organizing and defining the behavior of its members, one to another; enculturating its children; and maintaining cohesion through various positive and negative sanctions, myths, ceremonies, and other social and ritual arrangements by which the members of the group are induced to think, feel, and act as good Hopis, Zulus, or middle-class Americans. In short, I am suggesting that the most useful orientation a foreign student can have is one that helps him—whether through special lectures, regular classes, reading, guided experiences, or a combination of any or all of these means—to understand what culture is and how it operates, and to see himself, his own people, and the Americans he encounters in terms of their respective enculturations.

There are various approaches one can make to culture. We can look at it descriptively, that is, simply describe what it looks like, the form it takes. The differences in material culture are obvious to us—whether we use fingers, forks, or chopsticks, whether we sleep in beds or hammocks or on mats on the floor, whether men wear loin cloths, dhotis, trousers, or robes. Moreover, we can observe marriage customs and say that one society is monogamous while another practices polygamy, and we can talk about different patterns of classifying relatives, performing the marriage ceremony, handling a corpse, or approaching the gods or spirits.

But descriptions of other customs do not in themselves help us understand another people. We could compile a whole book of such descriptions and come out with the idea that other people are a queer lot who have never learned the proper way to do things. A culture consists not only of elements or traits (or discrete patterns of behavior) but also in their interrelationships and organization. Different cultures may have many specific patterns that are similar but within each culture there is an organization or configuration that makes it an integrated whole. One of the basic tenets of anthropology is that cultures must be studied as wholes and that any custom, pattern, or way of behaving can be understood only when seen within the total context of which it is a part.

Culture, of course, has almost as many definitions as there are people who use the term, but for purposes of understanding cultural differences the most useful way to view culture is to see it as an adaptive mechanism. In this sense, a culture is a body of ready made solutions to the problems encountered by the group. It is, as someone has expressed it, a cushion between man and his environment. It is thus the sum total and organization of all the patterned ways by which any given group copes with the physical world, with one another and with other groups, with the psychological and aesthetic needs of its members, and with those intangibles that fall into the categories of values, ethics, religion, the supernatural, or right and wrong. The resulting culture has form and pattern. There is a degree of order and system that gives to the people who participate in it a certain style of life that is peculiarly their own.

When looked at from this point of view we see that while cultures are specifically different they are basically alike—as we should expect when we note the essential likeness of the human organism, when we see that the essence of being human lies in our relationship with other humans, when we consider the long period of dependence of the human infant, and when we observe the essential likeness of the world in which men live. At first thought, Eskimos, Hottentots, and Dobuans may appear to live in very different worlds of snow, desert, and tropical island, but they all have the resources of air, land, and water; they all are dependent in some degree on the behavior of the sun; they all must reckon with weather and with whatever plants and animals their environment provides. They all perceive forms, colors, and texture. They all must eat and sleep; they must cope with the presence and peculiarities of their neighbors, and protect themselves from natural if not human enemies. They all go through the same life cycle, and they all must cope with illness, misfortune, and death. None can survive without the cooperation of his fellows and if the group is to perpetuate itself people must procreate, and they must rear the young in such way that they will in time carry on the work of their fathers.

There is actually a limited number of ways in which any of man's necessities, physical or social, can be provided, so that a study of the variety of ways in which any given human problem has been met gives us cues and clues to the meaning of man's behavior anywhere. This does not mean, of course, that behavior can be interpreted out of context, or that similar forms of behavior necessarily imply similar functions. Quite the contrary. In some cultures it is impolite to stand in the presence of a more important person who is seated or to walk behind rather than in front of someone else. And there are parts of Africa in which spitting at the feet of the judge is not an insult but the equivalent of our laying the hand on a Bible when taking a solemn oath. What we do discover is that all societies appear to have some way by which people in given situations show respect to other people, and that they all have ways of giving ritual recognition to sacred obligations.

There is one other factor that must be taken into account in the understanding of culture and that is man's seemingly almost universal bent toward ethnocentrism. Because we ourselves are ethnocentric we are usually surprised to discover ethnocentrism in others. Our ways seem to us so natural and right that we may be shocked to find that other people do things differently, and when we discover that they actually consider their ways superior to ours we are sometimes affronted.

Ethnocentric behavior is both old and widespread if not universal. Long before scientific studies of other cultures were made shrewd observers had noted ethnocentric behavior in their neighbors if not in themselves. Herodotus wrote of the Persians that they looked upon themselves as greatly superior in all respects to the rest of mankind. He apparently considered this behavior as common for he adds at a later time that if one were to offer men the choice of all the customs of the world, they would examine the whole number and end up by preferring their own.[7] Xenophanes observed that men even created their gods in their own images. "Aethiopians," he wrote, "have gods with snub noses and black hair. Thracians have gods with grey eyes and red hair." [8]

The Greenland Eskimos who first encountered Europeans thought their visitors had come to learn virtue and good manners from their hosts, and Europeans who did business with the Dahomeans during the days of the slave trade reported that the Dahomean king was so proud that he trod the earth as if it were honored with its burden.

It is an anthropological commonplace that people of the simplest cultures tend to see themselves as superior to their neighbors, and their ofttimes barren environment may appear to them as the best of all possible worlds. The Hottentots' name for themselves was *Khoisan* or "men of men" and countless other peoples referred to themselves by terms that can be translated as "men" or, as with the Navaho, simply "people."

All of this discussion of culture may sound very elementary but the student whose experience has been limited to his own culture, and who has had no such introduction to what culture is and what it does, lacks the theoretical framework within which to organize his new experiences in a different culture or to evaluate his home culture in any objective way. It has been my own experience that even American graduate students are often incredibly naive and ethnocentric. Many of them are not only ignorant of other cultures but also lacking in any objective view of their own culture.

In summary, I would emphasize again that information is not enough. There must be insight and understanding which comes of an awareness of what culture is and what it does. Only in this way can the student acquire a theoretical framework within which knowledge and experience can be organized and brought into a meaningful whole.

All of these factors add up to a formidable set of problems with reference to the foreign students in our midst. These problems involve the students, the institutions they attend, and the relationships of our government to the governments of the countries from which the students come. Our specific goals and the goals of the sending countries may be different but we should be able to meet on the plane of a common desire for better international understanding.

I have purposely ignored the question of our relationship to countries dominated by communist or other totalitarian ideologies. We can have no direct influence or control over their policies as host countries, and they do not generally permit their students to come to the United States or to go to other countries where they would be exposed to democratic ideas. Our primary opportunity to promote international understanding lies in our role as host country to students from democratic or ideologically uncommitted nations, and in the preparation of our own students who go abroad to study.

To the extent that perceptions can be changed at all, they are changed by different experiences, and the mere fact of living in another culture may help to clear away some false ideas and reduce the number of unreal stereotypes held about one's own and other countries. But the goal of international understanding is too important to be left to chance or wishful thinking. Our concern here is to find ways in which this process can be speeded up by conscious attention to the nature of the problem and to the means by which objectivity, insight, and understanding may be developed.

The possibility of success in promoting such understanding through student exchange will be increased to the extent that we are able to develop, both in ourselves as host country and in the students who come here to study, the ability to make objective evaluations of our respective countries, and to understand why we each think, feel, and act as we do. Certainly, the foreign students are helped to make such evaluations when they, their teachers and advisors, and their American fellow students, are made aware of the significance of cultural differences and the way in which such differences can be understood. An awareness of the fact that we do perceive the same reality in different ways and why this is so, in itself helps the individual to develop objectivity toward his own and other cultures. We do not have to like one another's ways to get along. We do need to understand why we are each as we are.

The goal may well be a degree of objectivity but not disengagement. Human beings cannot be fully human without culture and the person who rejects his own culture may be worse off than the man without a country. It is naive and foolish as well as unrealistic to attempt to make the world over in our own image. If we attempt to convert foreign students to the "American way" we shall usually find that our goals are in direct conflict with the goals of their countries, and we ourselves will be guilty of sabotaging the cause of international understanding. We can, in good conscience, seek to help students, both American and foreign, be constructively critical of both their own and other countries.

Nor does a world culture seem to be the answer though we do seem to be moving inevitably toward the world wide diffusion of modern technological patterns. Actually two seemingly contradictory movements appear to be dominant in the world today—one, the fragmentation of the large, formerly Western controlled, areas into smaller, highly self-conscious national entities, and the other, the spread of Western technology. Both of these movements, which often occur together, must be taken into account. Moreover, the nature of this concurrent political fragmentation and cultural diffusion may give the clue to a fruitful approach to international understanding that is acceptable to the free world and at the same time in keeping with our own national interest and goals. In a provocative article on "Evolution, Cultural and Biological," Julian Huxley takes the position that:

. . . the properties of the culture (including the speed and direction of its change) must be considered not only in relation to the more effective utilization of its environmental resources, but also in relation to the more satisfying enjoyment, by its human members, of their capacities for experience and achievement, for knowing and feeling, willing and acting. The scale of culture thus has a dual measure: it is related not only to efficiency of exploitation but also to fulfilment of potentiality.[9]

Western man has made far greater and more rapid advance in the efficiency of exploitation of environmental resources than in the fulfilment of human potentiality, and even this efficiency of exploitation rests on an earlier base not of Western man's making. To use Gordon Childe's formulation, man's conquest of the physical world rests on a series of what he calls revolutions, beginning with the agricultural revolution that gave man a stable food supply, followed in turn by an urban revolution that involved a system of writing and an extended division of labor, and then an industrial revolution culminating in modern technology and based on the scientific method. Only the third of these revolutions can be credited to Western man and without the earlier ones the third one would not have been possible. Civilizations had risen and fallen before northern and western Europeans had emerged from a tribal existence. Through long centuries, while the foundations of modern civilization were being laid, the Europeans were, as William Howells expresses it, "just natives." Our recognition and acknowledgement of this debt to the non-Western world is long overdue and to make such an acknowledgement now could have important ramifications in our relationships with the rest of the world.

To return to Huxley's analysis, he points out that biological and cultural evolution resemble each other in that both show a combination of two major trends, one to differentiation or divergence, the other to improvement or advance. In addition, cultural evolution shows a trend toward convergence and consequently toward a final unity superimposed upon diversity. Huxley thus sees the problem of acculturation in the world today as an inevitable accompaniment of the emergence of a new dominant cultural type. He sees in this development the possibility of a variety of cultural expression within a unitary frame of knowledge, ideas, and purposes in which conscious direction could help to minimize the evil effects of the process and maximize the desirable results.[10]

The majority of non-Western peoples are clearly eager for the results of the efficiency of exploitation developed by the West, and the technological revolution seems destined to supplant earlier and less efficient means of utilizing the world's natural resources. We are still far behind in the fulfilment of human potentiality, and the non-Western world has made it clear that it wants neither political nor cultural domination of the West. Perhaps this is the point at which we can not only allow for diversity in the satisfying enjoyment of man's capacity for experience and achievement, for knowing and feeling, willing and acting, but we can also learn from, enjoy, and be enriched by, the contributions of the various cultures whose diverse experiments in living open up new and different avenues for the fulfilment of human potentiality.

NOTES

1. *Open Doors 1964,* Report on International Exchange (New York: Institute of International Education, 1964), p. 4.
2. Benjamin Paul, editor, *Health, Culture and Community* (New York: Russell Sage Foundation, 1955), p. 2.
3. See the chapter "Philosophy and Human Conduct" in Charles A. Moore, editor, *Philosophy and Culture East and West* (Honolulu: University of Hawaii Press, 1962), p. 16.
4. Julian Huxley, *Evolution in Action* (New York: Harper and Brothers, 1953), pp. 105–107.
5. For the relationship of social structure to perceptions and attitudes in Negro-white relations, see Ina Corinne Brown, *Socio-Economic Approach to Educational Problems,* Vol. I, National Survey of Higher Education of Negroes (Washington, D.C.: U.S. Office of Education, 1942), pp. 22–45.
6. For an elaboration of this point, see Ina Corinne Brown, *Understanding Other Cultures* (Englewood Cliffs, N.J.: Prentice-Hall, 1963), p. 16.
7. Herodotus, *The History of Herodotus,* translated by George Rawlinson (New York: Tudor Publishing Co., 1939), pp. 52–53, 160.
8. For the full quotation see Kathleen Freeman, *Ancilla to the PreSocratic Philosophers* (Oxford: Basil Blackwell, 1948), p. 22.
9. The article appears as a guest editorial in William L. Thomas, editor, *Current Anthropology: A Supplement to Anthropology Today* (Chicago: University of Chicago Press, 1956), p. 20.
10. *Ibid.,* pp. 22–24.

CHAPTER 5

Education Comes of Age Around the World

OLIVER J. CALDWELL

Historically speaking, education, like Gaul, has had three principal manifestations. The first was the informal education of primitive man. Through his elders, and with the help of experience, this man learned how to survive in the face of a savage environment. Later there was a second kind of education which gave a small number of men and women the skills and understanding they needed to be leaders of the great majority. Still later there developed a special minimal education which gave a man or a woman a minimum of necessary information and skill necessary to serve effectively his superiors; a modification of this was education for the purpose of enabling people to read the Bible, the Koran, or some other holy book. At about this time visionaries began to talk about education for everybody, but it usually was in the context of helping to propagate within a single society a particular religion.

Thus little Jane Grey, at a time when women received little formal education, was given a rigorous training which encompassed most of what men in England knew in the fifteenth century; her father wanted her to be ready for the crown, which she wore for a few days before dying on the block in the Tower. For a long time the ability to read and write was akin to magic. Later it became the privilege of the aristocrat, and still later, of the free man.

Today we are witnessing some drastic changes in the function of education around the world. These changes are part of a great social, economic, and political revolution which has many manifestations. The gap between the very rich and the very poor seems to be narrowing, and in the more prosperous societies the gap between the well

61

educated and the less well educated also seems to be declining each year.

There are many new forces operating in human society; there is clearly a new understanding of the importance of education to the individual and of the role of education as a creative force in society.

As a result of these new concepts of the function of education a much larger proportion of children that are of school age, all over the world, are now in school than ever before and the proportion increases every year. It is probable that more children are staying in school longer than ever before. In the more sophisticated societies it is not enough today merely to have an introduction to the three R's. The complexities of modern life require that people know vastly more than their parents did if they are to make a decent living, and if the society of which they are a part is to prosper.

In many parts of the world class distinctions are beginning to break down, partly as a result of a mixing of social classes in schools. Thus education, which long was a chief support of class distinctions, is becoming an important tool in the demolishing of such distinctions.

At the same time there is a real possibility that a new system of class distinctions may grow out of the many narrow parallel intellectual channels into which people are being forced to travel in order that society may be supplied with high level skills. This has caused C. P. Snow and others to claim that Western society has been already split into groups whose languages and thoughts are mutually incomprehensible.

Finally, educational planning claims to have developed into a new science. Young people are studying to be educational planners and many of their elders have undertaken the responsibility of planning appropriate programs of education to meet the special needs of new nations in spite of limited specific qualifications for such responsibilities. Personally, I doubt if enough is known about the varying effects of different kinds of education on social development to warrant the belief that educational planning has achieved intellectual maturity.

To sum it up, there is a big boom in education in our times. We hope this boom will not rise too fast and collapse, leaving behind it a depressed and cynical concept of education and its importance.

The following summaries will attempt to describe dominant educational concepts in various parts of the world, and to indicate ways in which these ideas are being implemented. On the assumption that we are fully aware of the drastic changes now taking place in American education, these remarks will focus on the rest of the world.

Western Europe today is attempting to cope with an overdue revolution in education. One reason so much is happening is that so much needs to be done to enable Western Europe to compete with the rest of the world in manpower development. Traditional Western European education has been aristocratic, with the majority receiving relatively limited schooling, while a small elite has been trained for elitehood.

European economists have discovered, somewhat later than some of their colleagues in the United States and in the U.S.S.R., that there is a direct relationship between economic, political, and social development and the universal development of human resources. This awareness is sharpened by intensified economic competition with Japan, the U.S.S.R., and with the United States.

Therefore in most of the countries in Western Europe there is a public debate on these points:

1. Dare any country in today's world be content to give a good education to only a few and to leave the talents of the vast majority of people quite undeveloped? Is it possible for a nation which follows this policy to survive in today's intense economic and political competition?

2. Is it right and is it feasible to divide young children between the ages of eleven and thirteen into two groups, the gifted and the nongifted, and then to give these two groups of children very different kinds of education designed for the majority to produce workers, and for the minority to produce leaders?

This debate with local variations is going on all over Western Europe and each nation is coming up with its own answers. Some leaders in some countries believe that Europe in another generation will be crippled economically and politically if it does not give all of its children a chance to develop all of their talents. A more conservative group believes that prosperity is the egg out of which education hatches, and that only the prosperous can afford good education.

Generally, the newer opinion that education fosters development seems to be dominant. In France in 1954 only 37 per cent of the sixteen-year-olds were in school but ten years later the percentage had risen to 55 per cent. In England in 1958 only 19 per cent of the sixteen-year-olds were in school as compared to 29 per cent of this group in 1964, and the Robbins Report in England and other reports elsewhere advocated making education more truly universal.

The principal obstacles to giving every child an adequate opportunity to develop his talents are survivals of class distinctions, and the great cost of universal education.

Developments in education in the U.S.S.R. have been taking place at such a rate that what was true last month may be considerably less true today.

In this volatile society education consistently holds a high priority:

1. Communism teaches that everyone is entitled to enough education to enable him to be a productive citizen of the communist state. Education is also responsible for helping to identify those who have special talents and enabling them to develop such talents for the welfare of the collective.

2. Communism teaches that the socialist state cannot become a communist Utopia until the citizens of the state have grown wiser, more unselfish, more dedicated, more materialistic, and more communist in nature. Thus the school has a mandate to bring pressures to bear on the young to change them into the "new Soviet man."

3. At the same time education must be related directly to social, political, and economic need which requires a high degree of educational planning to satisfy the established goals of the State. Recent studies by the Office of Education indicate that Soviet schooling is geared to meeting specific estimates of probable needs for developed manpower in every segment of the Soviet economy. As the needs change, commensurate changes take place in the educational structure.

4. Finally, certain adjustments are taking place in the Soviet system of education based on changing concepts of the needs of the state. Among these changes are a reduction in the amount of time young people spend in school brought about by reducing the period of time devoted to industrial training. The years required to achieve advanced degrees are also being reduced. Both changes will make it possible for young people to enter the labor market more quickly than they do now. One notable step in the constant effort to improve Soviet education is a recent increase by 25 per cent of the salaries of all elementary and secondary teachers. Another important development is the new course in social studies required of all secondary school graduates. This is the New Testament of communism and is intended to indoctrinate boys and girls with the correct communist concept of the nature of human society and of their own roles in that society. It teaches that before the end of the century the Soviet socialist state will have metamorphosed into communism.

Africa South of the Sahara, where live over 200 million Negroes, is another area where strenuous efforts are being made to promote education. Most of the people were until recently members of colonies controlled by other countries.

Immediately after such a colony has received its independence there has customarily been an effort to enhance both the quantity and the quality of schooling available for all of the people. These efforts are generally handicapped by the extreme shortage of trained Africans competent to teach in or to develop or administer modern systems of education.

Another difficulty lies in the fact that in these new nations the only existing formal systems of schooling usually were transplanted more or less intact by the previous colonial masters, and may not form adequate foundations on which to build modern systems of education in a different environment. While there are some educational concepts which have more or less universal applicability, many of these foreign ideas have little relevance to the actual needs of the people in these newly independent states.

Many of the new nations achieve independence in a condition which approximates an educational vacuum. Almost all of the newly independent states seriously need technical assistance in designing and creating national systems of education. Thus education has become in a few short years a major business in Africa between the Sahara on the north and the Union on the south. In the beginning there is sometimes considerable naiveté among the political leaders of the new nations, some of whom seem to think that they can wish into existence adequate systems for training their manpower and womanpower. In recent months there appears to be the beginning of a sober realization of the nature of the difficulties they face and of the sacrifices they will have to make to enable their people to achieve both decent living standards and political freedom. Unfortunately the educational assistance they are receiving from the outside world varies considerably both in quality and motivation.

In Southern and Eastern Asia there has long been a strong intellectual tradition. Possibly in no other part of the world is the intellectual customarily more honored than he is in the nations between Tokyo and Karachi. Universal availability of education for all boys was advocated in China as early as 500 b.c., but was never to be a reality in ancient China. By this time there was also a clear idea of the function of education; it should create the Tsuin Tse, or Superior Man who would be the professional ruler under the Emperor. Confucius and his school of philosophers espoused ideas concerning education which often were similar both to the ideas of Plato, and to those of the more imaginative Soviet philosophers today.

There has long been a wide variation in the level of educational achievement in this area. Japan has one of the highest standards of literacy ever achieved by any nation, but some small nations which recently emerged from colonialism believe, rightly or wrongly, that their colonial masters deliberately kept the masses of their citizens in a state of ignorance.

While there are serious internal rivalries, most of the nations in this region seem dedicated to the proposition that economic and political growth and social stability cannot be achieved without universal literacy and high standards of development of their human resources. In some of these countries disproportionately large sums of money are annually appropriated for education. In most of them the level of poverty is such that there just is not enough money to implement national educational policies. These people do not seek to emulate Europe or America, but rather to revive the grandeur of past civilizations, and to achieve a new synthesis of Eastern and Western traditions. Considering the general level of intelligence and of determination in Eastern and Southern Asia, some Western observers believe that the balance of power in another generation may rest in this part of the world.

I vividly recall a visit to a mountain town in Korea which had several times been leveled by the war with the communists. Here I collected statistics concerning the sacrifices being made by the adults in this town to enable almost every boy and girl to receive an education. I received the impression that nowhere else in the some three score and ten countries in which I have had the privilege of visiting schools, had I seen such a grim determination by the adults to sacrifice a better life for themselves today on behalf of a much better life tomorrow for all of their children. One of the unique features of this particular situation was the system whereby older people who were not parents of young children accepted the responsibility for paying tuition to enable the children of the poor to go as far in school as their abilities would take them.

For a thousand years the Arab world was distinguished for its scholars, its warriors, its armies, and its universities. Recently there has been a rebirth of nationalism in the countries of Islam and the Arab nations. There is a fascinating diversity among the peoples who live in the nations between Morocco and Pakistan. They are united by a common faith which traditionally has taught its people to respect learning.

Today there is a great shortage of every educational commodity in these nations including teachers, school books, buildings, and equipment. But there is no shortage of a desire to achieve again not only political independence but equality in every way with the rest of mankind. Education is generally accepted as the tool of policy both to perpetuate religion and to promote economic development.

There are strong tendencies towards the preservation of national differences through the schools. This involves changing curricula to meet specific national goals and frequently requires a high degree of centralized control. There is also a widespread trend away from the old ritualistic learning towards a new emphasis on mathematics, science, and vocational education.

Characteristic of the new wave in the lands of Islam is the reorganization of the Al Azar, the oldest university in the world which has for more than a thousand years, in Cairo, trained both the secular and religious leaders of Islam. If published reports are correct, the Al Azar is rapidly assuming some of the characteristics of a modern university.

The weaknesses of education in Latin America are probably one of the greatest barriers to full development of the fabulous material resources possessed by most of our Latin neighbors. Clark, in his studies of the relationship of education and development, chose Colombia as an example of how a lack of education perpetuated poverty in a land of incredible natural wealth.

The problem here has been accentuated by a class system exemplified by the proud and often beautiful descendants of the Spanish conquerors, who in some areas own most of the arable land, and dominate a large majority consisting of Indians and people of mixed blood. Great distances, inadequate transportation and communication, and limited educational opportunities have combined to keep many of our Latin neighbors poor.

Recently there have begun a series of determined efforts to build a foundation of intelligent and well-trained manpower sufficient to the needs of these emerging societies. It is hard for a North American educator to travel among these people without being strongly attracted to them personally and without wishing it were possible to give them overnight the educational foundation they so desperately need.

Within the past ten years real progress has been made in developing in some fortunate areas systems of education aimed directly at helping people to live better in their particular environments. In the high Andes this has to some extent been achieved by the unique nuclear schools, which have helped many descendants of the Incas to build better lives for themselves and their children. But most Latin Americans still need access to the technical achievements and social ideals of Europe and America. These proud people need help to develop a planned approach to education in which all children will have opportunities to learn similar to those now available to North American children.

There are, of course, immense cultural differences between the countries of Latin America and perhaps no generalization is possible other than this: Most of these people are determined that their children shall have a better chance to develop their native capabilities than any other generation before them.

It is impossible to consider what is happening in education in our time without referring to that mysterious new science which was named cybernetics by its first exponent, Norbert Wiener. Cybernetics is an immense subject which covers many aspects of philosophy, mathematics, physics, psychology, and biology. The combined effect of the linking of many facets of this new science to human needs is to create in more advanced societies an ability to produce vastly more of the world's goods with vastly less effort. Some of our philosophers maintain that with existing hardware it would be possible, as social and other factors permitted, to develop in a few years a society in which only two per cent of the population would have to work to provide all of the food and all of the material goods required by the remaining 98 per cent. Whether this estimate be true or not, it seems clear that the world tomorrow will be a different place from the world today as a result of the new relationship between man the thinker, and the machine which is the doer and also sometimes a thinker.

What I am trying to say is that it is impossible to conceive of education as a creative force in our world unless we take into account the social changes which will be caused by automation and the other results of cybernetics. Men and women will possess vastly more leisure in an automated world than they now enjoy. They will have to be prepared to make use of that leisure. By implication, this means that people will have to develop new and stronger moral standards. It means that they will have to become much wiser than they are today because their opportunities will be so much greater. From a philosophic and moral standpoint, cybernetics is a new and major challenge to education.

Possibly no other generation has faced so many crises as we face today. But man as a species has always lived with danger, and always has survived. We hear too much about the various dangers inherent in the crises of our time and not enough about the opportunities they afford us. Whether man succumbs to the dangers or wins his way to a better and more stable order depends in large measure on what education does for man in the next decade.

I suggest that in the immediate future we should seek to promote, among others, these educational objectives:

1. We should try to develop a clearer understanding of the function of education in society. There has been enough talk about edu-

cation as the foundation of material advancement, but this should not be the total function of the school. Material advancement is only a means to the achievement of an end, which is the complete life of the individual and the society.

2. If we are to achieve the complete life then education should place more emphasis on the humanities, the arts, the social sciences. Someone recently commented that the Utopia which some of our cybernetics experts are predicting would be something like the old concept of heaven in which one would be rewarded for a good life by sitting forever on a white cloud strumming a harp. Those not musically inclined might spend most of their lives sitting on the banks of a river communing with the fish. Other possibilities come to mind, none of them attractive as a permanent occupation. I suggest therefore that education both for the understanding of one's environment and for the development of one's latent creative skills will be imperative in the age of automation.

3. The world of tomorrow is likely to present to mankind two alternatives. In one, society would freeze in a given mold, content with what it was and suspicious of changes. In the other, society would use new leisure and new wealth to open up new frontiers—intellectual, physical, and moral. But if society is to choose the second alternative, then education must be constantly flexible, prepared to change with the development of new knowledge to enable man to make a full use of his new opportunities.

4. We need a constant cross-fertilization of ideas between the many cultures of mankind. A logical function of education, in a world in which men and women everywhere have no alternative but to live as members of one community, is to serve as the medium whereby people become acquainted with each other.

5. If education is to remain constantly flexible and if it is to adjust constantly to a changing environment then we need a vastly increased component of research which would constantly seek out not only new realities but new ways to teach. One of the greatest weaknesses in our educational situation today is the weakness of educational research in all areas including comparative education.

6. Out of this research and out of our increasing wisdom should come a new and higher concept of man and his destination which would be in harmony with the teachings of our great religions. Man's achievements may make him only a little lower than the angels or almost as low as the devil. Which role he plays will to a large extent be determined by the kind of education we give the next generation.

Part **II**

Institutional Studies

CHAPTER 6

The Program of
the Comparative Education Center,
University of Chicago

C. ARNOLD ANDERSON

There is no single, best formula for a graduate program in comparative education. We at Chicago do believe that there are certain essentials of a sound program, and we give high priority to features that others would regard as idiosyncratic. The advantages of the program we have followed will perhaps become evident in the following pages; its defects are revealed by some of the successful endeavors of colleagues at other universities.

A broad charter for the Center was established before the director was employed; the staff have found it quite congenial to live with those initial expectations. The program has remained on the whole congruent with the original plans made by an interdepartmental committee. That advisory group continued to assist in making plans during the first years.

One purpose in launching the Center was to bring additional social science personnel into the Department of Education. The Department has for many years included several faculty members whose original association lay in one or another social science discipline outside the professional field of education. This emphasis has remained a distinctive feature of the Center program.[1] The Department is part of the social science division and awards the Ph.D. degree.

It was intended also that the Center be an instrumentality for bringing a greater measure of cross-cultural flavor into the program of the Department. The committee sensed that comparative education was gaining stature as an educational specialty and that it might help relate professional education to the many overseas responsibilities of universities.

Since Chicago is a small university with strong faculty autonomy, it has always been easy to establish research and teaching ventures bridging departmental boundaries. The staff of the Center represent separate social science disciplines. Andreas Kazamias is a specialist in the history of education.[2] Philip Foster, assistant director, was trained in anthropology and sociology. Mary Jean Bowman is an economist. Robert Havighurst from Human Development gives part time to the Center. The director, C. Arnold Anderson, is a sociologist. Two of the staff hold joint appointments in other departments, and two have served as editors of major social science journals. Two have received training in professional education and have taught in schools below university levels and in "underdeveloped" countries. The staff are associated with the Committee on African Studies and with the Committee for the Comparative Study of New Nations. It has, then, been quite natural to establish ties with other departments and programs, and we have been able to draw freely upon faculty elsewhere in the University for the benefit of our students and ourselves.

We have taken the position that Comparative Education is an approach to educational topics, not a discipline. Though hybrid disciplines are continually emerging in the learned world, there is little profit in debating our point of view on this question. We are content with maintaining that there is a fruitful and interesting cross-cultural and cross-disciplinary way of dealing with the more important aspects of education. In its details this approach can be interpreted differently in each university. Participants can be drawn from innumerable academic fields according to common interests in particular problems. Irrespective of one's position on this issue, comparative education is a growing field with diversified membership, a field in which this Center would like to play an active part.

There has seemed to us to be little profit in modeling our program on that of area centers. In grounding research on a cross-cultural basis, the societies chosen for study, and hopefully for comparison, will vary with the problems in hand, and there are solid reasons against becoming identified with any particular area of the world.[3] The interests of faculty and students will shift from one society to another. The topic should have priority over an area commitment. On the other hand, a center is fortunate if it has strong area programs accessible in the university.[4]

The Center was established with the aid of a substantial grant from the Ford Foundation, and this assistance has continued. The Carnegie Foundation supports one large project. Another, being carried out in collaboration with Teachers College and research agencies abroad, has been underwritten by a grant from the Office of Education—which has also given a few Small Contract grants. A few NDEA awards are available.

In line with general policies of the University, no overseas operations are carried on. While this policy creates some disadvantages, especially financial ones, it has enabled us to be more flexible in choosing the topics on which we will work. But it follows that most of the considerable amount of work underway at the Center is supported on a very modest scale.

Some of the advantages we would otherwise reap from overseas projects come to us as a result of a considerable amount of consulting work. On several small problems and on a couple of more important projects we have benefited from discussions with the UNESCO secretariat. One member has taught in a Peace Corps orientation course and another shares in awarding Ford Foundation fellowships to veterans of that program. Most of the staff have been active in the international committees of professional associations. Participation in the board of consultants of the International Institute of Educational Planning has proved most stimulating to our work in that area, as did service on a World Bank mission. We have participated in conferences designed to strengthen the international programs in universities and in international conferences on research in comparative education. It has been possible to attend workshops and conferences of the "comparative" committees of other social science disciplines. Our economist has been drawn into discussions regarding federal policy for human resources in our own underdeveloped areas. Along with colleagues from many universities, we assess and review proposed research projects for several agencies.

The Center teaches only graduate students, few of whom seek the masters degree except as a preliminary stage. Initially a large proportion of our comparatively few students were from overseas; interest among American students in this field was at that time limited, and the Center's program became known only gradually. Progressively we have shifted toward a preponderance of American students. We were quite unhappy with the difficulties of identifying foreign students with adequate preparation, especially in the social sciences. And it had been the original intent that the Center would put principal stress upon preparing American students for overseas assignments.

Only a few courses are offered in the Center. Some courses and seminars are cross-listed in other departments. The course in comparative education sets forth our basic methodological position and reviews the logic of comparative study as developed in other disciplines. Other topics vary from time to time; for example: factors encouraging the formalization of socialization, the role of education in formation of elites, recruitment of students to secondary and higher schools, status of teachers, economic aspects of education, decision making in educational policy.

Members of the Center staff play a key part in the department's course on the sociology of education. The Center offers one course and a seminar on the economics of education; this topic is timely, the staff includes one of the active people in that field, and economic considerations are becoming more important in educational policy and planning. A new course on "education and social change in the new states" is a codification of work previously given in seminars.

Beyond this list, we work with seminars. The topics vary in accordance with student interests, availability of fresh materials, or current activities of the faculty. These seminars have dealt with the following topics, some of which are occasionally repeated: university policy in Europe, education and elites, secondary school selection in Africa, culture and personality, educational planning, economics of education, education and religion, statistical interrelationships of national characteristics.

Within the Department the Center is part of the section called "Education and the Social Order" that includes also sociology, history, and philosophy of education. In the doctoral examinations our students must face questions in those several areas as well as on comparative education specifically. They of course take also the common examinations in statistics, educational psychology, and so on. After passing this examination students normally take much of their further work in other departments: usually in sociology or anthropology but also in the South Asia program, political science, and so forth.

A critic might comment that the Center too much resembles an ivory tower—a remark occasionally made about this whole University. Certainly disengagement from operations does in some respects isolate us. More important is the University tradition of giving priority to research. We think there is a place for a more strictly analytical approach to educational topics, and we endeavor to do creditable work in this mode. Every university has its ethos and the Center reflects its milieu.

It is only candour to admit that one outcome of this particular academic climate—facilitated no doubt by the personalities of the

Center's staff—is a "critical" view on many of the most widely discussed topics in comparative education. We try to examine important topics, especially those that are used to undergird public policy, from a fresh point of view. Perhaps we could achieve a more balanced alignment, but every group of scholars must work along the lines of its interests and by the aid of its particular skills, handicapped also by its particular prejudices. This has meant, as is discussed later on for example, that in taking up the questions of educational planning, we have been more impressed with the defects than with the positive features of that technique. Again, in looking at the recruitment function of schools, it has seemed to us that formal education does not in itself play a major part in the restructuring of a social system. On the economics of education it has seemed prudent to warn against premature or exaggerated conclusions from what is a quite new line of research. Revision of accepted views about the political context of policy on education emerged from work on English educational history.[5] In so rapidly changing a field as comparative education one can be confident that the errors of one group will be corrected by work done elsewhere. And, as research on one or another topic becomes consolidated, we can hope that our seemingly divergent conclusions will find their place.

In the short history of the Center, the advantages of enjoying that corporate title have been numerous, though "institute" would have served equally well. This organizational device is a favored one in the Department as a means for focusing interests, teaching responsibilities, and research in small clusters of faculty and their students. It facilitates policy making in the department and relationships with other parts of the University, and it aids in recruiting students.

The advantages of that identification have been most apparent in our external relationships. A name such as Comparative Education Center serves as a signal to the academic world, to international agencies, to other universities, and to foundations that it is possible to mobilize academic resources on this particular kind of problem. As successive similar centers are opened in other universities, the cumulative impact of this field increases. Obviously this favorable attention is matched by the obligation to keep busy on important topics and to speak responsibly for one's colleagues in comparative education at large.

Soon after the Center began operations an effort was made to outline a basic methodology for comparative education and at the same time to set down a working definition of the field. Comparative education is the cross-cultural study of (a) the relationships between education and other aspects of society, and (b) of the interrelationships among the various aspects of education. An example of the first approach would be a comparison of the social status of teachers (and with other occupations) in several societies. Analysis of the impingement of external examinations upon curricula in various nations would illustrate the second part of the definition.[6]

Each staff member and each student would weigh these two aspects of the field differently and would find more interest in topics from one rather than the other part. Since extended abstract discussions of methodology rather quickly become sterile, further attention to methodological questions has been incidental to technical problems of specific projects. Thus one will find a good many observations about the merits of different ways of assessing the functions of schools scattered through reports of the various recruitment studies. Similarly, the papers on educational planning recur often to the merits of various techniques for estimating educational "needs."

The Center has enjoyed one special opportunity for espousing its methodological position. For three years (1959–1961) we offered a one day workshop for members of the *Comparative Education Society* who were in Chicago to attend the annual meetings. In a sense those sessions were the first midwest regional meetings, which now take place at other universities of the region. By special request from members of the *Society* these meetings were resumed in February of 1965. The Center will present papers by invited scholars not on our own staff, and in these discussions there will be a good deal of attention to methodology.

Our point of view on research was exemplified by the articles in the October 1960 and 1962 issues of the *Comparative Education Review,* the full copy for which was supplied by staff, visiting lecturers, or students. The titles of those articles are listed below.

World Patterns of Education
Loss of Talent in Selective School Systems: Sweden
Economics of Vocational Training in the U.S.S.R.
The Dilemmas of Education in Ceylon
Some Social Aspects of Brazilian Education
A Historical and Social Note on Moral Education in Japan
Primary School Leavers in Uganda
Comparative Methodology and the Study of African Education
The Task of the Public School in the United States and Canada
Sociological Framework for Comparative Study of Educational Systems
Problems of Secondary Education in Iran

Compulsory and Free Education: a Content Analysis of 19th Century British Opinion

Religion, Politics, and Popular Education: Historical Comparison of England and America

Converging Concerns of Economists and Educators

Factors Related to Educational Output Differences among the Canadian Provinces

Ethnicity and the Schools in Ghana

Educational Plans and Teacher Supply

Conceptions and Images of the Physical World: Japanese and American Pupils

Sponsored and Contest Mobility in America and England

Education, the Muslim Elite, and the Creation of Pakistan

Socioeconomic Determinants of Expenditures for Education: Southern and Other States

An acute reader would immediately ask whether this is comparative or foreign education. The distinction between study of schools in one other society and comparison of the features of two or more systems is a legitimate one. But in returning a soft reply to critics we would point out that opportunities for research reflect a conjuncture of importance of topic, researcher's interests, and availability of data, as well as a passion for logical neatness. And time always presses upon the investigator. On many of the most fundamental topics we can obtain data for few societies, and accumulation of matched data for numerous countries will come slowly. By keeping the perspectives of comparative education and the need for generalizations in view and by skillfully drawing upon principles from the social sciences, opportunities for comparative assessment will prove plentiful. Each effort to widen our comparative view provides an incentive to improve the range and quality of data. We do not need a dozen studies to make it clear, for example, that youth's conceptions of occupational prestige are not produced by the courses they study in school.

Juxtaposition of the foregoing list of papers with the titles of later work will demonstrate that there has been a broad continuity in our program. But there have also been changes; quite unexpectedly, for example, educational planning moved to a central place. Among the reasons particular to ourselves were experience on a World Bank mission and the research on schools in Ghana. But the simultaneous rise of interest in that subject within international agencies and our own program in the economics of education played their part also. As a result, serious effort has been put into unraveling the logic of educational planning and into examination of the methodological and substantive work in that area.[7]

Other topics have come forward in a seemingly random way. For example, UNESCO asked us to prepare a broad report on discrimination in education, part of which will appear in journals.[8] Invitations to prepare chapters for the *Yearbook of Education* led us to sketch out discussions, with due attention to comparative aspects, on talent-centered education, the contribution of schools to international understanding, and the economic and sociological ramifications of "the educational explosion." We may anticipate similar shifts of interest over the years, not least as a result of the spreading interests of our students.

The cross-cultural study of intra-educational relationships is represented by a major international venture in cooperative research.[9] In his first efforts to survey the research potentials of comparative education the director found the "missing link" to lie in the absence of solid dependent variables. In the flood of books contending that French or Soviet or some other educational system was superior to our own, it was obvious that "students" were a fluctuating population and that none of the writers had any objective evidence. Until we could ascertain the actual patterns of pupil achievement in different countries, it seemed futile to speculate whether it might be better teachers, firmer discipline, or something else that produced the alleged differences in learning.

It turned out that others were suggesting the same line of attack on the problem. Consequently the Center joined with colleagues in this country and abroad [10] to plan an international study. The pilot study had proved that international cooperation on a large study was feasible, and the Office of Education made a large grant for the project. National teams prepared blueprint tests in mathematics; these were consolidated into an international test, tried out, and revised. The tests were administered to carefully drawn samples at different ages. Analysis is underway and a report will be available in 1965. Meanwhile committees are considering tests for a possible second wave of testing.[11] These data for a dozen countries (all developed and all Western except Japan) will for the first time give us reasonably dependable profiles of achievement. Through supplementary data on pupils' homes and ability, teachers, schools, and curricula it will be possible to go some way toward explaining any varying outcomes.

On a much smaller scale and with much less precise methods, a few smaller studies have dealt with other sorts of intra-educational problems, some of which were included in the two issues of the *Review*. The special difficulties of multilanguage nations with respect to the language of instruction were explored in one dissertation and the approaches to history teaching in the Imperial and Weimar periods in Germany contrasted in another study. Some of the problems of reconstructing secondary education in Pakistan were explored by Peshkin.[12] A recent paper explores the problems generated in university systems as they expand.[13] Studies of education in developing countries inevitably deal with the effects of rapid expansion of schools upon curricula and teacher quality and raise questions about the appropriate "profile" of an educational system under varying conditions. Under consideration as possible dissertation topics are the role of inspectorates and the intricacies of teacher supply.

The studies conducted by the Center that deal with the interrelationships between various aspects of education and one or another aspect of the social structure are considerably more numerous and diversified than those that we call intra-educational. In the nature of the case, our own studies have dealt with only a small portion of these possible relationships.[14]

European Education. A majority of the staff publications relate to the developing countries; nevertheless, a special effort has been made to maintain a special emphasis upon European education. In part this interest reflects European education or prolonged European residence by the staff. Through our interest in educational planning close ties have been maintained with OECD because of the leading role played by that organization in planning, particularly in its Mediterranean Project. Along with all American colleagues, we have been sensitive to the interest of the American educational profession in the possibilities of borrowing better practices. Then, most of the participants in the cross-national testing project are Europeans. But even with respect to research on education in developing countries there has been a sound reason to be familiar with European systems; the schools of a large part of the world are copies of European systems and the borrower can be understood better from knowledge of the model.[15]

Cross-Polity Studies. By this rather vague title I refer to statistical comparisons among all the countries of the world by mass data. Until recently it has been very difficult to carry out such studies because no one had undertaken the arduous task of compiling the available data. In one major paper of this sort educational indices were related to per capita income for the whole gamut of countries, as a test of some familiar assumptions about the relationships between those variables.[16] Students have been making some preliminary soundings in two recent compilations of statistical indices, and one can expect that such studies are going to multiply. Despite all their defects, these gross correlations of data for the whole world do make it possible to test some of the more sweeping generalizations that abound in the field and they suggest problems for exploration with other types of data.

Studies of Teachers. The Center has sponsored two studies dealing with the factors that affect the supply of teachers,[17] and preliminary studies have been made for more ambitious investigations in a couple of countries. A good deal of attention has been given to many facets of the teacher-status problem in seminars within the context of the sociology of occupations. Data are now being processed from a comprehensive inquiry among teachers in Kenya. The English-American contrasts in the political influences surrounding emergence of professional teachers associations are the subject of one dissertation, and a couple of students are exploring other phases of the situation of teachers for possible dissertations.[18]

Ecology of Educational Development. The possibilities of this way of attacking certain topics came to be realized only gradually. One of us had carried out several analyses of the intraregional variations of education in the American South. The Ghana study of secondary pupils revealed that there were marked regional differentials in aspirations for schooling. Numerous European investigations had identified large gradients in schooling, even in centralized systems. And of course the concept of "spatial multipliers" is much used by economists.

Our first broad statement of this approach appeared in a UNESCO-sponsored conference at Chicago.[19] The Ghana study and its subsequent Ivory Coast twin provided abundant evidence, as did the Kenya inquiry. In two dissertations on Nigeria this topic received special attention, and it has recurred in several of the articles on the economics of education.[20] Even the most rudimentary probing into the problems of educational planning made it clear that sound planning must link educational developments to other (especially economic) forces in spatial congruence. The essentially local character of a mass educational system connects public responsiveness to educational opportunities with other processes of modernization. And in countries using vernaculars in teaching, the localization of schools gives rise to major difficulties.

Four dissertations fall under this heading. Two parallel studies relate educational indices to other indices of social change for Mexico and Iran, using matrices from the computer. Another dissertation is exploring the historical changes in this kind of ecological pattern for France, and one student is working with data from Iraq.[21]

Economics of Education. The inauguration of the Center coincided with the florescence of interest among economists in this new specialty, and a desire to foster this line of work was a consideration in planning the Center.[22] The economist on the staff has been actively at work in this area.[23] Especially in the projects dealing with recruitment to schools and teacher supply, an effort has been made to link the economic with other approaches. And in the discussions of educational planning, particular attention has been given to distinguishing the economic from the technological approach.

As the study of "development" has spread throughout the world of the social scientists, the lack of historical depth in the literature has become a serious handicap. In particular, amidst all the voices calling for the universalizing of literacy and elementary education in the less developed countries, the lack of knowledge about the role of education in Western economic development is proving an obstacle to reaching sound conclusions. The Center was fortunate in being able to join with the Committee on Economic Growth of the Social Science Research Council in an exploratory conference on this question.[24]

To the economist, a theory of "human resources" is in part a branch of capital theory, yielding a theory of "human capital." Any attempt to assess the contribution of education to productivity or to economic growth or to cope with the intricacies of teacher supply must be related to broader relationships in economic theory.

As byproducts of two of our studies, inquiries have been made into the afterschool occupational careers of secondary school graduates. In both the large study in Brazil and in the Ivory Coast study, samples of graduates were used to investigate the relationships between schooling of various kinds and occupational opportunities.

Studies of Recruitment to Schools. Analysis of the functional contribution of schools to societal life must embrace a long and diverse list of specific topics. The Center has worked on only a few problems in this area, and our particular way of looking at these "functional" questions reflects a strong commitment to the sociological approach. It has seemed to us that data about pupils' backgrounds, schooling, and aspirations offer a promising way into this matrix of relationships. Especially in the developing countries, the pattern of recruitment of pupils and students largely determines the composition and character of the national elites. The same kind of data also enables one to explore how the distribution of opportunities among subpopulations and regions of a country contribute to development. This approach facilitates cooperating with the economist, because it raises questions about alternative investments in human and in other forms of capital. A central theme in the literature on educational planning is the production of high-level manpower; on this topic quantitative data about recruitment to schools are requisite for any definite analysis.[25]

Four students have adopted this approach in studies of universities as sources of national elites: in Egypt, Lebanon, Indonesia, and Nigeria.[26] Another dissertation will analyze the relative importance of region, religion, and social class in the secondary schools of the Netherlands. There is also a rather similar dissertation on Denmark underway. An earlier study contrasted the secondary recruitment patterns in the three Guianas.[27] And the most recently completed dissertation compares the political leaders of northern, southern, and frontier states before the Civil War with respect to their education, considering also section of residence, family background, and occupation.[28]

The most ambitious of our projects in this area has been carried out in Turkey.[29] Through favorable circumstances, an unusually comprehensive sample of secondary students were studied, and much historical material procured as well. The earlier Ghana study (in which many of the techniques used in subsequent studies were worked out) likewise had given special attention to the history of education in the area. Of special importance was the picture of struggle between colonial officials seeking conscientiously to introduce "useful" education and the local populations' aspirations for European education. Particular attention was paid (as in the other studies of secondary schools) to the dialectic between children's aspirations for jobs and their realistic appreciation of opportunities and to the changes in these attitudes and in educational aspirations as the educational system expanded.[30] As mentioned, the Ivory Coast study replicates that in Ghana, but particular attention is being given to the question of whether the difference in European control was accompanied by any important differences in the educational system.[31] A parallel study is being conducted in Brazil,[32] in which particular attention is directed to regional differences in that very large country. The Kenya data on secondary pupils also parallel those for these other countries.

Some Tasks Neglected. To list significant lines of research that have not been carried out at the Center would, in part, be to enumerate the many studies carried out at other centers. But it may be of interest to mention a few topics to which we have not been able to give attention for lack of personnel or resources.

Perhaps the major gap is our comparative neglect of the political side of education. This is of course not at all identical with consideration of educational policy and we have given a good deal of attention to policy. Numerous important issues have been discussed in the Ghana study, for example, and naturally policy was foremost in the work for the World Bank in Kenya. Numerous papers on one or another aspect of education in developing countries take up salient policy issues. Any work on educational planning is implicitly dealing with policy. But we would like to have sponsored research on other political questions. The tension between centralized and decentralized administrations of educational systems, and especially the contradictory tendencies that appear in any system formally structured in one of those ways, needs the skill of the political scientist. There are numerous questions for which exploitation of the archives of poll data would be useful. The processes by which countries make up their collective minds on university policy, illustrated by the quite different English and Swedish royal commissions, are an open field for study. We hope we may find personnel to take up some of these types of questions.

One might also mention such other policy questions as the adoption of a suitable curriculum for the schools in developing countries. This is a topic on which almost everyone concerned with education in those nations makes pronouncements, yet one must say that nearly all this fund of comment is superficial.

Conclusion. The man responsible for administering a program in comparative education is bound to be dissatisfied with what is accomplished. The gamut of topics suitable for comparative research is awesome, especially as educational topics have moved into the forefront of high policy in so many of the world's nations. The selection of a budget of projects involves many disturbing compromises that affront principles of balance. Each piece of research seems to take too long and cost too much. It is difficult to insure that the various studies fit into some coherent pattern. There is also the problem of keeping the needs of the students in mind, in view of their uncertain future careers, while at the same time attending to the standards of good research. Demands for advice on policy questions can easily absorb disproportionate energy and entice one into premature and superficial comment. We have so little solid information on most of the topics about which responsible officials must make judgments. At the same time it is necessary to give thought to building not only the data but also the conceptual apparatus of the field in which one is working while at the same time keeping abreast of the leading studies and ideas in the many disciplines that contribute to the amorphous activity that we call comparative education. Just the effort to entice one's colleagues in other disciplines (to give attention to what our field does) and if possible enlist their energies in joint research, absorbs much of the time of the administrator of a center. We at Chicago are constantly anxious about the balance and focus of our work; we hope what we do may retain the confidence of our colleagues and sponsors. The enterprise has certainly proved to be exciting and has brought us many stimulating professional associations.

NOTES

1. From time to time mimeographed reports of Center activities have been issued; copies of the latest one can be obtained. In the citations throughout this paper only part of the publications of the staff are mentioned.

2. To our regret Professor Kazamias has left the Center; he is directing the comparative education program at the University of Wisconsin.

3. One could even compare education in the American North and South, or Flemish with Walloon Belgium. But comparison of slum with suburban schools does not seem congruent with the connotation of the field.

4. Serious attention was given at one time to developing a program on the Soviet Union. But in view of the concentration of archives in the East and the number of excellent programs already underway, it was decided not to move in that direction.

5. A. Kazamias, *Politics, Society, and Secondary Education in England* (in press).

6. "Methodology of Comparative Education," *International Review of Education,* Vol. VII (1961), pp. 1–22. See also A. Kazamias, "History, Science, and Comparative Education," *ibid.,* Vol. VIII (1963), pp. 383–398.

7. C. Arnold Anderson and Mary Jean Bowman, "Theory of Educational Planning," in Don Adams (editor), *Educational Planning* (Syracuse University Press, 1964, pp. 4–46).

8. C. Arnold Anderson and Philip Foster, "Sociological Factors in Educational Discrimination," *Sociology of Education,* no. 38 (Fall 1964), pp. 1–18.

9. The discussion of the second part of the definition is being taken up first.

10. Professor Benjamin Bloom with the director represent Chicago; Professors Arthur W. Foshay and Robert L. Thorndike represent Teachers College; Professor Torsten Husén of the University of Stockholm is the technical director. The pilot project is reported in Foshay et al., *Educational Achievements of Thirteen-Year-Olds in Twelve Countries* (Hamburg: UNESCO Institute for Education, 1962).

11. Twelve other countries have requested that the study be replicated on their pupils, and consideration is being given also to testing in underdeveloped nations.

12. G. B. Kanungo, *The Language Controversy in Indian Education,* Com-

parative Education Center Monograph 1, 1962; H. Bruen, "The Impact of Social and Political Factors upon the Teaching of History in the Secondary Schools of Imperial Germany and the Weimar Republic" (dissertation, 1961); A. Peshkin, "Education in East Pakistan: A Case Study in Planned Change" (dissertation, 1962, now in press).

13. C. Arnold Anderson, "Emerging Common Problems of Universities," paper for 1964 Midwest Fulbright Conference.

14. Many of these are represented in the two issues of the *Review;* these papers will not be further cited.

15. The circumstances determining when and how much the copy will diverge from the metropolitan model are as yet unexplored.

16. C. Arnold Anderson and Mary Jean Bowman, "Concerning the Role of Education in Development," in C. Geertz (editor), *Old Peoples, New Nations* (Glencoe, Free Press, 1963, pp. 247–279).

17. W. Lee Hansen prepared one paper for the *Review* and a longer analysis for the conference cited in note 24.

18. Emogene Trexel, "Relationship between the Education Profession and the Political System in England and the United States" (dissertation in progress).

19. C. Arnold Anderson, "The Impact of the Educational System on Technological Change and Modernization," in B. Hoselitz and W. E. Moore (editors), *Industrialization and Society* (Paris: UNESCO, 1963), pp. 259–279.

20. G. Awani-Alele, "Dynamics of Education in the Birth of a New Nation: Nigeria" (dissertation, 1963); Charles Okpala, "Origins and Development of University Education in Nigeria" (dissertation, 1963).

21. A. Fattahapour-Fard, "Educational Diffusion and Modernization of Iran" (dissertation, 1963); P. Goldblatt, "The Role of Education and Social Change in Mexico" (dissertation in progress); J. Batt, "Interrelationship of Educational and Economic Change in France, 18–20th Century" (dissertation in progress); B. Khoshaba is also preparing a dissertation on the relationship of educational and economic developments in Iraq.

22. The initiative of T. W. Schultz of the Chicago Department of Economics in this area of research is well known.

23. For citations to the Center's work in economics see under Bowman in the name index of M. Blaug, *A Selected Annotated Bibliography in the Economics of Education,* Supplement 8 (University of London Institute of Education, *Education Libraries Bulletin,* 1964).

24. See *Education and Economic Growth* (Chicago, Aldine Publishing Co., 1965).

25. An example of some of the issues we have tried to deal with in this area is found in C. Arnold Anderson, "Economic Development and Post-Primary Education," in D. C. Piper and T. Cole, *Post-Primary Education and Political and Economic Development* (Durham: Duke University Press, 1964), pp. 3–26.

26. M. A. R. Shafshak, "The Role of the University in Egyptial Elite Recruitment: A Comparative Study of Al-Azhar and Cairo Universities" (disserta-

tion, 1964); M. A. Bashshur, "The Role of Two Western Universities in the National Life of Lebanon and the Middle East: A Comparison of the American University of Beirut and the University of Saint-Joseph" (dissertation, 1964); Joseph Fischer, *Universities in Southeast Asia,* Kappa Delta Pi, International Education Monograph, no. 6, 1964, which reports part of the data to be included in his dissertation; C. Okpala, *op. cit.*

27. The Netherlands study is by J. Ehrenberg, and the Danish one by M. Rudisch; L. W. Bone, *Secondary Education in the Guianas,* Comparative Education Center Monograph 2, 1962.

28. F. E. Cobun, "Educational Concomitants of Political Leadership in Five States of the Ante-Bellum North and South" (dissertation, 1964).

29. The first results of A. Kazamias' study in Turkey will be reported in a forthcoming Kappa Delta Pi *International Education Monograph;* the study was jointly supported by that organization and the Center.

30. Philip J. Foster, *Education and Social Change in Ghana* (University of Chicago Press, 1965).

31. Remi Clignet, a former civil servant in the Ivory Coast, is joint author with P. J. Foster of the study in that country. A preliminary comparison of Ghana and Ivory Coast schools will be found in an article by those two authors, "Potential Elites in Ghana and the Ivory Coast," *American Journal of Sociology,* Vol. LXX (1964), pp. 349–364.

32. The Brazil study is directed by R. J. Havighurst, with Aparacita Gouveia as research associate.

CHAPTER 7

The Development of
the National Association for Foreign
Student Affairs from "Idea to Institution"

M. ROBERT B. KLINGER

INTRODUCTION: WHAT IS A FOREIGN STUDENT?

One of the first problems in reference to the foreign student is that there is no completely accepted definition of a foreign student. Over the years, for example, four definitions have been used by the University of Michigan alone. In 1943, the published statistics of the University stated:

> In October, 1942, the definition of a "foreign student" was changed from "a student who is not a citizen of the United States." The distinction based on residence is, however, still kept for students from Alaska, the Canal Zone, Hawaii, Puerto Rico, and the Virgin Islands.[1]

In September, 1950, the statistics [2] omitted the students from United States Territories and possessions, and starting in October, 1953,[3] they added "Exchange Visitors and Visiting Professors." One of the most complicated definitions can be found in the statistics of foreign students in the United States published by the Committee on Friendly Relations Among Foreign Students in 1953, which states:

> The numbers recorded here do not include students from the outlying possessions of the United States, foreign born wives of American citizens, students who have taken out naturalization papers, or are registered as displaced persons, American citizens born abroad or any high school or prep school students. Those students are included, however, who are at present exiles from their own countries, but have not applied for citizenship here

or elsewhere, awaiting some turn of events which would make it possible for them to return or else would make it seem wisest to acquire citizenship in this or some other country not their native land.[4]

At times the same publication will give different figures for the same group. In *The Foreign Student in America*, Y. Y. Tsu's article speaks of "the approximately two thousand Chinese students. . . ." A footnote on the same page states:

> This estimate is somewhat widely at variance with the figure for 1920–21, cited on p. 12 as 1,443, or that for 1921–22, given on p. 16, as 1,218. It should be borne in mind, however, that both these totals represent college and university students only.[5]

A search of the literature can find other definitions at various times and places, and for various purposes. Any statistics used in this paper, therefore—or in any publication—may not be compared necessarily with any degree of accuracy with other statistics since the likelihood is that different definitions have been used.

EARLY HISTORY OF FOREIGN STUDENTS IN THE UNITED STATES AND THE EVANGELICAL CONCERN FOR THEM

The earliest known foreign student in the United States was Francisco de Miranda, later a liberation leader in Latin America, who studied at Yale in 1784. The earliest Chinese student was Dr. Yung Wing who also studied at Yale, and who returned to China in 1859. Joseph Hardy Neesima, who later founded Doshisha University, first studied at Philips Andover Academy and later at Amherst College from which he graduated in 1874. In 1925, Henry H. King, in his "Outline History of Student Migrations"[6] names many foreign students who became famous later: Fernando Bolivar, a nephew of the Liberator, former Presidents Errazuriz of Chile, Menocal of Cuba, Lefebre of Panama, Foreign Ministers and Ambassadors Bonillas of Mexico, C. T. Thomas Wang, and Wellington Koo of China.

Another chapter in the same book, bearing brief articles on "Representative American Opinion Concerning the Potential Influence of Returned Students," edited by Robert L. Kelly,[7] assesses the influence of study in the United States both as to "the foreign policies of their governments and on the attitude of their people toward other races and nations" and to "the Church and the Kingdom of Christ in their own lands and in the world."[8] Respondents to the questionnaire (used in this chapter to elicit information) seemed almost unanimously agreed on the possible influences as being good or bad, according to how the foreign students are treated here in the United States.

The 1925 reference "to the Church and the Kingdom of Christ in their own lands and in the world" seems peculiar in comparison with the present-day emphasis on secular goals in the foreign student movement. While it could be expected that the replies from Church-connected agencies would retain the evangelistic emphasis, as they do, the statements from Stephen P. Duggan, founding Director of the Institute of International Education, Harry E. Edmonds, Director of the International House, New York, and Dr. George M. Stratton for President Barrows, University of California, also bear the same evangelistic emphasis. In a latter chapter of this pioneering work,[9] Charles D. Hurry deals largely with this evangelistic direction of thought in reference to the foreign student.

A clear statement of the evangelistic emphasis is given by Professor J. Raleigh Nelson, first Counselor to Foreign Students at the University of Michigan, and believed to be the first such counselor to be appointed in the United States:

It is important to remember that the actual establishment of the University occurred at the beginning of the great evangelistic movement in the Protestant churches which sent American missionaries into the most remote and hazardous corners of the world. It is significant that a member of the very first class to be graduated from the University, the class of 1845, was destined to be the first missionary sent to China by the Methodists . . . Judson Dwight Collins. . . . From the class of 1848 Horatio W. Shaw . . . went to Allahabad, India, returning just in time to escape the Sepoy Rebellion. Tillman C. Trowbridge ('52 LL.D. '80) . . . went to Turkey . . . and Thomas Spencer Ogden ('53, A.M. '57) was sent to Corsica. Scores of Michigan men and women, as the great missionary movement swept to its climax, went out, not only to preach the gospel and minister to the sick but, whether intentionally or not, to become alumni centers of interest in the University of Michigan. Whatever opinion one may hold regarding the theological and denominational dogmatism of that period, one cannot fail to recognize the heroism and sincerity of these men and women; certainly the foreign students who were soon to come in such numbers to the University were the fruits of their sowing.[10]

In the late nineteenth century evangelic efforts culminated in several organized efforts at consolidation, as exemplified by the organization of the United Board for Christian Colleges in China and the foundation of the Near East College Association.

By 1904, whatever the causes, there was a total of 2,673 students from abroad in colleges and universities in the United States; British North America was represented with 614, Mexico with 308, Cuba with 236, Japan with 105, China with 93, other Latin American countries with more than 150, and the Philippines with 46.

In seven years, by 1911–1912, there was close to a doubling in numbers—4,856 students and 471 more in summer sessions. Canada had 898, West Indies 698, China 549, Japan 415, Mexico 298, United Kingdom 251, India and Ceylon 148, Germany 143, Russia and Finland 120, Brazil 76, Argentina 51, Peru 28, Colombia 28, Chile 19, and other Latin American countries 72.

By 1920–1921 the figures had risen 50 per cent to 6,901 students. China led with 1,443, Canada was second with 1,294, South America 563, Japan 525, West Indies 396, Russia 291, Mexico 282, India 235, Africa 223, France 160, and Great Britain with 149.[11]

ESTABLISHMENT OF ORGANIZED EFFORTS
ON BEHALF OF FOREIGN STUDENTS

The remarkable proliferation of agencies dealing with students from other lands in the past fifty years makes it impossible here to attempt to cover them all. A consideration of some of the pioneer efforts, culminating with the establishment and growth of the National Association of Foreign Student Advisers with its annual Conference on International Educational Exchanges is, therefore, all that is contemplated.

The pioneer effort for a national organization on behalf of the foreign students was, appropriately enough, an organization of the students themselves. Despite the evangelical and humanitarian efforts of the Churches, the Boards of Missions, the Young Men's Christian Association, and the Young Women's Christian Association, they were superseded, on a national level, by the Association of Cosmopolitan Clubs of America (ACCA).[12] The first Cosmopolitan Club was organized at the University of Wisconsin, in March, 1903. Before 1910 several had been founded and the leaders had banded together to found the ACCA. The general policy of the individual clubs was to discuss international relations, forms of government, habits and customs, the government of the United States, economic conditions in various countries, and the youth movements of these countries. American students and foreign students were banded together in these clubs. The constitution of the ACCA stated the purposes of the national association as follows:

The object of the Association shall be the development in the world of the spirit of human justice, cooperation and brotherhood, and the desire to serve humanity unlimited by color, race, nationality, caste, or creed, by arousing and fostering this spirit in college and university students of all nationalities. The membership of the organization is confined to all college and university clubs and clubs made up of alumni of such college and university clubs having for their object the uniting for mutual social and intellectual benefit of persons of different nationalities.[13]

The individual clubs grew and diminished, and the ACCA itself flourished, but gradually it withered and ultimately disappeared. In 1924, L. H. Pammel, President of the ACCA, lists thirty-one clubs in twenty-four different institutions, and three intercollegiate clubs in city associations. By 1942 [14] there was only one representative of a Cosmopolitan Club, Cornell's, present at a national conference. The ACCA had for all practical purposes left the foreign student scene.

Pammel's article does not mention any connection with the Christian Churches. From the recollection of former members, with whom the author has talked, there was little connection with the churches, except on some individual campuses, and in fact there was conflict and jealousy between some Cosmopolitan Clubs and local YMCA's. Pammel's only reference is:

> The work of the Young Men's Christian Association and the Young Women's Christian Association for the foreign students is highly appreciated by the various Cosmopolitan Clubs, but these two organizations cannot fully attend to the matter of organizing the work of foreign students, especially in its application to the forum.[15]

THE COMMITTEE ON FRIENDLY RELATIONS AMONG FOREIGN STUDENTS

The next two national organizations on the scene were the Committee on Friendly Relations Among Foreign Students (CFR), organized in 1911 by the foreign division of the International Committee of Young Men's Christian Associations, and the Committee on Friendly Relations Among Foreign Women Students, organized in 1914 by the National Board of the Young Women's Christian Association.[16] The Christian concern for the students from other lands had culminated in a national agency. The Committee was founded under the leadership of the eminent Christian statesman and student organizer, Dr. John R. Mott.[17] Mott, in 1924, was General Secretary of the International Committee of Young Men's Christian Associations; Chairman of the World's Student Christian Federation; and Chairman of the International Missionary Council, and his son, John L. Mott, was for many years Director of International House, New York.

Dr. D. Willard Lyon was first General Secretary of the Committee on Friendly Relations in 1915 and was succeeded by Charles D. Hurry. Hurry was present, as the retired secretary of the CFR, at the Conference of Foreign Student Advisers in Cleveland, 1942, as was his successor Samuel Mills.[18] Mills was succeeded by Louis Wolferz who was in turn succeeded by J. Benjamin Schmoker, one of the organizers and later President of the National Association of Foreign Student Advisers.

The Committee originally rendered services both in and from the New York office and in field travel by its secretary. The personnel was drawn from several Christian organizations. Through the years it has performed services by correspondence with missionaries and educators throughout the world and with prospective students in other lands. It has engaged in studies and statistical services including publication of *The Unofficial Ambassadors* which includes statistics on foreign students, and also articles and quotations from foreign students. This service, which began in 1915 as a series of directories, became a formal census report in 1919, and was entitled *The Unofficial Ambassadors* in 1928.[19] In more recent years the Institute of International Education cooperated in gathering data for the census which now is reported annually in the Institute's publication, *Open Doors*.

The Committee is also well known for its port-of-entry services to incoming students from abroad. By 1956 ships and planes were being met at seventeen ports of entry in the United States and three in Canada, and services provided for these students. The Committee has served local campuses, through forming hospitality committees, and also by coordinating efforts as a clearing house of information. It also performs a variety of other services of a general nature for foreign students. Throughout it has maintained its Christian character though emphasizing more the humanitarian strain of endeavor rather than the evangelistic spirit.

RECENT EVANGELICAL ORGANIZATIONS

While it is not chronologically appropriate, the evangelistic devotion to converting the non-Protestant foreign student to Christianity, and the "strengthening of the spirit" of the Protestant student, must take into account the more recent organizations in this area, namely International Students Incorporated and its action arm, Fellowship of Christian University Students, known as FOCUS. The evangelical missionary endeavor of some Protestant churches has always been in evidence, but not until the 1950's had those of the strongest evangelical concern banded together. These organizations are now on the scene, actively promoting the conversion of non-Protestant students from abroad to what some would describe as the "fundamentalist" strain of Protestantism—through carefully designed services to foreign students, through volunteers and a professional staff, such as port-of-entry, home hospitality, camps and conferences, and other similar endeavors.

THE INSTITUTE OF INTERNATIONAL EDUCATION

Not from a concern for Christian evangelistic endeavor but from one of international understanding, grew the Institute of International Education, founded in 1919. Three distinguished men, Elihu Root, lawyer and statesman, also Secretary of State in President Theodore Roosevelt's cabinet, Nicholas Murray Butler, President of Columbia University, and trustee since 1910 of the then newly founded Carnegie Endowment for International Peace, and Stephen Duggan, Professor of Political Science at the College of the City of New York and member of the subcommittee on international educational relations of the American Council on Education:

. . . sat before a log fire in the Columbia University Club in New York City in late fall of 1918. The Armistice had been signed in a railway coach in the forest of Compiègne only two weeks before. Their talk centered on the implications of peace and of future relations among the nations.[20]

Root's point was that free discussion in dealings with foreign governments was hampered by language and inadequate acquaintance of individual nations with other cultures. He is quoted as saying:

Something must be done on a large scale to make the people of various countries more familiar with other languages and viewpoints.

Butler mentioned that he noted that even intelligent Americans were comparatively unfamiliar with international affairs, and that "we live in an intellectual vacuum, and the only hope is for us to become internationally minded." Duggan reported that the subcommittee's discussions indicated a need for a clearing house of information, which would stimulate greater interest in the study of international relations and increase the flow of students, specialists, teachers, and trainees between the United States and other countries. He noted that:

If done on a large and carefully selected basis the exchange of such people might prevent war. But we should go ahead whether it might or not, because the world is shrinking and yesterday's foreigner is today's neighbor. We have to live next door, and the only sensible thing is to get acquainted.

The talk went on far into the night and the concept of the Institute of International Education was the result. The purpose was to be a two-way exchange of persons between the United States and all areas of the world with all fields of study to be included. Students would be expected to return to serve in their home countries, the measure of participation was to be ability, and scholarships were to be established for those students without sufficient funds.

Each person was an integral part of the structure, and personal attention to proper placement, orientation, and hospitality was to be the goal.

On February 1, 1919, the Institute opened its doors with Stephen Duggan as Director, a post he was to hold for twenty-eight years. Shortly after it was established a statement of policy was sent out stating the Institute's objectives:

The possibilities of service exist, of course, in an infinite number of directions. The Institute does not itself contemplate undertaking the establishment of courses, scholarships, or exchange professorships, much less financing these activities, but it hopes to help in making the existing facilities known and to act as an intermediary between persons who may suggest opportunities of service in international education, and persons who may make these opportunities available. The Institute will be grateful for the cooperation of the educational institutions of the country, and for suggestions from anyone interested in its efficient functioning.[21]

Associated with Duggan, as staff members, were Arthur W. Packard, later Director of the Rockefeller Brothers Fund, Edward R. Murrow, later radio commentator and Vice President of the Columbia Broadcasting System, and Edgar J. Fisher, recently of Sweet Briar College. Duggan's successor was his son, Laurence Duggan, who served from November, 1946 until his death in December, 1948. Under Laurence Duggan's direction there was a doubling of staff, budget, and total programs. Donald J. Shank, Vice President, then directed the Institute work. He was formerly with the American Council on Education and Cornell University. The present president, Kenneth Holland, assumed the Presidency in the Spring of 1950. He is a graduate of Occidental College and Princeton University and has studied abroad. He has served in governmental posts in the office of Inter-American Affairs, the Department of State, and other agencies. He has also been United States Counselor on UNESCO Affairs in Paris.

The roster of the Trustees and the Advisory Council of the Institute include many eminent names among whom have been Nicholas Butler, Henry Morgenthau, Sr., John Bassett Moore, Alice D. Miller, Dwight W. Murrow, Thomas W. Lamont, John Foster Dulles, Joseph P. Chamberlain, Virginia Gildersleeve, Jane Addams, Henry L. Stimson, Harry Emerson Fosdick, Julius Sachs, James T. Shotwell, Charles Evans Hughes, and Quincy Wright.

The Institute of International Education has made vast and important contributions. Ten thousand students, professors, specialists, technicians—foreign and American—were exchanged, and additional thousands advised in the first thirty years of the Institute's history. Some of the projects in which the IIE has pioneered are as follows:

The Institute published the first comprehensive list of scholarship opportunities for foreign students in the United States and for Americans abroad; the first guide books for foreign students; and the first monthly publications in this country exclusively concerned with international education.

The Institute pioneered in sending American professors to universities abroad and bringing foreign professors to the United States.

The Institute was the first organization to arrange on a large scale noncommercial lecture tours for distinguished scholars and men of affairs from abroad to speak at American colleges and universities.

In 1922 the Institute assisted in securing a change in existing immigration regulations to permit foreign students to enter the United States on special visas.

The Institute was instrumental in the establishment of "student third class" travel arrangements on ships, later to become the popular "Tourist Class."

The Institute has worked unceasingly to establish more uniform evaluation of academic credits in all educational systems.

In cooperation with the United States Department of State, the Institute pioneered in the establishment of uniform selection standards and the development of bi-national selection committees, so that only qualified students would come here or be sent abroad.

The Institute cooperated with the United States Department of the Army and other organizations to bring to the United States after World War II the first large groups of students from Germany, Japan, Austria, and the Ryukyus.

Since the end of World War II, the Institute has assisted in the establishment of programs for education in the United States of students and technicians from underdeveloped and colonial areas which had not sent students before.

The Institute encouraged the development of the office of Foreign Student Advisers on college campuses in the United States.[22]

The IIE has become preeminent in its field and was assigned responsibility for much of the implementation of Public Law 584 (19th Congress), known as the Fulbright Act, under contract to the Department of State. It was chosen by the Department of the Army to administer the educational program for over two hundred persons from occupied areas after the Second World War, and was asked to administer the UNESCO specialist program. The roster of some of the agencies, associations, and departments which have asked the Institute to administer programs is long and varied, and includes the National

Education Association, the American Chemical Society, the Institute of Scientific Research in Industry and Agriculture, the Republic of Korea, the English Speaking Union, the American Scandinavian Foundation, the Belgian American Educational Foundation, the Atlantique (French-American Society for Cultural Exchange), and the Rockefeller Foundation. To give a history and assessment of its importance in the field would require a volume of its own.

INTERNATIONAL HOUSES

The International House movement started with the International House in New York, opening as it did in September, 1924 with Harry Edmonds as its first director. The funds for the undertaking were provided through the generosity and international mindedness of Mr. and Mrs. John D. Rockefeller, Jr. Additional prominent international houses were built, through Rockefeller donations, in Berkeley and Chicago. The history of these houses and of the international camaraderie they have featured, I leave to other chroniclers.

THE LISLE FELLOWSHIP

There are a number of private groups with rather similar goals concerned with world understanding and cooperation, such as the American Friends Service Summer Seminars, the Experiment in International Living. One of the oldest, or at least a typical representative of the group which has been in operation for a number of years, is the Lisle Fellowship.

While they were in Burma for ten years, Dewitt and Edna Baldwin, felt the need for a:

. . . new kind of education for world mindedness, which should create in every individual an appreciation for other cultures and the recognition of the interdependence of people.[23]

They came to believe that the experience of living thoughtfully together with people of many backgrounds is essential to this kind of education. The core of the program would be the experience of participating as teams in actual community life and the thoughtful examination of this experience as a group. The Methodist Board of Foreign Missions, of which Baldwin was Secretary for Student Work, endorsed an experimental group as a summer session at Lisle, New York, in 1936. Called subsequently, the Lisle Fellowship, it took, in 1942, the subtitle "An International Institute of Human Relations," and was incorporated in New York state as a nonprofit membership association operating for educational purposes.

In recent years units have been in operation in the eastern part of the United States, in the far west, in Colorado, and in Denmark. By 1953, Lisle alumni had numbered over fifteen hundred persons throughout the world.

THE FOREIGN STUDENT ADVISER: ONE EXAMPLE

The office of foreign student adviser, under whatever title and with whatever organizational structure, was a later movement. While the establishment of such offices was not a national but a local campus phenomenon, the history of one such office is pertinent in describing who these "advisers" were who met first at the Cleveland Conference of Foreign Student Advisers in 1942, and who formed subsequently the National Association of Foreign Student Advisers in 1948.

One of the earliest such offices, if not the first, was at the University of Michigan, where Professor J. Raleigh Nelson was appointed Counselor to Foreign Students in 1933.[24] Professor Nelson first became interested in foreign students when, as an undergraduate, he met two women medical students from China on the Ann Arbor campus. His mother had been a missionary teacher to the Ojibway Indians in the Northern Peninsula and he was also imbued with the missionary spirit. Not long after returning to the University of Michigan, in 1908, to develop English courses for engineering students, he noticed that the foreign students required special help with their English. He organized a program of teaching English as a foreign language in 1911. In the same year the College of Engineering authorized the establishment of a Committee on Foreign Students in the College of Engineering, and Nelson was made permanent chairman of this committee with the title of Counselor to Foreign Students in the College of Engineering. In the College of Literature, Science, and the Arts, Professor Jonathan A. C. Hildner served as adviser to foreign students. In 1933, the University appointed Nelson as Counselor to Foreign Students for the whole University. Five years later, through Professor Nelson's efforts and President Alexander Ruthaven's active support and interest, a part of the Michigan Union was set aside as the International Center, and Professor Nelson was given the additional title of Director of the International Center. His course in English grew until two agencies for the teaching of English were founded on the Michigan campus—the English Language Service, to help students enrolled in the University, and the English Language Institute, to teach a concentrated prestudy two month course to new students.

By 1943, when Professor Nelson retired, there were 326 foreign students on the Michigan campus, from fifty-six countries, in the fall semester. In the same year there were 7,244 foreign students in 533 colleges and universities in the United States.[25] Thirteen campuses each had over one hundred students: New York University (528), Columbia University (359), University of Michigan (326), University of California (288), Harvard University (272), Massachusetts Institute of Technology (225), Teachers College, Columbia University (174), University of California at Los Angeles (167), Cornell University (132), University of Southern California (123), University of Chicago (117), University of Texas (111), and Louisiana State University (100).

UNITED STATES GOVERNMENT SERVICES

This paper is chiefly concerned with nongovernmental national services to foreign students, since governmental services would occupy at least as many pages. But some mention of them must be made. Except for sporadic interests and occasional agencies, such as the Cuban, Philippine, and Boxer Indemnity programs of the early twentieth century, the real effort by the United States government has dated only from 1936, when the exchange of persons started to become one of the main channels of our foreign policy through the Advisory Committee on the Adjustment of Foreign Students. First manifest through the "Good Neighbor Policy," then through "Point Four" and other concepts, the United States government has been involved through various departments and independent agencies: the Department of State, the Department of Justice, the Department of Labor, the Department of the Army of the Department of Defense, the Department of Health, Education, and Welfare, the Department of the Interior, the Department of Agriculture, the Department of Commerce, have all had or now have programs in the area of "exchange of persons." The United States Office of Education has been operating as long as any other in the field—performing special services, among others, in the evaluation of foreign credentials. Others are the United States Information Agency, Agency for International Development, the International Educational Exchange Service in the Department of State, to mention a few.

By 1956 the International Educational Exchange Service in the Department of State, alone involved an annual interchange of about six thousand people between the United States and over seventy countries of the world.[26]

THE NATIONAL ASSOCIATION OF FOREIGN STUDENT ADVISERS

All of the previous mentioned organizations, with others, came together in the organization of the National Association of Foreign Student Advisers. In the Association we find foreign student advisers from colleges and universities working at different levels. Some are working full time with a large staff under them, others, full time with a secretary, and some, part time giving service in addition to serving as a Professor of Spanish, or English, or Political Science, or Education. They are banded together with United States government representatives, International House Directors, personnel of the Institute of International Education, and the Committee on Friendly Relations, teachers of English as a foreign language, chairmen and members of community programs, the evangelists, the humanitarians, admissions officers, college presidents, deans and professors, cultural attaches and ambassadors, an occasional senator or governor, delegates, observers, and members from AAUW, YMCA, YWCA, Rotary International, the Pan-American Union, the Rockefeller Foundation, the Ford Foundation, and others, to form the National Association of Foreign Student Advisers. There were the professionals, such as James M. Davis, who served in the IIE before going to the University of Washington, then to the University of Michigan, and now back to the IIE as a Vice President; Joe Neal who attended the 1942 conference is still with us at the University of Texas; Harry Pierson occasionally in the government, and for a long time a key person in the IIE, is now with Asia Foundation; and Robert Klinger from 1938 to the present in the International Center of the University of Michigan. There are other professionals, of course—many of them—and there are the neophytes. How did this mixture come to be, this banding together of such varied persons all with a common concern for service to the student and visitor from other lands?

In 1938, Sumner Welles, Undersecretary of State under Cordell Hull, was impressed with the value of the international exchange of persons as an important factor in the Good Neighbor Policy. Perhaps from the IIE, or perhaps from other sources, had come the idea of an "Advisory Committee on the Adjustment of Foreign Students in the United States." The appointments had gone out in 1936 for a first meeting and the Committee was expanded in 1938. In 1941 the personnel consisted of Edgar J. Fisher of IIE as chairman, John L. Mott from International House, New York, and seven foreign student advisers or interested persons: Rollin S. Attwood, University of Florida, Gladys Bryson, Smith College, Ben M. Charrington, University of Denver, Charles W. Hackett, University of Texas, Charles B. Lipman, University of California, Martin R. P. McGuire, Catholic University, and J. Raleigh Nelson, University of Michigan. They considered many topics in their meetings but one seemed uppermost in the 1941 Committee sessions held in Nashville of those people working with foreign students. The IIE was asked to organize such a conference and an organizing committee was appointed which consisted of Fisher as Chairman, Bryson, McGuire, and Mott of the "Advisory Committee" mentioned previously, and Kenneth Holland, then Director, Division of Science and Education, Office of the Coordinator of Inter-American Affairs, John C. Patterson, Chief, Division of Inter-American Educational Relations, United States Office of Education, and Harry H. Pierson, Senior Divisional Assistant, Division of Cultural Relations, Department of State.

The first major conference was called for April 28–30, 1942, in Cleveland, under the auspices of the Institute of International Education in cooperation with the Department of State, the United States Office of Education, and the office of the Coordinator of Inter-American Affairs.

The scope of the Conference was broad but at the same time definite and realistic. The main emphasis was on problems resulting from the war situation: difficulties of transportation, selective service regulations, the evacuation of Japanese-American students from the West Coast, the need for funds and work opportunities for stranded students. Because of the . . . particular interest in Pan Americanism and the large numbers of Latin American students now in the United States, special problems relating to these students were stressed.[27]

Those persons clearly identified as foreign student advisers (FSA's as they are now more commonly known) at the 1942 conference numbered only thirteen. At the next conference, in 1946, which was called by the Institute of International Education in cooperation with the Department of State from April 29 to May 1, in Chicago, there were thirty-one representatives with a title similar to FSA.

By the fall semester of 1945 there were 10,341 students from abroad in colleges and universities in the United States. They were from ninety-nine countries, and whereas two years before there had been thirteen institutions with over one hundred students registered, now there were nineteen.[28] The leaders, with over two hundred students were: New York University (534), University of Michigan (507), Columbia University (385), Massachusetts Institute of Technology (319), Cornell (301), Teachers College, Columbia (293), Harvard (273), University of California (211), University of Washington (206). The University of Minnesota was unreported. Of note is the presence of Pasadena Junior College with 131 foreign students.

The goals of the 1946 conference, entitled the "Conference of Col-

lege and University Administrators and Foreign Student Advisers,"
were clearly stated by Stephen Duggan in a letter expressing his re-
grets at his inability to attend. The letter was read by the conference
chairman, Dr. Edgar J. Fisher, of the Institute of International Education. The concern of the IIE and the Department of State, and of
many others present as noted in the discussions, was that the conges-
tion in the colleges due to the influx of returned veteran students
would push out the foreign students. Duggan noted:

> My own information is to the effect that while the number of foreign
> students will unquestionably be reduced, there is a strong desire upon the
> part of college administrators to retain the practice of welcoming foreign
> students. Too many Americans forget that the universities in foreign coun-
> tries have either been closed for the past six years or drastically reduced in
> their activities. . . . It is to be hoped that no *numeras clauses* upon foreign
> students will be enforced in our country.[29]

The conference in Chicago in 1947, also sponsored by the Institute
of International Education and the Department of State, was chiefly
notable for the creation of a Conference Steering Committee to guide
the 1948 conference, and for a resolution to form a Committee on By-
Laws for a "National Association." The foreign student advisers and
friends of foreign students were ready to form an association. There
was much discussion on a possible name, on membership, and on
structure but it was left to the Committee on By-Laws to work out
by meetings and correspondence a tentative structure to be voted upon
at the 1948 meeting.

In Ann Arbor at the "Conference on International Student Exchange," May 10–12, 1948, called by the Institute of International Education, assisted by the W. K. Kellogg Foundation at the request of
the Steering Committee of the 1947 conference of foreign student advisers, the new association was born.[30] There were forty-eight persons
present, out of 224, at the conference, who clearly had titles that could
be interpreted as "Foreign Student Advisers." Before the close of the
meetings the bylaws had been discussed, modified, and passed, and
officers elected under the bylaws. The conference selected Professor
Clarence Linton, Adviser to Students from Other Lands, Teachers
College, Columbia University, as president; Allen C. Blaisdell, Adviser
to Foreign Students, and Director, International House, University of
California, as vice president; Harry H. Pierson, Director of Program,
Institute of International Education, as secretary; and Joe W. Neal,
Adviser, Foreign Students' Advisory Office, University of Texas, as
treasurer. Twenty-four members were elected to the Board of Di-

rectors—eleven were FSA's, three were college presidents, three were teachers of English as a foreign language, two were from binational agencies (China Institute in American and the English Speaking Union), two were directors of International Houses, one was in charge of a community program for foreign students, and one represented a national religious organization (The American Friends Service Committee). The directors also included Laurence Duggan, President of the Institute of International Education and J. Benjamin Schmoker, general secretary, Committee on Friendly Relations among Foreign Students. All of the major national groups previously considered, with the foreign student advisers, the teachers of English, and local community groups were now joined in an endeavor devoted to service for the student from abroad.

The number of foreign students in the United States continued to expand. There were 29,432 reported enrolled in the fall semester of 1950 in 1,254 institutions.[31]

By the fall semester of 1954 there were 34,232 students reported enrolled, with 635 foreign faculty members reported teaching in these colleges and universities, and 5,036 foreign doctors reported working in hospitals in the United States. There were seventy-eight institutions enrolling over one hundred foreign students, and of those, thirteen reported four hundred or more.[32] These were Columbia University (all campuses) (1,254), New York University (946), University of Michigan (610), University of California at Berkeley (798), Harvard (721), Massachusetts Institute of Technology (602), University of Illinois (594), University of Southern California (569), University of Minnesota (530), Cornell University (488), University of Wisconsin (477), University of Washington (442), and the University of Texas at Austin (411).

For a brief history of NAFSA since its formation in 1948, the best source will be found in a forthcoming NAFSA publication by Ivan Putman, which is Volume I of the *Handbook for Foreign Student Advisers*. I shall plagiarize here boldly and deliberately, giving full credit to author Putman:

From the beginning what happens to the foreign student in his period of study in the United States, the quality of his experience both in the classroom and out, has been the central concern of NAFSA. Key people in determining the quality of his experience are the foreign student adviser, the teacher of English as a foreign language in the college or university he attends, and those who introduce him to the American community in which he lives. Since inevitably many of these people are part-time and volunteer people, and because of the turnover from year to year in these positions over the country, NAFSA has always considered its major responsibility to be in-service training of those who work with foreign students. This has been a major focus of NAFSA's entire program. All of NAFSA's conferences, both national and regional, have been working conferences to help those who attend serve foreign students with greater understanding and professional competence.

NAFSA's publication program, one of its most significant contributions to the field of foreign student work, was launched in 1949 when the NAFSA Newsletter was established with Katherine Bang as its first editor. Following an extensive program of campus visits by J. Benjamin Schmoker during the period 1952–54 in his dual capacity as Executive Secretary of NAFSA and General Secretary of the Committee on Friendly Relations among Foreign Students, NAFSA's Regional Development Program was launched with Ivan Putman, Jr., as first chairman of the National Committee, again with in-service training as its major function.

The first grant for travel abroad to be made available through NAFSA was established by the American Friends of the Middle East [AFME] in 1952, and has continued on an annual basis ever since. The task of selecting the recipient of the AFME award was the initial charge of what is now the NAFSA Professional Development Committee. Since that first award nearly a hundred NAFSA members have had opportunities for significant experience abroad through the good offices of NAFSA, and another 150 or more have had opportunities to attend regional or national conferences and two-week seminars in the United States under grants through the NAFSA Regional and Professional Development Programs.

Other NAFSA services that have been significant have been its government liaison activities, development of relationships with educational and cultural officers of foreign embassies in this country, its cooperative relationships with other organizations interested in international educational exchange of persons, the work of its Research Committee in encouraging, conducting, and reporting research in intercultural exchange, and its recent work in developing a code of ethics for the profession of foreign student work.

The most recent major development in NAFSA history is the launching of the NAFSA Field Service project under a grant from the Department of State to provide consultative services to colleges and universities desiring to improve their foreign student programs, and to provide more extensive materials and opportunities for in-service training of foreign student advisers than have heretofore been available. Katherine Bang is the Director of the Field Service and opened her office in Cleveland, September 1, 1963.

NAFSA's record of service has been made possible over the years by a series of grants from foundations, beginning with a five-year Ford Foundation grant in 1951 (?). Two additional five-year grants have been received from this same source. Support for training opportunities abroad has come from the American Friends of the Middle East, the Asia Foundation, the Creole Foundation, and the Fulbright program of the Department of State. A major research project on the status of foreign student advising in the country was made possible by a grant from the Dean Langmuir Foundation, and a second grant made possible the preparation of a significant publication, "The College, the University, and the Foreign Student," which has been an important factor in encouraging institutions to improve their foreign student programs. A Danforth Foundation grant made possible the 1960 seminar on the uses of research in foreign student work, our first attempt at in-service training in depth. The Asia Foundation has supported a series of three two-week seminars on Asian cultures held in the summers of 1961, 1962, and 1963. Membership dues from both individual and institutional members and the sale of publications are other sources of support for NAFSA's program. In recent years, through the efforts of the Corporate Liaison Committee, significant financial support has also been obtained from major corporations having substantial overseas interests.

The English Language Section of NAFSA was formally organized in 1951 only three years after the formation of NAFSA itself with Clifford H. Prator of the University of California at Los Angeles as its first chairman. It has been a growing and very active unit promoting professional interest and competence in the teaching of English as a foreign language. The Community Section was organized in 1961 with Hugh Jenkins, Director of the Foreign Student Service Council in Washington, D.C., as its first chairman. It has effectively coordinated the interests of those NAFSA members concerned with community programs for foreign students. A section for admissions officers was formed in 1963 with Eugene Chamberlain of MIT as chairman.

In recognition of this diversity of interests and professional concerns within NAFSA the name of the organization was changed in 1963 from the National Association of Foreign Student Advisers to the National Association for Foreign Student Affairs, thus preserving the "NAFSA" designation which has become so well known in educational exchange throughout the world.

Again let me note that these last paragraphs are direct quotations from a forthcoming NAFSA publication written by Ivan Putman.

NAFSA itself is moving forward apace. The events of the last year are so fresh in our minds, and are still evolving, still developing. They are not yet definite enough to qualify as history. The best we can say is that we hope they will uphold the long traditions foreshadowed even by Thomas Jefferson in his friendship for Francisco de Miranda nine score years ago.

NOTES

1. M. Robert Klinger, *Statistical Relationship between Latin American Students and Other Data, University of Michigan, 1938–43,* mimeographed (Ann Arbor: University of Michigan, The International Center, n.d.).

2. *Enrollment of Students from Other Lands, Fall Semester, 1950,* mimeo-

graphed (Ann Arbor: University of Michigan, The International Center, 1950).

3. *Enrollment of Students from Other Lands, Fall Semester, 1955,* mimeographed (Ann Arbor: University of Michigan, The International Center, 1955).

4. *The Unofficial Ambassadors* (New York: The Committee on Friendly Relations among Foreign Students, 1953).

5. *The Foreign Student in America,* edited by W. Reginald Wheeler, Henry H. King, and Alexander B. Davidson (New York: Association Press, 1925), p. 44.

6. Henry H. King, "Outline History of Student Migrations," *The Foreign Student in America,* Chapter I, pp. 3–38.

7. "The Careers and Influence of Returned Students in Their Homelands," *The Foreign Student in America,* Chapter III, pp. 82–127.

8. *Ibid.,* p. 82.

9. Charles D. Hurry, "The Foreign Student and American Life," *The Foreign Student in America,* Chapter IV, pp. 135–144.

10. *President's Report 1935–1936,* see Appendix to the Report of the Dean of Students (Ann Arbor: University of Michigan, 1936), pp. 54–55.

11. *The Foreign Student in America,* Bureau of Education report for 1904 . . . , United States Commerce Reports, August 28, 1912. . . . George F. Zook, Specialist in Higher Education, Bureau of Education, "The Residence of Students in Higher Institutions" (Washington, D.C.: Department of Interior, Bureau of Education, Government Printing Office, 1922), pp. 11–12.

12. L. H. Pammel, "Cosmopolitan Clubs," in *The Foreign Student in America, op. cit.,* pp. 268–272.

13. *Ibid.,* p. 268.

14. *Report of the Conference of Foreign Student Advisers, Cleveland, April 28, 29, 30, 1942* (New York: Institute of International Education, 1942).

15. *The Foreign Student in America,* p. 269.

16. *Ibid.,* p. 13.

17. *Ibid.,* pp. 228–230.

18. *Report of the Conference of Foreign Student Advisers, 1942, op. cit.*

19. *The Unofficial Ambassadors* (New York: Committee on Friendly Relations among Foreign Students, 1950).

20. *Blueprint for Understanding: The Institute of International Education, Inc., a Thirty Year Review* (New York: Institute of International Education, December 1949).

21. *Ibid.,* pp. 9–10.

22. *Ibid.,* pp. 29–30.

23. See Celeste McCullough, *Information Material about the Lisle Fellowship, Inc.,* pamphlet (April 1953), no place listed. (Quotations in this paper are from the section on "History.")

24. See M. Robert B. Klinger, "The International Center," in Chapter IX, "The Student Life and Organizations, Athletics," *The University of*

Michigan: An Encyclopedic Survey (Ann Arbor: University of Michigan Press, 1958), pp. 1843–1849.

25. *The Unofficial Ambassadors* (New York: Committee on Friendly Relations among Foreign Students, 1943).

26. See *Federal Government Agencies and International Educational Exchanges,* Inter-Agency Committee on Technical Training Programs, Exchange of Persons, and Overseas Cultural Activities (Washington, D.C., 1956).

27. *Report of the Conference of Foreign Student Advisers, 1942, op. cit.,* p. 111.

28. *The Unofficial Ambassadors* (New York: Committee on Friendly Relations among Foreign Students, 1946).

29. *Report of the Conference of College and University Administrators and Foreign Student Advisers,* Chicago, April 29–May 1, 1946 (New York: Institute of International Education, 1946), p. 1.

30. *Special Report: Conference on International Student Exchanges, May 10–12, 1948, University of Michigan* (New York: Institute of International Education, 1948).

31. *The Unofficial Ambassadors* (New York: Committee on Friendly Relations among Foreign Students, 1951).

32. *Open Doors 1954–55* (New York: The Institute of International Education, 1955).

Part **III**

International Education
under Communism

CHAPTER 8

Government Encouragement and Control of International Education in Communist China

THEODORE H. E. CHEN

In the discussion of government encouragement and control of international education in Communist China, I have been asked to deal with three specific topics: (1) Chinese students studying abroad, (2) foreign students studying in China, and (3) overseas Chinese students who return to China for study.

It should be stated at the outset that there are no activities under any of these categories except those sponsored and controlled by the government. Moreover, the slogan "Let politics take command," which is to guide all individual and group activities in China, applies thoroughly and relentlessly to all phases of education. Therefore, we should expect not only a strict government control of the process, but also the domination of political motives in all phases of education, including international educational exchange.

CHINESE STUDENTS STUDYING ABROAD

Scope. Reporting to the National People's Congress in June, 1957, Communist China's Premier Chou En-lai stated that in the first seven years of the new regime China had sent more than 7,000 students to study abroad. No one goes abroad, of course, unless permitted by the government. According to Chou En-lai, the government selected students for foreign study on the basis of three criteria: political acceptability, academic achievement, and health. He frankly said that political qualifications were considered to be of paramount importance. Noting regretfully that carelessness in selection had allowed

111

some politically undesirable students to go abroad, he urged that more attention should be given to the political qualifications of candidates. He also announced a modification of policy which would terminate the practice of allowing graduates of middle schools to go abroad.[1]

Most of the 7,000 students who went abroad before 1957 went to the Soviet Union. According to the Chinese Minister of Higher Education, 6,288 students went to the Soviet Union between 1950 and 1956.[2] René Goldman, who went from Poland to study in Communist China from 1953 to 1958, wrote in 1962 that "China sent an average of 2,000 students yearly to the Soviet Union and a hundred or so to the Eastern European countries."[3] In his report to the Central Committee of the Communist Party of the Soviet Union on February 14, 1964, Mikhail Suslov said:

Between 1951 and 1962 about 10,000 Chinese engineers, technicians, and qualified workers, and about 1,000 scientists were afforded training in our country. In the same period over 11,000 students and post-graduate students finished courses at Soviet higher educational establishments.[4]

The disparity in statistics may in part be explained by the fact that relatively few students went abroad in the first three years of the regime, and the government did not send large numbers of students abroad till after the first five-year plan had gotten under way.

Besides the Soviet Union and Eastern Europe, Chinese students have been sent to North Korea, Mongolia, and a few other countries. The first group of "selected government cadres and students" went to the Soviet Union in 1951.[5] More than one hundred of them returned to China in the summer of 1955 after four years of study.[6] The first five-year plan, 1953–1957, provided for sending 9,000 students a year to the Soviet Union.[7] By 1955, between 1,800 and 1,900 students were going to Russia each year, with a few hundred going to more than ten countries in Eastern Europe.[8] Approximately 70 per cent of the students were to specialize in science or engineering.

Students in Russia. The students stayed in Russia for three to six years. Many of them completed the five-year course in Soviet universities. Before going abroad, they were required to spend a year in the study of Russian at the Peking Russian Language school or at one of the universities where there was a special course to prepare students for study abroad. In the spring of 1955, 2,260 students were studying at the Peking Russian Language school in preparation for study in the Soviet Union,[9] and in the following year, more than 2,400 were chosen by the Ministry of Education for a year of preparatory study prior to going to Russia.[10]

After 1955, each summer saw an increasing number of students returning to China after their completion of study in the Soviet Union. In 1958, more than 600 were reported to have returned after graduation from Russian universities,[11] and in 1959, 1,300 had completed their study and were given a farewell banquet by the Chinese Ambassador to the U.S.S.R., at which profuse appreciation of the generosity and kindness of Soviet teachers and students was expressed in various speeches. Most of the students had specialized in science and technology. One girl had studied music, and she declared that her fond ambition was to return to China and go to distant areas to introduce Russian classical music and the works of Soviet composers to the Chinese people.[12] In the following year, another group of 1,300 graduates returned from the Soviet Union and other communist countries.[13]

Besides students that enrolled in universities, China sent "advanced workers," technicians, and factory administrators for practical training in Soviet factories and industrial enterprises. Thousands of such persons were given special training in Russian factories to enable them to take up key roles in the 156 enterprises which the Soviet Union had undertaken to construct in China as a part of Soviet aid in China's first five-year plan, 1953–1957.[14]

Political Control. While Chinese Communist spokesmen profusely praised Soviet teachers and Soviet universities for the assistance they rendered to Chinese students, reports of observers in the Soviet Union gave the impression that the Chinese students did not mix much with Russian students or participate actively in life outside their studies. They were described as hard-working students who took their studies seriously and were anxious to complete their study as quickly as possible, but they remained relatively aloof. Whether they were under orders to avoid too many contacts, it is hard to say. There is no doubt, however, that the students were under the close supervision of their government. They were selected by the government for study in Russia, and upon arrival in Russia they came under the jurisdiction of the Chinese Embassy. The students were assigned to courses of study at various universities by the Embassy. At the time of the "blooming-contending" in 1957, it was reported in a forum of the Chinese Academy of Sciences that the period of waiting for an assignment could be wastefully long and that one student actually waited a whole year before he received his assignment.[15] Instances were also reported of students assigned to study in fields unrelated to their interests and previous preparation.

The control of Chinese students in the Soviet Union by the Chinese Embassy is not surprising in view of the fact that politics is a dominant factor in the entire program of sending students abroad for study. Party loyalty took precedence over academic qualification in the selection of students, and members of the Communist Party and the Communist Youth League with inadequate academic preparation were favored over others with better academic records.[16] Despite criticism, the policy remained unchanged and was reaffirmed in the rectification campaign of 1957. Authoritarian elements in the Party even demanded more emphasis on politics and charged that anti-Communist reactionary elements had infiltrated the Preparatory Class for Study in the U.S.S.R. of the Peking Russian Language school.[17] They criticized the Ministry of Education for having been careless in the selection of students for foreign study. Their criticism carried enough authority and pressure to lead the Ministry to write a letter to the *Peking People's Daily,* official organ of the Communist Party, apologizing for the neglect of politics and pledging closer attention to political criteria in the future.[18]

Recent Changes. It is to be expected, of course, that the policy of sending students to the Soviet Union cannot escape the effects of the political relations between the two countries. There has been no abrupt withdrawal of Chinese students from the Soviet Union comparable to the withdrawal of Soviet advisers and experts from China. There is no question, however, that the earlier campaign for learning from the Soviet Union has lost its impetus and that there has been a decline of Soviet influence on Chinese education and culture in recent years. While English was pushed out of the school curriculum to make room for Russian, it is being taught again in Chinese schools, and this furnishes a clear indication of the change of climate which must have its effect on study abroad.

The Soviet government has expelled some Chinese students for distributing anti-Soviet propaganda. The strained relations between China and Russia were further aggravated when a Chinese train carrying forty-two Chinese students and fifty other passengers enroute to Russia was stopped at the Russian border on September 9, 1963, because they were charged with attempting to bring anti-Soviet documents into the Soviet Union. All the passengers were detained and searched; since they were found to be in possession of Chinese statements on the Sino-Soviet ideological dispute, they were not permitted to continue their journey. Their return to China became an occasion for mass demonstrations, angry editorials, and protest meetings denouncing the high-handed manner in which the Chinese students were treated by the Soviet authorities. This incident was preceded by the expulsion of a Chinese student and the staff of the Prague office of the New China News Agency by the Czechoslovak government on the charge of distributing news releases and documents on the Sino-Soviet dispute which were in conflict with the position of the Czechoslovak government. It seems safe, therefore, to assume that the number of students going to the Soviet Union and Eastern Europe will decrease in the near future. There is, however, no dramatic announcement of policy change as yet. Cultural relations between China and the Soviet Union are still being maintained, though with decreased enthusiasm. As late as December, 1963, China still welcomed the arrival of an Educational Delegation from the Soviet Union in fulfilment of a cultural exchange plan agreed upon in 1963.

FOREIGN STUDENTS IN CHINA

Scope. When the Communists began sending students abroad in 1950, they also invited foreign students to come to China. The first arrivals were entirely from the Communist bloc. Whereas the majority of Chinese students went to the Soviet Union, Russian students did not come to China in large numbers. The first three years saw the arrival of 266 students from nine countries. In 1953, more than 500 were reported to have arrived from East Germany, Czechoslovakia, Poland, Hungary, Rumania, Bulgaria, North Korea, Mongolia, and North Vietnam.[19] In addition to the students, there were trainees who came for practical experience in Chinese industries; 306 trainees came from North Korea in 1954.[20]

A news release on the arrival of 348 students from thirteen countries in 1955 specifically mentioned the U.S.S.R. together with Eastern European and Asian countries. Fifty Soviet students who came to China early in 1957 were hailed as the largest group of Soviet students up to that time. These news items, together with René Goldman's statement that seventy Soviet students entered Peking University for the first time in 1951, seem to support the observation that no large number of sudents came from the Soviet Union.[21]

It was reported in 1955 that there were 1,200 foreign students attending "42 universities and 49 secondary training schools in 27 cities."[22] The total number of foreign students appears to have reached the highest peak between 1958 and 1960. With students from more Asian and African countries, the number of countries represented rose to more than forty. According to available statistics, the total number remained under 2,000 students. Most of the students were in Peking, with a sprinkling in such large cities as Tientsin, Shanghai, Wuhan, and Sian. According to René Goldman, European students were allowed to study in Peking only.

Later Developments. In the early years, the North Koreans constituted the largest group of foreign students. Later, they were outnumbered by students from North Vietnam. Other relatively large groups came from Indonesia, Cambodia, Ceylon, and Algeria. As an expression of his admiration for Communist China, Prince Norodom Sihanouk of Cambodia sent his young son to China to study in a junior middle school. Political interest in Africa led to a greater effort to attract students from African countries. There were 118 African students in 1961–1962, but most of them had left by the end of the year.[23] René Goldman stated that almost all European and Soviet students had left by 1960.[24] Recent reports, however, seem to show that the withdrawal is not complete. Reports of 1964 still claim that forty countries are represented among the foreign students in Peking.[25]

Nevertheless, it is safe to say that Euroepan students have dwindled to an insignificant handful and that foreign students in China at this time consist largely of students from African, Asian, and Latin American countries. A report on a foreign students rally in Peking early in 1964 supporting the "Panamanian people's anti-United States struggle" mentions representatives from fifteen countries including Vietnam, Korea, Laos, Cuba, Chile, Somali, Cameroon, and Albania, and it seems significant that Albania is the only European country specifically mentioned.[26] A later news release in April, 1964 regarding a protest by foreign students in Peking against the arrest of Chinese trade workers and newsmen by the Brazilian government lists Thailand, Chad, Cameroon, Nepal, Mongolia, Japan, Ceylon, Iraq, Vietnam, Korea, Albania, Rumania, East Germany, Indonesia, and Belgium.[27] Inferences may also be made from a news dispatch on foreign students graduating from twenty institutions of higher learning in Peking in the summer of 1964. It was stated that nearly one hundred graduating students had come from sixteen countries such as Burma, Indonesia, Cambodia, Nepal, Venezuela, Albania, Vietnam, and others.[28]

Life in China. All foreign students must study the Chinese language before admission into specialized study. They usually spend the first year in intensive language study; for those in the humanities, two years of language study are required. Since the regular college course consists of five years, it takes six or seven years for a foreign student to complete his study. A special school was established in Peking to prepare foreign students for admission into higher institutions. There is also a special language course in Peking University serving the same preparatory function.

There is very little free association between foreign students and Chinese students. The foreign students live in dormitories set aside for them, with their own dining halls and facilities which are not available for Chinese students. They enjoy better food and many other special privileges. While Chinese students are given a monthly allowance of at most ten *yuan*,[29] students from Africa and Asia get one hundred *yuan,* and European and Soviet students received the generous amount of two hundred and fifty *yuan.* No charge is made for room and tuition; a student pays for his food from his allowance. Allowances are a part of the scholarships granted to foreign students by the Chinese Communist government. One reason why European students are given a larger allowance is that they are served Western food instead of Chinese food.

The foreign students not only live in better dormitories and have more money to spend, they also enjoy special privileges in regard to buying food, clothing, and other commodities denied Chinese nationals. They are not limited by ration coupons; they do not have to stand in waiting lines. They can get things entirely beyond the reach of Chinese students.

Special Treatment. The special privileges accentuate their segregation from the Chinese. They are not permitted to invite Chinese students to eat in their dining halls. As a matter of fact, they are not encouraged to make friends among the Chinese, and there are restrictions preventing them from choosing Chinese friends. Communist reports praise the wonderful friendships developed between foreign students and the Chinese students, but reports by foreign students complain that the only Chinese friends they could have with official approval are those who are instructed by the Party either to help indoctrinate them or to spy on them.

In Peking University, which enrolls the largest number of foreign students, a Foreign Student Secretariat was in charge of all the activities of foreign students, and "conflicts between this body and the foreign students were frequent and sometimes harsh." [30] So close is the supervision, that the foreign students feel they have been deprived of freedom of action. A writer under official auspices frankly states that "the students' association and the China New Democratic Youth League make it their special job to help foreign students." [31] Unfortunately, their "special job" has not been appreciated by the foreign students.

An extremely critical report on Communist China and its program for foreign students came recently from the pen of Emmanuel John Hevi, who went from Ghana to China in 1960 with the purpose of studying medicine, but left China in disillusionment and disgust at the end of two years. "Out of a total of one hundred and eighteen African students who studied in China during my time," he wrote, "ninety-six have actually left and a further ten had signified their intention to leave by the time I packed my bags. This means that all together approximately 90 per cent of the original number have found something wrong with China—something which made it impossible for them to stay longer." [32] He pointed out the following "causes of the student exodus": [33]

1. Undesirable political indoctrination.
2. Language difficulty.
3. Poor educational standards.
4. Social life—or, the lack of it.
5. Hostility to foreigners enjoying special privileges.
6. Racial discrimination.
7. Spying on foreign students.

Sources of Dissatisfaction. Several of the previous mentioned causes may be considered as the outgrowth of the policy of segregating the foreign students. Because they could not mix freely with the Chinese students, they had very little social life and few friends of their own choice. They were especially unhappy about the lack of feminine company. They felt that they were not trusted and were always under close watch or what they considered to be spying.

A second major source of dissatisfaction was the emphasis on political indoctrination. The foreign students were fed large doses of political indoctrination even in their language study, because the language textbooks were full of Marxist clichés and political propaganda. Attempts were made to change the political ideas of the students to conform with Communist thinking. Says Hevi, "The Chinese had brought us to their country for a definite purpose: to absorb their indoctrination." [34]

Foreign students are asked to participate in various political activities. They are encouraged to raise their voice in protest on such occasions as the annual Anti-Colonialism Day on April 24. They attended meetings to denounce United States pressures on Latin American and Asian countries—for example, Ceylon—and United States discrimination against Negroes. They supported the Indonesian claim to West Irian, the Cuban struggle against American imperialism, and so on. In the early years of Sino-Soviet amity, foreign students were asked to join the Chinese people in "learning from the advanced experience of the Soviet Union," and to study the Russian language while in China.[35]

Communist China has signed cultural cooperation agreements with various countries, and an important activity of cultural cooperation is to offer scholarships to bring foreign students to study in China. No doubt, the original expectation was that the foreign students would promote goodwill and cement political ties. This expectation, however, has not been fulfilled. On the contrary, many foreign students have left China in bitterness and disillusionment. Goldman wrote as follows: [36]

Despite their relatively good living conditions the prevailing mood of the foreign students was not one of satisfaction. Some reacted by devoting themselves exclusively to their studies and paying no attention to events in Pei-Ta and in China generally, while many others, including the Soviet students, privately expressed bitterness and disappointment.

Mr. Goldman's observation is supported by that of Mr. Hevi, who reports that thirty out of thirty-two Cameroonian students in China were expelled on account of organized protests against the Chinese authorities, and 90 per cent of the African students left China "in disgust" without completing their study.[37]

It seems that the Communists are also disillusioned in regard to their foreign students program. According to Goldman, a revised Communist policy after 1958 allowed only one or two students from each country to come for one or two years of study of the Chinese language. No more large groups were wanted and no foreign students were admitted for the full university course of five years. "According to the most recent reports," he wrote, "in 1960 there were almost no European or Soviet students left; they had been largely replaced by students from Africa and Latin America." [38]

OVERSEAS CHINESE STUDENTS IN CHINA

Scope. Since its inauguration, the Chinese Communist regime has attached great importance to winning the support of overseas Chinese. A special commission of the Central government is in charge of affairs concerning overseas Chinese. One phase of the work is to promote the education of Chinese youth abroad and to induce promising overseas youth to return to China for study and service.

Various methods have been used to lure overseas Chinese youth to the mainland. In countries having diplomatic relations with Communist China, the Chinese consulates and embassies are a major channel through which propaganda materials are made available to overseas Chinese youth. These materials range from Chinese language textbooks to vivid descriptions of the new conditions of stability and progress on the mainland. Chinese language newspapers under Communist auspices help impress on young people the new opportunities for taking an active part in the construction of a new China. Student organizations on the mainland write letters to overseas young people and invite them to return. Scholarships are offered and travel arrangements carefully planned. Upon arrival, the overseas students are given a warm welcome and assistance in initial adjustments.

The response of the overseas students reached its peak of enthusiasm in the years 1955–1957. It was reported in 1957 that 40,000 overseas students were studying in China and that the number of students who arrived in 1957 was twenty times the number in 1949.[39] A report in 1961 stated that 60,000 overseas students had returned to China,[40] but another writer estimated that the total had reached 73,000.[41] Official releases state that overseas students have come from thirty countries including Japan, Canada, Australia, various countries in Africa, and the Americas, but the great majority are from Indonesia, Hong Kong, Singapore, and other Southeast Asian countries. More than half of the total are from Indonesia, where political conditions led to the repatriation of large numbers of Chinese residents. In 1960, for example, 94,000 Chinese left Indonesia for the mainland, and there were 13,000 students among them.[42]

Incomplete statistics show that up to 1955, about 20,000 young people had returned from abroad, and by 1955 each year saw 8,000 to 10,000 new arrivals.[43] With the exception of the mass repatriation of Chinese from Indonesia in 1960, the number of arrivals sharply declined after 1958, and the influx of overseas students has dwindled in recent years. It was reported that 11,000 students from mainland China got permission to visit their families in Hong Kong in the summer of 1962, and only 600 returned within the time limit granted for their visit.[44] Another report stated that until 1958, approximately 1,000 students used to go to the mainland each year, but after 1958 only a handful went each year.[45]

Schooling Provisions. The Communists say that their policy with respect to the returned overseas students is that of "centralized reception and dispersed enrollment." Students upon arrival on the mainland are directed to reception centers where they are given "assistance" in adjustment to new conditions. After initial orientation, they are then assigned to different schools and universities.

A few universities make special provisions to accommodate overseas students. Amoy University, with its affiliated *Chi Mei* Middle School, has always had a large contingent of overseas students. It even offers a correspondence course for teachers in Chinese schools abroad.[46] *Chi Nan* University, which was established specifically for the benefit of overseas Chinese in pre-Communist China, was reactivated in 1958 and is now located in Canton. *Hua Chiao Ta Hsueh*, the "Overseas Chinese University," was established at Chuanchow, Fukien, in 1960. The students, however, are not concentrated in these few institutions. The 6,000 overseas students in Peking in the summer of 1963 were reported to be attending one hundred different schools and universities in the city.[47]

Many overseas students are not ready for enrollment in the regular courses of the schools or universities. They are found to be deficient in their knowledge of the Chinese language and in academic subjects. They are, therefore, put in specially established Preparatory Schools for overseas Chinese. After at least a year of study, they take examinations for admission into the regular schools or universities; if they fail, they must either spend an additional year in preparatory study or they are assigned to production work or labor.

The purpose of the preparatory school is not only to give instruction in language and academic subjects, but also to provide political education to initiate the students into the new Chinese society. It is frequently pointed out that most of the students have been brought up in bourgeois society and saturated with bourgeois ideas which must be eradicated. In other words, they must undergo "thought reform." They must be taught to think in the proletarian way or in socialist terms. They must study Marxism-Leninism. They must overcome their aversion to physical labor. They must engage in production. They must rectify their "blurred political viewpoint." This political and ideological "remoulding" is not confined to the preparatory school but constitutes an integral part of all education in Communist China. Overseas Chinese, no less than all Chinese students, must strive toward the unquestionable goal of combining "Redness" with "expertness."

Throughout their schooling, the overseas students are exhorted to strive for the "Three Good," which means good in thinking, good in study, and good in labor. Members of the Communist Youth League make it their responsibility to make friends with overseas students and help them in their political ideological remoulding. Thus politics and ideology are given a high priority no matter what the academic field of specialization is. Patriotism, socialist construction, and the proletarian revolution are recurrent themes that are constantly stressed. Overseas students are taught to distinguish between the capitalist society from which they came and the socialist system they are now helping to build. They are told that they must accept the leadership of the Communist Party in the new society. Upon graduation, they are to take up any tasks assigned to them by the state and the Party, just like all other graduates of schools and universities in Communist China.

Much attention is given to moral education so that the overseas students may learn the "new morality" of proletarian society. Individualism, love of ease and comfort, and free spending are condemned as common faults of overseas Chinese. Their schooling, therefore, has stressed the value of collectivism, hard work, thrift, discipline, and the "labor viewpoint." The students are led to acquire "worker-peasant sentiments" by laboring and living with workers and peasants in factories, farms, mines, and so on. In pursuit of these objectives, overseas students in various middle schools in Peking launched a "five emulations" campaign, in which they endeavored to emulate one another in study, solidarity, labor, discipline, and endurance of hardship.[48]

Participation in labor and in political activities is expected of all students in China, and the overseas students are no exception. Approved political activities range from the support of Chinese troops in the Korean war and in the Sino-Indian border conflict to the anti-American and anti-imperialism campaigns and the support of "liberation movements" in Latin America, Africa, and other Asian countries.

Problems. Communist reports speak of the success of the education of overseas students in terms of their progress in ideological remoulding as well as in academic study. At the same time, they frankly admit that a large number of overseas students have not responded to the efforts to reform their attitudes and their thinking. A writer on the subject said in 1957 that overseas students often lacked "revolutionary knowledge and the new morality and philosophy of life" so that they became easily discouraged by difficulties and unstable in their thinking.[49] A report given in a session of the National People's Congress in 1960 stated that in the evaluation of the activities records of several hundred overseas students in nineteen middle schools, only 45.4 per cent were judged good or "activist," and the performance of only 48 per cent on the steel drive measured up to the standard of "activist elements." [50]

The overseas students have expressed dissatisfaction with their experience in China. They complain, as foreign students in China do, of being saddled with political requirements which overshadow their academic objectives. They have no taste for political indoctrination, and they feel that the study of Russian in addition to the study of Chinese means too much time consumed in language study. They object to compulsory labor; "we came to China to study, not to engage in labor" is a common retort. [51]

A major source of discontent is the lack of freedom. The Communists do allow overseas Chinese some special privileges. Because so many of them receive remittances from abroad, they are permitted to spend more than other Chinese students and enjoy more material comforts. But, in the Communist view, the overseas students are addicted to the libertine ways of bourgeois living and need to learn the discipline of revolutionary life. The students, on the other hand, complain that their study and their living are much too regimented and controlled. At the outset, they are assigned to schools and courses of study which are not of their own choice. Upon graduation, they are assigned to jobs not to their liking. They are not free to decide whether to go on for further study and/or what kind of employment to seek. They are told that they should always be guided by the needs of the state, rather than by their personal preferences. [52]

A practical problem confronting the Communists is the shortage of schools. Since there are not enough schools in the country, it is necessary to limit advance to higher schools by means of rigid entrance examinations. Overseas students are not exempted from entrance examinations. Even the completion of the prescribed course in the Preparatory School for Overseas Students does not guarantee admission into the regular schools. Those who do not pass the entrance examinations face an unpleasant future. They do not have a free choice of occupations, and they do not relish being sent to farms and factories for labor, notwithstanding the exhortation to join the production front as a patriotic duty. Discouraged and depressed, many become terribly pessimistic while others seek to return to their overseas home.

The Communist authorities try very hard to dissuade the students from leaving China. The Commission on Overseas Chinese Affairs holds forums and publishes newspaper interviews to explain to the students that in view of the shortage of schools the inability to enter higher schools for continued study must be considered a normal condition, and young people should welcome the opportunity of serving the Fatherland by taking up labor and production. It seems that some students have even expressed a wish to go to Taiwan. To be misled by the enticement of Chiang Kai-shek's agents, warned the Commission, would be truly dangerous.[53]

In reply to their demand for freedom in the choice of schools, the students are reminded that the aim of study is to build socialism, not to seek personal advancement. When the needs of the state do not correspond with personal desires, the new morality dictates the surrender of selfish ambitions. After assignment to a school, the students should not ask for transfer to some other school, because enrollment quotas have been set for different types of schools in different areas of the country, and transfers would interfere with the quotas.[54]

To counteract the disgruntlement of the overseas students, the Communists launched a campaign to rectify their "bourgeois thinking." One phase of the campaign was to urge the students to join the rest of the country to "learn from Lei Feng," a soldier who died in 1962 and was posthumously exalted to be a paragon of Communist virtues in the thought reform campaign of 1963. Overseas students were exhorted to study the deeds of Lei Feng and to emulate his love for the Communist Party, his love for Chairman Mao Tse-tung and his love for the new society.[55]

The Overseas Chinese Affairs Bulletin published testimonies of "enlightened" overseas students who, after studying the example of Lei Feng, adopted the correct ideological position enabling them to accept without complaint the arrangements made for them by the Communist Party. As Seniors of middle schools, they declared that if they should fail in the entrance examinations for higher schools, they would gladly obey the Party and accept assignments at the agricultural front. They pledged to remould themselves through labor and turn themselves into cultured laborers with a socialist consciousness.[56]

Bad behavior of overseas Chinese has led to the expulsion of those who led protests and disturbances in schools. A report on the Preparatory School in Peking blamed "bad elements" for instigating "group fighting" among the students and stated that order was restored after the expulsion of some students and sentencing others to labor.[57] "Group fighting" has also been reported in other schools and universities attended by overseas students. The eruption of violence is an indication of frustration and pent-up emotions.

Another cause of discontent is the Communist distrust of the bourgeoisie. The Communists lay great emphasis on the importance of class origin, and their educational policy accords special privileges and high status to students of "worker-peasant class origin." The overseas students are constantly reminded that they are products of bourgeois society, and in most cases their families are classified as landlords or bourgeoisie. Even with successful remoulding, they can at best become "reformed" activists, and they do not have the full confidence of those who call themselves leaders of the proletarian revolution. They are not admitted into the inner circles of trusted cadres, Party members, and the Communist Youth League.[58]

Many young Chinese originally frustrated by the lack of opportunity overseas had responded with enthusiasm to the Communist appeal to return to help build the Fatherland. They had returned to China with high hopes and idealistic dreams of becoming a part of a big force building a new nation and a new society. Great was their disillusionment when they found that, though welcomed as a part of the labor force and technical manpower, they were treated as suspect and denied the opportunity of making their maximum contribution. Even in universities and in scientific research, "security" measures compel them to stand on the sidelines and deprive them of equal opportunity of study and research with the trusted Party members. Only Party members, for example, have access to certain types of data in nuclear research.

There is no doubt that the experience of overseas students in the past accounts in no small measure for the marked decrease in the number of overseas youth deciding to return to the mainland in recent years. At the same time, evidently aware of the disillusionment of overseas students, Communist authorities have adopted a restrictive policy to discourage the return of overseas students who are not likely to make successful adjustments in China. They urge overseas Chinese communities to establish more schools abroad for their children, so that they can receive proper education abroad. Students are advised to complete their middle school education abroad before returning to China for further study.[59] Students physically too weak for labor are advised against coming to China. Modification of policy, however, does not mean a loss of interest in overseas Chinese youth. By offering correspondence courses for teachers of overseas schools, the Communists hope to be able to influence the education of Chinese youth abroad. The restrictive policy seems to be dictated by (a) the shortage of schools and (b) the disgruntlement of students who have returned to China. To relieve the shortage of schools, the Communists have encouraged overseas Chinese to provide funds to establish new schools on the mainland. Hundreds of schools have been established with money contributed by overseas Chinese. The integration of overseas students into Chinese society, however, remains a problem for which there is no easy solution.

CULTURAL EXCHANGE

There is another aspect of international education in Communist China that we can only touch upon in the limited space of this article. It is the exchange of cultural delegations, student groups for brief periods of visitation rather than study, scholars and experts to attend professional conferences, sports teams, song and dance ensembles, musicians and artists, theatrical troupes, entertainers, and goodwill missions.

It was reported that from 1950–1960, China received 1,500 cultural groups and delegations from 122 "countries and regions" all over the world.[60] In 1960, 400 cultural delegations from seventy-nine countries were reported to have visited China, while 200 Chinese cultural delegations visited forty-eight countries. More than half of this exchange of persons took place within the Communist bloc; but there were fourteen groups from eighteen capitalist countries, and seventeen Chinese groups went to a dozen capitalist countries.[61]

The exchange was not limited to persons. In 1958, arrangements were made for the exchange of animals with sixty zoological gardens and institutions engaged in zoological study. In exchange for antelopes, zebras, giraffes, and other rare specimens, China sent giant pandas, Manchurian tigers, leopards, and cranes.[62] From 1950 to 1956, the Chinese Academy of Sciences received 157,100 books and publications from foreign countries and sent abroad 39,300 publications in a project of exchange involving 733 organizations in fifty-one countries, including North and South America.[63]

Much of this exchange, as well as the student programs discussed in this article, is an implementation of the cultural cooperation agreements China has signed with various countries. Different organizations within China have been active in promoting the exchange. The All-China Students' Federation tries to promote contacts with student organizations abroad, and professional organizations have been in touch with their counterparts in other countries. In 1955, for example, the Chinese Medical Association played host to visiting delegations from twenty different countries, including Japan, Australia, France, and the Union of South Africa.[64] Among the most active agencies in promoting cultural relations are the Friendship Associations. There are some fifty such Associations in China, such as the Sino-Soviet Friendship Association, the Sino-Polish Friendship Association, the

Sino-African Friendship Association, the Sino-Latin American Friendship Association, and so forth. They have counterpart friendship organizations abroad. The most active and one of the biggest "people's organizations" in the country is the Sino-Soviet Friendship Association, which was organized under the personal direction of Liu Shaoch'i, now Communist China's Chief of State.

In a way, the cultural exchange program has not met with such conspicuous failures as the other three programs discussed in this paper. We have not read or heard of serious complaints or expressions of disillusionment regarding various projects of cultural exchange. As a matter of fact, the visitors usually bring back rather favorable impressions after their brief visits to China, and they are generally well pleased with the reception and assistance accorded to them during their visit.

Politics, however, still plays a central role. Cultural relations with specific countries are closely linked with political relations. Relations with Cuba, Albania, and the African states are given more attention as their political ties grow stronger or are considered more important. In the same token, cultural relations with the U.S.S.R. are bound to become less important. An indication of the trend was the absence of Soviet participation in an international scientific symposium that convened in Peking in August, 1964, to which were invited some three hundred and fifty scientists from forty countries in Asia, Africa, Latin America, Australia, and New Zealand. Its stated aim was to break the "imperialist monopoly of science" and "enhance cooperation and solidarity among scientists of Asia, Africa, Latin America, and Oceania." [65] The fact that no one from the Soviet Union was invited to the conference is significant in view of the close cultural ties of the past decade between the two countries.

Cultural relations with the Soviet Union, however, have not ceased, just as the political relations have not been severed. One still reads in Chinese Communist newspapers of the arrival of cultural delegations from the Soviet Union. A Plan for Sino-Soviet Cultural Cooperation was adopted in 1963, and another agreement was signed on February 29, 1964. Nevertheless, there is a vast difference between the temper of today and the earlier enthusiasm for the Sovietization of education and culture in China.

It was not so long ago that the Chinese Communists ordered a nation-wide campaign to "Learn from the Soviet Union." The Soviet Union was held up to be the model for Chinese education and cultural development. On the fortieth anniversary of the October Revolution, the Chinese Minister of Higher Education declared: "To learn from the Soviet Union is a firm and unshakeable policy of our nation's socialist construction." [66] There are two roads for higher education in China, he said, the road represented by the British and American capitalist countries which serves the interests of the bourgeois ruling class, and the road represented by the U.S.S.R. which serves the masses and produces cadres for the building of a socialist and Communist society. He related how Soviet scholars had guided the reorganization of Chinese universities, how they had trained teachers and graduate students, and how they had supervised the production of new textbooks and teaching materials for various subjects. From 1952 to 1956, he reported, 1,393 Russian textbooks had been translated for use in Chinese universities and more were being translated. The study of the Russian language was considered essential for higher education, and the Soviet system of specialization and academic degrees [67] were arduously followed.

Since the adoption of modern schools early in the twentieth century, Chinese education had been moulded by American and European influences. American influence on Chinese education was especially great and extensive. The Chinese Communists, however, made a determined effort to eliminate American and European ideas, methods, and institutions, and to replace them with Soviet reforms. The whole country—the lower schools and the population outside the schools as well as the colleges and universities—was urged to study the Russian language and Russian ideas. Russian was taught in evening schools and by radio broadcasting. It was reported in 1957 that 85,000 people had registered as listeners to Russian language radio broadcasts, and in 1956, 777,551 Russian books were imported.[68] In the same period, 12,400 Russian books were translated, with 191 million copies printed; they included selected works of Lenin and the complete works of Stalin.[69]

Throughout China, lectures and forums were organized under official direction to learn about the Soviet Union. Teachers and workers who were sent to visit Russia returned to tell the people of the marvelous things they had seen in Russia. In the city of Chungking, students and workers who had returned from their Russian visit spoke to audiences totaling 150,000 people.[70] When the Soviet Army Red Flag Song and Dance Ensemble visited China in 1952, a broadcast program was said to have been heard by 1,200,000 listeners.[71] Within the short period of two weeks in a month officially designated as Sino-Soviet Friendship Month, over 20 million urban inhabitants were drawn to see Soviet films; at another time, 4 million people in twenty-six cities saw Soviet films in one week of the Soviet Film Festival.[72]

Within a little over two months, an Exhibit on Economic and Cultural Achievements of the U.S.S.R. in Peking drew 2,600,000 visitors, of whom nearly half a million reportedly came from other parts of the country.[73] When the Exhibit was later held in three other cities, the total number of visitors was estimated to be 11,250,000.[74] In Peking, a special effort was made to urge people to see the Exhibit on October 10, 1954, the day that the Chinese used to celebrate as Independence Day (from the Manchus) from 1912 to 1949 and still do in Taiwan today, but a day which the Communists did not allow the people to celebrate after they came to power. Evidently it was considered more worthwhile to divert the people's interest to the Soviet Union, and on that day it was proudly announced that 103,000 people had come to visit the Soviet Exhibit.[75]

What amounted to a wholesale introduction of Soviet ideas and practices, practically to the exclusion of other influences, might have produced a significant change in the direction and the pattern of Chinese education and culture. It did not last long, however, and it is difficult to judge the extent of the impact within the few peak years of enthusiastic Sovietization. From the beginning, the efforts of the Communists met with little genuine enthusiasm on the part of China's scholars. As late as 1957, the Minister of Higher Education criticized "a small group of bourgeois Rightists" who opposed learning from the Soviet Union and "want to pull higher education back to the old road of learning from England and America." [76] Now, with Sino-Soviet relations growing less and less cordial, the earlier campaign for Sovietization has definitely lost its momentum and its appeal.

SUMMARY

1. Communist China has made a definite effort to develop the three phases of international education discussed in this paper. Government scholarships were offered to all three categories of students: Chinese students abroad, foreign students in China, and returned overseas students. The programs, however, cannot be considered as successful from any standpoint. The foreign students and the overseas students have been dissatisfied and have not grown in their admiration of the "New China," and the overseas students have often been contentious and restless.

2. The Communist authorities themselves have not been happy with their experience. In extreme cases, they have expelled foreign students and overseas students. For both, they have adopted restrictive measures limiting future arrivals. From the standpoint of international understanding, the policy of secregation which applied to both Chinese

students abroad and foreign students in China made impossible what promoters of exchange programs hope to achieve in the increase of "people to people" contacts and the development of friendships free from political interference.

3. Even in the case of the returned overseas students, reports of "group fighting" suggest the existence of barriers preventing their integration with other Chinese students and with the Chinese community.

4. In all three phases of international education, there has been a noticeable decline of interest and activity in recent years. The dwindling numbers are an indication of the decline of enthusiasm. Partly on account of excessive political control, the exchange of students has not produced goodwill or led to closer cultural ties. Brief visits of student groups and cultural delegations have not been subjected to so much criticism, but with the waning enthusiasm for Sino-Soviet ties, the total amount of activity in the broad field of cultural exchange is probably considerably less than in former years.

5. The Chinese Communists are not averse to cultural contacts with other countries. They are, in fact, eager to promote contacts, especially when such contacts can help strengthen political ties. There seems to be a greater inclination today than in previous years to promote educational and cultural exchange with non-Communist countries, and there is considerable activity in various projects of exchange with countries with which Communist China has not established diplomatic relations; take Japan, for example. It is possible that the Communists may revise their policy so that they may be able to attract foreign and overseas students again and so that Chinese students may be sent to more countries in the future. At this moment, however, with the failure of the early projects and without the inauguration of a new policy to bring about a change, one does not find in mainland China a favorable climate for international education and the free flow of ideas and cultural influences.

NOTES

1. *Jen Min Jih Pao* [People's Daily] (Peking, June 27, 1957).

2. Report by Yang Hsiu-feng, in *Kuang Ming Jih Pao*, daily newspaper (Peking, November 6, 1957).

3. René Goldman, "The Rectification Campaign at Peking University: May–June, 1957," *The China Quarterly*, no. 12 (October–December 1962), pp. 147–148.

4. *Text of Suslov Report to CPSU Plenum, 14 February, 1964* (United States Department of State, External Research Staff), p. 34.

5. *People's China* (September 10, 1951), p. 39.
6. *Kuang Ming Jih Pao* (August 5, 1955).
7. *Kuang Ming Jih Pao* (September 2, 1955).
8. *Kuang Ming Jih Pao* (August 7, 1956).
9. *Kuang Ming Jih Pao* (March 10, 1955).
10. *Kuang Ming Jih Pao* (August 31, 1955).
11. *Kuang Ming Jih Pao* (June 21, 1958).
12. *Kuang Ming Jih Pao* (August 2, 1959).
13. *Survey of China Mainland Press*, No. 2301 (Hong Kong: United States Consulate General, July 21, 1960), p. 21.
14. *Kuang Ming Jih Pao* (October 22, 1957).
15. *Kuang Ming Jih Pao* (May 30, 1957).
16. This was a specific criticism made by students of Peking University during the brief "blooming-contending" season of 1957. See *Kuang Ming Jih Pao* (May 26, 1957).
17. *Kuang Ming Jih Pao* (August 9, 1957).
18. *Jen Min Jih Pao* (September 26, 1957).
19. *Kuang Ming Jih Pao* (September 18, 1953).
20. *Kuang Ming Jih Pao* (March 25, 1954).
21. René Goldman, "Peking University Today," *The China Quarterly* (July–September 1961). Mr. Goldman, a student in Peking University from 1953 to 1958, said that when he arrived in 1953, there were about 150 North Koreans and 150 European students in the university. Before 1957, there were some Russian students in the Chinese People's University.
22. Ma Ho-ching, "Foreign Students in China," *People's China* (December 16, 1955).
23. Emmanuel John Hevi, *An African Student in China* (New York: Praeger, 1963), pp. 116, 141.
24. Goldman, *op. cit.*, p. 110.
25. Li Shih, "Foreign Students in Peking," *Evergreen*, English language bimonthly magazine published in Peking (April 1964). Dick Wilson, in "Portrait of Peking," *Far Eastern Economic Review*, Vol. XLV (July 16, 1964), p. 118, reports the presence of 150 foreign students from twenty countries in Peking University in April 1964. They were students from Russia, France, Japan, and other Asian and African countries.
26. *Survey of China Mainland Press*, no. 3150 (January 30, 1964), p. 22.
27. *Survey of China Mainland Press*, no. 3212 (May 5, 1964), p. 31.
28. *China Daily News* (Chinese language newspaper published in New York every Wednesday and Saturday) (August 8, 1964).
29. By the official rate of exchange, a *yuan* is the equivalent of forty cents United States currency, but its actual worth is much less. Goldman reports that the monthly allowance for Chinese students is one to five *yuan*. *Op. cit.*, p. 110.
30. René Goldman, *op. cit.*, p. 110.
31. Ma Ho-ching, *op. cit.*, p. 28.
32. Hevi, *op. cit.*, p. 141.

33. *Ibid.,* pp. 119–136.

34. Hevi, *op. cit.,* p. 117.

35. *Kuang Ming Jih Pao* (September 18, 1953).

36. Goldman, *op. cit.,* p. 110.

37. Hevi, *op. cit.,* pp. 117, 141.

38. Goldman, *op. cit.,* p. 110.

39. Article by Huang Tun-jen in *Jen Min Chiao Yu* [People's Education] (February 9, 1957).

40. *China News Analysis,* No. 362, Hong Kong (March 3, 1961), p. 7.

41. *Communist China 1961,* Vol. II (Hong Kong: Union Research Institute, 1962), p. 161.

42. *Ibid.,* p. 162.

43. *Kuang Ming Jih Pao* (July 7, 1955).

44. *Communist China 1962,* Vol. I (Hong Kong: Union Research Institute, 1963), p. 168.

45. A dispatch from Hong Kong, in *The Chinese World* (Chinese language newspaper in San Francisco) (July 22, 1964).

46. *Kuang Ming Jih Pao* (December 16, 1956); also (March 22, 1959).

47. *Kuang Ming Jih Pao* (July 28, 1963).

48. *Survey of China Mainland Press,* no. 1741 (March 28, 1958), p. 32.

49. Huang Tun-jen, *op. cit.*

50. *Jen Min Jih Pao* (April 15, 1960).

51. Report to the National People's Congress in *Jen Min Jih Pao* (April 10, 1960).

52. See "Questions and Answers on Schooling of Overseas Students" in *Wen Hui Pao,* Hong Kong (July 3, 1959).

53. *Survey of China Mainland Press,* no. 1530 (May 15, 1957), p. 15.

54. "Questions and Answers Regarding Overseas Students" in *Ch'iao Wu Pao,* Overseas Chinese Affair Bulletin (June 20, 1959).

55. Editorial in *Ch'iao Wu Pao* (April 1963).

56. *Selections from China Mainland Magazines,* no. 377 (Hong Kong: United States Consulate General, August 12, 1963), pp. 19–22.

57. *Ch'iao Wu Pao* (January 1958).

58. *Chung Yang Jih Pao* [Central Daily News], Taiwan (October 17, 1964), reports that the Communist Ministry of Education has issued an order prohibiting girl students from making friends with boys from overseas for fear they may be lured by the anticipation of material comfort into marriage and subsequent application to go abroad.

59. *Kuang Ming Jih Pao* (September 18, 1957).

60. *Current Background,* no. 609 (Hong Kong: United States Consulate General, January 14, 1960), p. 44. See also "Closer Relations Between Nations," *People's China* (March 16, 1956).

61. *Survey of China Mainland Press,* no. 2398 (December 15, 1960), p. 26.

62. *Survey of China Mainland Press,* no. 1929 (January 8, 1959), p. 54.

63. *Kuang Ming Jih Pao* (October 26, 1956).

64. *Kuang Ming Jih Pao* (November 1, 1956).

65. Reuters dispatch in *New York Times* (August 20, 1964); also *China Daily News* (August 26 and September 1, 1964).

66. Speech by Yang Hsiu-feng, in *Kuang Ming Jih Pao* (November 6, 1957).

67. For example, the Soviet grading system; also, the degree of "Associate Doctor," midway between the Master's degree and the Doctor's degree.

68. Article on the study of Russian in *Kuang Ming Jih Pao* (April 16, 1957).

69. See report of Acting Minister of Culture in *Jen Min Jih Pao* (January 12, 1957).

70. *Survey of China Mainland Press*, no. 459 (November 25, 1952), p. 2.

71. *Survey of China Mainland Press*, no. 458 (November 22–24, 1952), p. 4.

72. *Survey of China Mainland Press*, no. 461 (November 27–28, 1952), p. 1; no. 949 (December 14, 1954), p. 10.

73. *Survey of China Mainland Press*, no. 949 (December 14, 1954), p. 10.

74. *Survey of China Mainland Press*, no. 1341 (August 1, 1956), p. 26.

75. *Survey of China Mainland Press*, no. 906 (October 12, 1954), p. 8.

76. *Kuang Ming Jih Pao* (November 11, 1957); see also Alan Whiting, "Communist China and 'Big Brother,' " *Far Eastern Survey* (October 1955).

CHAPTER 9

The Experience of Foreign Students in China

RENÉ GOLDMAN

The essential feature of the foreign student education program of the Chinese People's Republic is that this program is carried out under the auspices of government organs (in the case of intergovernmental cultural agreements), or semiofficial public agencies, which conclude agreements with private agencies in the non-Communist world, within the frame of China's cultural diplomacy. Such agencies are the China Overseas Liaison Bureau, the All-China Federation of Trade Unions, the Afro-Asian Solidarity Committee, and so forth.

The foreign student education program was initiated less than a year after the foundation of the new regime. In the fall of 1950 the first East European and North Korean students arrived. Large numbers of foreign students, however, did not begin to appear until three years later. In the academic year 1953–1954, Peking University had some one hundred and fifty North Korean and seventy European students. The next year, this Korean group was replaced by a North-Vietnamese party of similar size, while important groups (ten to fifteen persons) of Indians and Indonesians began to arrive, followed after 1956 by small groups (two to five persons) of students from various non-Communist countries of Asia and Europe. There were no Soviet students until the spring of 1957 when they arrived in two large groups, altogether over a hundred persons. In 1958 the composition of the foreign student body at Peking University amounted approximately to: Soviet students (120), East Germans (40), Vietnamese (30), Indians, Indonesians and Arabs (15), each, Poles (15), other East Europeans (35), West Europeans (15). There were foreign students in other schools, in and outside of Peking.

Chinese policies toward the foreign students were not uniform and there was a different attitude toward the North Korean and Vietnamese students, compared with the others (students from the Mongolian People's Republic were treated as Europeans). Among the latter a subtle gradation of preference, shifting with the mood of China's foreign policies, added further differentiation. After they had mastered the language, Koreans and Vietnamese were distributed through schools all over China, while the other foreign students were not allowed outside of Peking, unless their field of studies required it. This graduation was also reflected in the amount of the scholarships awarded and the kinds of privileges accorded them. Though the scholarships of the Koreans and the Vietnamese were lower than those of the others, they were regarded as closer to the Chinese and consequently treated with greater paternalism. Yet, taken as a whole, the living conditions of the foreign students were fundamentally better than those of the Chinese; their food was more substantial, their dormitories uncrowded. At Peking University the foreign students lived in separate dormitories, one or two to a small room of the type in which six to eight Chinese students were crowded, and ate in their own dining halls. They were frequently taken to shows and excursions during the year and on sightseeing tours during the vacations.

Most of the newly arrived students first had to learn the Chinese language in a special school established for that purpose on the campus of Peking University. Prospective science students (mostly Koreans and Vietnamese) as well as prospective fine arts and commerce students were graduated from the language school after one year, others after two years. The first would then enter the specialized schools of their choice (technical, agricultural, fine arts, commercial colleges, etc.) while the latter joined various art institutions, such as the departments of history and Chinese literature at Peking University. The curriculum of the language school provided for four to six hours of classes a day. Only in the first few months were foreign languages used as media of teaching; Russian and Korean until 1955 and afterwards also English, German, French, and Vietnamese.

Peking University remained throughout the 1950's the major center of foreign student education. It steadily counted from one hundred and fifty to two hundred foreign students, while other schools in Peking, such as the Chinese People's University, the Central College of Fine Arts, the Foreign Trade Institute, and the College of International Relations, had at most twenty foreign students each, many of whom had first studied Chinese at Peking University. The language school was run by the Foreign Student Office, which was also the supreme authority in charge of the foreign students on the campus of Peking University. As a result of its multiple activities this office had developed an impressive bureaucracy. In 1956 a third year program was created in the language school for those who did not intend to pursue university studies, but wanted to become professional interpreters.

There were two kinds of foreign students. The first kind, amounting to perhaps two-thirds of the total number in the 1950's, were the high school graduates. These came to China for a duration of as long as seven years (two years of language school and five years of university studies), and were, in their departments, subjected to the same discipline as the Chinese students, except for a somewhat lighter curriculum and the dispensation from participating in the political activities of the Chinese. The other kind were the advanced or postgraduate students who came to improve their knowledge of Chinese and to conduct research; they enjoyed higher scholarships, greater freedom and could negotiate individual agreements as to the curriculum of their studies. The center of foreign student life was transferred to the Foreign Language Institute, with the departure of most European students after 1959 and the arrival of nearly one hundred and twenty African students.

Of the problems faced by the foreign students in China, the two most irksome were the privileged segregation enforced upon them and the extreme politicization of their education. To many foreign students, the segregation was not unwelcome. They enjoyed their higher living standards (in the case of Soviet and East European students, these were even much above what they could ever contemplate at home) and the security of their seclusion, which permitted them to devote themselves entirely to their studies. But there were also some who were filled with ideals of international brotherhood and craved to share the life of the Chinese students, even if this meant to go cold and hungry. These were in for the most violent disillusionment, for the Chinese authorities were not interested in promoting intimate relationships between Chinese and foreign students. They were bent on keeping constant control over the foreign students in order to prevent them from disseminating alien ideas among the Chinese and disturbing the international picture created in their minds by official propaganda. The control was also meant to prevent foreign students from acquiring too close a knowledge of existing conditions, which would mar the image of the New China the authorities wanted them to carry back home. These were the reasons for concentrating foreign students, other than the Koreans and the Vietnamese, in Peking. Privileged living conditions further contributed to erect a psychological wall between foreigners and Chinese, though the authorities tried to keep these privileges down at moderate levels, a policy reflected in their repeated pleadings with East European embassies not to raise the scholarships of their students. It is only after they had joined the departments or schools of their choice, that foreign students had an opportunity to acquire a more intimate knowledge of the Chinese, thanks to the sharing of classroom life.

Though it affected the foreign students much less than the Chinese, the politicization of education was a constant headache. Students beginning to learn Chinese complained of the considerable amount of political vocabulary of little usefulness they had to memorize, while remaining ignorant of much colloquial vocabulary of daily necessity, for the texts dealt largely with political subjects. In the curricula of the various departments, especially those of the humanities, all the subjects were taught with a Marxist-Leninist interpretation; even science subjects could not be taught without adequate quotations from Marx, Engels, Lenin, Stalin, and Mao Tse-tung. Moreover, in the curricula were included special political lessons, rated high in the examinations and from which foreign students were not exempted. The curricula included Stalin's short course of the history of the Bolshevik Party which was taught until 1957, and political economy, historical and dialectical materialism, all based on translations of Soviet textbooks.

Much of the extracurricular time of the Chinese students was taken up by meetings and other political activities, in which, even if they had desired, foreign students were not permitted to participate in for fear they might become overly familiar with the seamy side of the political situation in China. Notable exceptions were May Day and National Holiday (October 1st), when we were urged to participate in the people's parade. Yet the authorities felt the need to indoctrinate us, for this was their primary reason for inviting foreign students to China and to do so the regular curriculum, no matter how politicized, was insufficient. Therefore, at times, meetings and political courses specially intended for foreign students in the language school were organized. But it proved impossible to restrain the foreign students' political horizon and prevent them from using the knowledge of Chinese they had acquired to read posters pasted over the walls during such political campaigns as the "Party Rectification" and the mass drive against the "right-wing elements."

A most irritating factor in the relationship between the authorities, particularly the Foreign Student Office of Peking University, and the foreign students, was the virtual impossibility of communication, even when there was good will on the part of the former. The responsible leaders of the Foreign Student Office were poorly educated people who, like all persons in positions of real power in China, had been appointed not because of their qualifications, but because of their political reliability. They were unable to understand the problems we faced, the habits, values and feelings of young people of such diverse backgrounds. As a result, their relationship was tense and characterized by mistrust and repeated frictions. The Office summoned monthly meetings of heads of all nationality groups to inquire into their current complaints and invite them to offer "precious criticisms"; we could not help but feel that this was done strictly *pro forma,* for hardly ever was anything done even about the most frequent complaints. Even in such matters concerning the unhygienic conditions in the dining hall, it was nearly impossible to wrest concessions. On the other hand, the multifaced surveillance exerted over the foreign students, could not but have a most irritating effect upon them. Two Chinese students were attached to every foreigner to tutor him after classes. Those tutors, many of whom were incompetent, regularly sent confidential reports on our ways of life, opinions, and attitudes, to the Foreign Student Office. Our accidental discovery of this fact in 1956 created a scandal hard to describe.

Under these circumstances, moods of disenchantment and dejection were not rare. Many students, who were inclined toward communism at the time of their arrival in China, slid in the opposite direction by the time they departed. They, including the Soviet students, were shocked by the attitude of the Chinese Communist Party toward the intellectuals, the relentlessness and crudity of the indoctrination, and the ruthless suppression of any opposition, as witnessed during the drive against the "right-wing elements" in the fall of 1957.

The foreign students of the 1950's might have improved their lot, had they been capable of collective action, as the African students did in 1962. The foreign student community of Peking University was like a miniature United Nations Organization without a general secretariat, ridden by national dissentions and working at cross-purposes, subjected to the pressures and interference of both their embassies and the Foreign Student Office. Yet, viewed from the Chinese angle, it appears that, from a strictly political point of view, the foreign student education program was a failure. They not only failed to make a single convert, but drove many people away from Communism. Only a few die-hards remained unchanged by their Chinese experience. As we now know from *An African Student in China,* a book recently published by Praeger, the Chinese were no more successful in indoctrinating the African students they invited in 1960 than they were with the European students before. The Cambodian minister of education was shrewdly aware of this reality when, some three years ago, he declared in an interview granted to a correspondent of the Parisian daily *Le Monde* that Cambodia did not fear Communist subversion from the Cambodians who were studying in Peking, but from those who were studying in Paris.

However, more important than the political aspect of the foreign student's experience of China are two other aspects, in which lasting, positive acquisitions have been made: The academic aspect, which is evident, and the human aspect. Socio-political opinions may fluctuate with the mood of the time and the enrichment of our life experience, but feelings of sympathy and admiration born in China for the Chinese people remain firmly encrusted in our hearts and minds.

Though many students left China in anguish and frustration, after the passage of years they came to the realization that theirs was a most valuable experience, which sheds light on how people adjust and react to external forces. To have lived and tried to understand people, whom their original civilization and peculiar history have molded so differently, makes one realize wherein lies the fundamental similarity of all human beings and helps one to revise and circumscribe more clearly one's own values.

CHAPTER 10

Foreign Students in the Soviet Union and East European Countries

JOSEF MESTENHAUSER

Communist Aims and Objectives

The topic of this paper might well have been "The problems of studying the problems of International Education," for there are some formidable methodological difficulties hampering research into this topic. While admittedly any type of research involving the Soviet Union would be handicapped by a lack of reliable data, research into education—and especially international education—is even more difficult. The subject matter is widely scattered throughout a number of disciplines in the social sciences, and spreads across the entire world: relations with other bloc countries, the developing countries of Asia, Middle East, Africa, and Latin America, and the uneasy relations with Western countries.

SECRECY

The first and most difficult problem to face is the lack of information even of an insignificant nature which is implicit in the Soviets' mania for secrecy.[1] Their extreme tendency toward concealment and distrust as demonstrated by the endless regulations, gate passes, and locked doors limits both the researcher and the foreign student studying in the Soviet Union. This trait was particularly evident in the policy of the Soviet Union to consistently withhold basic statistical information about the composition of the foreign student population there. However, the Polish and Rumanian governments have been cooperative in releasing information of a basic nature. The sources of

141

this extreme suspicion can be traced to Russian tradition and the psychology of long-standing repression, even if self-imposed, and to the Communist ideology which has served for several decades to reinforce the idea of Soviet encirclement by hostile forces. The emphasis on secrecy is important in its implications for international education in which much happens in a free give-and-take on the part of participants. In a restricted atmosphere the Soviets are neither likely to be borrowers of ideas—a trait which has never been particularly Russian —nor are they likely to encourage the kind of intellectual freedom in which a free flow of ideas, typical of the ideal of international educational exchanges of the West, occurs.

COMMUNIST EDUCATIONAL SYSTEM

The second and perhaps most basic difficulty is the assessment of the very basis of education in the Soviet system and the scope and method of its relationship to foreign student training to meet the needs of communism. Although there is a wealth of easily accessible material about the educational systems in the Communist countries, and their recent revisions,[2] there is virtually no information about the specific accommodation of this system to foreign students. Several features of the current system now in operation deserve special attention because they have relevance to the problems of training foreign students.

The first point of special interest is that in Russian there are at least four different meanings of the word "education":

1. a systematic influence on the development of the child;

2. a systematic influence on the development of society;

3. the process of assimilating knowledge, instruction and enlightenment; and

4. the combination of learning received as a result of systematic education.[3]

All four aims of education thus defined are to be found in the educational system, with the second goal resembling most closely the well-known system of "indoctrination." The foundation of political education is expressed in Article 27, Section IV of the Supreme Law on Education: "The main task of Soviet Education is the training of specialists on the basis of Marxist-Leninist teaching." [4] Higher education, as declared by the statute of March 21, 1961, lists among the seven main tasks of higher education the following:

The training of highly qualified specialists brought up in the spirit of Marxist-Leninism to be well skilled in the developments of recent science and technology, both in the U.S.S.R. and abroad, and in practical matters of production, who should be able to make use of modern technical knowledge to the utmost and be capable of themselves creating the technology of the future.

The carrying through of research work which should help in the solving of problems of the building of full communism.[5]

A second point, which is a matter of record and does not need to be especially documented, is nevertheless of more than organizational importance. In the Soviet Union the decision making and the every day supervision of educational life is performed by the Communist Party of the Soviet Union.[6] This indicates that the educational system is a part of Communist ideology and is subject to manipulation by the Party, thus reflecting several main assumptions of a Communist system. The primary assumption, recently confirmed, is the elite basis of the educational system and indeed of Party work.[7] A second is the ability to mold and form students in accordance with preconceived ideas and plans. The third such assumption is that the manipulating occurs differentially according to the "person's place and role in society and by the productive process. . . ."[8] The fourth pertinent assumption is that related to the ideals of the Communist society (officially called full communism) in which education has a special task to produce the ideal communist through the system of character education.[9]

The third important factor in the system of Communist education is the realization that the existing system has not actually produced the desired results, that the "new" Soviet intelligentsia is ideologically insecure,[10] and that the creation of the new "monism"[11] between work and study has not sufficiently bridged the gap between the toiling and the studying classes of people. Thus, the entire thrust of the educational reforms, not only in the Soviet Union but in all East European countries under review, and the entire attention of the corresponding bureaucracy from the Party down to the government organs is upon the recipients of these extraordinary energies.

THE ROLE OF COMMUNIST IDEOLOGY

The preceding discussion has suggested several terms which have ideological meaning to the Communist world: capitalist encirclement; socialist countries; full communism; Marxist-Leninist teachings; character education; and Party cadres. Every student of Communist affairs must reckon with these terms and is often forced into some assessment of the role of ideology in the Communist system in general. Some writers have stressed the importance of the Communist ideology out of proportion because it attempts to furnish a complete, scientific, integrated, and simple way of life and way of thinking about the world, in addition to combining ideas and actions and ideals with realities. Others have dismissed this ideology because it is admittedly too simple and because it allows multiple explanations and courses of action. In research covering the topic of education and international education, ideology has been assessed across this range of extremes—from a mere coverup for power [12] to a passionate credo reaching beyond the cognitive imagery of external life,[13] often associated with a Slav tendency toward messianism and a feeling of personal self-sacrifice.[14] In the middle of this range are realistic analyses of ideology as coupled with nonideological motivants such as the Russian tradition, which still plays an important role in the formulation of the educational system,[15] and the ever-present, practical considerations which are "largely a response to needs and forces generated by and within the Soviet economy." [16] Nicholas DeWitt suggests here that a trained manpower supply is the main motivation for the recent educational reforms which swept the entire Communist world. These reforms also produced an unusual development in international education by increasing the numbers of foreign students studying in Communist countries.

The impact of communism should be neither exaggerated nor underestimated; there is strong evidence of the role which ideology is meant to play, even if it is not always consistent. We cannot avoid these ideological implications, because without taking them into account, it would be impossible to address ourselves to the question of what aims the Soviet Union and her East European allies have adopted to justify the extremely high expenditures and top priorities given to the development of their foreign student programs. In an earlier study this writer attempted to analyze the role of ideologies, the dynamics of their development, dissemination and institutionalization, and the processes of validation and reinforcement.[17] Ideologies were found to accompany change as carriers of change and served as motivants of both leaders and followers. Ideological goals were found to be defined independently of events and concrete situations and were frequently changed and adjusted to these situations. In times of crisis, however, ideologies served as frames of reference in decision-making, as a point of departure in case of alternative courses of action, and as independent forces toward ideological conformity in spite of temporary compromises.

COMMUNISM IN INTERNATIONAL RELATIONS

The first evidence of ideological thinking is usually an attempt to interpret events in strict accord with ideological prescriptions. Clearly defined ideological statements are, however, missing from Communist discussions of foreign student programs. Official statements are very cautious so as not to offend the foreign student population from the neutral countries. Foreign students from these countries have been ostensibly exempt from the "philosophy" requirements, those with which the native students must struggle in order to satisfy requirements of Marxism-Leninism.[18] What we know about the process of decision-making in the Soviet Union would strongly suggest that the foreign student program developed as a result of decisions in the highest organs of the Party, and that it was justified by ideological reasons stemming from the Communist conception of international relations in the process of transition to socialism. While earlier explanations required a revolutionary accession to power and an "imperialist" war as the last stage of transition, most recent theories of "peaceful coexistence" hold that the present strength of the "socialist camp" no longer requires military solutions even under conditions of imperialism [19]—the stage into which capitalism is predetermined to degenerate in the face of strong, determined and demoralizing Communist opposition. If ideological reasons are not voiced for the presence of foreign students, they are very active in determining the stages of history in which the so-called "poorly developed countries" [20] find themselves at any given stage of history. Once such determination is made, the course of action with respect to that country is more or less automatically prescribed by ideological reasoning. One interesting insight which we have been able to obtain into the Communist assumptions about international relations was from the development of various institutes for study and research into other cultures, comparative education,[21] and even the study of capitalist economy. These institutes have been encouraged to study, among other things, "bourgeois theories" because in certain countries the "anti-imperialist struggle of the workers" may be headed "at a certain stage" by the national bourgeoisie.[22]

IDEOLOGY AS MANIPULATOR

The ideological basis for the reform of the educational system in most of the Communist countries of Eastern Europe should not be underestimated in spite of strong evidence that nonideological considerations also played a crucial part. Following Party decisions to inaugurate educational reforms which, among other things, emphasized ideological training and ideologically based "monism" between work and study, Soviet educational literature abounds with evidence of emphatic reinforcements of Communist doctrine and with attacks on Western pedagogy.[23] Implicit and explicit in these debates are ideologically based assumptions about Lenin's elite system,[24] reinforced throughout by the system of higher education which is conducted on a highly selective basis in spite of manpower shortages. Another ideological assumption is the Communist inspired notion that human nature can be modified at will. The manipulative nature of education —one of the four Communist concepts of education—has been well described by Profesor Cantril:

> . . . since the Soviet leaders have been remarkably successful in manipulating their own subjects, they have rather "naturally" acquired a belief that Communist morality can be instilled more or less universally. They bolster this belief with the assumption that there are no important internal forces for personal development that they need to worry about or to respect, hence relieving themselves of any limitations on the extent to which this transformation can occur. Hereditary factors are assigned only a minor role in the confident belief that learning by conditioning can create the desired uniformity and guided morality.[25]

IDEOLOGY AND THE "NEW INTERNATIONAL INTELLIGENTSIA"

There is particular evidence of a strong ideological orientation in the training of foreign students which was demonstrated in the creation of the Friendship University and has been ably described by David Burg.[26] Since the Communist Party is supposed to be the Party of the workers, social origins of students are carefully analyzed and assessed. Even if the results of foreign student recruitment are disappointing in this respect, the ideological urge is present to offer higher educational facilities to those who would otherwise be deprived of them by virtue of their humble background. The early history of Soviet international educational ventures indicates that foreign students from non-Communist countries came primarily as a result of governmental agreements and that the composition of this student population proved disappointing to the Soviets. In an attempt to gain the "unprivileged" students from the emerging countries, the Soviets have drawn on their experience "with training personnel from youth of this type in the 1920's and 1930's." [27]

> . . . it was clearly shown that, when unexpectedly presented with the opportunity of receiving higher education, such young people are usually too much absorbed in the process of acquiring knowledge—any kind of knowledge—to regard this knowledge critically.[28]

These "Rabfaks" schools are of historical significance, especially in the light of the creation of the Patrice Lumumba University which appeals to these "underprivileged" classes of students.

Since the Soviets have been actively involved in international contacts they have developed an increasingly sophisticated concern about
the life and cultures in other countries. There is some evidence that
the Soviets have been especially aware of the changing role of youth
in many underdeveloped countries. While we generally tend to underestimate the political power of youth, the Soviets would tend to
overemphasize it because of their urgent need to find evidence of a
revolutionary trend in any given society which shows signs of dissatisfaction with the existing system.[29]

In addition to traditional teaching of skills, the Soviets have undertaken the training of a "new intelligentsia" which is different from,
and thus noncompetitive with, Western trained foreign students. An
interesting fact drawn from the few known statistics about foreign
students in Communist bloc countries is the predominance of students
in engineering fields, agriculture, and medicine—all "developmental"
fields—in contrast to the literary, administrative, basic scientific or
philosophic fields. This writer expected a much larger proportion of
"social and political sciences" which, in Soviet terminology, would
have indicated training in Marxism-Leninism. This emphasis on the
developmental fields,[30] coupled with official Soviet pronouncements
about their intention to "help other countries train highly qualified
people,"[31] has led one observer of Communist policy to identify a set
of long- and short-range goals for training of students from developing countries:

The long-run bloc aim in expanding its educational program is the creation
of cadres sympathetic to communism and capable of running the economic,
educational, and governmental institutions in their home countries. Short
term objectives include the expansion of the bloc influence and of personal
contact between the bloc and the developing countries, as well as the screening of sympathetic students for intensive communist indoctrination.[32]

We must, however, try not to overemphasize the importance of ideologically oriented goals in international education for there are several indications of nonideological motives. The first appears to be the
typical, Soviet boasting of technological and scientific accomplishments
which, translated into propaganda media, have created strong pressures from all over the world for sharing these accomplishments with
underdeveloped countries. A second motive is Soviet concern over the
spread of the English language as a medium of communication, even
in countries such as Ghana in which the Soviet bloc exercises some
measure of influence. The tremendous efforts which are today being
spent on the teaching of East European languages in intensive courses

of as long as one year's duration suggest that the Communist world is responding to Western programs with the same defensiveness that has often been demonstrated by their self-isolated and insecure feeling of importance, coupled with a determination to succeed and to never give up. In this the Soviet Union as well as several of its allies act as the trainers of the world, the source of knowledge, and as the powers which ought to be listened to.

Background, Administration, and Scope of International Educational Programs in the East European Countries

THE UNION OF SOVIET SOCIALISTIC REPUBLICS

Although the training of foreign students in the Soviet Union is a distinctly post-Stalin phenomenon, Soviet interest in training foreign youth dates back to the October revolution of 1917. A most astute student of Soviet "cultural diplomacy," Professor Barghoorn, has related the backstopping of coexistence propaganda by cultural diplomacy[33] to the period of 1925 when the All-Union Society for Cultural Relations with Foreign Countries was established. The main purposes of this organization were to popularize "Soviet culture abroad" and to "mobilize foreign intellectuals against alleged plans for military attack on Soviet Russia."[34] This organization was restructured in 1958 and renamed the Union of Soviet Societies for Friendship and Cultural Relations with Foreign Countries. It plays a very active role in recruitment, selection, orientation, and administration of the current foreign student programs.

Another student of Soviet foreign educational policy goes farther back to relate the foreign educational programs to the developments immediately following the October revolution when several higher schools were established to train young Communists from other countries. The most important of these, at least for Americans, was Lenin University which was organized in Moscow to train American citizens.[35] Another such school, the Sun Yat-sen University, was established for training Communist revolutionaries from China, Japan, Korea, Vietnam, and other Asian countries. These institutions have been shrouded in secrecy and not even the currently published *Soviet Encyclopedia* has described these institutions.[36]

The first and only statistical record of post-war scholarships for foreign students was announced by the U.S.S.R. through UNESCO in 1958. The growth of foreign student programs was recorded as follows:[37]

Academic Year	Number of Foreign Students
1950–51	5,200
1951–52	6,622
1952–53	8,897
1953–54	10,344
1954–55	9,275
1955–56	12,289
1956–57	12,565

Considering the countries of origin of these students, it would appear that the majority came from other communistic countries: [38]

Communist Countries		Non-Communist Countries	
Albania	312	Afghanistan	5
Bulgaria	921	Burma	3
China	4,963	Egypt	14
German Democr.	880	Finland	2
Hungary	786	France	13
Korea	510	Iceland	2
Mongolia	667	India	6
Poland	1,184	Indonesia	8
Rumania	774	Nepal	3
Czechoslovakia	1,107	Syria	3
		Vietnam	394
		Others	7

It was reported that pressures had been building up in the Soviet Union for the expansion of scholarships for foreign students. These pressures came primarily from "front" organizations whose members have extensive foreign contacts, especially the youth and labor organizations, many of which applied to the government for approval of such scholarships as early as 1957.[39]

Following the Suez crisis the Soviet government entered into special training agreements with the United Arab Republic and this pattern of intergovernmental agreements has since prevailed for educational programs in the neutral countries of the Middle East and Asia. In 1958 there was evidence that the leaders responsible for the "Soviet cultural offensive," especially Georgi Zhukov, were aware of American and Western efforts in this field. Zhukov took issue with the so-called "free cultural exchanges" in an important article in *Mezhdunarodnaya Zhizn* (International Affairs), an organ of the All-Union Society for the Dissemination of Political and Scientific Knowledge. He attacked the Institute of International Education, the Inter-Governmental Institute and other such institutes in the United States and

Table 1 *Estimated Numbers of Academic Students from Developing Countries of the Free World Being Trained in the Bloc as of December 1962* a

(By Country of Origin) b

Area and Country	Total	Area and Country	Total
TOTAL	11,865		
Latin America	2,770	Africa	4,520
Argentina	20	Algeria	470
Bolivia	100	Angola	5
Brazil	80	Basutoland	35
British Guiana	55	Bechuanaland	30
Chile	35	Cameroon	195
Colombia	30	Central African Republic	5
Costa Rica	25	Chad	10
Cuba	2,160	Congo	85
Ecuador	30	Ethiopia	60
El Salvador	15	Federation of Rhodesia and	
Guatemala	10	Nyasaland	45
Haiti	15	Ghana	415
Honduras	20	Guinea	525
Mexico	45	Kenya	310
Nicaragua	5	Liberia	5
Panama	15	Libya	5
Paraguay	10	Malagasy Republic	15
Peru	40	Mali	280
Uruguay	15	Mauritania	30
Venezuela	45	Mauritius	5
Middle East	3,250	Morocco	145
Cyprus	35	Niger	200
Iraq	2,230	Nigeria	380
Jordan	5	Senegal	25
Saudi Arabia	5	Sierra Leone	80
Syrian Arab Republic	290	Somali Republic	450
Turkey	40	South Africa	5
United Arab Republic	245	Sudan	215
Yemen	400	Tanganyika	90
Asia	1,325	Tunisia	40
Afghanistan	60	Togo	200
Burma	70	Uganda	80
Cambodia	75	Zanzibar	80
Ceylon	45		
India	130		
Indonesia	650		
Laos	185		
Nepal	110		

a Taken from *The Education of Students from Developing Countries in the Soviet Bloc,* p. 7, chart 3, paper duplicated by the Department of State, Washington, D.C., 1964.[45]

b Numbers rounded to nearest 5. Includes Cubans, excludes Chinese living overseas.

concluded that Soviet citizens must be protected from harmful influence which sought to "utilize cultural exchanges and tourist travel to carry on propaganda in favor of capitalism." [40] Quoting Khrushchev, Zhukov suggested that the "only satisfactory type of cultural exchange was that which proceeded through channels designated and approved by the Kremlin." [41] The defensive tone of this article was evident from the conclusion in which Zhukov asserted "that those in the West who thought that they could score a political victory over the Soviet Union by provoking it into closing its doors to any kind of exchange would not be successful." [42]

Once the basic decisions had been made, the programs expanded rapidly. In 1959 the U.S.S.R. negotiated several new agreements on cultural exchanges, including educational exchanges, with Iraq, Afghanistan, Indonesia, and many other countries.[43] Simultaneously, special preparatory language facilities were set up for the incoming foreign students. Official announcements designated this special faculty for students from the Middle East and Asia and revealed that some subject-matter courses were to be included. A statement by *Radio Moscow News* "reflected Soviet concern for improving foreign students' appreciation of the Soviet system, declaring that the students would get familiar with the life and culture of the Soviet people and their achievements in various fields of science and technology." [44]

By 1962 the Soviet and Communist programs for foreign students had expanded radically, as is revealed in the following table from a non-Communist source, indicating the statistics of foreign students in all bloc countries in East Europe from all developing countries, not including either students from the West, or other Communist countries:

Tass announced in 1964 that in the Soviet Union alone there were 29,000 foreign students, an increase of 6,000 students over the previous year. Estimates for the other East European countries are as follows: [46]

Poland	1,200
Czechoslovakia	3,200
Hungary	500
Bulgaria	1,300
Rumania	1,200
East Germany	2,000

The total of all foreign students studying in the East European countries is thus estimated at 38,400. While the majority are students from other Communist countries including Cuba and China, the non-

Soviet bloc countries are represented by at least 12,000 to 15,000 students. Considering the fact that these exchanges started in 1956 and were developed more intensively since 1960, it may be anticipated that the first graduates of Soviet training institutions will return from their long-term study opportunities (five to seven year scholarships) in approximately 1965 and 1966.

THE PATRICE LUMUMBA UNIVERSITY OF FRIENDSHIP

By 1960 the Soviet experiences in training foreign students had not been altogether satisfactory. The United Arab Republic program backfired and many African students openly rebelled against restrictions and lack of intellectual freedom. It appeared that the only students not openly dissatisfied were those from the West who knew what was in store for them, and those convinced Communists who had vested interests in the outcome of their study in the Soviet Union.[47] Mr. Khrushchev announced at Gadjah Mada University in Djogjakarta, Indonesia, on February 22, 1960, that a new university would be created especially for students from Asia, Africa, and Latin America. At first it appeared that this new university was created to remedy the problems of dissatisfaction of students whose early experiences have shattered the utopian concept of the Soviet Union as "devoid of the social and racial inequalities of the non-Communist world." [48] Some have speculated that the establishment of this university came so rapidly as to surprise even Soviet Party and policy officials who looked with apprehension towards the problems of security connected with the presence of large numbers of non-Communists in the U.S.S.R.[49]

Considering the large numbers of foreign students already in the Soviet Union and the relatively small capacity of the Friendship University—it was to grow to a maximum of 5,000 enrollment—it is unlikely that the isolation of Latin American, South and Southeast Asian, African and Middle Eastern students was the sole objective. The Friendship University was also intended to become the new kind of university of which David Burg spoke in his discussion of the "Rabfak" experiences. From what we know about the system of controls in Soviet universities, it would appear that whatever problems the Soviets may have had with their foreign students they could have been more effectively handled by distributing the foreign students among the native students in already existing institutions.[50] The new university resembled the new boarding schools, "internats," which were designed in part to strengthen ideological influences over the students. Khrushchev's speech at Gadjah Mada University strongly implied that the international experience for the underprivileged was the prime objective of the regime in order to supplement traditional training programs based on bilateral exchange agreements. In this new approach Khrushchev "hinted that in the future the communist countries mean to get into the village." [51]

> Many students from all countries of the world are now studying among us. But the majority of these students are sent by government agencies, and of course, these agencies cannot satisfy all requests. Therefore, many talented young people from underprivileged families are deprived of the opportunity of realizing their desire to study in the Soviet Union. We think that both those sent by government agencies and those who express their wishes personally should study at the new university.[52]

Literature about the Friendship University, while not abundant, is significant and instructive.[53] The university opened in the fall of 1960 with one faculty, the preparatory faculty, and enrolled 597 students of whom 140 were from Africa, 112 from Asia, 95 from the Middle East, 191 from Latin America, and 59 from the U.S.S.R.[54] When the six regular faculties were opened in 1961, the university expected to have 600 foreign students and 100 Soviet students in attendance. Total enrollment in the third year of operation was 2,000, representing eighty countries, while in 1963 there were 2,600 students registered. Throughout its short history the university has attracted tremendous attention both outside and inside the U.S.S.R. The university council reflects the interests of the scholarly and "front" organizations which are fully represented there through twenty organizations.[55] From a recently published speech by the rector of the university we may infer that special efforts have been exerted by the Soviets to prepare syllabi and instructional materials to suit the "special needs of foreign students." [56] Although the contents of these are not available, the composition of the faculties reflects the concerns of the regime. In addition to the specialists, teaching their respective fields, there are full-time staff members "with considerable experience in teaching foreign students"; [57] regular Moscow institutions release, in addition, some of their instructional staff to teach part time at the Friendship University.

The hard work which has gone into this university and the seriousness with which the Soviets have set forth their goals to train the new underprivileged class are not to be underestimated. Nevertheless, interest by potential foreign students in applying to this university seems to have declined as applications fell from 43,531 in 1960 to 6,000 in 1961.[58]

SELECTION AND RECRUITMENT

Among the most difficult problems of United States programs for international education are the proper method of selection of participants, accreditation of previous education, production of satisfactory linguistic skills, and establishment of special counseling services.[59] By a process of trial and error, the experience of Communist countries has indicated the existence of similar problems, though their solutions have been radically different. Early foreign student participants were Communists or Communist sympathizers who selected themselves for the educational experience and whose ultimate fate depended entirely upon the regime since many of them could not return to their home countries. Later, post-Stalin foreign student programs were conducted primarily on the basis of the cultural agreements. Students have been selected by their own governments and have been sent for training needed by these governments. It was only after the establishment of Friendship University that the Soviet government attempted openly to side-step foreign governments in the screening process and to utilize to a greater extent its own resources for selection and recruitment. Placement of students is for the Soviets no problem; with the exception of applicants to Friendship University, which collects and screens its own applicants, students from other countries are assigned by the Ministry of Higher Education to the respective universities, as are domestic students. From the onset of these programs the Soviets are reported not to have expected such high standards of scholarship as those traditionally required by the Western universities.[60]

Applications may be made in one of several ways. The first method is *through official exchange agreements,* such as those with the United Arab Republic, China, Sudan, or the United States. This arrangement is apparently preferred in all cases where reciprocal exchanges are involved. Here the ideological motive is evident that the non-Communist world should not be permitted to pass judgment in accepting or rejecting Soviet and other Communist participants in the exchanges. A second way of seeking scholarships is through *Communist front organizations,* especially International Union of Students, World Federation of Democratic Youth, the various Friendship Societies, Societies of Progressive Artists, Women's Peace Leagues, Leagues for Anti-Colonialism, and so forth. These organizations are the only "private groups" which participate in the formulation of exchange programs. But final selection is performed completely by the governments of the bloc countries, themselves, rather than by these organizations, even for scholarships offered and advertised by the International Union of Students.[61] The third method of selection assures some degree of ideological uniformity by selecting properly "receptive" students. This screening is done by the *local Communist Parties,* especially in countries where Soviet diplomatic representation is lacking. Several Latin American countries and some Asian countries, including Japan, are often reported to use this channel. A Latin American informant suggested that the Communist Parties attract youth with "progressive" ideas and that often a simultaneous judgment is made regarding the high mental abilities of that individual as going "naturally" together. A fourth way of attracting students is through *East European and Soviet Festivals, Seminars, Tours, or Cultural Activities* organized through cultural agreements or by front organizations. Often students are recruited on the spot by organizers of the conferences. The fifth channel is *United Nations and UNESCO* organized scholarships which often operate through local ministries of education, educational associations, and even through student organizations, themselves. The *front organizations of the East European bloc are the sixth channel* for scholarships; through their own contacts abroad with other professional—and not always—front organizations they are said to have been particularly interested in promoting the scholarship programs. An obvious channel for applications is, of course, the *embassies of the Communist countries* which are reportedly prepared to offer advice, counseling and information, to collect applications, and to make recommendations regarding the potential of the candidates. Last but not least are the *participants in these scholarship programs themselves.* Their organizations have been most active in their home countries and in other countries of the West, helping to recruit students and to disseminate favorable information about study opportunities in Communist countries. It may be of special interest to note that in all countries reported here there are officially financed and recognized organizations of foreign students sanctioned in accordance with government decrees setting forth rules of conduct, scholarship provisions, responsibilities of holders, and obligations to the universities.[62] Since many of these foreign students are participating in governmental exchanges, their organizations may actually have a degree of freedom not altogether anticipated by the Communist regimes. Although the official pronouncements of many of these nationality groups would suggest that they are front organizations being used primarily for the purposes of surveillance and indoctrination, it should be remembered that many were organized by the students themselves, during periods of racial troubles to act as a pressure group for the purposes of representing collectively the grievances of these students. The fact that

some 550 foreign students have left or have been expelled from the
bloc countries up to 1963 and some fifteen per month are estimated
to be leaving at present, should indicate the extent of the problems
which students face. It is likely, of course, that leftist students may
capture the leadership of these organizations which are so structured
as to make this possible; yet these possibilities should not mislead us
into believing that the organizations represent wider groups. So long
as these students have their own embassies to report to, their counseling problems are well handled. One of the most significant developments to be reported is the creation in Prague of a "Secretariat of
the Union of African Students in Europe and East Europe area"—
with a corresponding secretariat in London. This secretariat has been
functioning since March of 1964. Among its objectives are the breaking down of the barriers of suspicion which African students in Western Europe have against those studying in Eastern Europe and vice
versa, and the launching of a full-scale attack on prejudice at home
against the qualifications of the students studying in the Eastern bloc.
The group is well supported by the Czech government which sponsors conferences, seminars, and meetings among African students
studying in all Soviet bloc countries and arranges occasional visits
to the West.

ADMINISTRATION OF PROGRAMS AND HANDLING
FOREIGN-STUDENT PROBLEMS

As has been suggested, Soviet educational policies are made by the
Party Central Committee where it is likely that the international educational commitments of the Soviets also originated. The main department of the Central Committee concerned with higher education is
the Department of School Affairs, Higher Education, and Scientific
Research, with its counterparts in all central committees of the Soviet
republics down to regional, city, and district levels.[63] The universities and institutes where the foreign students are assigned by the Department of Foreign Affairs of the Ministry of Higher Education are
likely to have special divisions in both the Party organs and in the
Republic Ministries, paralleling each other's interest in the foreign-
student programs. At present foreign students are found in Moscow
(at the State University and Friendship University); in Leningrad State
University, Kiev State University, in Tashkent's Central Asian University, Tashkent's Agricultural Institute, and in the Georgian Polytechnical Institute in Tbilisi.[64] Although there is no evidence of decentralization, the Department of Foreign Affairs in the Ministry appears to enjoy a degree of autonomy in handling foreign-student pro-

grams.[65] Professor De Witt has suggested, however, that there is a general trend toward decentralization of functions which "appears to be" a manifestation of the "process of replacing control of the functional ministry type." [66] Whether or not this is true in the field of foreign student affairs remains to be seen; indications are that stipends, selection, placement, negotiations, general correspondence, and even establishment of "scattered dates" for payments of stipends, are handled centrally, but that on-the-spot supervision is performed locally.

All through the system there is a close link between the Party and the individual institutions. The proportion of Party members is highest at Moscow State University. At the U.S.S.R. Academy of Sciences, for example, the proportion of Party members among scientific workers is 42 per cent [67] and Party affiliation appears to be growing. The individual universities have very likely established some foreign student "advisers" outside of the "major advisers," but the only evidence found so far has been a department for "Foreign Affairs" at Moscow State University where some 2,000 foreign students are reported to be studying.[68] This department handles, among other things, permission to travel outside Moscow on educationally related trips. The entire system, from the Party through the Ministry to the Universities, is well supported financially, especially at Friendship University. Rector Rumyantsev told a reporter from Harper's Magazine that "they gave us a blank check. They gave us tens of millions of rubles and said 'spend them.' " [69]

As Professor Barghoorn suggested, Soviet cultural diplomacy, even outside of the foreign student programs, "requires massive financial and organizational support." [70] Outside of the Party and the Ministries, the most important body dealing with international education is the State Committee for Cultural Relations with Foreign Countries, a ministerial committee organized in 1957. This body, headed by Georgi Zhukov, former editor of *Pravda*, is attached directly to the Council of Ministers and works in close cooperation with the Foreign Ministry. Zhukov continued to serve as head of this committee even after he became the Deputy Minister of Culture in 1959. Several supporting organizations with regional specialties have come into existence. These include the Soviet Society for Friendship and Cultural Relations with Foreign Countries.[71]

Of special relevance to foreign student programs are the Foreign Language Institutes which have been heavily supported financially and whose services were most urgently required in connection with teaching the Russian language to foreign students. In addition, the Soviet Academy of Pedagogical Sciences formed, in 1955, a special department called "Department of Contemporary Education and Schools Abroad"; this department has been responsible for the production of literature related to the international educational system. In 1956 it published *Educational Systems in Foreign Countries;* in 1957, *Syllabi and Curricula of Foreign Schools;* in 1958, *School and Education Abroad Today;* in 1959, *Education for Life and Work;* in 1960, *Character Education in Foreign Schools.* Projected for future publications was the topic, "Theories of Education Abroad." [72] The content of these publications, as is suggested by other publications of this Academy, is heavily ideological in orientation and is anti-Western.[73]

Other recently established institutes have made corresponding effort to learn about other countries, their languages and cultures, including those of the "capitalist" countries. In 1956 a reference was noted regarding an Institute of World Economy and International Relations of the U.S.S.R. Academy of Sciences, apparently under the supervision of the Foreign Ministry.[74] The content of its curriculum is of interest in that it reinforces our assumptions about the ideological content of Soviet interests: political economy, history of the Communist Party of the U.S.S.R., foreign languages, economics of the capitalist countries, general economic problems of imperialism, the situation and the struggle of the working class of the capitalist countries, economics and politics of the capitalist countries, agrarian problems of imperialism, contemporary international relations, problems of militarization of the economy of capitalist countries.

The linguistic emphasis is well reflected in the attention which Soviet educators give to foreign students studying the Russian language. Friendship University reportedly had 120 teachers of Russian on its staff in its first year of operation, following a directive from the Ministry of Higher Education which specified that classes should be conducted for every six students, each having the same level of preparation.[75] Although we have no specific evidence, there is reason to believe that the instructional staff in the subject-matter necessary for the training of foreign students is at least in the same ratio as that for the native Russian students. In 1959 the student-staff ratio for full-time students was 8.4 per cent when total student enrollment represented 6 per cent of the total population of college age.[76]

A discussion of Soviet higher educational administration would not be complete without mentioning the "security" personnel who are reported to have special tasks and assignments connected with the foreign students' stay. Since all foreign students live in dormitories there is evidence that special supervision is provided there, both for foreign students and for those Soviet students who may maintain an unusual degree of contact with their foreign counterparts. This supervision pertains equally to students from other Communist countries, especially those from China. The maintenance of strict rules is reinforced by the requirement that no visitors are allowed in the dormitories.[77] The surveillance is evident for students who visit their embassies too often. Soviet students have apparently been briefed before the arrival of foreign students to expect spies among them. Additional source of supervision is provided by student groups of a semipolice character with the power to make arrests. These "druzhina's" are charged with maintaining order and enforcing the rules of socialist community life.[78] The well-known but poorly understood system of "criticism-and-self-criticism" is the most commonly reported technique of social control. A social psychologist has recently suggested that this system is similar to recent Western experiments on small groups in which the majority was able to enforce its view on the minority.[79]

It is easy to understand why relationships between the foreign students and their native counterparts are not conducive to the same degree of intellectual give-and-take which is being promoted in the West. Competitiveness for university training, segregation, different social life, and alleged preferential treatment for foreign students are the most common criticisms by the Soviet students.[80]

POLAND

Although most attention has been given to foreign student programs in the Soviet Union, a few remarks must be made to explain corresponding programs in other East European countries. Poland, next to the U.S.S.R., has the most systematic program of scholarships and appears to maintain considerable independence in carrying them out. Many generalizations which apply to other Communist countries with respect to the educational systems do not apply to this country because of its individuality, Catholic faith, Western orientation, and more liberal approach to communism.[81] The regime must, of course, maintain its ideological direction and there is every evidence that it does, even in foreign student programs. Yet there is, unlike in the U.S.S.R., a measure of academic flexibility, some degree of internal freedom, and the students are more influential in policy-making decisions. In fact, the Polish student organizations have been recognized by the government (in the special instructions issued to foreign students) as agencies designated to administer certain phases of the foreign students' stay including their health insurance schemes and social and recreational life. Very little emphasis is paid in the Soviet programs to recreation and relaxation—a hard and Spartan life prevails.

Regular English language announcements are printed in attractive format and are distributed by Polish diplomatic missions and other auxiliary organizations to prospective students. The brochures, brought up-to-date periodically, list degree programs, scholarship opportunities, general cultural background about Poland, and "orientation" information about living and study conditions. In 1960 there were some 1,000 foreign students from sixty-two countries studying in many institutions of higher learning, including the private Catholic University in Lublin. Most foreign students are concentrated in the National University in Warsaw, in Cracow, Wroclaw, Gdansk, and Lodz—the last of which has been designated as the orientation center for a Polish language preparatory course of one year's duration.

Almost 50 per cent of all foreign students in Poland study geology, varieties of engineering, mining, hydromechanics, and shipbuilding. About 10 per cent are in medicine and an equal number in agricultural sciences. In addition to students from the other Communist countries and the developing nations, Poland has a strong representation of Western students and appears to attract students from several Latin American countries who are either unwilling or unable to go directly to U.S.S.R., for example, Colombia, Ecuador, and Haiti. In 1962 the total foreign student population was approximately 1,200, a small amount considering the student population was 160,000, which, in turn, represents only some 2 per cent of the entire college-age population. An interesting feature of the Polish program is the "private student" who may apply directly and go by his own financial support to the Polish universities.[82] Rules and regulations issued for the conduct of foreign students are instructive in that they give the basis for possible disciplinary action for behavior which is defined only loosely:

All foreign students are obliged to abide by the rules and regulations compulsory for Polish students, as well as to meet the requirements specified herein. In particular, foreign students are obliged:
1. to pursue their studies systematically and diligently;
2. to conduct themselves morally and properly;
3. to strictly observe all regulations relating to the organization of studies, all rules affecting students within the area of the educational institution and of the students' hostels;
4. to conduct themselves properly toward their superiors, the teaching staff, other employees of the educational institution and their fellow students;
5. to respect institution property and to oppose any improper attitude in this regard;
6. to avoid any action which might prejudice the reputation of their educational institution and the good name of the student.[83]

Another outstanding feature of the Polish educational program not evidenced in other Communist countries is the setting up of special, post-graduate seminars conducted in the English language by Polish professors in three areas of academic activities. The first is the special course for Slavic Language Scholars; the second is the International Cooperative Seminar in Warsaw; and, finally, the "Advanced course in national economic planning for developing countries" held also in Warsaw at the School for Planning and Statistics. The outline of the cooperative seminar is related to "socialistic" theories:

1. Polish cooperatives and planned economy
2. Basic economic problems and social problems of Polish People's Republic especially with regard to Agriculture
3. Basic principles of Poland's planned economy
4. Opportunities for cooperation between the cooperative organizations of Poland and those of the developing countries.[84]

An outline of the course on economic development is the only evidence of Communist training in statistical methods. While we may assume that the course is also heavily Communist in content, it is apparent from this outline that the ideological thinking operates on a higher level of abstraction:

1. Planning for growth in developing countries
2. Problems of concentration and efficiency of investment
3. International economic relations
4. General principles and techniques of planning
5. Planning in an underdeveloped country
6. Theory of linear programming
7. Selected problems of statistics.[85]

The official objectives of the Polish government in educating foreign students are to strengthen "mutual understanding between nations" and to help "establish broader cultural and economic contacts. This lively contact between young people from all over the world, cannot help but strengthen peace." [86]

CZECHOSLOVAKIA

The Czechoslovak Communist regime, from its early inception, appeared to be more concerned with Party work training than with academic training. The Party ideologue, Jan Kozak, made a distinct contribution to the theory of peaceful coexistence in a pamphlet entitled, *How Parliament Can Plan a Revolutionary Part in the Transition of Socialism.*[87] Both this pamphlet and the experience of the Czech *putsch* in 1948 have convinced the Russian Communists that conditions for a successful take-over by the proletariat are possible without military solutions. Having accomplished the "ideological first," the Czechoslovak Communists played a leading role in the Communist conference in Calcutta in late 1948; and Musso, the leader of an unsuccessful Communist uprising in Indonesia, came through Prague in 1949. Outside of Party training, however, the long-standing international educational commitments of the previous regime have come to a standstill.

The first post-Stalin, cultural agreement was signed with Ghana in 1957. It provided for 115 scholarships for foreign students to study in Prague. By 1964 there were 3,200 foreign students, 66 per cent (or 2,100) of them from Africa, Asia, and Latin America.[88] Since very few Western students study in Czechoslovakia, it may be assumed that the rest of some one thousand students are from other East European countries.

That the regime is more ideologically zealous than its Russian mentors—even if less refined—is evident from several pronouncements which have come to attention recently. At the opening of the "University of the 17th November" on November 9, 1961—this University is the Czech version of the Soviet Friendship University—the Minister of Education and Culture stated that "the main purpose of the foundation of the new university is to give active support to the struggle of Asia, Africa, and Latin America for political, economic and cultural independence." [89] Present at the inaugural ceremony was the rector of Friendship University, who presented a commemorative medal "as proof of the common road and future close cooperation of the two institutions." Even before the university was created, the Ministry of Education had published and on several occasions explained their directives on the relations of Czechoslovak institutions of higher learning to international education. An official of the Ministry announced that "we shall do our best to make certain that the foreign contacts of our institutions of higher learning appropriately help the political and educational activity of the Communist Party." [90] In assigning the Czechoslovak Youth Organization (*Svaz Ceskoslovenske Mladeze*), a leading role in administering foreign student programs, the directive continues: "We want to ensure that our foreign students return home not only as outstanding specialists but also as devoted friends of Czechoslovakia and adherents of Socialist ideas." [91] Writing in the same article, Dr. Ludek Holubec spelled out the concerns of the Ministry:

> The admission and training of students is considered the most important part of our cultural relations with countries of Asia and Africa. The work

with scholarship students from Eastern countries creates many political and pedagogic problems. . . . An institution for the education of foreign students will be created at Charles University which will become the center of the solution of those problems. In its advisory council should gather all the most experienced people in both the political and technical fields to weigh the best methods of instruction of organizing political work, and of the influencing of the cultural and social life of foreign students here.[92]

And finally on May 16, 1961, the official organ of the Czech Communist Party, *Rude Pravo,* stated editorially that the main reason for training foreign students is, ". . . to make the foreign students, after their return to their homelands, apostles of the ideology of the Czechoslovak Socialist Republic—Communism." [93]

Czech problems in handling foreign students were similar to those in Soviet and Polish universities and their solution required the creation of the University of November 17th. Unlike the Soviet Union where foreign students are also trained in other, regular institutions, in Czechoslovakia after 1961 all foreign students have had to register here, even if they take courses elsewhere. Upon arrival students take compulsory language training which is heavily mixed with indoctrination and preparatory subject matter. Students who do not fulfill educational requirements receive special tutorial and seminar assistance. The political content of the preparatory work is evidenced in several ways. For example, examinations periodically administered would contain questions about the "successes of Socialistic countries" or "benefits of the working people from the February Revolution," and so on. Another example is the use of *Rude Pravo* as a text for line-by-line analysis of the news of the preceding day.[94] A third example is a special tutorial in which each first-year student must spend eight hours per week with his instructors in addition to twenty-one hours of formal instruction. In the second half of the first year, two hours of the twenty-one hours of lectures are devoted to "Czechoslovakia: Past and Present" and fourteen hours of work are added in the field of study.[95]

Unlike Friendship University, the University of November 17th is narrower in its training scope. It has only three faculties: the Faculty of Language and Preparation; the Faculty of Natural and Technical Sciences specializing in construction, engineering, agricultural engineering, and agriculture; and the Faculty of Political Science specializing in teacher training for secondary schools in the developing countries.[96]

The Czechoslovak training programs include an interesting refinement of the Soviet procedure for using domestic students as special enrollees of the University of November 17. Although little is known about the Soviet students at Friendship University, we may assume that they are young Soviets attending regular university courses, simply on assignment to this university. As all students are officially placed, this matter creates no special problems for the Soviets. The Czechoslovak innovation is that a few carefully selected Czech and Slovak "students" who are already trained technicians are assigned to the university in order to train themselves for foreign assignments as technicians in the countries of the foreign students, thus gaining a practical knowledge of foreign cultures and peoples through personal contacts and associations.[97]

Even if the foreign students qualify for regular degrees, the University of November 17th also issues certificates and diplomas. Approximately 70 per cent of all foreign students receive government grants and approximately 10 per cent are self-supporting. The others receive various kinds of subsidies, mostly from their own governments or from national and international organizations including the International Union of Students.[98]

There is evidence that relationships between foreign students and the local student and nonstudent population leaves much to be desired in spite of the resources at the disposal of the system. Official notice had to be given in the press that foreign students do *not* live in luxury accommodations, that they are *not* eating better than the local population which is subject to food rationing, and that they *must* undergo thorough medical examinations—as assurance that they do not bring with them "venereal diseases from somewhere in Africa."[99]

BULGARIA

In spite of the sometimes sensational articles about racial discrimination against African students in Sofia, relatively little is known about the scope and extent of foreign student programs in Bulgaria. Following the U.S.S.R., the first scholarships were offered in 1958 through the International Union of Students and UNESCO. It is estimated that by August of 1962 when the first racial difficulty occurred, there were some 1,000 foreign students in residence. Following the second racial incident in February of 1963, which also caused a great deal of embarrassment to the regime, it was announced that in November 1963, a special Institute for Foreign Students would open in Sofia. When this Institute was opened it absorbed some 1,300 foreign students from fifty-six countries who were in residence at the time. Of these, 850 came from the "newly liberated and underdeveloped countries." [100] The only variation from the pattern for special schools in other bloc countries is that all students, including East Europeans, remain attached to the Institute for the duration of their stay, taking courses on Bulgarian language, history, and "histories of national liberation movements in various countries." This attachment does not preclude transfers to regular institutions of higher learning after the first year for courses in the specialties. Significantly, there are no private students in Bulgaria as all foreign students are on Bulgarian Government Scholarships.

RUMANIA

Trends toward nationalism and the idea of Communist grandeur are evident in the foreign student training programs in Rumania. Although there is no major innovation in programming, the Rumanian government has apparently drawn on its own experiences with the minorities and applied it to foreign students. Unlike Czechoslovakia, Bulgaria, and to some extent the Soviet Union, foreign students in Rumania are scattered throughout almost all of the thirteen universities of that country. Policies toward minorities have been described as a shift away from "unfair assimilation" to the so-called "socialist assimilation." [101] In 1963 there were some 1,200 "young students from 53 countries getting higher education in Rumania." [102]

A most attractive, pictorial brochure has been published by the Rumanian government and is freely distributed to prospective students. This pamphlet speaks very highly of the "Socialist Republic of Rumania" and her technological achievements and especially stresses technology, oil engineering, and chemistry as being the most attractive fields for foreign students. Foreign students are said to "enjoy particular concern on the part of the teaching staff and are shown consideration and friendship from their Rumanian colleagues and the whole of Rumanian youth." [103] According to official announcements, government scholarships are not the only source of support for foreign students.[104] There is no evidence in Rumania that the foreign student program is attempting to reach the underprivileged students. The minimum requirement is a "school leaving certificate" and the preparatory course is not set up to provide background in the discipline for students lacking such background. It is possible that the regime may incorporate the "underprivileged students" in its productive branches for technical training, but on this we have no special information. However, a transition to university training from such practical training is apparently not possible. Compulsory language training is substantially shortened to only six months unless progress reached is inadequate to assure educational benefits from a university course. It appears that this regime expects political indoctrination and ties of friendship to develop more spontaneously than in other East European countries, through mere contacts and special "fringe" benefits such as vacations on the Black Sea or in mountain skiing resorts. The brochure states confidently that foreign students "express their satisfaction and a high appreciation of the high level of Rumanian higher education, and the optimum conditions for life and study they are ensured in Rumania." [105]

EAST GERMANY

Least is known about the foreign students in East Germany although there is evidence of some 2,000 students enrolled there in some forty-six institutions of full or affiliated university rank. Special interest in foreign students is evident at the University in Leipzig where foreign students have been in attendance since the early 1950's.[106] The rector of the University of Leipzig has shown keen interest in Friendship University in Moscow and attended the special inauguration of the University of November 17th in Prague in 1961. The foreign student program was apparently started at this university under the direction of the State Secretary for Universities and is reputed to have allowed a good deal of free mixing between German and foreign students. In 1959 the German government signed a cultural agreement with Ghana according to which fifty students would receive scholarships in East Germany.[107] Other areas represented in East Germany are: "colonial Africa"; South America; Asian countries; Middle East; Albania; Bulgaria; Finland; France; Greece; Iceland; Poland; Rumania; Hungary; and the U.S.S.R. Discreet sources have identified, in East Germany, a strong group of Iranian students who have reportedly received East German government support for publications and organizational work among Iranian students in Western Europe. The context and organization of foreign student training programs are not known; it may be assumed that foreign students are subject to the same rules and regulations as domestic students and that their political indoctrination follows the same pattern of structured and extracurricular organization.[108]

In addition to the German government support, the students receive scholarships from the following organizations: International Union of Students, the World Federation of Trade Unions, the World Federation of Democratic Youth, and the World Peace Council.[109]

Communist Regional Interests

AFRICA

The discussion of Communist participation in international education would be incomplete without examining their specialized interests in the various regions of the world from which their foreign students come. Since the aims of communism continue to be the change of capitalism and democratic socialism into the Communist conception of "socialism," it is highly instructive to consider the Communist involvement in international education in terms of that change and in terms of the principles according to which the change is to be produced. In this section consideration is given to the application of these principles primarily to Africa and the Western countries; time and space prohibit a more thorough treatment than is accorded to interests in Asia, the Middle East, Latin America, and the Communist countries.

Africa was included in more depth primarily because more is known about the treatment of African students in the bloc countries and because the Soviet position on Africa, with respect to the stages of international development, has been formulated only recently. It is to be regretted that the problems which the African students have had in East Europe often have been exploited for propaganda purposes by those who find a special consolation in knowing that the Soviets practice racial discrimination as well. Examined objectively, the stories told by many young, ambitious and knowledge-thirsty men and women have revealed the tragic split among the rising intelligentsia which is urgently needed for development. Although these stories are most fascinating and revealing, they are of concern only as they may be related to the main topic under consideration.[110]

Lenin has always been considered as the father of the special Communist doctrines applicable to the stages of historical development of colonial people and capitalist countries. There is, however, almost nothing in his prescriptions which applies to Africa. Before his death, when he saw that the world revolution would not materialize immediately, he turned toward Asia where the greatest masses of people were located and where the most pressing ideological problems were to be found.[111] His official strategy for Africa, it would appear, was that which outlined the role of the Communists in more backward areas "in which feudal or patriarchal and patriarchal-tribal relations predominate":

The Communist International must support the bourgeoisie-democratic national movements in the colonies and backward countries only on condition that the elements of future proletarian parties in these countries, which will be Communist not only in name, will be brought together and educated to understand their special task—the task to fight the bourgeois-democratic movements within their own nation.[112]

This confusing strategy was followed throughout the entire period of the International, the Comintern, the theory of "Socialism in One Country," and the Second World War. In 1950 the Soviet Institute of Ethnology published a paper on Africa by I. I. Potekhin supporting this same view. It was repeated again in 1954—one year after Stalin's death—in a book entitled *Narody Afriki* (Peoples of Africa).[113] In a 1957 conference in Moscow where leading Soviet Africanists gathered, representing several organizations including the Academy of Sciences, the Institute of Ethnography, the Institute of World Economics, and others, Potekhin complained that "we haven't even one work which deals with the question of how the working class, the national bourgeoisie and the intelligentsia appeared on the African political scene." [114] The following year Potekhin went to Accra as an observer to attend the conference of African Peoples and returned impressed by the following unexpected phenomena which he observed: first, that the "liberation movement" had already acquired a "national character"; second, that there was a strong spirit of Pan-Africanism; third, that this spirit had racial overtones; fourth, that the "working class" lacked in political maturity; fifth, that the ethnic, social, economic, religious, and tribal variables defied the traditional Marxian prescription for African development; and, finally, that the Soviets were insufficiently prepared to cope with these newly discovered complexities.[115] Apparently on his initiative a new Institute of African Studies was established in 1960 with I. I. Potekhin as director. It was organized under the tutelage of the Soviet Academy of Sciences into four departments: history, linguistics, culture, and contemporary problems. Potekhin published an eighty page pamphlet for the first meeting of the Learned Council of this Institute, *Afrika smotrit v budushchee* (Africa Looks to the Future),[116] in which such terms as "negritude" and "African personality" were discussed. It was interesting to note that this pamphlet took issues with both racial feelings and African socialism. Since the only meaningful "working classes" are in Arab Africa (Algeria) and in South Africa, these two areas are apparently to be included in the Soviet conception of future African unity and liberation movements. The negative attitude toward African socialism was expressed through a subsequent resolution by the 22nd Congress of the Communist Party of the Soviet Union:

. . . socialism of the national type . . . are socio-philosophical doctrines that are, as a rule, variations of the petty-bourgeois illusion of socialism, an illusion which rules out class struggle. These theories mislead the popular masses, hamper the development of the national-liberation movement and imperil its gains.[117]

The new institute formulated a six-year plan for study and research which was to be primarily historical.[118] This Institute is of more than passing interest even though it does follow the usual Soviet pattern of writing its own history. It can be related to the need within Communist doctrine to know precisely, from the Marxian point of view, at what stage of history Africa is at present; understanding this point is necessary in order to apply specific strategies for change. It has been the contention here that training of students from Africa has been a part of this total pattern, even if a confusing one at times. It appears that the most urgent task in dealing with Africa was to avoid the capitalist stage of development in the transition to "socialism" and to develop an intermediate political system which would place Africa within the fixed Marxist laws of historical development applicable to the rest of the world.[119]

This concept was later enunciated by Khrushchev, himself, as the concept of the "independent national-democratic state." Khrushchev explained: "The Communists are revolutionaries, and it would be bad if they failed to see the new opportunities that are arising and did not find new methods and forms that lead most surely to the achievement of the established goals." [120] Potekhin explained that the study of Africa "is not only a scientific, but also a political task. . . . It is an organic part of the struggle against the threat of neo-colonialism impending over the African people, of the struggle for genuine independence and free choice in the method of further development." [121] An even more definitive answer embodying Communist "truth" was given by Potekhin in answer to an American reporter who had questioned him about the Marxist-Leninist explanations for Africa:

There is no other truth . . . and I can assure you that no one working in this Institute has any other truth. . . . There is no other truth and it is within this framework that we shall write the history of Africa. The falsifiers and distorters are finished. . . . Their work is over; now the time has come for the only truth. . . .[122]

The programs of training for African students in the East European countries including the emphasis on long-range study, underprivileged youth, and developmental fields, are now more comprehensible. The Soviets are well aware that "many African countries still do not have a single engineer who has come from the local population." [123] It is also easy to see why the Soviets and the Czechs are willing to spend great sums of money to support travel and conferences among the various nationality organizations of African students in the Soviet orbit with those studying in the West in order to promote better acceptance there of the Communist-trained intelligentsia.[124] Also, not without logic, is the Soviet effort to actively recruit African students already studying in European countries; it was reported in 1960, for example, that a young Kenyan in London was paid $28,000 in United States currency to recruit and send African students to study in Communist countries.[125]

OTHER DEVELOPING COUNTRIES

As we have seen in Africa, Communist strategy concentrates on "strength." This is evident from the statistics of students from Ghana, Guinea, and Algeria who represent nearly one-third of all Africans studying in the bloc countries, while the other two-thirds have their origins widely scattered throughout the remainder of the African continent.

Asia presents a similar picture. Almost half of all Asian students—their totals are relatively small—come from Indonesia alone—the country reputed to have the largest Communist Party outside of the Communist bloc. Since many of these Asian countries have already attained their independence, the short-range objectives of the Soviet Union seem to be to undermine whatever Western influences remain in these countries, to present an appealing picture of the Soviet Union and her technological achievements, to establish organizational links between the Soviet and Asian intelligentsia, and to influence non-Communist Parties of these countries.[126] These objectives seem to be supported by the relatively recent Soviet interest in the role of the national bourgeoisie, and the revival of high quality institutes for Oriental studies in the bloc countries. At the same time, several language textbooks have been published for the study of Asian languages, for example, Vietnamese, Hindu, and Pushtu.[127]

The study of Soviet interest in Asia allows a casual speculation of the impact which scholarly interest in Asia may have had upon the Soviets themselves. In international education we usually consider mutual learning to be the result of cross-cultural contact. Our experiences with cross-cultural research indicates that a complex process of learning and mutual adjustment occurs even if the final outcome may not be a very dramatic change of attitude. This kind of speculation begs the question in which many scholars, diplomats, and politicians are interested, namely whether there is any possibility that the Soviet system and the participants in that system may be positively or negatively affected through exposure to cultures and peoples about whom they have had only an ideologically distorted perception.

We have found two examples of such adjustment by Soviet scholars to Asian cultures, which are reported to hold genuine fascination for them. Professor Barghoorn reported the experience of an American anthropologist with the Soviet military in Korea: "While both Russians and Americans displayed amusement at Korean culture, the Russians treated the Koreans as individuals, with more respect than Americans, and in contrast with Americans, displayed no racial prejudice." [128] This kind of human and scholarly interest in Asian countries is apparently sufficiently widespread that the Communist press has to take official recognition of it:

. . . many institutes and scholars do not participate in solving the most important practical problems of the building of communism and occupy themselves with abstract themes and, in fact, separate themselves from life. . . . The work of Soviet Orientologists is still far from satisfying the demands which present-day life sets before them. . . . It is a matter of honor for our Orientalists that they should produce works . . . which would promote a further creative elaboration of questions connected with the foreign policy of the Soviet Union in relation to the countries of the East. . . . Orientologists-Africanists in Moscow, Leningrad and the union republics are to intensify their activities in the study. . . .[129]

India, the largest Asian country outside of China, has displayed a relatively cautious policy toward Soviet and East European study programs. Most Indian students in the bloc countries are officially sponsored by the Indian government, with the diplomatic missions carefully supervising the grantees. Selection is performed by the Indian Ministry of Education, and courses of study and academic programs are defined by that agency. Only a handful of Indian Communists, who do not intend to return to India, are at present reported to be enrolled in Soviet and East European universities as guests of those governments.

The policy of the United Arab Republic is similar to that of the Indian government. Although at one time large numbers of Egyptian and Syrian students were sent to the Soviet Union for training, many of them were withdrawn *en masse* as early as 1959 and 1960 because of their unfortunate experiences. At present modest numbers of Egyptian students are in East Europe primarily as a result of official exchanges. Only a very few Syrian and Egyptian students have elected to remain in the Soviet Union. Syria and Iraq were, for a short period, the countries best represented in the Soviet Union. Iraq is still in that category, although many of the Iraqis in the Soviet Union today only represent the minority Communist front parties. Commencing in 1963, non-Communist Iraqi students were being gradually withdrawn from the Soviet Union.[130] Several students from the Middle Eastern countries, who once studied in the Soviet Union, have told this writer of the difficulties which were encountered in receiving appropriate training and of the "drab" life behind the Iron Curtain.

Least is known about the recruitment and training of Latin American students in Soviet bloc countries other than Cuba. A few reports suggest that the position of "strength" is followed and that the countries most systematically solicited are Bolivia, Brazil, Chile, Venezuela, Panama, Guatemala, Mexico, and Uruguay. A Latin American student familiar with Soviet recruitment and scholarship procedures reported that academic credentials and records are not the most important criteria, but rather the student's organizational associations, especially those indicating strong positions in favor of the policies supported by the Soviet Union.

EXCHANGES WITH THE WEST

Exchanges with the West are the only "true" exchanges in which the Soviets participate equally on the basis of a very strict reciprocity. Professor Barghoorn makes the point that while the Soviets have been particularly restrictive in permitting West Europeans to come to Communist countries, they feel a special affinity for the cultures, technologies, and arts of that continent. The psychology of this relationship is, however, defensive, as if the Soviets were trying to prove themselves in technology, techniques, and communications.[131] Dealings with Americans and Western Europeans have been unpredictable, ill-defined, and changeable. Exchanges with Britain and France materialized first shortly after the celebrated visit of Mikoyan to Britain; but exchanges included only scholars.[132] The Soviets were much less suspicious of France, which they defined in socio-economic and ideological terms as a developing country, but as one having an interesting culture and an impressive artistic history.[133]

The pattern of negotiations for the British contact was between the National Union of Students and the Soviet Anti-Fascist Committee of Soviet Youth which resulted merely in summer travel exchanges. Then followed an exchange of scholars between Oxford and Cambridge and the University of Moscow. Official exchanges were negotiated between the Soviet government and the British Royal Society, in which the Soviet Academy of Sciences became the Soviet representative. The French exchanges, typical of their governmental procedures, were negotiated intergovernmentally and resulted in a formal treaty which established a permanent Franco-Soviet commission to review periodically problems involved in these exchanges.[134] In accordance with the principle of reciprocity, the receiving governments accepted full responsibility for the exchanged students; it has been reported that until the French government undertook financial sponsorship of its own students, the political complexion of the French students in the U.S.S.R. was primarily Communist. Subsequent selectees have been more broadly representative of French students.[135]

West German students have been studying in the Soviet Union since 1960, preceded by Norwegian, Belgian, Swedish, Icelandic, and Danish students. Norwegian and Belgian exchanges, negotiated prior to the events in Hungary, were delayed until 1957 with the Danish Parliament failing to ratify its treaty with the U.S.S.R. for several years. These exchanges, while numerically very small, have repeatedly produced the most "free" experiences in the Soviet Union. Unfortunately we have not been able to obtain sufficient data on exchanges between the East European and Scandinavian countries in recent years. They do exist, and together with Finland, operate on a larger scale than that typical of other West European countries. Similarly, no records are available for any programs with the Netherlands. Most West European students studying in the Communist countries are non-Communists although there are steady connections with the Communist parties in West Europe, especially in France and Italy, which often result in academic programs. In most European countries the common channels for such exchanges are specially established organizations usually called "Soviet Friendship Societies."

Exchanges with the United States, successfully established in 1958, have been supported by three administrations and by varied public and private support. Students and scholars took part in only one out of a total of 520 exchange projects since the inception of these programs. A recently published State Department report and a report to Congress, have assessed the goals of the Soviets as two-fold: first, to obtain scientific and technical information about the United States; and second, to paint a favorable picture of the Soviet Union and Soviet policies.[136] The report went on to assure the American public that the exchanges have been a two-way traffic. Most writers, commenting either on United States–Soviet Union exchanges or on West European programs in the Soviet bloc countries, have expressed equally reserved optimism about the future of these exchanges in which our own ultimate goal is restoration of a free flow of information to the total populations in East Europe.[137] Officially there have been no published accounts of experiences of American scholars in the Soviet Union and it appears that too much publicity in this country may prejudice the constantly tense atmosphere surrounding the negotiations of East-West exchanges. For those dealing with some aspects of the administration of these programs, it is apparent that many small-scale problems such as fees, lodgings, English language training, travel restrictions, and research inhibitions constantly clog the daily relationships on both sides. Coupled with our knowledge that the Soviets have established a rather sophisticated Institute of Capitalist Economy and that they have decided to look at us in a much more different way than was the case earlier, one must conclude with Stephen Wiederman that the exchanges have been a bridge of understanding—even if a narrow one and even if that understanding often produces negative results.

Two recent official pronouncements have been recorded, one in the Soviet Union and the other in the United States, regarding the aims of these exchanges. The Soviet Minister of Higher and Specialized Secondary Education, V. P. Elyutin, has stated concerning exchanges with the West:

We maintain useful ties of a mutual character with a whole series of capitalist countries. On this basis we are prepared to go on developing our cultural and scientific ties with all countries of the world. We are convinced that in developing and expanding cultural and scientific ties between countries we are helping to increase mutual understanding among peoples and to strengthen peace throughout the world.[138]

A recent American government report expressed a cautious attitude, stating that exchanges "are not a strong enough vehicle to reform the Soviet Union or to solve fundamental problems." The report added, however, that these exchanges "are useful in learning more about the world's second largest power, and over the long term they may help to influence that power in a more constructive direction." [139]

There should be no doubt that the East-West exchanges are very carefully administered and are supervised on governmental levels, and that they are "directional" with some changes expected to occur as a result of them.

CONCLUSION

It remains for us to sum up and to assess the efforts of East European countries in their relatively new, international educational ventures. While much specific evidence is still lacking, and programs are in the process of development and change, it is possible to draw some conclusions.

It has been said of the West that our educational exchange efforts are aiming toward change which is urgently needed, both in the so-called "developed" and "developing" countries. This would be an understatement if applied to the Soviet bloc countries; for them change in the direction of communism is the sole purpose of foreign student programs. The direction of change, methods to be applied, and even the speed of program development are subject to ideological determinations. There is some hope for us to note that the educational efforts in bloc countries have changed in emphasis from "revolutionary" to "developmental" programs, and that the attainment of ideological goals appears to be postponed. Present educational programs seem to suggest that the Soviets and other satellite countries have a reasonably long-range objective in mind even though their Chinese counterparts wish for a speedier, revolutionary change. This long-range planning may well signal a postponement of ideological goals in the face of the strength of Western countries, which the Communists claim have reached a stage of imperialism; during this period capitalism is alleged to be dangerous in that it may attempt a war of desperation in the face of its forthcoming disintegration.

In spite of temporary set-backs and problems which have reached embarrassing proportions and have deeply offended the neutrals whom the Communists have attempted to win, East European countries have apparently reached a point of greater sophistication through painstaking work which has led to invaluable experience. The rector of Friendship University has remarked that "in the course of our work we are finding answers to many urgent organizational and methodological problems." [140] It may be very difficult to speculate about the long-range impact of the set-backs which the Soviets and their allies have suffered in Asia and Africa; yet their financial outlay and massive efforts are evidence that, "as long as the bloc countries continue to expand and to finance their programs, they believe that educational exchange will contribute to their objectives." [141]

The number of students involved in these efforts is rapidly expanding even if the statistics reveal that the bloc countries are well behind the West. Such statistical comparisons are small consolation, however, if we consider the elite nature of Communist education and the activism which this education generates. This elitism was evident not only from the process of recruitment and training but also from the selection of countries and the emphasis put on the underprivileged background of selected students. Here is a variable—the income level— which Western exchange programs have not coped with satisfactorily. As one observer pointed out, "a situation my well develop in which the professional posts in the towns are staffed with Western-trained graduates, while technical positions at the all-important local level in the countryside are occupied by Communist orbit-trained men." [142] The seriousness of objectives and toughness of the Soviet approach has been observed recently following their difficulties with foreign student programs. Foreign students who "abused Soviet hospitality" are encouraged to "quit our country at any moment" if the Soviet system is not to their liking.[143] Furthermore, foreign students have been advised that legislation was enacted under which such students are subject to deportation proceedings and to criminal prosecution.

On the positive side it may be helpful to recollect that many Soviet and other Communist scholars have actually held a great admiration for the cultures they study or have contact with, and that they have developed a corresponding respect for cultural differences. In addition, observers have often insisted that the impact of foreigners upon the Soviet bloc has been greater than official pronouncements and government propaganda would suggest.

It is only speculation, but one which this writer cannot avoid, that the process of cultural adjustment which we have studied in the United States recently in connection with foreign student programs may actually be at work in the East European countries. Many reactions of the foreign students there toward the regimes may well be a reflection of cross-cultural adjustment with which we are familiar from our own programs. The reaction of receiving cultures in the East European bloc has also shown similar tendencies which accompany the reception given to strangers, ranging from suspicion to complete acceptance and fascination as an object of experimentation. If it is indeed true that cultural anthropology is at work, the result of the educational impact upon the Soviets may not be favorable attitudes and friendship in international cooperation, but it may be a more realistic assessment of the "adversaries," a more realistic understanding of the processes of cultural change and the urgency of development. We should not assume, either, that the training of students in the Soviet Union and her satellites will automatically produce Communists; while it is obvious that all efforts in that direction will be made, it is also likely that the process of cross-cultural learning will produce attitudes confirming both positive and negative reactions.

Regardless of the short-term outcome, it is evident that we are in competition with the East European bloc by their own definition whether or not we like it or take cognizance of it, in our academic procedures. The political nature of their objectives may well force a greater intensification of the political objectives of exchanges in this country and elsewhere. Moreover, it is likely that the Soviet appearance on the world scene of educational opportunities will have focused even more sharply the political attitudes of youth in developing countries in which the Western and Communist programs are competing. Our problems may well multiply and intensify should we, for example, have to extend our scholarship programs to include the "under-privileged" students, or should foreign governments exclusively select such students on their own scholarship programs. At any rate, the massive Soviet efforts may at least help in producing an equal effort here since the normal course of development has not succeeded in accomplishing this long overdue necessity.

NOTES

1. For an excellent analysis of the meaning of "secrecy," see Urie Bronfenbrenner, "Secrecy: A Basic Tenet of the Soviets," *The New York Times Magazine* (April 22, 1962).

2. The writer is especially indebted to the recently published series on various phases of education in East European countries by the U.S. Department of Health, Education and Welfare, Washington, D.C., especially the following:

Nellie Apanasewicz and Seymour Rosen, *Education in Czechoslovakia,* Bulletin no. 27, OE-14090 (January 1963).

——— and ———, *Selected Bibliography of Materials on Education in Czechoslovakia,* OE-14053 (August 1960).

——— and ———, *Soviet Education: A Bibliography of English-Language Materials,* Bulletin no. 29, OE-14101 (1964).

——— and William Medlin, *Selected Bibliography of Materials on Education in Poland,* OE-14030 (February 1960).

Randolph Braham, *Education in the Rumanian People's Republic,* Bulletin no. 1, OE-14087 (1964).

Herta Haase and Seymour Rosen, *Education in Rumania,* OE-14050 (July 1960).

William Medlin, Clarence Lindquist, and Marshall Schmitt, *Soviet Education Programs,* Bulletin no. 17, OE-14037 (1960).

Nicholas Rokitiansky and William Medlin, *Bibliography of Published Materials on Russian and Soviet Education,* OE-14033 (February 1960).

Seymour Rosen, *Higher Education in the U.S.S.R.,* Bulletin no. 16, OE-14088 (1963).

——— and Nellie Apanasewicz, *Higher Education in Poland,* Part I, Bulletin no. 19, OE-14082 (1963).

Vera Tomich, *Education in Yugoslavia and the New Reform,* Bulletin no. 20, OE-14089 (1963).

U.S. Department of Health, Education and Welfare, *Bibliography, 1959 Publications in Comparative and International Education,* OE-14004 (1959).

———, *Education in the U.S.S.R.,* Bulletin no. 14 (1957), Division of International Education.

———, *Soviet Commitment to Education,* Bulletin no. 16, OE-14062 (1959), report of the First Official U.S. Education Mission to the U.S.S.R.

———, *Teaching in the Social Sciences and the Humanities in the U.S.S.R.,* OE-14025 (December 1959).

In addition, a few official government publications in the English language have been circulated by the various East European governments:

Ministry of Education, *Development of Education in the Rumanian People's Republic in the 1962–1963 School Year* [report submitted to the 26th International Conference on Public Education, Geneva, July 1963, Ministry of Education, Rumanian People's Republic] (Bucharest, 1963).

Ministry of Higher Education, *Institutions of Higher Education in Poland* [Information and Statistics Bulletin] (Warsaw, 1963).

National Commission of the Rumanian People's Republic for UNESCO. *Education, Work, Recreation of Youth in Rumania* (Bucharest, 1963).

Apart from governmental sources, the following writings of individual specialists and scholars have been examined for the purpose of this paper:

C. Arnold Anderson, "World Patterns of Education," *Comparative Education Review,* Vol. IV, no. 2 (October 1960), pp. 68–70.

Jeremy K. Azreal, "The Educational System as an Agency of Political Socialization in the U.S.S.R.," *Education and Political Development,* James A. Coleman (editor) (Princeton, N.J.: Princeton University Press, 1965).

George Z. F. Bereday and Jaan Penner (editors). *The Politics of Soviet Education* (New York: Praeger, 1960).

———, William Brickman, and Gerald Read (editors). *The Changing Soviet School* (Cambridge, Mass.: The Riverside Press, 1960).

Randolph L. Braham, "The Rumanian Schools of General Education," *Journal of Central European Affairs,* Vol. XXI, no. 3 (October 1961), pp. 319–349.

Thomas J. Blakeley, "Marxism-Leninism in High School," *Studies in Soviet Thought* [Institute of East European Studies, University of Fribourg], Vol. III, no. 2 (June 1963), pp. 139–147.

Urie Bronfenbrenner, "Soviet Methods of Character Education: Some Implications for Research," *Cornell Soviet Studies Reprint No. 5*. Ithaca: Cornell University, n.d. Reprinted from *American Psychologist*, Vol. XVII, no. 8 (April 1962), pp. 550–564.

———, "Soviet Studies of Personality Development and Socialization," *Cornell Soviet Studies Reprint No. 6*. Ithaca: Cornell University, n.d. Reprinted from *Some Views on Soviet Psychology* (New York: American Psychological Association, 1962), pp. 63–86.

George S. Counts, *The Challenge of Soviet Education* (New York: McGraw-Hill, 1957).

Nicholas DeWitt, *Education and Professional Employment in the U.S.S.R.*, National Science Foundation, NSF-61-40 (Washington, D.C.: U.S. Government Printing Office, 1961).

Stewart Fraser, "Notes on Sino-Soviet Cooperation in Higher Education, 1950–1960," in *Melbourne Studies in Education, 1961–62*, E. L. French (editor) (Melbourne, Australia: Melbourne University Press, 1964), pp. 36–55.

Edmund J. King (editor), *Communist Education* (Indianapolis: The Bobbs-Merrill Company, 1963).

Kenneth V. Lottich, *Poland, Champion of Latin Christianity* (Zurich: International Institute of Arts and Letters, 1963).

Richard Pipes (editor), *The Russian Intelligentsia* (New York: Columbia University Press, 1961).

Herbert C. Rudman, *Structure and Decision-Making in Soviet Education*, Bulletin no. 2, OE-14094 (Washington, D.C.: U.S. Department of Health, Education and Welfare, 1964).

3. Hadley Cantril, *Soviet Leaders and Mastery over Man* (New Brunswick: Rutgers University Press, 1960), pp. 62–63.

4. Seymour Rosen, *The Peoples' Friendship University in the U.S.S.R.*, OE-14073 (Washington, D.C.: U.S. Department of Health, Education and Welfare, April 1962).

5. King, *op. cit.*, p. 177.

6. DeWitt, *op. cit.*, pp. 43–44. See also a more recent document by Herbert C. Rudman, *op. cit.*

7. Counts, *op. cit.*, p. 280.

8. This is apparently the psychological meaning of "individual differences" in the Communist conception. Cantril, *op. cit.*, p. 52.

9. Bronfenbrenner, "Soviet Method of Character Education: Some Implications for Research," *op. cit.*, pp. 550–564. Peter H. Juviler, "Communist Morality and Soviet Youth," *Problems of Communism*, Vol. X, no. 3 (May–June 1961), pp. 16–24. F. F. Korolev, "Rounded Development of the Human Personality: The Paramount Task of Communist Construction," *Soviet Education*, Vol. IV, no. 3 (January 1962), pp. 3–19 [translated from *Sovietskaia Pedagogika*, no. 7, 1961].

10. In several recent articles there has been a discussion of the problems of changing values of Soviet Youth; for example, see Juviler, *op. cit.*

11. This "monism" was well described in Kenneth V. Lottich, "The Educational Outlook in East European Satellite Countries," *Journal of Human Relations*, Vol. XII, no. 4, p. 492. The author called attention to a different interpretation of the relationship between work and study which is often not clearly understood in the West.

12. Nicholas P. Vakar, "Creeds and Communism," *East Europe*, Vol. X, no. 12 (December 1961), pp. 6–14.

13. King (editor), *op. cit.*, p. 15.

14. Azrael, *op. cit.*, p. 8.

15. King (editor), *op. cit.*, p. 179.

16. DeWitt, *op. cit.*, p. 45.

17. Josef A. Mestenhauser, "Ideologies in Conflict in Indonesia: 1945–1955" (unpublished Ph.D. dissertation, University of Minnesota, Minneapolis, 1960).

18. "New Type University for Developing Countries (U.S.S.R.)," *Times Educational Supplement*, no. 2367 (September 30, 1960), p. 386.

19. Richard V. Burks, "Perspectives for Eastern Europe," *Problems of Communism*, Vol. XIII, no. 2 (March, April 1964), p. 74.

20. This is Khrushchev's term.

21. Nicholas Hans, "The Soviet Approach to Comparative Education," *Comparative Education Review*, Vol. VIII, no. 1 (June 1964), pp. 90–94. V. A. Veiksham, "The Moscow Center in Comparative Education," *Comparative Education Review*, Vol. III, no. 1 (June 1959), pp. 4–5.

22. Frederick C. Barghoorn, *The Soviet Cultural Offensive* (Princeton, N.J.: Princeton University Press, 1960), p. 188.

23. E. I. Afanasenka, "The Decisions of the June Plenary Meeting of the CPSU Central Committee and the Tasks of Public Education Bodies," *Soviet Education*, Vol. VI, no. 5 (March 1964) [translated from *Uchitel'skaia Gazeta*, August 17, 1963]. Arcadius Kahan, "The Economies of Vocational Training in the U.S.S.R.," *Soviet Education*, Vol. V, no. 3 (January 1963) [translated from *Sovietskaia Pedagogika*, No. 9, 1962]. Z. Malkova, "Pragmatism and Pedagogy," *Soviet Education*, Vol. V, no. 7 (May 1963), pp. 42–45 [translated from *Uchitel'skaia Gazeta*, May 9, 1963]. Leonard Shapiro, "The Party's New Rules," *Problems of Communism*, Vol. XI, no. 1 (January, February 1962), pp. 28–42. B. Vulfson, "Existentialism and Pedagogy," *Soviet Education*, Vol. V, no. 7 (May 1963), pp. 45–47 [translated from *Uchitel'skaia Gazeta*, May 11, 1963]. ———, "The Crisis of Bourgeois Pedagogy," *Soviet Education*, Vol. V, no. 7 (May 1963), pp. 40–42 [translated from *Uchitel'skaia Gazeta*, May 7, 1963].

24. Counts, *op. cit.*, p. 280.

25. Cantril, *op. cit.*, p. 43.

26. David Burg, "The Peoples' Friendship University," *Problems of Communism*, Vol. X (November, December 1961), pp. 50–54.

27. *Ibid.*, p. 53.

28. *Ibid.*

29. There are several excellent sources about the changing values of youth in other countries, especially the developing countries in which cultural change is rapid and political insecurities great. Understanding of the Soviet educational involvement in foreign student programs will be greatly enhanced if the processes of change in general are better understood. In fact, understanding of foreign student programs in the United States and elsewhere is incomplete without insight into the position of the student generation and "student culture" with respect to change. The students from these countries of rapid change appear to exhibit some of the same characteristics both in the United States and in the Soviet Union:

J. B. Amstuty, "The Indonesian Youth Movement, 1908–1955" (unpublished Ph.D. dissertation, Fletcher School of Law and Diplomacy, Tufts University, Medford, Mass., 1958).

G. B. Baldwin, "Foreign-Educated Iranians, a Profile," *Middle East Journal,* Vol. XVII (Summer 1963), pp. 264–278.

J. W. Bennett, "Innovative Potential of American-Educated Japanese," *Human Organisation,* Vol. XXI (Winter 1962–1963), pp. 246–251.

W. A. Douglas, "Korean Students and Politics," *Asian Studies,* Vol. III (1963), pp. 584–595.

J. Fisher, "Universities and the Political Process in S. E. Asia," *Pacific Affairs,* Vol. XXXVI (Spring 1963), pp. 3–15.

J. Gullahorn, "Role of the Academic Man as a Cross-Cultural Mediator," *American Sociological Review,* Vol. XXV (June 1960), pp. 414–417.

C. I. Eugene Kim and Ke-soo Kim, "April, 1960 Korean Student Movement," *Western Political Quarterly,* Vol. XVII (March 1964), pp. 83–92.

Charles G. McClintock and Henry Turner, "The Impact of College upon Political Knowledge, Participation and Values," *Human Relations,* Vol. XV, no. 2 (May 1962), pp. 163–177.

S. S. Robin and F. Story, "Ideological Consistency of College Students," *Sociological and Social Research,* Vol. XLVIII (January 1964), pp. 187-196.

U.S. Department of State, Bureau of Education and Cultural Affairs, "Changing Roles of Youth in the Developing Nations" (mimeographed, n.d.).

U.S. National Student Association, "The Rise of the Latin American Left," Political Background Project, USNSA, Philadelphia (mimeographed, n.d.).

U.S. Information Agency, "The Comparative Image of the U.S. vs. the Communist Powers among Philippine University Students," Research and Reference Service, May 1960 (mimeographed).

———, "The Arab Student Attitudes toward the U.S. versus the U.S.S.R.," Research and Reference Service, June 1958 (mimeographed).

———, "Attitudes of Turkish Students Toward the U.S. Military and Indications of the Present and Future Standing of the U.S.," Research and Reference Service, October 1958 (mimeographed).

————, "The Image of America among Vietnamese University Students," Research and Reference Service, December 1959 (mimeographed).

30. *Times Educational Supplement,* "The New Type University for the Developing Countries (U.S.S.R.)," *op. cit.* Commitment to economic development, or entrepreneurship in this respect is a relatively recent phenomenon. For an interesting analysis of an early development of entrepreneurship, see Arcadius Kahan, "Entrepreneurship in the Early Development of Iron Manufacturing in Russia," *Economic Development and Cultural Change,* Vol. X, no. 4 (July 1962), pp. 395–422.

31. Quoting Khrushchev's speech delivered at the inauguration of the Friendship University, *International Student Conference,* "Problems of Overseas Students in Europe," report by the Research and Information Commission, submitted to the 11th International Student Conference, New Zealand, June 22–July 1, 1964 (mimeographed, n.d.). See also the speech of the Minister of Higher and Specialized Secondary Education, V. P. Elyutin, "Higher School at a New Stage: The Higher School's Foreign Ties," *Soviet Education,* Vol. IV (January 1962), pp. 35–52.

32. United States Department of State, "The Education of Students from Developing Countries in the Sino-Soviet Bloc" (mimeographed, n.d.), p. 1.

33. Barghoorn, *op. cit.,* p. 17.

34. *Ibid.,* p. 17.

35. Counts, *op. cit.,* pp. 283 ff.

36. Training in Party work remains an important phase of the Soviet educational system, but detailed information is not available. It has been suggested to this writer that foreign communists are generally not allowed in the Russian Party schools of the higher order.

37. Jane B. Webbink, *African Students at Soviet Universities* (Cambridge, Mass., Harvard University, 1964), p. 3.

38. UNESCO, *Study Abroad: 1958/1959,* Vol. X; see also O. J. Caldwell, "What Others Are Doing," *Annals of the American Academy of Political and Social Sciences,* no. 335 (May 1961), pp. 112–121.

39. *Times Educational Supplement, op. cit.,* p. 386.

40. Barghoorn, *op. cit.,* pp. 96–97.

41. *Ibid.,* pp. 96–97.

42. *Ibid.,* pp. 96–97.

43. *Ibid.,* p. 98.

44. Seymour Rosen, "The Preparation and Education of Foreign Students in the U.S.S.R.," *Information on Education Around the World,* no. 44 (Washington, D.C.: U.S. Office of Education, 1960), p. 3.

45. U.S. Department of State, "The Education of Students from Developing Countries in the Sino-Soviet Bloc" (mimeographed, n.d.), p. 7. Additional statistics can be found for 1960 in Webbink, *op. cit.,* p. 5, and in SEATO, *Free World Students in Communist Bloc Countries,* SEATO Document No. 1–451 (12), p. 11, n.d.

46. *Christian Science Monitor* (March 21, 1963) and (September 4, 1964);

also "More Foreign Students Come to U.S.S.R.," *School and Society*, Vol. XCII, no. 2241 (March 21, 1964).

47. Burg, *op. cit.*, p. 52.

48. *Ibid.*, p. 51.

49. Professor Barghoorn has also suggested that "foreigners with wide experiences in the negotiation of exchanges have gained a strong impression that the scholars, professors and experts, and even, to a degree, some of the bureaucratic personnel with whom they deal on the Soviet side, are far more enthusiastic regarding exchanges than are the party and perhaps police officials . . ." Barghoorn, *op. cit.*, p. 161.

50. Burg, *op. cit.*, p. 51.

51. Jan S. Prybla, "Soviet Aid to Foreign Students," *Queen's Quarterly*, Vol. LXVIII (Winter 1962), p. 649.

52. *Ibid.*, p. 650, and Seymour Rosen, *The Peoples' Friendship University in the U.S.S.R.*, OE-14073 (Washington, D.C.: U.S. Department of Health, Education and Welfare, April 1962), p. 4.

53. In addition to sources quoted in this paper, there are three further useful articles with references to the Friendship University: Martha B. Lucas, "Behind the Doors of Friendship University," *Overseas: The Magazine of Educational Exchange*, Institute of International Education (May 1962); also "Recent Developments Concerning the 'University of Friendship of the Peoples,'" in *SMSE Bulletin*, Vol. II, no. 10 (Munich: Union of Emigre Youth of the People of the U.S.S.R., 1960), pp. 2–3; also "The 'Peoples' Friendship University and What Is Behind It," in *SMSE Bulletin*, *op. cit.*, Vol. II, no. 10.

54. Webbink, *op. cit.*, p. 11.

55. Rosen, *op. cit.*, p. 5.

56. See S. V. Rumiantsev, "The First Academic Year of the University for the Friendship of Peoples," *Vestnik Vysshei Shkoly*, no. 5 (1961) [translated in *Soviet Education*, Vol. IV, no. 2 (January 1962), pp. 61–63].

57. Rosen, *op. cit.*, p. 11.

58. Burg, *op. cit.*, p. 51.

59. Unless otherwise indicated, this section of the paper is based on a hitherto unpublished document from Europe which the authors requested not to quote. This document contains information from systematic interviews with over three hundred foreign students who have left the Soviet Union and other East European countries because of their unsatisfactory experiences. They have sought to better their study opportunities in the West.

60. Research and Information Commission, International Student Conference, *Problems of Overseas Students in Europe*, *op. cit.*, p. 75. Also Webbink, *op. cit.*, p. 1. According to the latter source, Dr. Nichol, principal of the University College in Sierra Leone, suggested that many students who seek scholarships to the U.S.S.R. are those who have failed to obtain admission to the local university.

61. The International Union of Students (I.U.S.) is reported to have administered some 200 scholarships for all East European countries in 1964.

62. "Rules on Foreign Students and Their Organizations: Regulations on Foreign Citizens Studying in Higher and Specialized Secondary Educational Institutions of the U.S.S.R.," *Current Digest of the Soviet Press,* Vol. XVI (May 13, 1964), pp. 24–25.

63. DeWitt, *op. cit.,* p. 44.

64. Rosen, *op. cit.,* p. 2; also *Problems of Overseas Students in Europe, op. cit.,* p. 78; and Webbink, *op. cit.,* p. 7.

65. DeWitt, *op. cit.,* p. 225; and Rudman, *op. cit.,* p. 11.

66. DeWitt, *op. cit.,* pp. 224–225.

67. Bereday, et al., *The Politics of Soviet Education, op. cit.,* p. 47.

68. *Moscow University—A Campus Report: Recollections of a Western Exchange Student,* compiled by the Audience Research and Evaluation Department of Radio Liberty (mimeographed, n.d., n.p.).

69. Burg, *op. cit.,* p. 51.

70. Barghoorn, *op. cit.,* pp. 158–159.

71. *Ibid.,* p. 160.

72. Veiksham, *op. cit.,* pp. 4–5.

73. Vulfson, *op. cit.,* pp. 45–47, and Malkova, *op. cit.,* pp. 42–45.

74. Barghoorn, *op. cit.,* p. 178.

75. *Times Educational Supplement, op. cit.,* p. 386, also *Problems of Overseas Students in Europe, op. cit.,* p. 77; also "The Preparation and Education of Foreign Students in the U.S.S.R.," *op. cit.,* p. 3.

76. DeWitt, *op. cit.,* pp. 316–317, 370.

77. *Problems of Overseas Students in Europe, op. cit.,* p. 77.

78. Darrell P. Hammer, "Among Students in Moscow: An Outsider's Report," *Problems of Communism,* Vol. XIII, no. 4 (July, August 1964), pp. 11–18; also *Moscow University—A Campus Report, op. cit.,* p. 3.

79. Urie Bronfenbrenner, "Soviet Methods of Character Education," *op. cit.,* p. 561.

80. United States Joint Publications Research Service, "Soviet News Reports Tension between Komsomol Youth and Foreign Students" (Washington, JPRS: 19, 106, May 15, 1963), p. 11.

81. King (editor), *op. cit.,* p. 197. On the other hand, Professor Lottich suggests that this liberalism is rather misleading and beneath a facade of liberalism there is hard-core communism. See Kenneth V. Lottich, *Poland, Champion of Latin Christianity, op. cit.,* pp. 70–72. See also Z. A. Jordan, "The Philosophical Background of Revisionism in Poland," *East Europe,* Vol. XI, nos. 6–7 (June, July 1962).

82. Ministry of Higher Education, *Information on Application Procedures for Admission to Institutions of Higher Education in Poland Affecting Foreign Candidates* (Warsaw: People's Republic of Poland, 1963), p. 54.

83. Halina Zalewska-Trafiszowa, *Educational Opportunities for Foreigners in Poland* (Warsaw: Polonia Publishing House, 1963), p. 54.

84. *Ibid.,* p. 54.

85. *Ibid.,* pp. 47–48.

86. Halina Zalewska-Trafiszowa, *Foreign Students in Poland* (Warsaw: Polonia Publishing House, 1962), p. 92.

87. Jan Kozak, *How Parliament Can Play a Revolutionary Part in the Transition to Socialism* (London: Independent Research Centre, 1961) [translation from Czech original first published in 1957].

88. *Problems of Overseas Students in Europe, op. cit.,* p. 29.

89. *Youth and Freedom,* Vol. IV, nos. 3–4 (March 1962), p. 10 (New York: Institute for International Youth Affairs).

90. *Youth and Freedom, op. cit.,* Vol. II, no. 2 (June 1959), p. 4.

91. *Ibid.,* p. 4, quoting from *Vysoka Skola* [Higher Institution].

92. *Ibid.*

93. *Problems of Overseas Students in Europe, op. cit.,* p. 36.

94. *Youth and Freedom, op. cit.,* Vol. IV, no. 2 (October 1961), p. 9.

95. *Problems of Overseas Students in Europe, op. cit.,* p. 31.

96. *Youth and Freedom, op. cit.,* Vol. IV, nos. 3–4 (March 1962), p. 10.

97. *Ibid.*

98. *Problems of Overseas Students in Europe, op. cit.,* p. 31.

99. "Be Nice to Foreign Students," *Kulturni Tvorba,* Prague (November 14, 1963) [translated in *East Europe,* May 1964, pp. 23–24].

100. *Youth and Freedom, op. cit.,* Vol. VI, no. 4 (1964), p. 10.

101. Braham, *op. cit.,* pp. 319–349.

102. Stefan Balan, *Higher Education in Rumania* (Bucharest, Rumania, mimeographed, n.d.).

103. *Foreign Students in the Rumanian People's Republic* (Bucharest: Meridiane Publishing House, 1963), p. 19.

104. *Ibid.,* p. 30.

105. *Ibid.,* p. 19.

106. *Times Educational Supplement,* "Foreign Students in East Germany," no. 2331 (January 22, 1960), p. 114.

107. Prybla, *op. cit.,* p. 634.

108. This indoctrination has been described well by Kenneth V. Lottich, "Extracurricular Indoctrination in East Germany," *Comparative Education Review,* Vol. VI, no. 3 (February 1963), pp. 209–212.

109. *Times Educational Supplement, op. cit.,* p. 114.

110. Since a comprehensive bibliography of articles and pamphlets dealing with the stories of African students in the Soviet bloc countries has not yet been compiled, it may be advisable to direct attention to some of the main works:

AFL-CIO Free Trade Union News, "African Students in U.S.S.R. Denounce Discrimination, Deceit, Brutality," Vol. XV (December 1960), pp. 4–6.

African Diary, "Rioting between African and Bulgarian Students," Vol. II (September 15–21, 1962), pp. 761–762.

Andrew Richard Amar, *A Student in Moscow* (London: Ampersand, 1961), p. 64.

Michel Ayih-Dosseh, "Les Sovietiques et L'Afrique," Supplement de Est et

Ouest, *Bulletin D'Etudes et D'Informations Politiques Internationales,*
no. 261, 1–15 (Paris: Juillet, 1961), p. 53.

Jordan Bonfanta, "African Students at Iron Curtain Schools Flee a Hateful Epithet 'Cherni Maimune,'" *Life,* Vol. LIV (March 15, 1963), p. 19.

Christian Science Monitor, "African Students Flee Soviet Bloc" (March 28, 1964).

R. Cox, "Segregation in Moscow: An African's Story," *U.S. News and World Report,* Vol. L (March 6, 1961), p. 94.

Wilton Dillon, "Wandering African Intellectuals," *New Republic,* Vol. CXLVIII (March 9, 1963), pp. 17–19.

E. Dunbar, "African Revolt in Russia," *Look,* Vol. XXVIII (May 5, 1964), pp. 31–35.

East Europe, "Bulgaria—African Students Leave after Clash," Vol. XII (March 1963), pp. 36–37.

———, "Ethiopian Student Tells of Disillusionment," Vol. XII (March 1963), pp. 40–41.

Economist, "Africans in Russia: Le Rouge et Le Noir" (December 21, 1963), pp. 1247–1248.

Darrell P. Hammer, "Among Students in Moscow: An Outsider's Report," *Problems of Communism,* Vol. XIII, no. 4 (July–August 1964), pp. 11–18.

Emmanuel John Hevi, *An African Student in China* (New York: Praeger, 1963).

J. C. Kennedy, "African Students in Russia," *Commonweal,* Vol. LXXVIII (May 3, 1963), pp. 161–163.

Life, "African Lesson for the Russians," Vol. LVI (January 3, 1964), p. 4.

Liu Shui Sheng, "Life in a Chinese University," *Institute of International Education News Bulletin,* Vol. XXXVI (February 1961), pp. 20–26.

C. McCarry, "African Students Who Quit the Soviet Union," *American Federationist,* Vol. LXX (January 1963), pp. 18–21.

I. Mulehezi, "I Was a Student at Moscow State," *Reader's Digest,* Vol. LXX (July 1961), pp. 99–104.

New Republic, "Girl Trouble," Vol. CL (January 11, 1964), p. 9.

New Statesman, "Trouble in Paradise," Vol. LXVI (December 27, 1963), p. 931.

Newsweek, "Good-by Lumumba U: African Students Leave Russia," Vol. LXIII (February 10, 1964), pp. 80 ff.

———, Huldah Clark, "Daddy's Little Girl," Vol. LIX (January 8, 1962), p. 40.

———, "Red and Black: African Demonstration in Moscow," Vol. LXII, no. 28 (December 30, 1963).

———, "Segregation in Sofia," Vol. LXI (February 25, 1963), p. 42.

S. O. Okulio, "Negro's Life in Russia: Beatings, Insults, Segregation: Interview," *U.S. News and World Report,* Vol. XLIX (August 1, 1960), pp. 59–60.

G. Pfeifer, "Red and the Black: Racism in Moscow," *Reporter,* Vol. XXX (January 2, 1964), pp. 27–28.

Lazar Pistrak, "Soviet Views on Africa," *Problems of Communism,* Vol. XI, no. 2 (March, April 1962), pp. 24–31.

Seymour Rosen, *Soviet Training Programs for Africa,* Bulletin no. 9, OE-14079 (Washington, D.C.: U.S. Department of Health, Education and Welfare, 1963).

Senior Scholastic, "Anger in Red Square: Demonstration Protesting Racial Discrimination by African Nations," Vol. LXXXIII, no. 17 (January 10, 1964).

———, "Soviet Schools," Vol. LXXVI, no. 6T (March 2, 1960).

SMNSE Bulletin, "African Students in Moscow" (Munich: Union of Emigre Youth of the Peoples of the U.S.S.R., 1960), pp. 6–9.

Time, "Free Ride in Moscow: Friendship University," Vol. LXXVII (January 6, 1961), p. 38.

———, "Three Who Went to Moscow: African Students," Vol. LXXVI (October 3, 1960), pp. 27–28.

———, "U.S. Students in Russia," Vol. LXXX (November 30, 1962), p. 66.

———, "We, Too Are People: African Students vs. Soviet Police," Vol. LXXXII (December 27, 1963), pp. 20–21.

The Times (London). "East-West Race to Teach Afro-Asians" (July 27, 1961), p. 11.

U.S. Department of State, *U.S. Exploring Ways to Help African Students,* Bulletin no. 48 (March 11, 1963), p. 375.

U.S. News and World Report, "Now, Race Riots in Moscow," Vol. LV (December 30, 1963), p. 5.

Jane B. Webbink, *African Students at Soviet Universities.* Cambridge, Mass., Harvard University (lithographed), 1964.

111. Pistrak, *op. cit.,* p. 25.
112. *Ibid.,* p. 25.
113. *Ibid.,* p. 26.
114. *Ibid.,* p. 27.
115. *Ibid.,* p. 27.
116. *Ibid.,* p. 25. Also see Christopher Bird, "Scholarships and Propaganda," *Problems of Communism,* Vol. XI, no. 2 (March, April 1962), p. 35.
117. Pistrak, *op. cit.,* p. 30.
118. Bird, *op. cit.,* p. 35.
119. Pistrak, *op. cit.,* pp. 29–30.
120. *Ibid.,* p. 30.
121. *Ibid.,* pp. 24–25, quoting from the *Kommunist,* no. 12 (1961), p. 51.
122. Bird, *op. cit.,* p. 36.
123. Rumiantsev, *op. cit.,* p. 61.
124. *Problems of Overseas Students in Europe, op. cit.,* pp. 37–38.
125. Webbink, *op. cit.,* p. 16.
126. Barghoorn, *op. cit.,* p. 189.

127. *The Preparation and Education of Foreign Students in the U.S.S.R.,* *op. cit.,* p. 3.

128. Barghoorn, *op. cit.,* p. 218.

129. Bird, *op. cit.,* quoting an editorial in *Problemy Vostokovedeniia,* no. 1 (1959).

130. *Christian Science Monitor* (February 4, 1963).

131. Barghoorn, *op. cit.,* p. 133.

132. *Ibid.,* p. 239.

133. *Ibid.,* p. 251.

134. *Ibid.,* p. 252.

135. *Ibid.,* pp. 254–255.

136. United States Department of State, *Report on Exchanges with the Soviet Union and Eastern Europe,* Report no. 22 (January 1, 1964). Also United States Department of State, *A Summary Report on the United States Exchanges Program with the Soviet Union,* Soviet and Eastern European Exchanges Staff, April 18, 1964 (mimeographed).

137. *A Summary Report . . . , op. cit.,* p. 4. For the discussion of problems of difficulties involved in administration of Soviet-American exchanges, see also the following:

Darrell P. Hammer, "Among Students in Moscow: An Outsider's Report," *Problems of Communism,* Vol. XIII, no. 4 (July, August 1964), pp. 11–18.

Moscow University—A Campus Report—Recollections of a Western Exchange Student, compiled by the Audience Research and Evaluation Department of Radio Liberty (mimeographed, n.d.).

S. Shabad, "Amerikanets in a Moscow School," *New York Times Magazine* (June 9, 1963), p. 44.

S. Viederman, "Academic Exchange, a Narrow Bridge," *Bulletin of the Atomic Scientists,* Vol. XVIII (February 1962), pp. 17–21.

Marianne Wannow, "A German Visitor Observes Soviet Student Life," *Our World* [bimonthly of the American Field Service] (October 1961), pp. 19–23.

138. V. P. Elyutin, *op. cit.,* p. 52.

139. *A Summary Report . . . , op. cit.,* p. 5.

140. Rumiantsev, *op. cit.,* p. 62.

141. United States Department of State, *The Education of Students from Developing Countries in the Sino-Soviet Bloc, op. cit.,* pp. 3–4.

142. Prybla, *op. cit.,* p. 650.

143. Webbink, *op. cit.,* pp. 17, 21, quoting respectively from *Tass* (December 21, 1963) and *New York Times* (March 27, 1964).

CHAPTER 11

Sino-Soviet Educational Cooperation: 1950–1960

STEWART FRASER

SOVIET INFLUENCE IN CHINESE EDUCATION

The role that American educational ideas played in China during much of the twentieth century has been in the last decade largely usurped by ideas imported from the Soviet Union. A large proportion of the better foreign colleges, private colleges, and mission colleges had been financed, staffed, and supported from America. America for the past hundred years, in fact, has provided an academic alma mater for a large percentage of the "returned Chinese intellectuals." But with the demise of the Nationalist regime on the mainland and the Chinese intervention against the United Nations forces in Korea, all this has changed. Private education has virtually ceased, and total control of education by the Communist government at all levels, national, provincial, and county, has been introduced. The elimination of the educational policies of the Kuomintang and those of "Sino-Deweyism" was followed by a spate of adoration for the Soviet Union and Russian teaching methods. An ideological reformation of the professors, at its height in 1952, and recurring in 1957, was aimed at debunking the "bourgeois" and American pedagogical ideas that were

This article was originally written for *Melbourne Studies in Education,* and its contents reflect Sino-Soviet educational relations during the first decade of the Chinese Communist regime; it does not cover subsequent developments after 1960. Kind permission to reprint this article has been given by E. L. French, editor of *Melbourne Studies in Education,* and the publisher, Melbourne University Press, Australia.

common in "preliberation" China. Into the vacuum have come Russian ideas, Russian experts, teachers, and technicians.

The ties established between the two nations are both formal and informal. The formal ties include the Sino-Soviet Non-Aggression Treaty of 1937, the Sino-Soviet Treaty of Friendship and Alliance of 1945 (both signed with the Nationalist government), the Sino-Soviet Treaty of Friendship, Alliance and Mutual Assistance of 1950, and the involvement of Russia in China's first Five-Year Plan, 1953, under which ten thousand Chinese students were to take advanced training in Russia. The informal ties are less clearly discernible, but are manifest in diplomatic, cultural, educational, and sports associations.[1] The trade union delegations, industrial conventions, literary congresses, and ideological campaigns, all transcend national boundaries at each level of organization. Whether for students or artists, a myriad of Communist-sponsored interchanges take place between the two countries. The extent and success of the links is not surprising in view of the fact that the Communist Party and the People's Government are modeled closely on their Russian counterparts, and the fact that over half the members of the Central Committee of the Chinese Communist Party have received training or education in Russia.[2] Doctrine and jargon are derived from the universal fountainhead, and the works of Marx, Engels, Lenin, Stalin, Khrushchev, and more recently those of Mao Tse-tung and Liu Shao-chi, have become widely known.[3]

Russian educational aid consists of the exchange of teachers and students, the consultation services of Soviet teachers and skilled industrial technicians, and the export of textbooks and classroom apparatus and scientific equipment. Estimates of the number of educational specialists in China vary. One Hong Kong journal some nine years ago indicated vaguely that they would "outnumber the total foreign population during the boom between war years."[4] But Professor Chang-tu Hu of Columbia University is probably nearer the mark when he writes:

> Higher education has received a considerable proportion of the total number of Russian experts working in China since 1950. It has been reported that up to 1956, 583 Russians had been assigned to institutions of higher education and that for the academic year of 1957 alone, 117 Russian experts were added to the already sizeable Russian staff.[5]

"This proportion," he says, "becomes quite impressive when measured against the total number of Russian experts working in all fields, which is given at 7,000 for the period 1949–1958." The decision to accept Russian educational assistance dates from 1949. At the Ministry of Education's "All China Educational Work Conference" of that year the Vice-Minister of Education, Ch'ien Chun-jui, stated that Communist educational policy would "construct education under the New Democracy based on the experience of the new education in the old liberated areas, absorbing the useful experience of the old education, and borrowing help from the experience of the Soviet Union." [6] Some three years later, Ma Hsu-lun, the Minister of Education, called together all university and college presidents in North China and indicated to them their duties and responsibilities. The country's central task in 1953 was, he said,

. . . to strengthen ideological political education and to learn the advanced experience of the Soviet Union, carry on the teaching reform and promote the quality and quantity of teaching. . . . We are trying our best to solve the problem of teaching plans and materials. We will revise the previously translated teaching plans and programs so that they may be better suited to the practical conditions of Chinese institutions of higher learning. We will systematically translate the teaching materials of the Soviet Union by unified efforts. It is decided that about 200 kinds of teaching materials are to be translated this year, thus creating conditions for the teaching reform. [7]

This, as he indicated earlier, represented a revolution for higher education in China.

While it is apparent that Russian teaching techniques and textbooks were most acceptable to the Ministry of Education, many of the professors were reluctant to accept them at face value. It took time for them to realize that careful adaptations of the Soviet material might have to be made. Until then a plethora of praise was offered up in support of Russian education as contrasted with that of the United States.

The scientific techniques of the Soviet Union are the most advanced in the world. If you read the scientific technical books of the Russians and then go to read the same kinds of books published in the United States, you would feel that the American books are boring in substance and tasteless, and you would never wish to read American books again. The merits of Russian scientific books are: (1) richness of content. The American books contain a lot of rubbish, some are boasting, some are flattery, with plenty of unnecessary pictures and photos. . . . (2) Association of theory with practice. The Russian books are far more profound than the American ones in theoretical aspects; when we read them we do not find them hard to comprehend. (3) Originality. The Russian books introduce to us the creations and inventions exclusively of the Soviet Union herself. [8]

This was the tenor of it.

In the face of this attempt at complete emulation of Russian classroom procedures there appeared to be relatively few Chinese academicians during 1955 and 1956 who would assert their independence of Soviet pedagogy. For obvious reasons it was difficult to show opposition to an educational methodology which was "so eminently suited for a revolutionary Marxist nation." The "ideological remoulding of the intellectuals" was still fresh in the minds of the professors, and was readily brought into play to correct any "reactionary tendencies." The plight of the Chinese intellectual is well stated by Allen Whiting:

> Torn between pride in the superiority of China's historic civilization and a growing sense of inferiority before the material accomplishments of other countries, this group is now forced to resolve all doubts in favour of complete subservience before Soviet institutions. The Russian intelligentsia, in a sense similarly torn between so-called Westerners and Slavophils, was free until the post-war period to "learn" from the capitalistic world, while denouncing its existence and predicting its downfall. The Chinese artist and scientist is denied the opportunity. He must shift his views—to suit political winds blowing in the Soviet Union.[9]

The conformity maintained in academic life eventually brought a reaction. The well-known story of the "Hundred Flowers and Blooming and Contending" was evidence of smouldering dissent, and it was possible to see evidence of a timid reappraisal of American and Russian scholarship. A Party member, Dr. Mao I-shen, presented the new official Communist line, stating:

> In the past, the aged engineers had a great esteem for the English and American technology, and consequently betrayed their resistance to learning from the Soviet Union at the initial stage. Later, having gained adequate knowledge of the Soviet science and technology, they dared not even mention English and American technology, and put away English and American books lest they be accused of political backwardness. In point of fact our government repeatedly called upon us to learn useful experience from all countries as regards science and technology; such apprehensions on their part are really unnecessary.[10]

Just how far the *détente* has proceeded it is hard to say.

SOVIET TEXTBOOKS, AND THEIR USE

The intrusion of Russian education on the Chinese scene is perhaps most clearly noticeable among teachers' textbooks. With the demise of the Nationalist government on the mainland, the Communists felt it necessary to revise the curriculum completely and make textbook changes. They were obliged, however, to make do for a time with what materials were available, and universal book burning was not a practical solution, although it was certainly carried out in some parts of China. School and college textbooks for the most part had always come under the close scrutiny of the Central Government, and a few publishing houses like the Commercial Press of Shanghai and the Chunghua Book Company maintained a virtual monopoly of official textbook production. Before these two largest publishing houses of "pre-liberation" China could recommence publication they were forced to examine their inventories of books. During fifty years of operation the Commercial Press published nearly 15,000 titles of books and periodicals. Of the 8,000 titles in stock during 1950, 1,234 titles or 13 per cent were found to be "fit" for circulation after Communist scrutiny. The Chunghua Book Company was allowed to circulate 2,000 of the 13,000 items on its catalogue, or 16 per cent of its original stock. Those items considered redundant were pulped as waste paper.[11]

The use of Russian translations and texts was "obviously" sound, and a great volume of new texts soon poured from the government-controlled publishing institutes. By December 1952 over 3,000 Russian books were said to have been translated, and six months later, in June 1953, it was reported that "more than 130 different textbooks translated from Russian had been adopted in Chinese institutes of higher learning." [12] In 1952, the Director of the Publications Administration, Hu Yu-chih, wrote:

Without the spiritual and material assistance of the Soviet Union, the nationwide victory of the Chinese Revolution would have been inconceivable. There is now a countrywide upsurge of interest in studying the Soviet Union and its advanced socialistic spirit. In the Field of publications this is reflected by the fact that Chinese translations of works on Soviet politics, economy, art, literature and natural sciences receive an enthusiastic welcome from multitudes of readers. Although Soviet publications on Marxism, literature, and science have been translated and printed in large editions since the liberation, they still fall short of the demand. Since we are on the threshold of large-scale economic construction and a readjustment of curricula has been made in our universities, we now stand in urgent need of large numbers of translated works to introduce us to advanced Soviet scientific theory and technique to take the place of the stale and outworn texts cribbed from bourgeois writers and scholars which were used for the education of Chinese students in the past.[13]

The *People's Daily* reported in March 1954 that over 10 million copies of Stalin's works had been published since 1949, while nearly 4 million Chinese translations from the Soviet Foreign Languages Publishing House in Moscow had been imported to be sold in China.[14]

In 1953 the Ministry of Higher Education began to organize the massive translation of teaching materials from institutions of higher learning in the Soviet Union. The task was divided between the various colleges and universities. Works in the fields of engineering and natural science used in the first two years post-secondary study received first attention. The distribution of these works among the constituent subjects was as follows:

Table 1 *Translation of Soviet Teaching Material* [a]

Subjects	Subdivisions of Subjects	Number of Volumes	Number of Characters (millions)
Geology, Mining	39	58	12.34
Methodology, Mechanics, Electrical Engineering, Aeronautics	57	88	19.08
Civil Engineering	30	41	9.48
Mathematics	20	31	7.68
Physics, Biology, Astronomy	13	28	6.46
Chemistry, Chemical Engineering	13	23	4.81
Agriculture and Forestry	18	36	6.83

[a] Chung Shih, *Higher Education in Communist China*, p. 64, quoting *Kwang Ming Jih Pao* (May 23, 1953).

It was expected that "before the end of June 1953, 107 kinds of teaching materials in 131 volumes and about 28,570,000 characters" would be recommended for publication. "Apart from these," it was said, "the Ministry of Education is inspecting the translation of Russian teaching materials concerning finance, economics, politics and law, which have been produced by the Chinese People's University in the past two years." It is estimated that there are fifty odd kinds in about 8 million characters which will be published." [15]

With the introduction of Soviet textbooks comparison between Soviet and American texts was inevitable. Initially, considerable powers of persuasion were needed to convince students and professors that the latest scientific achievements of Europe and the United States were not of comparable importance with those of the Soviet Union. However, since October 1957, when the first Russian Sputnik was launched, persuasion has apparently become rather easier. Nevertheless, institutions of higher learning that adopted Soviet textbooks without much alteration found that the books were often designed for a five-year curriculum, and were unsuited to the three- and four-year "crash" plans of the Chinese government. The simple way of meeting the difficulty was to lengthen courses where possible to five years. The slogan became: "Learn Less but Better." [16]

Side by side with the use of translated materials went the teaching of the Russian language. This has served to build a supply of partly and fully trained Russian linguists for both military and civilian purposes, and at the same time to overcome the traditional dominance of works in English in the universities. It seems that already there are nearly as many journals devoted to the study of Russian educational techniques and developments as there are journals devoted to the study of developments in Chinese education. To many native journals there appear to be complementary journals containing translations from the Russian. For example, *People's Education* is complemented by the *Journal of Education Translations; Teaching Russian* is complemented by Chung Hua's *Russian Language; Historical Research* by *History Translation* and the *Journal of Geography* by the *Journal of Geography Translations*. For the most part it appears that the translations are of Soviet scholarship, only occasional references being made to the educational developments in any of the People's Democracies other than the U.S.S.R. Likewise it appears that few references are made to educational developments in Western Europe, fewer still to British or American educational developments, except for critical comments.[17]

This policy has had its effect on the Chinese bookshops and on the range of books available to university students. After Frank R. Moraes, editor of the *Times of India,* had visited China with an Indian Cultural Mission, he wrote that

. . . the book shops are all alike confined largely to Chinese and Russian books. The New China Journals have been closely patterned on the Muscovite models and all sing the glories of Marxism. The few English Journals and books are hand picked.[18]

Continuing with observations on the foreign works generally available to university students, he said:

Walking on the campus of Peking's Tsinghua University one afternoon in May, I asked my Chinese student companion whether his textbooks had been changed with the "liberation." "Yes," he replied. "Were they out of date?" I asked. "No, they were instruments of American cultural aggression," he replied.[19]

It should be pointed out, however, that access to foreign works would appear to depend in any one instance on the nature and location of the institution of higher learning. A specialized technical or scientific institute concentrating on research would have a wider range of works than an undergraduate institution. A distinguished Canadian geophysicist, President of the International Union of Geodesy and Geophysics, who went to China in 1958 as a guest of the Academia Sinica, and visited the Academia's Institute of Geophysics and Meteorology, commented on the excellent library facilities available to the students and faculty.

I estimated that the reading room held about 400 current journals on geophysics and related subjects. It was impressively complete and up-to-date, having, for example, four Italian Geophysical journals published in English, French, and German. I went carefully through the stacks and opened a variety of volumes there. The sets of all important geophysical journals were complete and there were many marginally related publications such as the *Proceedings of the American Society of Civil Engineers.* The library and its indexes are all in their parts. There are large Russian and Chinese sections as well as that for the Western languages . . . there were good libraries to be found in every institute and university I visited. Back and current numbers of the more widely read journals which might otherwise be difficult to obtain in China have been multilithed and I repeatedly saw copies of some of the standard American, English, German and Russian journals and of textbooks in that form.[20]

Speaking of the library facilities in physics at the University of Peking, he commented:

Physics was housed in another of the old buildings. In the departmental library I noticed about 250 periodicals of which some fifty were in Chinese and fifty in Russian and the rest in various Western languages. I saw copies of the English journal *Nature* with back numbers to 1890, and of the American publication *Physical Review,* and of the *Canadian Journal of Physics.* The latest copies of all publications I saw there were with one exception dated 1958. The idea never occurred to me in China, but I have since wondered if there is an embargo on the export of American journals to China. Certainly there was no sign that it was effective.[21]

Professor Wilson visited the University of Sian, a newer foundation, and noted that the geological library was well supplied with standard journals such as *Economic Geology, Bulletin of the Association of American Petroleum Geologists,* and *Journal of Geophysical Research.* He makes the interesting comment regarding Sian and other university libraries that "many of the English and Russian journals were multilithed because of the difficulty in maintaining their regular subscriptions."[22] English was, apparently, widely known among the staff, and students were expected to read it in addition to Russian and German.

The development of Russian into the foremost foreign language in Chinese education has been effected by persistent use during the past decade. Russian is both patriotic and useful, English has been suspect and is considered "academic." The odds were a hundred to one that the foreigner in China during the 1950's was either Russian or a member of a Soviet bloc country fluent in Russian. The introduction of Russian into the middle school curriculum and as a necessary course for most college freshmen has increased its importance. The initial replacement of English by Russian, the proscribing of many English language magazines, periodicals and texts, and the exchange of Russian professors for Chinese students meant the promotion of slavonic studies on an unprecedented scale. Further support for the study of Russian was given by the flood of Sino-Soviet Friendship Societies which have been established. Short term Russian language courses have been given to workers and technicians using Soviet equipment, and many Chinese professors have been forced to go to evening classes in Russian to "improve their ideological consciousness" as well as to understand correctly the "advanced science" of the Soviet Union.

How effective has been the substitution of Russian for English is a matter for conjecture, especially in view of the rift between the two nations that has occurred during the last two years. Some notice should be taken of the view expressed in a research publication directed by Professor Shau Wing-chan of the China Project, Stanford University.

There is a lack of subtlety in the Chinese Communist attempt to reconcile their theory of patriotism with their thorough Russian propaganda line. When they directed the teachers to abandon the use of English except in foreign language classes they defended this by saying that Russian would be taught in certain schools in order to expedite the process of translating certain Russian works into English so that even this practice would be terminated as soon as the goal was obtained (*People's Education*, February 1952, p. 7), but they failed to specify the time when such practices would cease. Since learning of foreign language is no easy matter, such a substitution of Russian for English has been a controversial point and may remain an unresolved issue of the Communists' ideological orientation in education.[23]

It is doubtful if we have heard the end of the matter.

ORGANIZATION ON THE SOVIET MODEL

In 1952 there was a reorganization and redistribution of the institutions of higher education. In 1950 there were 227 institutes of higher education, including sixty-five universities, ninety-two specialized colleges, and seventy specialized schools. By 1953, the number was reduced to 182 by elimination of some institutes and the reorganization of others. While this reduced the total number of institutes there was yet an increase, as time went on, in the total number of students and institutions. Starting with just over 117,000 students, the new regime had enrolled over a million students by 1960.[24] The *Kwang Ming Jih Pao* of October 1, 1958 indicated that higher institutes of learning numbered over one thousand, eight hundred of which had commenced in 1958. Of these, sixty were controlled by organs of the Central Government, forty by provincial or municipal agencies, and sixty by industrial works; the rest were controlled by local organs.[25] By January 1960 the regime claimed 841 institutes of higher learning, "not including part-time and spare-time colleges." [26]

Chinese universities used to be modeled mainly on the American-type college, consisting often of semi-independent faculties spread over a single campus. The new organization, which has developed during the last decade, restricts the typical university to the nontechnical disciplines and concentrates the scientific, technical disciplines in polytechnical institutes, like the Tsinghua University in Peking. To supplement these two types of institutions of higher learning a variety of specialist technical colleges has been established, which concentrate their efforts on such fields as geology, petroleum science, iron and steel technology, engineering, agriculture, and medicine. Many regions that have been unable, so far, to develop a university or polytechnical institute have fostered specialized institutes to meet their local technical requirements. The idea of the general college within the university, as the Americans have understood it, has been virtually replaced by the Soviet idea of specialized courses and specialized institutes. All the institutions of higher learning are strictly controlled by central planning with private institutions abolished entirely and provincial ones enjoying only a limited degree of autonomy.[27]

In addition to the universities and polytechnical institutes there is the institutional complex organized under the Academia Sinica.[28] The importance of the Academia can hardly be overemphasized, because of its central role as the principal research body. While in the main the polytechnical institutes and specialist colleges concern themselves with training scientific workers and conducting local research, the Academia Sinica and its affiliated institutes concern themselves with pure research. The Academia's research is carried out under the direction of four academic departments: physics, mathematics and chemistry; biology and earth sciences; technological sciences; and philosophy and social sciences.[29] There are over ninety research institutes affiliated with the Academia Sinica.[30] This may be compared with the two hundred scientific institutes affiliated with the U.S.S.R. Academy of Sciences. The functions of the two Academies would appear to be almost identical. Altogether, it is fairly clear that the Chinese have carried out their reorganization of higher education on lines that are familiar in the Soviet Union.

CHINESE STUDENTS IN THE SOVIET UNION

The idea of sending Chinese students to study in Russia is not new, but since the Chinese revolution the idea has become a policy. The First Five-Year Plan, 1953–1957 (though some students started in 1951), envisaged a considerable flow of students to institutions abroad. In 1953, 700 students were to go abroad; 1,500 in 1954; 2,400 in 1955; 2,600 in 1956; and 2,900 in 1957.[31] To quote from the text of the First Five-Year Plan:

> The sending of students abroad to study or get practical training is an important measure for raising our general scientific and technical level and improving the management of enterprises in our country. In this five-year period, 10,100 students will be sent abroad to study, 9,400 of them will go to the Soviet Union and 700 to the People's Democracies and other countries.[32]

The organization of the scheme included the establishment of a Preparatory Department for further studies in the Soviet Union.[33] In expectation of a certain amount of wastage the Plan allowed for about 12,800 students to be enrolled in the Department.[34] It seems that in spite of a five-year plan and "superior proletarian selection methods" it was thought essential to select more than 25 per cent more students for the Preparatory Department than it was planned to send abroad, such was the likely rate of failure and withdrawal.

It appears, however, that the Five-Year Plan was not fulfilled. It was reported by a Hong Kong research worker in 1959 that the total number of students sent to the Soviet Union during the previous nine years was 6,561.[35] If only 6,561 students were actually sent to the Soviet Union to study during 1950 and 9,400 was the number planned to be sent in the years 1953 to 1957 it appears that perhaps less than half the planned number actually went to Russia during the currency of the Plan. Another indication that the numbers of students sent abroad fell short of the number planned is to be seen in a report of August 1956, according to which the Minister of Higher Education, Yang Hsiu-feng, was said to have held a farewell party for 2,169 students going abroad to study. Something like 1,800 or 85 per cent of these were destined for the Soviet Union, of whom 520 were research students. The majority of the students were to study engineering and natural sciences. But these figures only approximate those set out in the First Five-Year Plan, which estimated that 2,600 students should go abroad in 1956, 90 per cent going to the Soviet Union.[36]

Among the possible explanations (although not a sufficient one) for the difference between the number of students expected to study abroad and the number who actually did so is one suggested by some of the criticisms of the Chinese students who have returned from their Soviet studies. The Deputy Director of the Institute of Mechanical Sciences in May 1957 is reported to have said:

> There is a tendency for political qualifications to override cultural and technical qualifications. Many students sent to Soviet Russia find difficulty in keeping up with their studies. . . . The stock of the student who has been to Russia rises sky high on his return. He gets a cushy job and a princely salary and enjoys all sorts of privileges, including meals, special messes, without having to prove his worthiness.[37]

It is not difficult to detect here the old division between the Chinese scholars who had "returned" and those who had not traveled abroad. Once it was the vogue to have returned from Japan, then from America; today it is from Russia, though this too is now subject to rapid "revision." Another possible reason for the difference is the change, in 1957, in the procedure for selecting students, a change from the method of nomination by institutions to "the method of free examination."

By 1955 some 110 students had returned from Russia after having spent four years abroad. They were assigned work in the Academy of Sciences, the Ministry of Higher Education, the Ministry of Fuel Industry, the Ministry of Conservacy, the Public Health Ministry, and the Ministry of Railways.[38] During the summer of 1956 a further report[39] indicated that 260 students had returned after having been sent by the government to study abroad. The students sent to the Soviet Union studied metallurgy, machine building, geology, and mineral prospecting, while those sent to the other People's Republics studied languages, literature, history, and arts. Of these students 174 had studied in the Soviet Union and Mongolia, the rest in Korea, Poland, and Romania.

Parallel with the scheme for sending students to the Soviet Union for study went a scheme of "mutual assistance" by which Soviet experts came to China on exchange. The Chinese Communists have been reticent until recently about indicating in exact figures the numbers concerned in this scheme. However, the occasion of the tenth anniversary of the Mutual Assistance Treaty between the two countries brought forth some interesting statistics. An indication of the extent of the scheme may be gained from the following statistical summaries in five selected fields:

Industrial Units. During the currency of the First Five-Year Plan the Soviet Union assisted in building 166 large scale construction plants. In 1958, 125 industrial units were established with Russian assistance under the Second Five-Year Plan.[40]

Scientific Development. In 1956, a team of Soviet scientists came to China and assisted in the drawing up of a twelve-year plan for scientific development. In 1958, a protocol was signed between the two countries allowing for "122 important scientific and technological research projects which were to be carried out jointly by China and the Soviet Union or by China with Soviet aid." [41] In 1959, it was reported that Chinese and Soviet scientists had made eighty joint researches into scientific subjects.[42]

Soviet Experts in China. During the decade something like "10,800 economic and cultural and educational experts" were sent to China under the various cooperation programs.[43] It was also estimated that some 1,500 experts from other Communist bloc countries were sent during the decade.[44]

Chinese Workers and Students in the Soviet Union. A total of 38,000 Chinese engineering technicians and workers went to Russia during the period 1950–1958. Of these it is believed that 6,500 were students (though estimated for the period 1951–1958).[45] A somewhat larger number of students, 8,500, is said to have studied in Russia between 1950 and 1958.[46] The figure for Chinese students in 1960 studying in higher institutions in the Soviet Union was over 3,200.[47] For the whole decade 1950–1960 the total number of students receiving higher education in Russia would approximate to 13,500.[48]

Cultural Delegations. The exchange of cultural workers, artists, and writers has been an important facet of this cooperation, and 134 artistic groups from China were exchanged for 112 similar Russian groups during 1949–1958. The same period saw nearly 750 Soviet films exhibited in China, while over 100 Chinese films were sent to the U.S.S.R.[49] These figures, it must be remembered, are official figures.

THE CONTRIBUTION OF THE SOVIET UNION

It may be too early to judge the influence of the contributions of the Soviet Union to Chinese education. It can be said, however, that the contributions were felt to be valuable and the Chinese have readily accepted them. Also, there has been general acknowledgment of the "superior science, technology and education of the Soviet Union." It has also been clear that Soviet contributions have not been always accepted uncritically, and there have been indications that adaptation rather than mere imitation will be the watchword for the future.

Probably the most fruitful period of political criticism of Russian contributions occurred during the "Hundred Flowers" campaign. Chu Yu–hsien, Professor of Education, East China Normal University, indicated in May 1957 that:

> During the past few years the fundamental feature has been the mechanical copying of Soviet experiences. There has been a strong tinge of doctrinism. Up to the present Chinese institutions of higher education are still using only Russian textbooks in education. No textbook on education has been written and published by ourselves.[50]

Speaking about the same time of the teaching methods employed and the subservience expected of Chinese students to Soviet material Liu Pu–t'ung, a Professor in Northwest University said:

> The existence of dogmatism nowadays has made teaching a very convenient profession. There was a time when the "three-copy" teaching method was in vogue in Northwest University; the teachers' lecture notes were copied from Soviet teaching materials, which were without alteration of a single word copied out on the blackboard by teachers at classes, and then recopied into their notebooks by students. In the case of students not understanding the point, the teacher would confront him with the stick with the remark, "this teaching material originates from the Soviet Union." [51]

Criticisms of this type were legion. Two recent well documented works on this subject, by Theodore Chen and Roderick MacFarquhar, give a wide sample of the adverse comments emanating from students, scholars, and others, during the years 1956 to 1957 when "all forces contended." [52]

One might ask whether there was any response from the Soviet Union. Khrushchev had commented already on the contradiction in the notion that the affairs of the Communist country were entirely its own. Accordingly, one would not have expected any great sensitivity on the part of Russian pedagogues when their educational system was criticized by the Chinese. This, however, was not the case, and nearly a year later Professor T. N. Anastasyeva of the Stalingrad Teachers' College attacked the criticisms made by a group of highly placed Chinese educationists, a group that included the Professor of

Education and Assistant Dean of the Peking Teachers' College. Speaking of the "ring-leader" he said:

He published articles in the press with an elaborated anti-Party and anti-popular program in the field of education and launched a number of attacks against the study of Marxist-Leninist educational theory and the advanced experience of the Soviet school in the field of education and character training of the rising generation.[53]

Whether Russian national pride, the reputation of Marxist-Leninist dogma, or criticism of the "advanced experience of the Soviet school" prompted this Slavonic polemic against Chinese criticism of Communistic practice can only be guessed.

It is the task of the National Communist Parties in Russia and China to ensure that education is maintained at a "revolutionary" level, that the five-, seven-, and twelve-year plans be carried out and so increase material prosperity. Education is not regarded as a panacea; instead it is regarded as a vehicle for scientific progress.

The Sovietization of much Chinese higher education is encouraged by the Communist regime, which rarely fails to acknowledge Russia's assistance in educational matters. But to believe that the Chinese Communists are unoriginal, slavish imitators, is to ignore the whole history of the Communist relationship between China and Russia. Acknowledgment of assistance has not meant total acceptance as events of 1956–1957 have shown.

The necessity to develop an educational structure best suited to Communist China's own requirements has possibly been hastened by the developing ideological conflicts between the Soviet Union and China. It is believed that the major educational reforms proposed in China in 1960 could revolutionize and revitalize the primary and secondary educational structure; and through the "articulation effects," influence tertiary education to an unprecedented degree. While on the surface the new educational models would appear to be those of Russia, it is apparent that they are at last being adapted to the "present stage of development" in China, with lesser dependence on Soviet experimentation and tutelage as may have been the case during the past decade.

NOTES

1. "Premier Chou Visits Moscow University," *New China News Agency* (January 9, 1957). United States Consulate General, Hong Kong, *Survey of the China Mainland Press,* no. 1449. See also Peter S. H. Tang, *Communist*

China Today: Domestic and Foreign Policies (New York: Praeger, 1957), p. 392.

2. See R. C. North, *Kuomintang and Chinese Communist Elites* (Stanford: Stanford University Press, 1952), p. 72.

3. *Administration of Teaching in Social Sciences in the U.S.S.R.: Syllabi for Three Required Courses* (Ann Arbor: University of Michigan, July 1960), pp. 28, 32, 76, 134.

4. *Far Eastern Economic Review* (April 15, 1954), p. 459.

5. Chang-tu Hu, *Teachers' College Record,* Vol. LXII, no. 5 (February 1961), p. 361.

6. *Jen Min Jih Pao* [People's Daily] (January 6, 1950), quoted in Chung Shih, *Higher Education in Communist China* (Hong Kong: Union Research Institute, 1953), p. 9.

7. Chung Shih, *op. cit.,* p. 59.

8. *Chieh Fang Jih Pao* (August 1952), quoted by Chung Shih, *op. cit.,* p. 61.

9. A. S. Whiting, "Communist China and Big Brother," in *Far Eastern Survey,* Vol. XXIV, no. 10 (October 1955), p. 150.

10. Mao I-shen, "What We Aged Scientists Hope For," *Jen Min Jih Pao* (January 22, 1956). United States Consulate General, Hong Kong, *Current Background,* no. 379.

11. *Ta Kung Pao* (January 6, 1952). *Survey of the China Mainland Press,* no. 265.

12. See Richard L. Walker, *China Under Communism: The First Five Years* (New Haven: Yale University Press, 1955), p. 196.

13. Hu Yu-chih, "Publishing Serves the People," in *Culture, Education, Health, in New China* (Peking: Foreign Languages Press, 1953).

14. *Jen Min Jih Pao* (March 5, 1954), quoted in Richard Walker, *op. cit.,* p. 278.

15. *Kwang Ming Jih Pao* (May 23, 1953), quoted by Chung Shih, *op. cit.,* p. 64.

16. See Lu Ting-yi, "Our Schooling System Must Be Reformed," *New China News Agency* (April 9, 1960). *Current Background,* no. 623. R. D. Barendsen, *Planned Reforms in the Primary and Secondary School System in Communist China,* no. 45, Information on Education Around the World (Washington, D.C.: U.S. Office of Education, August 1960).

17. See *Current Background,* no. 387, for a translation of a brochure issued by the Peiping Post Office listing cultural and educational periodicals currently published in Communist China (1956–1957), and circulated through the post office.

18. Frank R. Moraes, "I Saw Red China," in *United Nations World* (October 1952), pp. 26–29.

19. See Walter Crosby Eells, *Communism in Education in Asia, Africa, and the Far Pacific* (Washington, D.C.: American Council on Education, 1954), pp. 208–209. This and the reference immediately preceding have been suggested by Eells.

20. J. Tuzo Wilson, *One Chinese Moon* (New York: Hill and Wang, 1959), p. 78. Quoted by kind permission of Longmans, Canada, Ltd.

21. *Ibid.*, p. 42.

22. *Ibid.*, p. 180.

23. Stanford University China Project, *Central South China*, Human Relations Area Files, Vol. I (1956), p. 298.

24. See "Educational Big Leap," in *Peking Review*, no. 7 (February 16, 1960), p. 5.

25. *Communist China 1958* (Hong Kong: Union Research Institute, 1959), p. 122.

26. "Educational Big Leap," *loc. cit.*

27. *New China News Agency* (August 27, 1958). *Survey of the China Mainland Press*, no. 1841.

28. See Nieh Yang-chen, "The Development of Science and Technology in Our Country over the Last Ten Years," in *Ten Glorious Years* (Peking: Foreign Languages Press, 1960), pp. 328–347. See also Kuo Mo-jo, "Development of Scientific Research in China: Report to the Third Session of the First National People's Congress," *New China News Agency* (June 18, 1956); and *Current Background*, no. 400.

29. Chang-tu Hu, *China: Its People, Its Society, Its Culture* (New Haven: Hraf Press, 1960), p. 446.

30. See "The People's Republic of China," in *The World of Learning, 1960–1961* (London: Europa Publications, 1961), pp. 201–207; and Nieh Yang-chen, *op. cit.*, p. 330.

31. *First Five-Year Plan for Development of the National Economy of the People's Republic of China in 1953–1957* (Peking: Foreign Languages Press, 1956), p. 183.

32. *Ibid.*

33. This Department was probably located, for administrative purposes, in the Ministry of Education.

34. *First Five-Year Plan . . . ,* p. 185.

35. Ch'en Lei-szu, "Education," in *Communist China 1958* (Hong Kong: Union Research Institute, 1959), p. 130. Note that these "official" figures to some extent conflict with those given by the Institute of International Education. See "North Asia," *News Bulletin* (New York: Institute of International Education, December 1960), p. 18.

36. *New China News Agency* (August 6, 1956). *Survey of the China Mainland Press*, no. 1346.

37. Lei T'ien-chueh, *Forum Held by First Ministry of the Machine Industry. Kwang Ming Pao* (May 20, 1957), quoted in Roderick MarFarquhar, *The Hundred Flowers Campaign and the Chinese Intellectuals* (New York: Praeger, 1960), p. 83.

38. *Communist China 1955* (Hong Kong: Union Research Institute, 1956), p. 141.

39. *New China News Agency* (August 1, 1956). *Survey of the China Mainland Press*, no. 1344.

40. Nu ssu ju t'i, "Magnificent Aid and Past Friendship" (Secretary General, Sino-Soviet Friendship Association of Sinkiang Uighur Autonomous Region), *Sinkiang Jih Pao* (Urumchi) (February 14, 1960). *Survey of the China Mainland Press*, no. 2233.

41. *Ibid.*

42. Speech by Hsieh-Miao-No-Wei-Ho at Banquet in Honor of Tenth Anniversary of Signing of Sino-Soviet Treaty of Friendship Alliance and Mutual Assistance, in *Hsin Hunan Pao* (Changsha) (February 14, 1960). *Survey of the China Mainland Press*, no. 2232.

43. *Ibid.*

44. Choh Ming-li, "Economic Development: The First Decade," *China Quarterly*, no. 1 (January–March 1960), p. 39.

45. Hsieh-Miao-No-Wei-Ho, in *Hsin Hunan Pao* (February 14, 1960).

46. Nu ssu ju t'i, in *Sinkiang Jih Pao* (February 14, 1960).

47. Hsieh-Miao-No-Wei-Ho, in *Hsin Hunan Pao* (February 14, 1960).

48. This is, necessarily, a "guesstimate." Thus if 8,500 students accounted for the period 1950–1958, at least 1,500 would account for 1958–1960. Hsieh-Miao-No-Wei-Ho stated that "at present" (1960) there were over 3,200 Chinese students in Russia. An approximation of 13,500 is therefore feasible for the period 1950–1960.

49. Hsieh-Miao-No-Wei-Ho, in *Sinkiang Jih Pao* (February 14, 1960).

50. *Kwang Ming Pao* (May 6, 1957), quoted by MacFarquhar, *op. cit.*, p. 91.

51. *Sian Kuang Ming Pao* (May 6, 1957), quoted by MacFarquhar, *op. cit.*, p. 97.

52. See Theodore Chen, *Thought Reform of the Chinese Intellectuals* (Hong Kong: Hong Kong University Press, 1960), and MacFarquhar, *op. cit.*

53. T. N. Anastasyeva, "The Struggle for a New School and Marxist Education in the Chinese People's Republic at the Present Stage," *Soviet Education*, Vol. I, no. 1 (1958), p. 65.

Part **IV**

Area Studies

CHAPTER 12

Governmental Policy and International Education: United States of America

JAMES M. DAVIS

In our interdependent world community with almost instantaneous communication, international educational and cultural affairs have assumed an increasing importance in government. Programs have emerged faster than the policy to implement them and before broad objectives were fully articulated and understood. In the United States, both the public and private sectors have moved ahead largely on the basis of vague presumptions of common interest. Numerous studies have probed these assumptions, but none have related them to the aims of the United States. This paper fails to do the comprehensive job that is needed. It might better be titled: a few introductory notes to suggest directions for a study of government policy and international education with regard to the aims of the United States.

Even that topic is too broad for I am dealing here largely with the aspects of the topic related to foreign students in the United States.

Following a brief historical overview, the aims of the major programs and of some of their components are examined. On the basis of this examination, a few questions are raised.

HISTORICAL OVERVIEW

The systematic promotion of international educational and cultural exchange programs by the government of the United States dates from 1936. In that year, the United States representatives at the Conference for the Maintenance of Peace in Buenos Aires proposed a convention for the promotion of inter-American cultural relations. Under this convention, ratified by the Senate in 1938, and under the Act for Cooperation with other American republics, which Congress passed the same year, there was developed the educational and cultural programs of the coordinator of inter-American affairs and of the Department of State, with its Division of Cultural relations and interdepartmental committee on scientific and cultural cooperation.[1]

During the Second World War, these programs expanded to other areas of the world, and soon after the war the passage of the Fulbright and Smith-Mundt acts established them as permanent features of the foreign relations of the United States throughout the world. Immediately following the war, the federal government moved heavily into educational exchange with the occupied areas and the Army in particular operated large programs for nationals from former enemy countries to come to the United States as students and as short-term professional observers.

Following the passage of the economic assistance acts stemming from the Marshall Plan and Truman's Point IV, the "technical assistance program" was operated by a series of agencies: the Economic Cooperation Administration, the Technical Cooperation Administration, the International Cooperation Administration, and the current Agency for International Development. This Agency is now a part of the Department of State. Its Administrator reports to the Secretary of State and holds a rank equivalent to Undersecretary of State.

Within the Department of State, the International Educational Exchange Service (IES) developed along functional lines with special branches to deal with programs related to particular types of people (i.e., with foreign students in the United States, United States students abroad, foreign professors here, United States professors and teachers abroad, etc.). These functional branches were to serve in relation to the entire world.

During the Eisenhower administration the chief of IES, who had been under the Assistant Secretary of State for Public Affairs, was made a Special Assistant to the Secretary of State, reporting directly to the Secretary.

Shortly after the War the United States Information Agency was established to support programs to interpret the United States in other countries. Educational and cultural exchange activities quickly emerged as a significant aspect of the USIA program. Its overseas staff, the Cultural Affairs Officers and Public Affairs Officers at American embassies and consulates abroad, became the agents of IES in the operation of its program. USIA was and is reimbursed by the Department of State for the cost of the time spent by these officers, primarily Cultural Affairs Officers, in overseas service to exchange programs.

Since the end of the Second World War, the military establishment of the United States has implemented its policies related to international educational exchange through two major programs. As already pointed out, in 1946 the Army embarked upon a program to reorient the people of Japan, Germany, and Austria from belief in totalitarian principles toward a more democratic approach to government. Large numbers of people from these countries were brought to the United States for higher education and for short-term professional observation visits. During the early 1950's this program phased out, with the exception of that operated for the Republic of the Ryukyus, an island group south of Japan still administered by the Army.

As the United States sought defense support in mutual security arrangements with other countries, the Defense Department invested heavily in equipping and training the military forces of friendly nations. This led to the operation of a large program of military educational exchange. Between 1950 and 1959, more than 100,000 foreign military personnel had received training in the United States through various military assistance programs.[2]

Shortly after his election in the autumn of 1960, the President-elect appointed a task force to advise him on major needs in the broad field of educational exchange and to recommend federal action to meet these needs. The writer, who was at that time President of the National Association of Foreign Student Advisers, was asked to chair this body.

The task force proposed certain action which the President could (and to a large extent did) take. It also recommended certain basic changes which required revisions in the existing laws governing exchange of persons for educational purposes.

Thus, it joined forces with a movement already started by Senator Fulbright and the Special Assistant to the Secretary of State in charge of the International Educational Exchange Service to up-date and revise the basic laws. This led to the formulation and passage of the "Mutual Educational and Cultural Exchange Act of 1961," the so-called Fulbright-Hays Act which consolidated in one piece of legislation the many existing provisions of law.

Against this background let us look at the programs and purposes of the major operating agencies and factors involved in this process in the United States.

DEPARTMENT OF DEFENSE

Any examination of federal programs of international education must recognize that the largest program is that operated by the Department of Defense to provide training and military skills to improve the effectiveness of the military establishment of selected foreign countries. In 1961, some 18,000 foreign military personnel received training at some 142 Army, Navy, and Airforce installations in thirty-one states. These individuals came as part of the worldwide military assistance training operations of the United States Government. It was estimated that in 1963, 50 per cent of the trainees were officers and 44 per cent enlisted men.

Between 100 and 150 foreign military personnel attend civilian colleges and universities each year under the military assistance program. For the 1961 fiscal year, 92 million dollars were spent. Yearly training expenditures now are about twice as much as they have averaged during the past twelve years.[3]

In a hearing before a Senate committee in 1962, Secretary of Defense Robert S. McNamara stated: "Possibly the greatest return on our military-assistance investment dollar comes from the training of selected foreign officers and key specialists at our military schools and training centers in the United States and overseas. These students are hand-picked by their own countries to become instructors when they return home. They are the coming leaders in their nations, the men who will have the know-how and will impart it to their own forces. I need not dwell upon the value of having in positions of leadership men who have first-hand knowledge of how Americans do things and how they think."

DEPARTMENT OF STATE

At present, the basic general legislation governing international educational exchange in the Department of State is Public Law 87-256, the "Mutual Educational and Cultural Exchange Act of 1961." This act updated and revised the "Fulbright" and "Smith-Mundt" acts which had governed the educational exchange program of the Department of State heretofore, parts of the Internal Revenue Code of 1954, the Immigration and Nationality Act, and certain other legislation.

Cosponsored by the Committee on Foreign Relations of the Senate and the Committee on Foreign Affairs of the House of Representatives, this act is known by the names of the chairmen of these committees, as the Fulbright-Hays Act.[4] Its statement of purpose sets the general tone of federal participation in educational and cultural exchanges, as follows:

The purpose of this act is to enable the government of the United States to increase mutual understanding between the people of the United States and the people of other countries by means of educational and cultural exchange; to strengthen the ties which unite us with other nations by demonstrating the educational and cultural interests, developments, and achievements of the people of the United States and other nations, and the contributions being made toward a peaceful and more fruitful life for peoples throughout the world; to promote international cooperation for educational and cultural advancement; and thus to assist in the development of friendly, sympathetic, and peaceful relations between the United States and other countries of the world.

Federal international education programs comprise a heterogenous and sometimes unruly flock of activities scattered among twenty-four federal organizations, but only two of these are operationally involved with large numbers of foreign students. The Secretary of State, through an Assistant Secretary for Educational and Cultural Affairs, who administers the Bureau for Educational and Cultural Affairs, is regarded by the President as a principal shepherd responsible for exercising primary leadership in persuading the members of the flock to move in more or less consistent directions.

The Assistant Secretary of State for Educational and Cultural Affairs is both the operator of one of the programs and the coordinator of all of them. There is a tendency within the bureaucracy of government for programs to be responsive to the sources of their funds rather than to moral suasion from officers charged to coordinate them, but not implemented with budget review powers.

In the further pursuit of federal coordination, the Department of State established on January 30, 1964, the Council on International Educational and Cultural Affairs, an interagency policy coordinating at the sub-Cabinet level. The responsibilities of the Council are:

to strengthen the coordination of educational and cultural policies for government programs which are essentially international in purpose and impact (including the development of better communication among agencies with programs of this type and the more effective use of common resources);

to provide a forum for the discussion of problems which affect other governmental agencies with domestic programs having international implications; and to act as the parent body for other interagency committees and working groups which deal with specific matters or problems which are related to the Commission's area of general concern.

Chaired by the Assistant Secretary of State for Educational and Cultural Affairs, the Council includes among its members representatives of A.I.D., the Office of Education, USIA, the Department of Defense, the Peace Corps, and an observer from the Bureau of the Budget.[5]

A number of other interagency bodies are at work. As the United States Advisory Commission on International Educational and Cultural Affairs states in its second Annual Report, "Much has been done in the past two years to coordinate international educational and cultural activities, but much remains to be done." [6]

From the outset, the government effort in educational exchange was seen as a cooperative one. The original concept under which the program was launched and under which it still operates was that the role of the government should be to facilitate and to coordinate international cultural and educational exchange, but never to dominate it. The program in the main should originate in the cultural institutions of the country. It has always been recognized that the colleges and universities carry the major share of the national program through their direct admission and services to foreign students. The federally sponsored program has always been a minor part of the total, usually accounting for not more than 12 or 13 per cent of all the students enrolled. This cooperative concept was written into the Fulbright-Hays Act which states, "Foreign governments, international organizations and private individuals, firms, associations, agencies, and other groups shall be encouraged to participate to the maximum extent feasible in carrying out this Act and to make contributions of funds, property and services which the President is hereby authorized to accept, to be utilized to carry out the purposes of this Act." (Section 105) (F).

Thus, the Department of State has contracted mainly with the Institute of International Education for the placement and supervision of foreign students in the United States. These students are funded in part, or in whole, by federal monies, with significant participation in their financing being provided by American institutions and organizations.

The selection of students who are given assistance to study in the United States is achieved overseas through the utilization of binational Fulbright commissions or selection committees. These volunteer bodies of distinguished educators, in the sending countries, are joined with Americans residing in these countries to review applications and often interview applicants individually. The binational commissions administer United States Government funds in local currencies in the operation of their two-way exchange programs and typically have their own staff organizations, some of which are headed by nationals of the respective countries and others by Americans. The Committees on Study and Training in the United States are given staff help by the Cultural Affairs Officer or from the binational center where they are located.

The comparatively modest size of the State Department's program is misleading. It is highly selective. It is apportioned by countries according to political judgments. It is carefully programmed. Its balance between the immediate and ultimate objectives is calculated. It combines United States dollars, foreign currencies, and private contributions, thus making up the pattern of complicated cooperative grants. It also stimulates and services a variety of nongovernmental exchanges.

The Department of State program is assisted by the U.S. Advisory Commission on International Educational Exchange and the Board of Foreign Scholarships. These citizen bodies are provided secretariats by the Department of State and deal with policy considerations in assessing the total program and in granting scholarships. The Advisory Commission was directed by the Fulbright-Hays Act to evaluate the total Department of State program. The conclusions of this evaluation were based on extensive research, including thousands of interviews, consultations, responses to letters and questionnaires, and other means. It has been published in a pamphlet entitled, "A Beacon of Hope— the Exchange of Persons Program." [7]

The findings of this evaluation are summarized as follows:

1. Testimony is overwhelming from all sources that the program as a whole is effective . . . The evidence is also conclusive that the program has proved itself an essential and valuable part of America's total international effort.

2. There is impressive testimony that the exchange program increases mutual understanding.

3. Evidence is abundant that the exchange program has succeeded in helping dispel among foreign visitors many misconceptions and ugly stereotypes about the American people.

4. The exchange program does not bring about a uniformly favorable point of view on all aspects of the American scene; the reaction of former grantees varies considerably with the country from which they have come, and with the particular aspect inquired about.

5. The program has been outstandingly successful in providing a valuable educational experience to foreign grantees.

6. The evidence is significant, though somewhat less conclusive, that the grantee's United States visit also benefited his home country, by enabling him to transmit to it valuable new ideas, skills, knowledge, and attitudes.

7. The program has effectively established channels of communication between the people in other countries and the United States.

8. In increasing mutual understanding, in demonstrating American character and achievements, in furthering the grantee's own development and career and the strengthening of his country, the exchange program has effectively supported one of the nation's most basic international objectives—of helping support strong free societies able to work together, in mutual trust and understanding, on the grave issues of our time.[8]

It is not difficult to extract aims from the foregoing conclusions on the extent to which the aims were achieved.

The Bureau of Educational and Cultural Affairs is also the principal link between the East-West Center in Hawaii and the federal government which provides funds for the Center. Located on the campus of the University of Hawaii, this unique Center for technical and cultural interchange between East and West has a special relationship both to the University of Hawaii and to the federal government. The Center is operated under the Regents of the University but has a new National Review Board to view the Center with regard to the implementation of national policies.

Some inference on the priorities of aims of the Bureau of Educational and Cultural Affairs may be drawn from the recent reorganization of the Bureau. Functional divisions based upon similarities in the types of persons served and of programs have been replaced by area divisions corresponding to the geographic regional organization in the rest of the Department of State. To these area divisions (Near East and South Asia, Far East, Africa, Europe, and Latin America) were added a United States division to handle certain interdivisional services. The foreign area divisions include programs for students, faculty, and others in two-way relationships and budgets include funds to these regional offices for all educational and cultural activities in their particular regions.

Through these arrangements the Department of State would appear to be seeking to achieve a more effective impact on particular countries and geographic regions.

AGENCY FOR INTERNATIONAL DEVELOPMENT

The United States seeks to further economic and social development in more than eighty countries through the programs of the Agency for International Development. A.I.D. identifies its trainees and students as "participants" and it speaks of training rather than education.

A.I.D. participant training is distinctively different from the cultural and educational exchange programs of the Bureau of Educational and Cultural Affairs of the Department of State. Training of foreign nationals is undertaken as one means towards accomplishing a particular development objective: for example, establishment of a local training school or an agriculture extension system; overhaul of country fiscal operations; or setting up an industrial productivity center.

Participant training has been a growing element in development operations, and is likely to become more important as A.I.D.'s technical and institutional assistance activities are further concentrated on key development areas.

A.I.D.'s Office of International Training directs the training of approximately 6,000 foreign nationals each year in the United States (and 2,000 to 3,000 in third countries). Of these 6,000, approximately 40 per cent enroll as students in a college or university for a term or longer.

FOUNDATIONS

American foundations operate their own programs. Some, such as that of the Ford Foundation, which are beamed on the development of indigenous institutions overseas, utilize United States educational facilities to train significant numbers of foreign nationals. Those who will return to teaching positions form the most numerous category of foreign students sponsored by foundations.

Other agencies, such as the American Friends of the Middle East and the English Speaking Union, reinforce ties between certain regions and countries and the United States through bringing students here for study in a wide variety of fields.

MANY MORE FACTORS

Certain aims of the United States as expressed through Federal agencies appear in the foregoing. Since all Federal programs account for only about one-eighth of the foreign students in the United States, and those of foundations and agencies an even smaller number, it is evident that this is a very complex and relatively uncoordinated business involving more than foreign students coming under specific programs. The facts that most of the foreign students who come to this country are self-sponsored and that many more come on combination programs sponsored in part by government, a United States college or university, private foundations, corporations, and foreign governments, suggest that the aims of all of these individuals and agencies are quite diverse and complex but that they tend to focus in this particular program under consideration.

Several studies of the purposes which individual students have in coming here have established the consensus that most students seek primarily their own professional and academic advancement through advanced degrees and more extensive knowledge gained in this experience.

The foreign governments bringing students here are interested in securing more competent specialists who can assist in the development of their economic and educational systems at home.

Numerous business corporations which provide financial assistance to students do so in order to strengthen their overseas establishments through the infusion of better trained manpower and also through establishing a more favorable climate of relationships with the countries in which they operate subsidiaries.

American colleges and universities have quite varied purposes in entering into this program. Many see the foreign student as a means of broadening the education of American students. They tend to find a cosmopolitan atmosphere on campus somewhat useful in their public relations. They seek qualified technical people to further research interests. They are aware of an obligation to support the foreign policy of the United States which is fulfilled in part through having foreign students on campus and through assisting them.

SOME FINAL CONSIDERATIONS

The aims of the Federal government in all of this activity are varied and complex, as indeed is the federal establishment itself. In reflecting on this recent history one must conclude, I believe, that the ultimate objective is peace. Peace has been seen as deeply involved with another aim; that is, to withstand the extension of communism. Communism may be curbed by helping people attain their expectations under governments that are not Communist (and are friendly to the United States), which have the capabilities to defend themselves from communist threats from within or without, and which are able to work effectively toward improving the conditions of their people. Wherever these United States educated people make their contribution at home—in military defense, business, production, education, public administration, health, or in whatever field of endeavor—they will be inclined to be more willing to have attitudes favorable to the United States and will be more competent in their jobs than if they had not been here. Governments must support the national interest.

In educational exchange that interest is bound up with a generally enlightened, long-range, goal.

A month after his inauguration President Kennedy stated his understanding of the national aims as follows: "There is no better way of helping the new nations of Latin America, Africa, and Asia in their present pursuit of freedom and better living conditions than by assisting them to develop their human resources through education. Likewise, there is no better way to strengthen our bonds of understanding and friendship with older nations than through educational and cultural exchange."

Within the framework of the operations of the Federal government, agency programs serve their aims, but must be justified in terms of national objectives, particularly at appropriation time. Original purposes related to offsetting communism have somehow decreased in their direct effectiveness and are now related to the resistance to communist extension overseas by developing sound countries with viable economies which depend upon improved human resources and thus are related to manpower development through educational exchange.

Few would disagree that Federal governmental activities must be justified in terms of national interest. The area of disagreement lies in the definition of national interest. Educational exchange represents a long range and delayed impact effect in relation to foreign policy objectives. A calculated risk is taken in bringing a student here in the hope that the future role he achieves in his maturity may make him more favorable to the United States. On the whole, most educators would not find much attraction in this justification. They would rather point out that the individual who gains an education anywhere which serves him well in his mature, productive life is more likely to be understanding in a favorable way toward the institution and country which helped him get that education. They would point out that national loyalties are not properly changed by temporary sojourns abroad but that these sojourns do give an individual a basis for a more fair and sometimes more favorable understanding of the country in which he studied. In the short run, some educators would point to the influence on their home countries by students in residence here, transmitted through letters and news stories to families, towns and villages, and national bodies at home.

Certainly many would hold that an overemphasis on short-run objectives and on external signs and statements about this country may well be self-defeating.

Most thoughtful people in this field recognize that academic achievement by the students is primary. They thus place great emphasis on selection of the best possible students and on their preparation in English adequate to advanced study in this country. They would also emphasize the values inherent in orientation programs which help the student who has been successful in another educational system and often in a different language to become quickly effective in this milieu. And they would point to the importance of good, nonacademic arrangements at the host campus: adequate housing, sufficient food which is acceptable, and the presence of a staff counselor interested in the student as a person quite beyond his academic problems and concerns and available to him for counseling on a wide variety of problems.

Recent studies suggest that foreign students do as well as American students at the same institution. Their more careful selection, involving a significant commitment by the institution to the individual who is so far from home, usually offsets the disadvantages which the foreign student experiences in relation to language difficulties, different background preparation for particular courses, and unfamiliarity with particular academic procedures used in American institutions.

This emphasis upon careful selection is embodied in the Immigration Law under which only those students who already have been accepted by an American institution are authorized visas to come here. However much difficulty the enforcement of this law may make for foreign student advisers and individual students, it is probably the soundest basis on which this program can operate. It is envied by people working with foreign students in countries in which the foreign student may enter without having obtained university admission and then present himself to the institution for reception as a student.

THE FUTURE

Educational exchange has become an important element in international relations. It offers an acceptable, potent, long range opportunity to combine an increase in individual competence with the national objectives of two different countries. The number of foreign students in the United States has approximately doubled each decade since the Second World War. That trend is likely to continue.

With the increasing attention being given to this process, it is certain to improve in quality at the same time that it expands. The United States Government will be one of the prime forces in support both of the expansion of quantity and of the improvement of quality.

The aims of the United States Government in educational exchange

Table 1 *Foreign Students in the United States, 1954–1964* [a]

Number and Per Cent Distribution by Academic Status and Geographic Region of Home Country

Academic Year	Number	Academic Status: Per Cent Distribution			Geographic Region: Per Cent Distribution [c]						
		Under-graduate	Graduate	Special [b]	Africa	Europe	Far East	Latin America	Near & Middle East	North America	Oceania
1953–54	33,833	54	29	17	3.4	17.5	24.9	25	13	14	1
1954–55	34,232	55.8	35.3	8.8	3.6	15	29.5	25	13	13	0.9
1955–56	36,494	56.6	37.4	6	3.3	15	30	23	13	14	0.9
1956–57	40,666	55	34	9	3.5	14.7	31.8	22.4	12.9	13.4	1
1957–58	43,391	54	35	10	3.5	16	33	21	13	12	1.1
1958–59	47,245	52.5	35.5	12	3.5	14	33.5	21	14	12	1.2
1959–60	48,486	52	38	10	4	13	35	19	14.7	12	1.1
1960–61	53,107	50	40	9	5	13	36	18	15	12	1.2
1961–62	58,086	51	42	7	7	12	37	17	14	11	1.3
1962–63	64,705	51	45	4	7.7	12	36.7	17	13.7	11	1.5
1963–64	74,814	48	41.6	10	8	12	35	17	13.5	11.4	1.4

a (These statistics were obtained from *Open Doors* and *Education For One World*, published by The Institute of International Education, 809 United Nations Plaza, New York 17, N.Y.)

b Includes "special" status and "not known."

c The percentage of foreign students in the Stateless category has increased slowly from 0.1% in 1959 to 0.2% in 1963.

have seldom been better stated than they were several years ago by Senator John F. Kennedy when he said:

To us the challenge is not one of preserving our wealth and our civilization—it is one of extension. Actually, they are the same challenge. To preserve, we must extend. And if the scientific, technical, and educational benefits of the West cannot be extended to all the world, our status will be preserved only with great difficulty—for the balance of power is shifting, shifting into the hands of the two-thirds of the world's people who want to share what the one-third has already taken for granted. . . . to thus extend ourselves will require a political decision. But such a decision will take economic and educational forms.

NOTES

1. Francis J. Colligan, "Exchange Programs," *The Social Welfare Forum, 1960* (New York: National Conference on Social Welfare, Columbia University Press, 1960).

2. *Military Assistance Training Programs of the U.S. Government* (New York: Committee on Educational Interchange Policy, Institute of International Education, July 1964).

3. *Ibid.*

4. The legislative history of this Act is summarized in a forthcoming publication which the writer was privileged to read in an early draft. Written by Walter Johnson and Francis J. Colligan, the prepublication title of this excellent and most significant volume is: *Fulbright—A Magic Name: A History of the Fulbright Exchange Program. 1946–1962.* Chapters 20 and 21 deal with the development and passage of P.L. 87-256.

5. *Second Annual Report of the U.S. Advisory Commission on International Educational and Cultural Affairs,* 88th Congress, 2nd Session: House Document no. 364 (August 1, 1964), p. 6.

6. *Ibid.,* p. 5.

7. *A Beacon of Hope—The Exchange of Persons Program* (Washington, D.C.: The U.S. Advisory Commission on International Educational and Cultural Affairs, 1963).

8. *Ibid.,* pp. 1–3.

CHAPTER 13

Government Policy and International Education: Canada

JOSEPH KATZ

Canada's role in international affairs has undergone some radical reorientations in the period since 1763 when Canada began to take shape as a distinct political entity on the world scene. In the intervening two centuries the first orientation took place when Lord Durham in 1839 spelled out a policy which in substance dictated that the then colony look to Britain for guidance and direction in all matters pertaining to foreign matters. This policy of dependence upon Britain in foreign affairs gave way to independence when in 1922 Canada gave notice that she would make up her own mind in this realm, and in 1923 signed the Halibut Treaty with the United States without benefit of Westminster's blessing. In 1931 the Statute of Westminster provided for coordinate status of Commonwealth Parliaments with the result that the Canadian Parliament, in effect, became an independent body no longer responsible to the British Parliament. In substance, December 11, 1931, became Canada's Independence Day. Since then Canada controls her own international affairs, and has managed thus far to reconcile her role in the Commonwealth with her role in the Atlantic Alliance as well as with her role in the United Nations.

This reconciliation has not been an easy task, since Canada has had to take into account her relations with the United States whose socioeconomic influence upon Canada has been, and is, a highly significant one; and it has also had to take into account the bicultural and bilingual character of her own society. In the first instance Canada finds herself adopting foreign policies different from the United States with respect to China, Cuba, and South America, and in the second instance Canada finds that internally Quebec and the other provinces differ as to viewpoints concerning the Commonwealth. Despite these and other internal and external, social, economic, political, and cultural pressures, Canada has demonstrated her ability to hammer out foreign policies which are at once consistent with her capabilities and with the needs of both developed and developing countries abroad.

Canada has had a long history of internationalism contributing to her present-day ethos. The French Canadian tradition in Canada reaches back to Cartier and Champlain in the sixteenth century and this tradition was later rooted in the Napoleonic code recognized by Britain in Quebec two centuries later. The nineteenth and twentieth centuries witnessed vast numbers of peoples from Europe each contributing to what came to be known as the Canadian mosaic of peoples. Canada's immigration and settlement policies during these centuries were such as to permit them to preserve their cultural identities with the result that there has emerged a pattern of respect for peoples of diverse languages, customs, and conventions within Canada enabling her peoples to appreciate the wide range of diversities abroad. At the same time the concept of the melting pot never did take root in Canada in consequence of which no isolationist policy developed. Furthermore, Canada's place in the Commonwealth of Nations brought her into constant communication with other national groups, thus ensuring that the Canadian peoples were always aware of the problems and perplexities beyond their shores.

Until 1914, Canada was essentially a self-governing dominion. Sir Joseph Pope, Undersecretary of State in 1907, recommended a Department of External Affairs which was established in 1909 under the Laurier Government. In 1921, the office of the High Commissioner in London was placed under the control of the department. In 1925, a Canadian Advisory Officer was appointed in Geneva and a Canadian legation opened in Washington in 1926. In 1927, correspondence from the Dominion's office in London and from foreign governments was addressed to the Secretary of State for External Affairs instead of to the Governor-General, marking full recognition of Canadian responsibility for its own external affairs. In 1939, Canada declared war on its own, marking a further step in its independence in respect of foreign affairs. In 1947, embassies were opened in India, Pakistan, and subsequently in Ceylon, Ghana, Malaya, Nigeria, and Sierra Leone. This list has since been extended to include most countries of the world.

Canada's participation in two world wars has helped place Canada as a middle power on the world stage. More important, these two wars taught Canadians that the world was one and indivisible, and that time had given way to technology, and space to speed. The rising expectations of underfed, underhoused, and underclothed peoples were seen to be the legitimate outcomes of the wars to end wars, the realities behind the ideals for which millions had fought and died. Canada's political ethos, her experiences at home and abroad ultimately shaped her international role in the image of her national conduct: peace, order, and good government. Because of this, Canada's foreign policy is directed to offering assistance whenever it is needed in the world in order that peoples everywhere may benefit from this sociopolitical trinity.

DEVELOPMENTS SINCE 1945

Canada's interests in international relations have always had an educational dimension stemming from the French regime when missionaries and educators came over from France in the seventeenth century, while the sons and daughters of the ruling classes went abroad for study. This tradition was continued after 1763 by both English and French, and today continues to a limited extent despite an elaborate educational system in Canada. More important than the numbers concerned, however, is the tradition itself which has helped shape Canada's role in international affairs as one contributing to human betterment through education at home and abroad. Thus, during the Second World War Canada helped train pilots from Commonwealth countries, and provided homes and schooling for large numbers of orphans from war torn Britain. At the same time Canada entered into schemes providing for the education and training of technical personnel for service overseas and at home.

In keeping with this history and tradition, therefore, it should come as no surprise to learn that in 1941 Canada had a total of 2,056 students from abroad of whom only 289 were from countries other than the United States, the United Kingdom, the British West Indies, and Newfoundland. In 1951, the 289 had increased to 1,014; and in 1956, to 1,696. In the 1959–1960 academic year there were 6,433 students from outside Canada in colleges and universities. In the 1961–1962 academic year there were 7,900; in 1962–1963, 8,544 of such students. Students from other countries have for the past several years constituted 6.1 to 6.4 per cent of Canada's enrolments in higher education.

AGENCIES

The agencies responsible for this increase include the Department of External Affairs which administers six programs: the Colombo Plan, the West Indies Program, the Commonwealth Technical Assistance

Program, the Canadian Commonwealth Scholarship and Fellowship Program, the Special Commonwealth Aid to Africa Program, and the Canadian Program of Educational Assistance for the French-speaking States of Africa. In 1957 the Canada Council was established to promote the arts, letters, and sciences in Canada, but this body has recently extended its program to include aid to those interested in education abroad. In addition, the Canadian National Commission for UNESCO, supported in part by the Canada Council, has played its part in furthering Canada's educational interests overseas. In 1962 the Canadian Universities Foundation established an international division for the express purpose of processing the increasing number of exchanges. The Canadian University Service Overseas, founded in 1961 as a volunteer agency supported by students and business men, has progressed from seventeen overseas volunteers in four countries that year, to 225 volunteers in 1964 to sixteen countries. In June, 1964, Paul Martin, Minister for External Affairs, recognized the work being done by CUSO by offering to provide government air transport for all overseas volunteers. More recently there has been established a Canadian service for overseas students and trainees which, though not offering scholarships or financial assistance, does provide information and assistance to students from abroad in respect of their residency in Canada. All of these agencies seek to cooperate with their counterparts abroad in order to facilitate so far as possible the objects of international exchanges. And most recently there has been established the company of young Canadians which will in effect be Canada's Peace Corps.

UNIVERSITIES

Canada's universities play a significant role in the realm of international education consistent with their personnel and resources. Canada's higher educational efforts began in 1635 with the establishment of the College des Jesuits in Quebec. Though few others were established until after 1800, there followed development of three classes of institutions, church-dominated, independent, and provincial. At present there are in Canada forty-seven degree-conferring universities, twenty-one of which are in Ontario, eight in Nova Scotia, six in Quebec, six in New Brunswick, four in British Columbia, and one in each of Alberta, Manitoba, Saskatchewan, and Newfoundland. Most of these universities have students from abroad on their campuses and have a variety of facilities specially geared to accommodate these students.

AID

The students from outside of Canada come from the United States, South America, West Indies, United Kingdom, Continental Europe, Asia, Australia, New Zealand, and Africa and receive Canadian aid in varying degree from different agencies. Thus, direct federal grants-in-aid account for the support of 26.9% of overseas students in universities, with major support going to students from Malaya, Pakistan, Australia, New Zealand, and Africa. Provincial grants-in-aid provide for 2.7% of assistance; universities and colleges provide for 42.9% of assistance; other assistance being provided by alumni associations, private foundations, church organizations, and by private business organizations. Canadian grants-in-aid as a per cent of all grants received by the students are of the order of 81.7%, the remaining 18.3% being taken care of by the student's home government. This 81.7% represents an income to the student of approximately 1,500 Canadian dollars. Financial assistance varies as between undergraduate and graduate programs, and again as between professional and nonprofessional programs.

ENROLMENT

Actual enrolment of non-Canadian students increased from 5,988 in 1958–1959 to 7,900 in 1961–1962, and has increased proportionately since. These 7,900 students came from 150 different countries; approximately half from countries of the Commonwealth, the remainder from other areas. The greatest number of students come from Rhodesia and Nyasaland, Ghana, Kenya, Nigeria, Ceylon, Hong Kong, China, Trinidad, and Jamaica. (See Table 1 for complete data.) The median age for all students is twenty-three years and five months, with male students averaging twenty-three years, nine months, and female students, twenty-one years and nine months.

FIELDS OF STUDY

Non-Canadian students are to be found in almost all university undergraduate programs. Thirty-five per cent are enrolled in Arts and Science, 19.2% in Pure Science, 6.4% in Commerce and Business Administration, 16.2% in Engineering, 0.8% in Architecture, 10.9% in Medicine, 2.0% in Dentistry, 1.0% in Nursing, and the remaining 8.3% in other faculties. The graduate and postgraduate distribution is significantly different. Here, 17.8% are in Arts, 39.7% in Pure Science, 2.2% in Commerce and Business Administration, 12.4% in En-

gineering, 5.6% in Agriculture, 3.2% in Medicine, 3.4% in Philosophy, 4.6% in Psychology and Sociology, and 11.1% in other faculties.

As regards the distribution of non-Canadian undergraduate and
graduate students across Canada, 21.9% of the undergraduate students are in the Atlantic provinces, 34.4% in Quebec, 25.6% in Ontario, and 18.1% in the West. The graduate student distribution is
significantly different. Here, 4.2% are in the East, 19.2% in Quebec,
42.9% in Ontario, and 33.7% in the universities of Manitoba, Saskatchewan, and British Columbia.

Thirty-four per cent of the non-Canadian graduate students held
degrees on arrival in Canada, but varied widely in respect of country
of origin. Thus, 91% of Indian students had degrees; whereas only
16% of the students from Hong Kong. Only Pakistan, India, Oceania,
and some of the Asian countries showed more graduate than undergraduate students. In so far as changes in program are concerned, only
7% changed to a related field, and only 4% to an unrelated field.

Cambodia may be cited as a particular example of the form Canadian aid may take. In 1962–1963 there were thirty-one training programs for Cambodian scholars and fellows in Canada. In 1961–1962
there were only thirteen of these. For the most part these Cambodians
were in engineering courses at Laval University and at the Ecole Poly-
technique in Montreal, although there were Cambodian nurses enrolled at L'Institute Marguerite d'Youville in Montreal. At the same
time there were four Canadians teaching in Cambodia under the Colombo Plan. From India there were 155 trainees in Canada, in 1962–
1963, while from Burma there were seven students. The Special Commonwealth Africa Aid Program accounted for 145 students in Canada
in 1962–1963, as contrasted with eighty-four the year before.

Another class of student is also to be found in Canada. In 1961 the
University of British Columbia sent a team to the University of Malaya to help establish a School of Business Administration. This project also involves bringing Malayans to Canada for training as replace-
ments for the Canadian staff at present in Malaya. This arrangement
is carried out under a contract between the University of British Columbia and the External Aid Office.

WORK

Non-Canadian students may work in Canada on a full or part-time
basis. In the 1961–1962 academic year, 32.0% of such students (ex-
cluding those from the United States of America) were engaged in
paid summer work. On the other hand, 58.4% did not look for summer work. Fourteen per cent were employed in part-time jobs, and

9.6% were unable to find summer work in that year. Of the 1,030 students engaged in summer work, 96 worked at universities, 322 at jobs related to their studies, 7 gave military instruction, 137 were in jobs requiring special skills, 43 worked as store clerks, cashiers, and receptionists, 194 as waiters, maids, cooks, guards, orderlies, 37 as recreation workers or entertainers, 40 as factory, truck or bus drivers, 109 as labourers, seamen, railway or highway workers, the remainder in unstated occupations. The median monthly pay was $242, and median savings $500 per year.

SELECTION

Selection procedures followed in the case of students receiving Canadian Government awards are quite thorough. For example, awards made under the Colombo Plan by the Canadian External Aid Office involve nomination by the government of the country of origin, preliminary screening there, and then a further screening by a Committee of Academics in Canada up to the point of deciding whether the applications are worth consideration by the universities. They are then forwarded to the universities where the final decision is made regarding acceptance or rejection. Awards made under the Colombo Plan and the comparable technical assistance programs administered by the External Aid Office are designed for people who can profit from educational experience in Canada and there is no element of competition on the basis of merit (E. F. Sheffield, personal correspondence).

The Canadian Scholarship and Fellowship Plan follows a slightly different procedure. This plan also involves a preliminary screening in the country of the student's origin and a further screening in Canada. In this case, however, there is competition on the basis of merit, and both in the country of origin and in Canada candidates are arranged in order of merit and only the best are offered awards. In this case too, the Canadian selection committee decides which students will be accepted and then invites appropriate universities to say whether they can offer places to them. Students who come from abroad without government sponsorship are subject to only one selection procedure, the procedure adopted by the university to which his application is made.

In mid 1963 the Canadian Universities Foundation established a service to universities for the interpretation of academic documents. According to Dr. E. F. Sheffield, Director of Research, the service provides for the interpretation of academic documents together with a description of the educational system in which the student has done his work, giving details as to levels, grading systems, and such data as is likely to be helpful to an Admissions Committee in making its assessment.

The selection procedures followed by the Canadian University Service Overseas program in placing students abroad is not too dissimilar. In this first instance, local committees located at forty-four universities and colleges across Canada interpret to volunteers the program as a whole and explain special problems in various developing countries. These committees interview and screen applicants, giving consideration to their academic record, personality, character, and health. The applicants finally recommended are then referred to representatives of the countries requesting their services. These representatives make the final decision concerning the acceptance and assignment of volunteers. Prior to undertaking actual assignments, volunteers receive orientation courses to prepare them for service overseas. An approximately similar procedure is followed by the Department of External Affairs in assigning professional personnel to teaching and supervisory basis abroad.

ADVISORS

So far as possible Canadian universities have placed their regular personnel services at the disposal of non-Canadian students, and recently have begun to appoint special advisors for them. At the University of British Columbia, Mr. John Thomas, Director of International House, serves in this capacity. International House has a varied orientation program for new arrivals on campus, and a continuing program designed to afford non-Canadian students extracurricular experiences of all kinds. More recently a research committee has been established to enter into cross-cultural studies and studies of transitional states.

TRENDS

Although the number of non-Canadian students in Canadian universities would appear to be numerous, it is only in the last decade that both private and public agencies have become more or less fully aware of the significance of this development. The Canada Council in its 1963–1964 report noted that: Asian, African, Latin American, and Slavic Studies are now of increasing concern to the Western World, and must take their place in any full-scale program of training in the Arts, Humanities and Social Sciences. The country lacks (a) departments and institutes, (b) graduate students, (c) trained teachers, (d) funds to supply (a), (b), and (c). Large sums of money must now be available for the rapid development of study and research for these ends in order that Canada may (*a*) develop among its people generally the greater knowledge and understanding of other countries that are so necessary in the world today; (*b*) train many more specialists for international service; (*c*) produce the experts who will become the teachers, members of government service, and journalists whom we urgently need; and (*d*) do its part in making the general contribution to knowledge that it ought to make. The Canada Council's recognition of Canada's responsibility in the realm of international education is a significant step forward and in sharp contrast with its position only a few years ago.

PUBLIC RESPONSE

Nevertheless, though the Canada Council, the government, and the universities recognize the increasing importance of Canada's role in international education both at home and abroad, the same is not necessarily true of many sectors of the public. All too many non-Canadian students of African and Asiatic origin find themselves unable to find satisfactory accommodations off university campuses, and all too many are subjected to discriminatory practices of one kind and another. Efforts are being made by public and private bodies to correct these practices when they do happen, and to try so far as it is possible to prevent their happening, but a much more effective publicity and educational campaign is indicated. In effect there must be a wider recognition that provides for human rights and applies to all residents in a country, and not only to its citizens.

FOREIGN STUDENT RESPONSE

A survey of student opinion concerning their stay in Canada revealed that 3,026 of 3,842 students reporting had no language difficulty; 2,917 had trouble following lectures; 2,761 had no difficulty in finding accommodation; but 2,801 encountered difficulty in making friends. Only 962 reported frequent invitations to Canadian homes, while 721 reported being hardly ever invited. Approximately half of the students travelled only in the province in which they were located, and only 548 stated that they were going to settle in Canada, showing that the largest majority were undecided as to settlement.

COSTS

In the realm of non-Canadian student expenditures the average single male undergraduate spent $1,805, while his female counterpart spent $1,665. The single male graduate spent $2,165, the female $2,091. In all cases single males and females spent less than their married counterparts. Almost two-thirds of the 544 families of married male students were in Canada, and 44% of the wives worked full time. It would appear from the foregoing that the non-Canadian student in Canadian universities is pursuing his education at a level which does not permit of many luxuries.

LENGTH OF STAY

The greatest number of students stay for a period of two years while the remainder stay anywhere from three to five years depending upon resources and performance. More specifically, 36.9% of students expect to graduate in one year, 39.4% in two years, 16.9% in 3 years, and 1.5% in 4 years. These expectancies are apparently realistic.

BILINGUALISM

Inasmuch as Canada is a bilingual country with possibilities for non-Canadian students to elect a French-language college or university, it is interesting to note the distribution of students across Canada by region since this enables an approximation: What has to be taken into account is that though Quebec has a majority of French-language institutions, McGill and Bishops, for example, provide English language instruction. It should be noted that there is a Canadian program of educational assistance for the French-speaking states of Africa, Cameroun, Congo Brazzaville, Mali, and Togo, most of the personnel being drawn from the province of Quebec. A natural consequence of this is the university intake of students from these lands. In July, 1964 the Canada Council announced that thirty senior French-speaking students, scholars, researchers, lecturers, and artists from France, Belgium, and Switzerland would be the recipients of new Canadian Government scholarships and fellowships designed to do for French-speaking countries what the Commonwealth scholarship scheme had done for English-speaking ones. A total of $250,000 has been earmarked for the 1964–1965 fiscal year for this new program.

THE CANADIAN CLIMATE

A further measure of the educational climate emerging in Canada with respect to accommodating foreign students is to be noted in Prime Minister Lester Pearson's announcement at the Commonwealth Conference that the Canadian delegation would place itself firmly beside the Africans and Asians in the struggle to bring about African majority rule in Southern Rhodesia. At the same time Pearson offered a crash program of education and specialized training for black Southern Rhodesians for roles in government. Yet, while it is true that

Canada has increased its external aid estimates from $50 million in 1963, to $75 million in 1964, only a small portion of which has been going into education at home and abroad, there has been a change of view and according to John Walker of the Province Ottawa Bureau News services, Canadian Aid Officials have discovered, as have the Americans and the Russians, that gaudy dams and power stations are of little help unless the people who run them are educated enough to do so. Hence, Canada is emphasizing student exchanges, help for CUSO, technical studies, school buildings, and similar projects. In this connection it may be well to note that the University Affairs Bulletin of April, 1963 reported that the Canadian Universities Foundation had entered into an agreement with the African students foundation to establish a final selection committee for AFS-sponsored students. According to this announcement the CUF will attempt to find up to fifty free tuition places in Canadian universities for African students beginning in the 1964–1965 academic session. These places are to continue for three to four years until the candidate receives his first degree.

FEEDBACK

In still another connection, W. T. Ross Flemington, Director of Education in the External Aid Office in Ottawa, reported that there were, in 1964, a total of 160 secondary school teachers from Canada in developing countries. Of these, about a hundred were in Africa, the rest in East Africa, the Caribbean, Hong Kong, British Honduras, and British Guiana. In addition, there were in the same year twenty-seven university professors abroad. With increasing frequency, numbers of teachers have mentioned in their reports the desirability of some of their students receiving further education in Canada. It would appear to be a developing trend, and a desirable one, to have teachers in service abroad identify those students in their homelands worthy of further education.

CONCLUSION

This examination of the nature and scope of government policy in International Education in Canada, though brief and selective, nonetheless indicates that Canada has recognized through its governmental and educational institutions the increasing importance of education for peoples both at home and abroad. This recognition has developed out of a bicultural tradition and a multipolitical heritage all of which have been rooted in a healthy respect for the role of education in society at large. The Canadian ethos of imperturbability has contrib-

Table 1 *Summary of Students, from Outside Canada at Canadian Universities and Colleges, by Region in Canada and Country of Residence, 1962–1963* [a]

	Nfld.	P.E.I.	N.S.	N.B.	Quebec	Ontario	Manitoba	Sask.	Alberta	B.C.	Total
Total Canada	15	72	940	295 (1,322) (45)	2,708	2,786	518	303	225	682 (1,727) (91)	8,544
Africa	1	1	30	13 (226)	153	217	20	23	15	33	506
Asia	10	12	130	74 (59)	593	673	149	76	83	195 (371)	1,995
Europe	1	—	26	32 (806)	587	431	66	119	50	136	1,448
North America	3	56	623	124 (20)	818	1,017	41	41	55	129 (33)	2,907
South America	—	2	12	6 (14)	126	65	6	5	1	21 (22)	244
Central America and Mexico	—	—	14	— (1)	26	20	—	—	1	21 (43)	82
Oceania	—	—	—	1	14	53	1	4	5	33	111
West Indies	—	1	105	45 (151)	391	310	235	35	15	113 (398)	1,250
Canadian forces Overseas	—	—	—	—	—	—	—	—	—	1	1
Total	15	72	940	295	2,708	2,786	518	303	225	682	8,544

[a] Maritime Provinces and Western Provinces show totals in parentheses.

uted in no small measure to exercising a carefully controlled pragmatic approach to International Education consistent with its temperament and resources. It is for these and similar reasons that Canada's contributions to International Education will continue to give expression to its basic belief that peace, order, and good government are the rights of peoples everywhere, and attainable primarily through a widespread sharing of educational programs and perspectives.

CHAPTER 14

Foreign Student Exchanges: France

JACQUES POUJOL

It is not at all certain that the word "exchange" is very appropriate in the expression "foreign student exchange." Cultural values have conformed to the economic and financial vocabulary; however, to consider cultural exchanges as more or less conforming to the laws of finance and economics would be committing an enormous error. There is no stock exchange for foreign students, and in this domain it is impossible to imagine a cultural balance of exchange measuring profits, deficits, and equivalences. There exists neither loser nor winner in international education—a unique world apart, where one is enriched by giving, and where the best way to make a profit is not to practice exchange, but to offer a gift without reciprocity or hope of even indirect benefit. In opposition to practices in commerce and business, disinterest is the Golden Rule in cultural affairs.

The cultural policy of France deems most important the reception of foreign students, which is what we intend to illustrate by the statistics which follow. However, it is indispensable to note that the essential effort made by France is not aimed primarily at attracting students, but rather at forming national elites at home, in their native countries. Thirty-eight thousand, the number of foreign students, might appear a very impressive figure. What is more important, however, is the number forty thousand—indicating those French professors teaching out of their country. France is the greatest exporter of teachers in the world. One out of every eleven French persons engaged in teaching teaches abroad. This effort in personnel is supplemented by an extremely important financial effort by France in regard to her resources. It is well established that in relation to her Gross National Product,

France is the country which gives the most aid to underdeveloped nations (2.41 per cent as compared to 0.97 per cent for the United States). This effort is in great part cultural: research institutes, universities, schools, built by French workers, with French funds, and staffed by French personnel.

The philosophy behind this attitude is that it is more valuable to set up institutions of learning in countries which need them, than to import to France an elite which at all times risks being more or less lost, far from its native soil. It is commonly admitted that it is wiser and more fruitful to set up institutions in overseas nations which will be progressively taken under the charge of local governments, than to create a dangerous dependence of populations of underdeveloped nations, in relation to the institutions of learning in France. This policy has borne fruit in several countries formerly placed under French domination, even where the errors of colonialism were permitted to corrupt the results. It is true that in the past France created elites to whom she later refused to accede responsibilities which should have been theirs. But now, to a large extent everywhere, in Africa, Viet Nam, Algeria, the schools have survived the end of the French rule, and the elites in these liberated countries have remained attached to certain forms of French culture. This explains how France contracted various moral obligations in the field of education with a great number of the emerging nations.

However, these problems of international education are not new for France. The tradition of foreign students in France is as old as the universities themselves. In the Middle Ages, the Sorbonne and the other colleges of the University of Paris received students coming from all the countries of Europe, who grouped themselves in "nations" according to their origins and formed a sort of international society with Latin as the common language. This long tradition, interrupted in 1940 for five years by war, was revived in 1945, and the first foreign students to rediscover the paths of the Sorbonne were American G. I.'s who had just been introduced to the French language, literature, and culture. At the present time, there is in French universities one foreign student out of every ten students. In addition to the students of the five traditional "facultés" (Law, Science, Letters, Medicine, Pharmacy),[1] there are those who attend other institutions which in the American system are also parts of universities: the Grandes Ecoles, Engineering Schools, Technical Schools, Fine Arts Schools, Schools of Architecture, Dentistry, Agriculture, Ecoles Normales, as well as all the private institutions (Catholic schools, Alliance Française, etc.). In addition to the 23,561 students of the "facultés" who were regularly counted by government census in 1961–1962, there are approximately 10,000 additional students in higher education (who are unfortunately not tabulated). To these two groups can be added a third important contingent: that of the "stagiaires" or trainees, who do not take a full load of courses in the universities or other schools, but who, during a year or more, are initiated into a particular profession under the supervision of an organization such as ASTEF (Association pour l'Organisation des Stages dans l'Industrie Française): 4,469 engineers and specialists came from foreign countries in 1962–1963 to spend time in French industry, business, or public administration. All together a total of 38,100 foreign students studied in France during 1962–1963 (not including summer courses).

The essential characteristic of this foreign student program is that it is placed almost completely under the authority of the French government. This is no wonder, since the nineteen universities as well as the majority of other institutions of higher learning are also under the authority of the Ministry of National Education. It is thus important to specify the role played by a certain number of agencies of the French government in the recruiting, the orientation, and the control of foreign students.

1. The *Direction Générale des Affaires Culturelles et Techniques* (DGACT)—37 Quai d'Orsay and 23 rue La Pérouse, Paris 16°—which is part of the Ministry of Foreign Affairs. It is responsible for the activities of the cultural services of the various embassies, which counsel foreign students desirous of going to France, and distribute scholarships for university study as well as for traineeships.

2. *Direction de la Coopération avec la Communauté et l'Etranger* (DCCE)—55 rue St. Dominique, Paris 7°—part of the Ministry of National Education, which handles the following: administration of international cultural agreements and university exchanges; administration of the training periods for foreign professors and students in the teaching of French; organization of French courses for foreign students. At the same time, the DCCE controls the following organizations: *Bureau d'Etude et de Liaison pour l'Enseignement du Français dans le Monde*—9 rue Lhomond, Paris 5°, *Centre International des Etudes Pédagogiques à Sèvres,* and *Centre de Recherches pour l'Enseignement de la Civilisation*—both at 1 rue Léon Journault, Sèvres, S. et O, *Centre de Recherche et d'Etude pour la Diffusion du Français*—6 rue de Tournon, Paris 6°.

3. The *Service de Coopération Technique* of the Ministry of Finances and Economic Affairs—administers, through the intermediary

of ASTEF (4 rue Foucault, Paris 16°), traineeships in France for recipients of scholarships from "Technical Cooperation"; assigns scholarships to cover periods of study in France for candidates presented by commercial counselors of French Embassies in countries which have bilateral accords with France on technical cooperation.

For students from certain countries, there exist special services, such as the following:

4. *Service de la Coopération Technique* and the *Service de la Coopération Culturelle* of the Secrétariat d'Etat in charge of Algerian Affairs (80 rue de Lille, Paris 7°)—is charged particularly with aiding Algerian students.

5. *Service de l'Enseignement et de la Formation* of the Ministry of Cooperation (20 rue Monsieur, Paris 7°)—is charged particularly with aiding students from the new republics of Africa and the Malagasy Republic.

In addition to all of the above, the following organizations devote a part of their activities to foreign students:

Direction de l'Enseignement Supérieur: 110 rue de Grenelle, Paris 7°;

Haut-Commissariat à la Jeunesse et aux Sports: 34 rue de Châteaudun, Paris 9°;

Institut Pédagogique National: 29 rue d'Ulm, Paris 5°;

Centre National des Oeuvres Universitaires et Scolaires: 69 Quai d'Orsay, Paris 7°: charged with the improvement of living conditions of both French and foreign students; this is the central agency which coordinates the action of the Services d'Accueil (welcoming and guidance services).

Services d'Accueil—When he arrives in France, the foreign student does not have to deal directly with the organizations cited above. He can, according to his particular case, make use of one of the following services:

Service de l'Accueil aux Etudiants Etrangers—6 rue Jean Calvin—coordinates the actions of regional centers; greets foreign students in the Paris region. This is where the foreign student receives his student cards, entitling him to university benefits. This service also takes charge of lodging, training periods and temporary work, placement in families, cultural activities, and contact with the population.

Services d'Accueil Spéciaus: Franco-Vietnamese Institute; *Services d'Accueil* for students from Tunisia and Morocco; Franco-American Commission for University Exchanges (for American Fulbright students—9 rue Chardin, Paris 16°).

Information centers to which foreign students may address themselves for special counseling: *Bureau Universitaire de Statistiques et de Documentation Scolaires et Professionelles*—29 rue d'Ulm, Paris 5°; *Office National des Universités*—96 Boulevard Raspail, Paris 6°; *Office National du Tourisme Universitaire*—137 Boulevard St. Michel, Paris 5°.

In addition, there are numerous student organizations which are open to foreign students, as well as hundreds of private organizations.

Finally, many of the "facultés" in Paris have organized services of guidance for foreign students in Letters, Law and Economics, Medicine and Science.

Naturally, foreign student programs are established in cooperation with the states concerned. A large number of states have signed bilateral agreements of cultural and technical cooperation or of technical and scientific cooperation with France. Certain special programs (such as those with Latin America) are negotiated with the interested governments so that the offers made by France might satisfy the economic or cultural needs of each of these countries. In many cases (as in India) it is the governments themselves which designate which students should benefit from a French government scholarship. At times it is a specialized agency (such as the Institute of International Education in the United States) which is in charge of selection of a large number of the scholarship recipients. The case of the bilateral collaboration of France with the United States is completely unique. A Franco-American commission in Paris selects the French scholars, professors, and students who will go to the United States, and controls the sojourn in France of scholars, professors, and students from America.

The problems of foreign students are sometimes negotiated with groups of states through multilateral accords. Thus the European ministries charged with education meet periodically: one of the innovations resulting from these conferences is the "carte d'identité culturelle du Conseil de l'Europe" which permits professors, men of letters, artists, and researchers to avail themselves of a certain number of advantages. The conferences of Ministers of Education from France, Africa, and the Malagasy Republic have also had a particular importance in determining the trends of cultural and technical cooperation: thus a certain uniformity in the programs of secondary education facilitates the transition to higher education. The problems of equivalences of diplomas can be discussed and corrected. In certain cases, an agreement easing entry conditions in certain "grandes écoles" or technical schools is reached. The raising of age limits, special competitive exams for admission, admission based on degrees and diplomas are also topics for discussion.

Finally, a large number of international organizations grant foreign students scholarships for study in France. The number of these awards is five times greater than it was four years ago, having now reached 982.

There exist among foreign students considerable differences in the duration of their studies:

1. Certain students come to France for their entire university education: such is the case of students from the Middle East for example, who complete *all* their medical studies in a medical faculty in France for six years until they obtain the medical-doctor's degree. This can also be the case of an African lawyer or a Vietnamese pharmacist.

2. Other foreign students come to France to complete that portion of their studies which is not offered in their home country. For example, in certain African universities only courses for the first one or two years are under way: thus a further two or three years of study will be necessary in France before a degree is obtained.

3. Certain foreign students come to France to study at the postgraduate level. In this case, they can prepare for either a Doctorat d'Etat (for exceptional students, as it requires at least five years of research), a Doctorat d'Université, or a Doctorat du Troisième Cycle (initiation to research). Often they take courses in an institution which specializes in their field, or become affiliated with a university: for example, Institut Henri Poincaré, for mathematics; Institut de Phonétique; Institut de Psychologie; and so forth. Others are attached to laboratories and might be appointed to assistantships at the French National Research Center. The length of the sojourn in France for these foreign students is in general one year, but might reach two or three.

4. One category of foreign students, whose number grows steadily, is that of young people who, either before or after having obtained a diploma in their home countries, come to France to spend a year in order to enlarge their horizons and acquire a human experience in an international context. A very large number of Americans (in particular those who participate in Junior Year Abroad Programs) belong in this category. It is these who most often take the special courses in French language and civilization given by almost all the universities of France. They are frequently accompanied by American professors who aid them in adapting to a new type of education. These programs are easily integrated in the cycle of studies of an American college, thanks to the control exercised by the organizers of Junior Year Programs over the courses taken by their students.

The statistics found at the conclusion of this paper classing foreign students by field of study are somewhat incomplete. For example, they do not show the large number of those who come to France to study Fine Arts. As has been indicated above, the students of the Grandes Ecoles, Schools of Engineering, and other technical institutions, are not on the list either, nor do they figure in the statistical totals. However, the statistics concerning foreign students enrolled in the "facultés" permit us to make the following observations:

The proportion of foreign students studying Letters and Humanities is the heaviest. This reflects a general trend in French universities. But whereas for the totality of students the proportion is only 31 per cent, it exceeds 34 per cent for foreign students. The proportion of foreign students in law and economics is normal, in relation to the proportion of French students taking these same subjects. The proportion of foreign students in medicine is slightly heavier than that of the whole student body. On the other hand, only 20 per cent of the foreign students are in the sciences, while the proportion of French students in this field exceeds 30 per cent.

Naturally these proportions vary enormously according to the home countries: students coming from countries which are highly developed technically tend to be mostly in Letters and Humanities (e.g., Germany and the United States). On the other hand, the countries which are less developed tend to send many more students in the sciences (e.g., Tunisia, Madagascar, Viet Nam, Iran, etc.).

The statistics concerning technical cooperation are useful in completing these observations on the distribution "by field" in the universities. Among the scholarships distributed, a large percentage go towards studies or traineeships in the technical and scientific domains.

No systematic study has ever been made on the successes and failures of foreign students. It is however predictable that this study would produce the same conclusions which are already known concerning French students. The university system is extremely competitive and based entirely on results achieved on yearly examinations. It is rather common for 50 per cent of the candidates for a certificate of "Licence de Lettres" to fail. A progressive selection is obtained, but this system is under severe criticism at present. One of the objects of the reform undertaken by the Ministry of Education is precisely to eliminate these very heavy losses of time and effort which are the ransom price paid under the present system. In this domain an improvement of the situation for French students will also serve the cause of foreign students. Most recent statistics show that out of 9,000 students beginning their medical studies, there are no more than 3,800 in the second year, and 3,000 in the sixth. The statistics for Law show a comparable decrease: 11,000 in the first year, 4,000 in the second, 3,000 in the third, and few more than 2,000 in the fourth year.

This very rigid and inhuman system often frightens foreign students, especially when they are used to a warmer treatment in their home countries. Although this is one of the reasons for the prestige of university studies in France, there remain great strides to be made to render the selective process more just and more effective.

If we now consider the living conditions of the foreign student in France, we will first notice that he benefits from a series of advantages which the French students enjoy as well, and in addition he has certain privileges reserved uniquely for the foreign student.

1. If he is taking the same courses as French students, the foreign student profits from an almost free education—except for minimal registration fees for courses and examinations. However, the "cours spéciaux" (French language and civilization, summer courses) must be paid for.

2. The foreign students profit from the social benefits granted to French students:

Social Security (sickness and maternity insurance): for those students coming from countries having concluded with France social security agreements. For others, there is available insurance from the National French Students' Mutuelle at only 15 francs per year.

Access to student lodging in the Cité Universitaire or in the "Foyers d'étudiants," although one must make reservations long in advance.

Access to university restaurants upon presentation of a student card —1.20 francs per meal (approximately $0.25).

Reductions in admission prices for theaters, movies, concerts, museums, and when traveling between France and their home country, a 30 per cent reduction on the railroads, and in certain cases, special reductions on planes and ships (of 15 to 25%).

3. The foreign student enjoys the same rights and is under the same obligations as the French students. He is bound by the formality of his visa (which may be obtained either upon departure from a French Consulate, or upon arrival in France at a Police Prefecture). If the foreign student desires employment, even temporarily, he must have special authorization to do so; the formalities are reduced to a minimum in the cases where the student's home country has an agreement with France for the exchange of trainees in industry, business, admin-

istration, and so forth. (N.B., the United States is not one of these countries.) Work-permits for the duration of the summer are issued without formality. Special permits are given to female foreign students who become "aides familiales."

As one can see, the French Government plays a role of primary importance in the financing and the general organization of foreign student programs. Is this control accompanied by an indoctrination and an ideological pressure? It is normal to ask oneself this question, because in certain Eastern countries, the political education of a foreign student is the fatal complement of his stay in the country. In France, the situation is completely different, because of the living and active traditions of "academic liberty" which reign in the establishments of higher learning. Religious and political indoctrination are forbidden subjects in the courses. No particular governmental line is imposed in French education: in this area foreign students study in the same atmosphere as French students. The political education of the young students who have come from every corner of France and the world is not carried on in the classrooms, but in the free ambience of discussion of the cafés of the Latin Quarter in Paris, or in the other university cities of France. All possible ideologies come to light in these cosmopolitan regions, where students of every origin meet. The official policy line followed by France is probably what is least discussed: but other ideologies are passionately debated: nationalism, pacifism, socialism, existentialism, surrealism, and so forth—with each person taking and contributing what he wants from these exchanges. When returning home, the student is sometimes converted to one cause or party: but French propaganda has not dictated his choice.

The French Government's intervention in foreign student programs is limited to the distribution of scholarships, to one or another nationality; therein resides the only real political choice. It is certain that the government and diplomats of France might have tried to attract many countries (in particular Africa and later perhaps South America) by offering a large number of scholarships. But they are not in a position to influence anyone once the student is in France, sharing in the privilege of independence of spirit enjoyed by the students of France.

In conclusion, one can state without the least doubt that in France, as elsewhere in the world, the exchanges of students are passing through a critical stage. At the present time, the foreign student in the majority of cases is the student from an underdeveloped country who has come to be educated in a country which offers institutions of higher learning and a superior intellectual level. Programs of this nature are destined to disappear progressively, as the underdeveloped countries become equipped with research laboratories and universities.

What will remain will be the exchanges which are not required by material or economic necessity; the free exchanges of students desiring to compare their education and culture with that of other countries. In this domain, the possibilities are immense. The foreign student of the future will be the man or woman who will leave his country already an educated individual, and will travel throughout the world in order to enlarge his horizons and to reassess his knowledge—discovering that there are many different paths which lead to the same truths.

NOTE

1. We must also keep in mind that the term "university"or "enseignement supérieur" (higher education) applies only to those students having received their "baccalauréat." Consequently, in the French system, the first year of "l'université" or of "enseignement supérieur" corresponds to the Junior year in an American college.

FOREIGN STUDENTS IN FRANCE: STATISTICAL NOTES

Ratio of Foreign Students to Local Students Enrolled
During 1961–1962 in the Five "Facultés"—Law, Science, Letters, Medicine, Pharmacy—there were:

Number of foreign students	23,561
Number of students in all	232,610 *
Ratio of foreign students	10.13%

Growth During Past Decade
During 1951–1952 the figures were as follows:

Number of foreign students	13,057
Number of students in all	136,942
Ratio of foreign students	9.53% †

Country of Origin
(1) During 1961–1962 the breakdown by countries of origin was as follows: (The figures below include only Foreign Students (FS) registered in French State Universities. Only countries with FS enrollment in excess of 100 are recorded.)

* N.B. In 1964 the total number of students will pass the 400,000 mark.
† From here on, the percentages of Foreign Students may decrease, even though the absolute numbers will increase.

North Africa	Algeria	4,434	Western Europe	Germany	1,563
	Morocco	1,603		Great Britain	892
	Tunisia	1,871		Greece	533
African				Spain	439
Republics	Senegal	321		Italy	446
	Mali	227		Luxembourg	312
	Ivory Coast	503		Belgium	247
	Dahomey	234		Turkey	144
	Cameroon	608		Low countries	126
	Togo	158		Portugal	123
	Congo-Brazza	145	Middle East	Iran	691
	Guinea	163		Lebanon	485
	Malagasy Republic	843		Syria	205
Rest of Africa	Congo-Léo	134		Israel	153
	Egypt	279	Asia Pacific	Vietnam	1,475
Eastern Europe	Yugoslavia	166		Cambodia	167
	Poland	161		Formosa	133
	Hungary	134		Japan	119
North America	United States	1,313	Latin America	Haiti	129
	Canada	211			

(2) During 1961–1962, 1962–1963 the breakdown by area was as follows: *

	Total Number of FS, 1962–1963	FS reg. in French Univ., 1961–1962	French Govt. Higher Educ. Scholarships, 1962–1963	Tech Co-op Scholarships, 1962–1963
Algeria, Morocco Tunisia	(11,000)	7,908	1,437 (Mor. & Tun. only)	12
African Republics	(9,800)	3,406	3,755	1,988
Rest of Africa	(800)	566	599	93
Western Europe	(6,000)	4,957	542	427
Eastern Europe	(800)	600	107	181
Middle East	(2,500)	1,612	288	377
Asia Pacific	(3,000)	2,318	572	505
North America	(2,500)	1,524	109	37
Latin America	(1,700)	653	618	849

* Figures in parentheses are estimates.

Field of Study

During 1961–1962 the figures were as follows (students from Algeria are not included in this survey):

Law * 3,927 (includes political science and economics)

* Note that the French "Faculté de Droit" includes economics and political science as well as law. The French "Faculté des Lettres et Sciences humaines" includes philosophy, psychology, geography, and sociology.

Sciences   4,472 (includes chemistry, physics, mathe-
                             matics, natural science)
Letters   7,922 (includes humanities and some of so-
                             cial science)
Medical schools   3,891
Pharmacy   519

There are considerable differences among the different nationalities regarding the various fields of study. Below are some typical examples, giving
one representative country from each area.

Country	Law	Sciences	Letters	Medicine	Pharmacy	Total
U.S.A.	43	41	1,176	51	2	1,313
Tunisia	320	550	353	563	85	1,871
Malagasy Republic	132	251	192	243	25	843
Vietnam	168	663	189	373	82	1,475
Germany	218	75	1,231	30	9	1,563
Iran	120	203	107	247	14	691

Financing and Source of Support

In 1963–1964, the French government awarded 8,027 scholarships to FS
for higher education (university students and others), and 4,469 scholarships
to trainees. A breakdown per area of those figures is given in the "Country
of Origin" table.

(1) The breakdown by field of French government scholarships granted
to FS from all countries except the African Republics, the Malagasy Republic,
and Algeria is as follows:

Higher Education Scholarships		Technical Cooperation Scholarships	
Letters and humanities	973	Technical education	858
Medicine, pharmacy, dentistry	462	Public administration	529
Sciences	426	Medicine, public health	359
Law, politics, economics	277	Sciences, research	356
Fine arts	203	Agriculture	283
		Architecture, urbanism	94
		Social welfare	95

The breakdown by field of French government scholarships granted to FS
from the following countries is as follows: Ivory Coast (784 + 287), Cameroon
(562 + 199), Malagasy Republic (379 + 355), Senegal (323 + 147), Mali
(302 + 72), Dahomey (258 + 163), Guinea (251 + 28), Upper Volta (173 +
77), Togo (156 + 36), Congo-Brazzaville (140 + 212), Gabon (118 + 78), Tchad
(113 + 68), Central African Republic (77 + 50), Niger (56 + 65), and Mauri-
tania (40 + 67). (The figures following the name of each of the above countries refer respectively to the number of Higher Education scholarships and
that of Technical Cooperation scholarships.)

(2)

Higher Education Scholarships		Technical Cooperation Scholarships	
Letters and humanities	286	I.H.E.O.M.*	501
Medicine, pharmacy, dentistry	517	A.S.E.C.N.A.†	131
Sciences	447	Finances	244
Law, politics, economics	291	Economy, statistics	79
Institutes of theology	97	Press and information	80
Grandes écoles, engineering		Teaching	204
schools	528	Agriculture	116
Preparatory to above schools	244	Technical	194
Technical, vocational schools	837	Medical and social work	84
Hygiene, social work	269	Telecommunication	114
Others	297	Others	309

* Institut des Hautes Etudes d'Outre Mer.
† Agence pour la Sécurité de la navigation aérienne en Afrique et à Madagascar.

(3) Grants from International Organizations to FS in 1962–1963 (they total 982 in 1963 as against only 167 in 1959):

U.N. Technical Assistance Program	71
International Labor Organization	130
UNESCO	176
U.N. Food and Agriculture Organization	45
World Health Organization	287
World Meteorological Organization	19
International Telecommunication Union	62
Universal Postal Union	8
International Civil Aviation Organization	1
International Atomic Energy Agency	45
Organization for Economic Cooperation Development O.E.C.D.	138

Number of Foreign Students in Various French Universities, 1961–1962

Paris	10,172	out of a total of	76,707	13.26%
Aix-Marseille	1,111	out of a total of	18,011	6.18%
Besançon	233	out of a total of	2,793	8.32%
Bordeaux	938	out of a total of	13,420	7%
Caen	484	out of a total of	7,364	6.63%
Clermont	98	out of a total of	5,251	1.88%
Dijon	299	out of a total of	4,532	6.41%
Grenoble	1,428	out of a total of	10,262	14%
Lille	451	out of a total of	12,240	3.61%
Lyon	565	out of a total of	13,781	4.12%
Montpellier	1,281	out of a total of	13,115	9.78%
Nancy	504	out of a total of	8,361	6.07%
Nantes	102	out of a total of	3,535	2.91%
Orléans	187	out of a total of	1,636	3.01%

Number of Foreign Students in Various French Universities, 1961–1962 (Cont.)

Poitiers	382	out of a total of	6,212	6.16%
Reims	69	out of a total of	1,339	5.30%
Rennes	234	out of a total of	9,159	2.59%
Strasbourg	1,116	out of a total of	10,803	10.33%
Toulouse	1,077	out of a total of	14,089	7.64%

French Students Going Abroad
(1) With French Government Scholarships, 1963:

By country   Total: 180   By field

United States	82	Engineers
Italy	24	Language and literature
U.S.S.R.	16	Artists
Great Britain	13	Law and economics
Other Countries	45	Medicine

(2) With Foreign Government Scholarships:

Germany	142
Italy	82
U.S.A.	50
Poland	21

(3) Fulbright Exchange Program, 1964–1965. French FS and scholars in U.S.A.:

Research scholars	27	One-way teachers	20
Visiting lecturers	33	Students	183
Summer scholarships for French teachers of English			20

(4) Of a total of 663 French students in the U.S. in 1962–1963:

Business administration	107
Engineering	129
Humanities	197
Medical sciences	34
Physical and natural science	79
Social science	93

Financing and Source of Support
(French government contributions to the FS program)

Scholarships awarded through technical cooperation:
29.9 million F = $4 million
Scholarships awarded to university students:
12.8 million F = $2.5 million
Scholarships awarded to French students studying abroad:
3.3 million F = $0.6 million

CHAPTER 15

Foreign Student Exchanges: Germany

WIEGAND PABSCH

Throughout the Middle Ages, Germany constituted a part of the free society of the sciences and of education which encompassed all of Europe. In those all but dark days, there were practically no limits to the migration of teachers and students. The migrant scholar was almost a pattern of social life in Europe. Many a students' song still popular among German students of today depicts the life of the mendicant student who traveled the "via latina" of monasteries, churches, and parishes to reach a university where a famous scholar taught. German law students went to Italy to study Roman law in Bologna, Pisa, or Padua. Great philosophers at the Sorbonne or in Salamanca attracted the German academic youth during the thirteenth to the sixteenth centuries. Shakespeare's Hamlet brings us back the memory of the times when young students interested in theology went to Wittenberg, the university where Martin Luther taught, to listen to the doctrines of the reformers.

In the eighteenth and nineteenth centuries, when outstanding philosophers of the German idealism like Kant, Fichte, or Hegel taught in Koenigsberg or Berlin, many students from France, England, and the United States came to Germany. Most young men who could afford it considered it part of their general training to undertake a "Bildungsreise," in most cases to Italy, but very often to France, not so much for serious academic study, but just to get acquainted with foreign countries and foreign civilizations.

The outbreak of the First World War cut off many of the flourishing relations of German universities with institutions of learning abroad. After the war had ended, the tide of nationalism withdrew. At that time, the German Academic Exchange Service was founded, and Britain invited German students to apply for her scholarships, notably the Rhodes Scholarship of Oxford. Governments everywhere took a growing interest in the exchange programs by granting scholarships and facilitating academic research in foreign countries.

The year 1933 brought a sudden break. German students and scholars were no longer allowed to go abroad. The acquiring of foreign degrees was greatly discouraged when a law was passed in Germany which required the official acknowledgment of foreign diplomas by the Nazi Ministry of Education. In the dark years of 1933–1945, Germany made a contribution, involuntary as it was, to the internationalization of education when many eminent scholars left the country because of persecution or because the freedom of research and teaching once so deeply rooted in Germany, suddenly was severely curtailed. Many of these scholars migrated to the United States. In the fields of theology, sociology, science, law, medicine, the arts and architecture, their achievements were valuable contributions towards American scientific and cultural life. What became America's gain remains an irreparable loss for Germany which had 40 per cent of all Nobel Prize Winners before the war and today only has 6 per cent.

When the war ended, German youth was thoroughly cured from narrowminded nationalism. Even in the years of distress of 1947–1948, students—many of them former soldiers—went abroad on their own to study at other European universities. There was a thirst for the experience of living abroad mainly due to the fact that German youth had been cut off from the main current of cultural life in the rest of the world for such a long time. Foreign scholars or students, on the other hand, felt little inclination at that time for life in a country of ruins and hunger.

When Germany recovered economically, these things developed rapidly. Not only did the number of German students going abroad increase year by year, but to a growing extent, foreign students came to Germany, at first perhaps only to see what was going on, later to stay and study.

Germany perhaps never before in this century took such an active part in international education as it has done over the last fifteen or sixteen years. The reasons for this are many; they largely reflect the overall development in the Western world in the post-war period.

After the clouds of war had vanished, the international community of nations soon overcame the decomposition it had suffered during the war. Enormous technical advances, notably in the field of transport and communications, contributed to make the free world an interdependent society. The advance of all nations towards greater affluence, the war against illness and poverty, the spreading of knowledge, the command and exploitation for useful purposes of nuclear power, the preservation of peace by the strengthening of international law and order became matters of concern to all mankind, at least on this side of the Iron Curtain.

People in Germany soon realized what was going on beyond the frontiers of their country and responded to this development. In fact, there would never have been such a rapid rise in the figures of both Germans going abroad and foreigners being attracted to Germany if a basic attitude both of official authorities and the public in Germany had not facilitated this. The year 1945 ended a long period of forced seclusion in German academic life. Soon a strong desire could be felt to join again the international community of the free mind. When the Federal Republic of Germany was founded in 1949, political forces determined to integrate Germany firmly into the free world prevailed and took the lead in the country. Diplomatic relations which the war had broken were taken up again with all non-Communist countries. Germany applied for admission to the Council of Europe and was granted it. She joined NATO and founded the European Community together with five other European countries. She was admitted to UNESCO and other specialized agencies of the United Nations. The German people firmly supported this policy and used the reopening of the formerly hermetically closed frontiers to their advantage. Millions of Germans of all walks of life began to spend their vacations abroad and thereby realized that establishing relations with foreign peoples not only meant enrichment of their own life, but also was the best means to strengthen the free society of the Western world; at the same time they learned to consider it a safeguard against any relapse into dictatorship, be it Communist or other.

Those who felt responsible that nothing like the rise of nationalism after the First World War should ever happen in Germany again, thought it of paramount importance to mold the younger generation in the spirit of international understanding. They advocated programs of exchanging young people to give them an opportunity of getting acquainted with foreign countries and making friends with youth abroad. Private foundations, churches, universities, high schools, and youth associations joined the government in an endeavor to bring this about. Happily enough, these aspirations met with an equal desire in other countries where, for largely the same reasons, a need for increasing international exchanges was felt.

In the academic sphere, conditions were even more propitious. The tradition of international cooperation in research, teaching, and learning had always been firmly established in the academic life of Germany, and even in the years from 1933 to 1945, the good relations existing between scholars and universities in Germany and other countries were not totally severed, but often continued on a private basis. When the Nazi regime collapsed, they soon were revived and multiplied. The war and post-war advances in all fields of science outside Germany added a special challenge to the German scholar and student to establish relations with the academic world abroad. This factor, however, only served as a first incentive. In the years since 1945, German science has largely recovered from the setback of the twelve years of isolation. It has joined the international community of research and teaching again, both in giving and taking. In the interdependent world of today of which international education is only one aspect, Germany has found its position, and she endeavors to take her share in the advancement of human progress throughout the world.

Before starting to discuss the part the German Government has taken in promoting international education, I would like to give an outline of the constitutional framework limiting governmental activities in the cultural field. Germany is organized as a federal state in which all cultural and educational affairs are the responsibility, not of the Federal Government, but of the governments of the eleven states, the so-called "Länder." There is no central legislation in domestic educational matters.

According to Article 32 of the German Constitution, however, the Federal Government is the only authority to deal with foreign affairs. Questions of international education—as far as governments are concerned with them at all—are considered to be foreign affairs both by constitutional theory and practice which no Länder government has ever questioned. From Article 32, the Federal Government derives its authority to deal with matters of education going beyond the German borders and involving relations with foreign governments or institutions. The Federal Government is authorized to conclude international agreements affecting education and it is generally held to be equally authorized to transform them into public law—though the latter is disputed by some of the Länder. Yet, implementation of an international agreement within Germany is not left to the Federal Government but to the Länder. Logical or not, once an international agreement in this field has been concluded by the Federal Government and enacted by parliament, the Government in Bonn has no possibility whatsoever to watch over its execution. This division of power, which may have its benefits in the domestic field, proves to be an important handicap for any administrative activity of the German Federal Government in international education.

So the German Federal Government is restrained to a rather indirect role in the promotion of international education. One of its instruments in this field is the conclusion of agreements with foreign governments stipulating mutual obligations to promote the exchange of scholars and students. Cultural agreements of this type are in existence between Germany and thirteen foreign countries, among them the agreement between the German Federal Govrnment and the United States Government for conducting certain educational exchange programs of November 20, 1962, substituting the Fulbright Agreement of 1952. Such agreements provide a basis for the cooperation with foreign governments and serve as a valuable instrument for the Federal Government in its dealings with the governments of the Länder. The role of agreements for the working of an exchange program, however, should not be overestimated; its existence is by no means a prerequisite for an exchange program to be carried through.

Another perhaps even more important instrument of the Federal Government, to attend to its responsibility in international education, is financial support to agencies working in this field, be it public institutions such as the universities or private foundations. In fact, there were more than 167 million DM in the 1963 budget of the Federal Foreign Ministry directly appropriated for this purpose; another 4 million DM of the budget are earmarked for international educational institutions. In execution of the 1962 Fulbright Agreement mentioned before a yearly 4 million DM go to the joint German-American Exchange Commission for educational exchanges with the United States. The decision how and for which particular program these funds are used is largely left to the discretion of the receiving institution.

Apart from financing there are few other possibilities of the Federal Government to take part in the promotion of international education. Much of the work of the cultural division of the Federal Foreign Office and of the educational offices of our Missions abroad is instrumental in this way, for example:

1. To encourage academic institutions, scholars and students in foreign countries to enter into exchange relations with partners in Germany.
2. To inform institutions and persons in foreign countries about the exchange possibilities with Germany.
3. To act as mediators between institutions or persons in foreign countries and in Germany interested in an exchange.
4. To assist occasionally in implementing exchange programs.

The degree of direct government intervention in exchange matters naturally depends largely on conditions existing in the partner country. Where education is under the direct control of the host government, the educational staff of our Missions when acting on behalf of the German partner institution, often has to take responsibility in the implementation of an exchange program, as the host governments often prefer to deal with a government representative on the spot rather than with a private body in Germany. In countries where the state-sponsored educational system is sufficiently developed or where education is the affair of independent private institutions, there usually is not much need for a German Embassy or Consulate to intervene directly. Educational institutions often prefer to make contacts with a German partner on their own. In these cases an educational officer may restrict his activity to information, advice, or occasional assistance. In many countries there seems to be an increasing tendency of the educational institutions, both public and private, to take up direct relations with corresponding institutions in Germany without governmental interference. In the years after the war, when an exchange with Germany still involved a number of problems, the task of our Missions in initiating exchange programs was enormous. Nowadays, as cultural relations between Germany and other foreign countries are well-established, many of the exchange programs between foreign and German universities run entirely on their own, and new contacts are established every year without the authorities in both countries even noticing it. Happily enough, in many cases the number of exchanges has outgrown the possibilities of our governments to attend to them under their direct responsibilities. The intensity of the exchanges, however, increased the need for indirect, i.e., mostly financial, assistance by our governmental agencies.

This is particularly true of the exchange relations between two countries, Germany and the United States. As an exception to the rule, the Fulbright Exchange Program has to be mentioned which is carried through under a special agreement made between the two governments in 1962 by an official joint German-American Commission. Besides the Fulbright Programs there are, however, a great number of exchanges on a private basis which do not require special attention of the governmental agencies.

As we have seen, the role of the German Government in directly implementing exchange programs—much as it is limited by constitutional provisions—has still been reduced by the rapid development of direct relations between educational institutions in Germany and abroad. We are far from deploring this; we feel, on the contrary, that it shows an increased sense of responsibility of the general public for the need of international education. This is particularly encouraging in the case of Germany where in the past too much private initiative was disliked by the authorities and people consequently tended to leave things to the government. Fortunately, this attitude has changed to the better, and there is not much need any longer to stimulate interest in international exchanges nor to intervene in the implementation of such programs.

In fact, the number of public and private institutions in Germany actively engaged in international education is quite considerable. A number of them work on a nation-wide basis and promote exchanges in all institutions of learning above high school level. Some of them are devoted to the exchange of scholars, others to the exchange of students, others have programs for both. Some have the exclusive aim of promoting international education, others have a more general scope, but are active in exchange programs as well. The latter are almost innumerable; there is no institution interested in education unaware of the international implications of research, teaching, or learning. Partly, there is a useful division of programs and activities between these numerous institutions, partly there is not. I shall try to give a general outline of the more important of these institutions and their scope of activities.

Beginning with the *West German Conference of University Rectors* I present to you the most important academic body in the field of international education. The university rectors, through their elected president, represent the whole of the West German universities with the government and the academic organizations of foreign countries. They help German university teachers returning from a stay abroad to face the difficult problems arising after their return; they determine the regulations and language requirements for the admission of foreign students for full-time study at a German university; they are consulted on the recognition of foreign degrees and advise the universities in all matters concerning the foreign student.

The Bureau for the Mediation of German Scholars for Research or Teaching Abroad assists both foreign universities and German scholars to meet each other; for the German scholar going abroad it gives valuable help in maintaining his rights while he is away and in finding academic employment upon his return.

The "Deutsche Forschungsgemeinschaft" (German Research Association) is another body the universities themselves founded together with some private institutions interested in the promotion of research. Its aim is to give financial support to specific research programs of German scholars both in and outside the country and to visiting foreign professors, using funds given by the Federal Government and private donors.

The *"Stifterverband fuer die deutsche Wissenschaft"* (Union of Donors for Science in Germany) is a foundation of private donors conscious of the importance of scientific progress and willing to make donations for research purposes. The funds raised go mostly to the Deutsche Forschungsgemeinschaft, but it also sponsors direct exchange programs in the field of research rather than programs for students.

The *"Deutscher Akademischer Austauschdienst"* (German Academic Exchange Service—DAAD) is entirely devoted to foreign exchange programs for both scholars and students. It was founded in 1925 by the German universities, suspended during the years 1933–1945, revived in 1950 and is perhaps the most universal body in the field of foreign exchange. It offers scholarships to both foreign scholars and students to attend German universities and to German students to study abroad, offers help to the universities in working out orientation programs for foreign students, gives financial support to study travels in Germany of academic groups from foreign countries, and acts as a mediator for foreign universities in procuring German language lecturers. It is the only organization to have representatives abroad, that is, in London, Paris, Cairo, and New Delhi.

The *"Alexander von Humboldt Foundation"* is a private organization founded in 1925 with the aim to give highly qualified scholars of foreign countries an opportunity to do special research in Germany. Its requirements are high as are the scholarships it offers; applicants must have at least two years' experience in research or university teaching. They have to submit their research programs and must be recommended by authorities in their field of research.

Once a foreign student has come to study at a German university there are the *German Students' Service* set up by the universities, and *World University Service* to offer him assistance in his daily problems.

Last but not least the forty-eight German universities and other institutions of higher education have to be mentioned, many of which carry out their own exchange programs. Almost every university has entered into a partnership with one or more foreign universities throughout the whole world. These partnerships often imply an exchange of scholars and students on a bilateral basis.

I cannot possibly mention the numerous other institutions devoted to education or international relations in general. Almost all of them are interested in educational exchanges and offer scholarships both for German and foreign students. These institutions include associations for the promotion of specific sciences or of the arts, societies interested in relations with a special country, business organizations, trade unions, religious bodies, and municipalities.

After this summary of the constitutional and institutional framework, I would now like to discuss a few characteristics of foreign educational exchange in Germany. The great complexity and diversity of the problem which has been explained in the introductory remarks, makes it difficult to make general statements. In a country where the basic philosophy of the government is not to repeat the excesses of past state control over education but to encourage private initiative wherever possible, it is not surprising to find a liberal diversity of programs and patterns.

Regulations and international agreements governing the exchange of scholars and students are few. There are the previous mentioned cultural agreements of the Federal Government with thirteen foreign countries, but they are by no means a prerequisite for exchange activities. As to other regulations, we have to bear in mind that there is no constitutional competence for the Federal Government to legislate in educational matters. The Conference of the Ministers of Cultural Affairs of the Länder has, however, acted as a substitute by setting up some basic rules binding on the universities. These rules govern the admission of a foreign student to a German university, but do not interfere with the granting of scholarships; in the exchange of scholars there is complete liberty.

These regulations provide that a foreign student who wants to be admitted for full-time study at a German university has to have a "leaving certificate" of an institution of secondary education of his home country entitling him to study at a university in his country and equivalent to the German "maturity certificate"; secondly, he has to prove a working knowledge of the German language. If a student does not fulfill the first requirement he will have either to pass a special examination or will have to attend at least a one year's course at a college specially founded to help foreign students acquire the admission standard. If knowledge of German is not satisfactory the student may take classes at one of the language schools of the "Goethe-Institut," an institution for the promotion of the German language.

Regulations other than those mentioned before do not exist, and where there is no legal provision there is liberty. The only possibility of the Government exercising a certain guiding influence on exchange programs lies in the fact that academic institutions receive financial support from the Government. Normally, a government official is appointed to the board of these institutions. He has to see that money from public funds is not wasted; he does not interfere with the running of exchange programs and leaves it to the decision of these institutions themselves to establish guidelines for the administration of the programs they sponsor.

It is therefore difficult to speak of a "government policy" in the field of international education other than the policy of encouraging exchanges whenever possible. There are no quotas for specific countries nor does the Government try to use international exchange programs for national ends other than the purpose to contribute by such programs to the promotion of understanding between Germany and other nations.

Let us now examine the functioning of an exchange program in practice. When we speak of "programs" as organized means to promote international education, we already exclude the ever increasing number of German scholars and students going abroad and foreigners coming to Germany entirely on their own, not asking for any help of an official institution in their own country or in Germany. A German *scholar*, well known among his professional colleagues abroad, may get an offer from a foreign university to join its staff as an ordinary member. His position at the foreign university will not be much different from what it was in his own country. The same applies to a foreign scholar accepting an invitation to teach at a German university.

When a foreign *student* is interested in studying in Germany, he may go to the university of his choice, register—provided he meets the enrollment requirements—and lead the life of an ordinary native student for as long as he might wish. He does not need any specific visa, since that is not required for nationals of most Western countries. Once he is at a German university, he may, if he likes, make use of the services the universities offer to foreign students. If he prefers not to do so, his life will not be different from that of any German student. He or she will have no difficulty in making friends with German students of both sexes since all German universities work on a coeducational basis. If his knowledge of German is good enough he should be able to follow the courses and, according to his achievements, succeed or fail in getting a degree as any other German student might succeed or fail. A large number of students from abroad are "private" students, and as such, do not require any special attention, and we are encouraged by this situation. Is this a more promising sign, for the dream ultimately to become reality, that one day there will be a free academic society encompassing all scholars and students irrespective of nations?

But we have not yet reached this stage, and organized programs to encourage the exchange of scholars and students are still very much needed. Let us examine the German contribution to these endeavors.

In the field of research, three hundred scholarships are offered each year by the Alexander von Humboldt Foundation for highly qualified scholars irrespective of sex, race, or religion. There are no quotas as to countries or field of research. The grantee is free to choose the university and professor he wants to associate with. Applications have to be submitted directly to the Foundation which decides on its own responsibility. If a scholarship is granted, the grantee is paid his transportation expenses to Germany; he receives DM 1,100 a month plus an additional DM 180 if he is married. He may take free language courses for several months if his knowledge of German is not satisfactory. While he is in Germany, he may receive additional grants for traveling in connection with his research subject, for attendance at scientific conventions, and the like. There are special tutorial programs run by the Foundation to help him become acquainted with cultural and social life in Germany.

The German Academic Exchange Service (DAAD) fosters scholar exchange programs on a mutual basis. In 1963, it initiated and gave financial support to an exchange of fifty-three German and sixty foreign scholars and gave grants for shorter periods of study to almost five hundred foreign scholars.

The foreign scholar who would like to work in Germany as well as the German scholar who would like to go abroad to do research may apply to the German Research Association for financial support to carry out his program.

The *German student* eager to study abroad may obtain one of the more than two hundred scholarships of the DAAD or a grant from a private German institution. There are also many scholarship opportunities offered by foreign governments and institutions as well as by international organizations.

The *foreign student* who would like to obtain a scholarship for a period of study in Germany may get basic information about the existing possibilities through the respective German Embassy or Consulate. In most countries, applications are to be submitted to a German Mission which will forward them to the DAAD. In the case of the United States, however, all DAAD grants are administered by the Institute of International Education in New York which selects the students to be recommended to DAAD for a grant.

Upon the recommendation of the screening agency, the selection committee of DAAD will decide; in recent years two out of three recommended applicants had a chance to be accepted. As to scholarships granted by institutions other than DAAD procedures of selection may vary.

Most student scholarships include transportation costs to and from Germany; in other cases application for a travel grant can be made, but some grantees have to pay for their own travel. Having arrived at the university, a grantee will receive his monthly grant of approximately DM 400,—. If he feels he should improve his knowledge of German, he may either register with a one-to-three months' language course of the Goethe-Institut already mentioned or follow one of the language courses most universities have specially set up for their foreign students. Recipient of a scholarship or not, a foreign student will have to face the fact that there are comparatively very few student dormitories at German universities. Though the academic bodies responsible for dormitories usually try to help foreigners by allotting to them places in student homes, the student from abroad may well have to rent a furnished room with some private landlord. To solve these and other problems of his daily life, he may find it useful to contact the Academic Service for Foreigners of his university which will give him any possible assistance.

As to the course of his studies, he may find himself rather lost in the beginning. Since Wilhelm von Humboldt had made the academic freedoms of teaching and learning the guiding line of his university reforms in 1809–1810, the German university system expects the student to draft his own schedule of study for himself. No academic authority will prescribe for him which courses or in which sequence he has to choose and how to fit the many subjects he will need for his final examination into a study time of three to four years. For a foreigner as well as for a young German student, this liberty is sometimes bewildering, but he has to cope with it. If he is reasonable enough he will ask the advice of the Academic Foreigners' Service or of one of his professors. If he is not, he might find academic life in Germany rather pleasing at first glance, but will have a cruel awakening if he ever cares to take an examination.

In this context, mention should be made of the exchange programs of the International Association for the Exchange of Students for Technical Experience (IAESTE). This program is handled on the German side by DAAD which has managed to place, in 1963, a total of 3,500 foreign students, most of them from developing countries, into various branches of German industry for practical training in the technical field. The same program has offered similar opportunities abroad to 1,200 German students. A corresponding program of the

International Association of Students of Economic and Commercial Sciences exchanged 700 foreign and German students in 1963; the equivalent Association for Students of Medicine gave 900 German and foreign students an opportunity to do practical training in clinics and medical institutions outside their own country.

Summer courses at German universities (courses in language and German culture) were attended in 1963 by 3,500 foreign students of whom 960 received a grant by DAAD. An estimated total of 14,000 German students attended summer courses abroad, of whom over 200 were given a DAAD grant.

Furthermore, the DAAD programs for study traveling of foreign students' groups should be mentioned which brought almost 5,000 foreign students to Germany last year. Many of these groups received financial support from DAAD.

Having now outlined the functioning of exchange programs let us deal now with some specific problems arising in an exchange. In the field of exchanges of scholars difficulties for a German scholar to go abroad for a limited period of time often arise from the fact that once he has left the country, he quickly loses contact with academic life at home. Whether a junior scholar receives an invitation to a chair in a German university faculty or not depends largely on the academic record he has acquired at home; legitimate or not, his recognition by scientific authorities abroad would not help him very much at home. So he is reluctant to accept an offer to go abroad because he might fall into oblivion at home once he is away, and would have to struggle hard again after his return. Scholars already established may have to fear that once they have given up their chair for a teaching period abroad, they might find it difficult to get it back upon their return. The West German Conference of University Chancellors, the Bureau for the Mediation of German Scholars for Research and Teaching Abroad, and the DAAD, however, have taken precautions to eliminate setbacks in the academic career of scholars devoting some time to study or teaching abroad.

The greater difficulties we have to face, however, do not lie in the field of exchange of scholars but of students. They arise from the great differences in the educational systems the various nations have developed in the course of their history. It is very tempting indeed to examine the historical reasons for these differences; but this would lead too deeply into analyzing the influence of the national character, the general social and economic conditions, religious convictions, and other factors in shaping the educational system of every country. In order to afford at least an idea how important these differences are let me draw a brief sketch of the educational system in Germany.

Since the reforms of Wilhelm von Humboldt, the German "Gymnasium," the institution of secondary education, aspires to introduce the pupil into the guiding principles of human life and nature, to teach him how to learn and to develop the faculties of judgement and independent thinking enabling him to study on his own and to grasp the scientific problems involved in his field of studies as soon as he starts studying at a university. Equally, since Humboldt, the university in Germany has emerged from the medieval pattern of preparatory general education in a liberal arts college leading to a bachelor's degree and of consequent advanced scientific studies leading to a master's degree. Humboldt conceived the university as an institution where research and teaching are closely combined. This concept requires the student to take an active part in scientific work right from the beginning of his studies. As a member of the free community of a university he enjoys great liberties; he is entirely free to choose his subjects of study and his professors, and he may change from one university to another as often as he likes. He can plan the course of his studies according to his preference; his presence in lectures is not controlled. Soon he may join a "Seminar," which is a working group consisting of a professor and a limited number of students dedicated to detailed studies of a specific problem. The structures of the secondary education and of the university system in Germany are clearly devised to complement each other. Since secondary education in Germany encompasses a task which is part of university training in many other educational systems, secondary education in Germany takes longer than in countries where the old system prevails; it takes nine years (after four years of elementary education). Many students from countries inspired by the Anglo-Saxon educational system, who want to register at a German university immediately after leaving high school at home, have to be told that their educational standards do not entitle them to university studies in Germany. If such a student has completed two years at a junior college in his country which is generally regarded equivalent to the nine years of high school in Germany, he may consequently be admitted to a German university; but he will often not be prepared to cope with the problems arising from the concept of academic freedom when there is nobody to tutor him, set his pace of learning and supervise his course of study. For a foreign student who is used to the rigid system of getting through term finals and amassing papers and certificates, which prevails in several countries, the difficulties the German system present to him may discourage him from doing part-time studies in Germany because he might feel he would lose time in studies that would not be counted for his degree at home.

For the German student, the difficulties arising from a different educational system in the country where he desires to study are less important. He usually adapts quickly to the necessity of following a fixed pattern of studies and therefore brings home good results. But in spite of this the disposition of German students to go abroad for part-time studies has diminished lately. There has not yet been a full explanation of this phenomenon. Some reasons may lie in the fact that the requirements for a final degree have risen greatly in recent years and that there is a growing trend among students—deplorable as I think it is—to obtain a degree as early as possible in order to finish their formal education and to take up a profession quickly. Though a German student has comparatively few tests to pass and certificates to acquire before he presents himself for the final examinations he, too, may find that going abroad for studies means loss of valuable time. Furthermore, to an increasing extent German students seem to feel that in order to get to know foreign countries, they might as well go abroad traveling during their vacations instead of studying abroad, and that studying for a degree can best be done at home.

The difficulties I mentioned are perhaps one of the main reasons why in the overall figures of students taking part in exchange programs with Germany, the number of participants from the highly civilized countries of Europe and the United States of America is rather low compared with the number of students from developing countries. As I have already mentioned, there are no quotas for students from these countries; therefore, the statistics do not reflect a policy, but a given trend. Students in highly civilized countries seem to be more tied to their native educational system; in these countries a degree from a native university is usually given higher credit than that from a foreign university so that there is little incentive to go abroad for a full-time study, and for the reasons discussed before the student often prefers not to interrupt his usual course for a part-time study abroad. Therefore, there is only a minority consisting mainly of language students or graduates interested in studying abroad to acquire a deeper knowledge of a foreign language or to do graduate studies or research.

On the other hand, a student from a developing country may find that taking a degree at a university in a highly developed country adds to his prestige at home. In many of those countries the university system is not yet developed enough to offer facilities of higher education to all who are interested in it; often such a country can satisfy its need for university-trained people only by sending large numbers of students abroad. As a result, students from developing countries seem to be more "internationally minded" in education than the students of Europe or North America. The rising numbers of African or Asian students may be explained by the fact that these students like to come to Germany because they find comparatively few difficulties in making contacts with people; furthermore, the average costs of living are still lower in Germany than they are in Britain, France, or the United States.

In closing, let me throw a brief glance at the statistics on foreign students in Germany. In 1963, there were approximately 27,500 foreign students enrolled at approximately forty-eight German universities and technical colleges, making up almost 10% of the total of students in Germany. This percentage is among the highest in the world, and even the absolute figure makes a good showing compared with nearly 70,000 foreign students in the United States during the academic year 1963–1964.

Among these 27,500 foreign students, Greeks are the largest single national group, constituting some 14%; Iranian students follow with 13%. The third largest group is made up by the students from the United States; they number almost 1,600 and constitute, together with the Canadians, roughly 6% of the total. Turks and Norwegians both constitute a percentage of over 5%. With the exception of Norway and Austria, there is no single European country which contributes more than 2% to the foreign student population of Germany. The number of French and British students in Germany is almost equal; each group constitutes 2% of the total.

A breakdown by geographic areas shows that Europe takes the lead, with 39% of all foreign students in Germany. This figure includes, of course, the 14% of Greeks and the 5% of Norwegians so that the total percentage of students from the remaining countries of Western Europe is less than 20%. The amount of students from the Near and Middle East is 32%. Students from Africa are about 8%, from North America roughly 6%, and from Latin America 5%. From the Far East there are another 5%. If from every geographic area we single out the developing countries, we will find that about 65% of all foreign students in Germany come from these countries.

Out of the 27,500 foreign students in Germany almost 10% receive a scholarship award from a German institution. Statistics, however, are only available for the about 2,000 scholarships granted or administered by DAAD. The lion's share, that is, 24%, go to European students; this percentage, however, does not correspond with the 39% the Europeans constitute of the total figure. Students from Latin America come next with 21%, a rather high amount compared with the small 5% Latin Americans constitute in the total figure of foreign students. Far Eastern students, too, had a fairly good chance to obtain a grant; 21% of the DAAD scholarships went to this group of only 5% of all foreign students. African students received 14% of the DAAD grants, Near East students 12%; North American students (United States and Canada) received a share of 8% out of the DAAD scholarship funds, a share slightly higher than their percentage of 6% of the total foreign students' population.

The survey I have presented of the German encouragement of international education could only be brief, and several important aspects of the problem have only been touched upon. I would be glad, however, if my remarks had at least conveyed the feeling that the German Government as well as private educational bodies in Germany make every possible effort to strengthen the ties which have so happily developed between our country and many other nations in the educational field after the Second World War. The challenges this nuclear age presents to the academic world of research, teaching, and learning are indeed great; the response can no longer be given by isolated nations alone. In many fields of science the tasks lying before us require forces and resources which surpass the possibilities of a single nation, and particularly we Europeans are fully aware of this. We are therefore prepared to cooperate. Our universities are open to all who want to use them to increase their knowledge, and we send our scholars and students abroad to take advantage of the high standards of science in the universities of other nations. We are proud of the relatively large numbers of foreign students who select German universities for their studies, and of the equally great numbers of German students who choose the adventure of studying abroad. We are convinced that by encouraging the exchange of scholars and students of all nations we contribute not only to the progress of mankind but to the spreading of freedom and to the preservation of peace.

CHAPTER 16

Modernization as Affected by Governmental and International Educational Influences: Japan

DONALD K. ADAMS and ROBERT BJORK

As interest has mounted in the underdeveloped areas around the world during the last few years, increasing attention has been focused on Japan's peculiar position. Japan is the only Asian nation excepting such European-settled areas as Australia and New Zealand that does not easily fit into the underdeveloped classification. Although the per capita income of Japan in 1964 fell well below that of the most advanced European and North American nations, it is exceeded by no Asian or middle African nation and by only six countries of Latin America.

Thus the intriguing question is raised. Why should Japan almost alone among the non-Western nations be able to break out of traditional ways and turn to new modes of living? Why did the Japanese leaders during the latter part of the nineteenth century—at the same time that Japan's neighbors, China and Korea, were attempting to shore up their nations against subversive modern influences—reach out to pluck the fruits of Western technology, military science, and education? And how was it possible for the Japanese people to accept so readily the personal and social consequences of new modes of production, new occupations, and a new education? Was modernization affected by foreign educational influences or through Japanese governmental initiatives?

The version of Japan's modernization popular in America, at least until recent years, depicts the startling effect of the arrival of Perry's black warships on the shores of Japan in 1853. After Perry had forced the feudal leaders of Japan to abandon their policy of seclusion and enter into intercourse with the advanced Western nations, so the story goes, the fruits of acquired modern knowledge ushered in a period of rapid modernization. More recently, however, economic and social historians searching for the roots of Japanese development have focused their attention on the Tokugawa Shogunate (1603–1868) as well as the early Meiji Period (1868–1912).

One observer, the economist E. E. Hagen, pushes the beginnings of Japan's period of change and progress even further back into history. Hagen argues that many of the manifestations of modernization found during the Tokugawa period, were but the natural result of personality transformation begun as early as 600 A.D. To Hagen personality is the chief causal factor for social and economic change. In his words:

> I suggest, therefore, that change in personality is typically the first step in the sequence leading to urbanization, increased media participation, increased literacy and further change in personality, and that the urbanization and communication aspects of the sequence are steps in the process of change but not its point of departure.[1]

A somewhat oversimplified synopsis of Hagen's story of Japan's modernization runs as follows: Since the early centuries, after the birth of Christ, the nature of Japanese social structure and culture promoted a sense of inadequacy during the late infancy of the child. This sense of inadequacy and its associated sense of shame was repeated century after century through a similar childhood environment. This sense of inadequacy when coupled with the accompanying pain and anxiety created "need dominance" and "need aggression," and one form of authoritarian personality was thus formed.

The "need submission-dominance" in Japanese personality greatly assisted in the formation and perpetuation of a hierarchical power structure. Not until the Heian period (710–1185), with the appearance of one form of Buddhism, did the belief in a social hierarchy begin to be questioned. Japanese Buddhist monks in the tenth century began teaching the doctrine of individual salvation through prayer, thus giving the individual increased stature and lessening his need to seek security within the hierarchical structure. Interestingly enough, Hagen does not view the Japanese concept of a debt to superiors as conflicting with a growing awareness of the individual. On the contrary he suggests that the obligation one owed to family, lord, and nation could not have arisen unless the individual had been conceived as having value as an individual.

The traditional order was further undermined during the period extending from the twelfth to the seventeenth century by the appearance of Zen Buddhism which emphasized the virtue of bravery and loyalty and the value of meditation (or rather freeing the mind from all thought) as a means of gaining insight. Two other important changes during this "feudal" period were: (1) an emergence of a greater awareness of the common people by those of higher status, and (2) a further nationalization of the Japanese religion.

The culmination of the increased worth and freedom of the individual, the blurring of status lines, and the introduction of a faith based on individual salvation was the initiation of economic and technological change during the Ashikaga period (1333–1568).

The breakdown of the traditional Japanese society, then, according to Hagen, began in the Heian period. The manifestations of the Hagen formula—withdrawal of status respect—retreatism—alienation from traditional values—increased productivity and technological progress, while noticeable from the twelfth century onward, reached their peak during the Tokugawa period. During the eighteenth and nineteenth centuries, two groups particularly, the wealthy peasants and lower samurai, sought through education to regain their lost power and status. Seeking new knowledge and a new route to power represented a rejection of old values and, because of the nature of this new knowledge, it led to the possibility for developing modern institutions.

Most students of Japan's economic development—not so concerned as Hagen with the role of personality change as the key to economic and social progress—limit their attention to the Tokugawa period. Levy,[2] for example, takes as the "initial stage" (the stage of a social system from which change takes place) in Japan's development, the reign of the Shogun Dyemitsu (1623–1651). For the student interested in the possible contributions of formal education to Japan's modernization, Levy's base line seems more appropriate. Though neither Levy nor Hagen mention the school as a contributing factor—indeed Hagen makes no mention of the role of education in his theory of social change—the virtual absence of organized schooling on any sizeable scale prior to the seventeenth century makes the Tokugawa period an appropriate time to start for our purposes. Moreover, some segments of the Japanese people had undergone a personality transformation, as Hagen suggests, by all the usual criteria applied, and the Japan of 1600 A.D. represented a traditional society.

THE HISTORICAL AND EDUCATIONAL SETTING

The Tokugawa Shogunate, established in 1603, has been identified with the beginning of the Japanese *universal state*. Under the military leaders of the Tokugawa clan unification and some two hundred and fifty relatively peaceful years were brought to a people who had been besieged by feudal strife for several centuries. But this was a period not only of tranquility but of orthodoxy as well, for the Tokugawa vigorously sought to spread an acceptable ideology, namely that of Neo-Confucianism, while prohibiting the entrance of Western ideas and peoples.

Under the highly centralized Tokugawa rule the emperor was allowed to keep his court but lived in splendid isolation, performing little more than ceremonial functions. That part of Japan not under the direct control of the Tokugawa was ruled by feudal lords known as daimyos who were allowed considerable autonomy in matters of primary concern to their fiefs but who owed ultimate allegiance to the Shogunate. Indeed, each daimyo was required to spend part of his time in the capital city and upon departure for his estate to leave part of his family behind, presumably as hostages. Yet, as long as the actions of the daimyo did not threaten the Tokugawa Shogunate, he could expect a free rein.

The Tokugawa society was rigidly stratified. During the early part of Tokugawa rule there were four separate social orders to be found within the population: the soldier, the artisan, the peasant, and the merchant. The daimyo and the upper class samurai (knights-in-arms) lived apart from the others and for all practicable purposes were inaccessible to the lower classes. The feudal lords and their retainers depended on the crops grown by the peasants for their income, and in turn the artisans and the merchants sold their wares to the lords. National unity was promoted by direct or indirect obligations to the ruling clan, and by a common racial and cultural heritage communicated to the people through familial education or by drama and edict. The unity of the "extended family" resulted from a strong binding force of filial piety which dictated the responsibilities and authority of each family member.

Social status in the early Tokugawa period was ascribed, and individuals fitted into their class on the basis of heredity rather than on achievement. Social, as well as economic, behavior was tied to kinship or to class and the family was the primary unit of social organization; although it was not always the recipient of the first obligation of loyalty. In Japan, unlike China, obligation to one's code or lord might well supersede familial loyalties.

But Tokugawa social structure was not quite so rigid as it might seem at first glance. Although the Shogunate gave detailed orders encompassing the behavior, dress, rituals, courtesies, and obligations of all people, on occasions allowances were made for excellence, and some mobility took place within the several classes. Ideally, one was expected to be born into and die in the same social position held by one's parents; yet exceptions to the ideal are important. A competent young samurai might be adopted by a daimyo and even replace the daimyo's eldest son in the line of succession and inheritance. Once elevated to that position, the adopted son was cut off entirely from former family and friends.

Nor did the relative lack of mobility between social classes act entirely to thwart development. The merchants who found higher status closed to them, were forced to concentrate their efforts on improving their wealth and security within their own class. The growth in power of the merchants, who became not only traders but all types of entrepreneurs, coincided with the disintegration of the old regime.

Iyeyasu, the first Tokugawa Shogun, was a scholar, and took a keen interest in the status of culture and learning in Japan. He urged his descendants to follow the golden rule: "Human happiness may naturally be found in learning, and should be sought therein." [3] There were four specific measures undertaken by Iyeyasu to foster learning:

. . . (1) investigation of old books and documents, (2) employment of learned men, (3) establishment of schools, (4) and publication of books.[4]

The ban on the importation of foreign books was temporarily lifted under the eighth Shogun, Yoshimune (1684–1751). Although this breech in the seclusion of Japan was later filled by the isolationist policies of the ninth Shogun, Western learning continued to seep into Japan through the small port and trading facilities the Dutch were allowed to maintain at Nagasaki. The international implications of the continued infiltration of "Dutch learning" will be considered later.

Yet, the formal learning, promoted during the first half of the Tokugawa Period can hardly be said to have been oriented towards the fostering of economic and social change. The educational institutions which were controlled directly by the Shogunate existed largely for advanced classical studies of Chinese learning or, more rarely, Japanese learning. The han or clan schools were established by the daimyo for the samurai and their curriculum consisted of the Chinese Classics and military arts. These schools were not numerous, however, in the early Tokugawa period, and not until the latter part of the period was a sizeable portion of the formal educational facilities extended to other than families of the ruling clan.

For the younger children, aged seven to thirteen, of lower class Bushi, merchants, and peasants, there existed the *Terakoya* schools.

The curricula of these schools included: caligraphy, reading, letter-writing, arithmetic, and etiquette. The lessons varied somewhat according to the future calling of the children, as determined by the parents' occupation, and an attempt was made to provide practical studies. The relationship between teacher and student frequently resembled that between father and son, and stories of the warm and lasting friendships which developed in these schools are legion. Accurate statistics on the enrollments of the Terakoya are not available. It is unlikely, however, that in the first half of the Tokugawa period more than a small percentage of school-age children received any formal schooling.

The Genroku era (1688–1703) is sometimes considered the turning point in the Tokugawa Period. The rise of Genroku culture reflects the growing commercial development and the creation of a "townsman" tradition. Growing wealth fostered opportunities for cultural growth, and experimentation among the bourgeois society and the life of the townsman took on a degree of social freedom unknown in rural life. The flamboyance, luxury and even dissoluteness of new urban living patterns contrasted sharply with the frugality, restraint, and discipline practiced by the samurai. Consider for example the difference between the spartan heroes in traditional Tokugawa literature and the hero of the very popular Genroku novel, *The Man Who Spent His Life in Love-Making*. By the turn of the eighteenth century literacy among the urban population was fairly widespread, and knowledge of the new culture penetrated Tokugawan society to a considerable extent, even converting some of the samurai.

But the breakdown of feudal society and the creation of a new value system did not depend entirely, nor even primarily, on Genroku culture. New religious and social thinkers were appearing on the scene, and their views were being heard. Ishida Baigan (1685–1744) founded a movement called the *Shingaku* which propounded, among other things, a defense of the merchant class and justified the accumulation of wealth. Further comment on the Shingaku will be made later.

Moreover, the displacement of Buddhism by Confucianism was, as Sansom points out, the triumph of the practical ethic over abstract speculation, or even over the kind of resignation implicit in Buddhism. The Confucian canon of traditional knowledge had thwarted innovation in the Chinese society and produced a highly conservative class of scholar-officials. Nevertheless, although heterodox schools of learning were prohibited, the doctrines of Confucius played a somewhat different role in Japan. Neo-Confucianism placed emphasis upon the legitimacy of the Emperor and thus cast the Tokugawa in the role of usurpers. This emphasis was made most apparent upon the appearance of *The History of Great Japan* produced by the Mito branch of the Tokugawa family; and though this history was the product of Neo-Confucian scholars, it stressed patriotism, nationalism, and Japanese literature.

Borton, Bellah, and Lombard [5] are in agreement concerning the undoubted influence of the Mito school on generations of teachers, and in turn upon those who became the leaders of the *Meiji Restoration* and later industrialization. The teachings of the Mito school seemed to combine Confucian philosophy, the historic findings of its research scholars, and Shinto beliefs. So important a figure as, for example, Yoshida Shoin was influenced by the Mito school, and spread its ideas widely among the young samurai. The particularly strong hold which these ideas took in western Japan in the 1850's might be interpreted as a cause for the country's early industrial development.

The work of one Japanese, Kaibara Ekken (1630–1714), illustrates the consequences of following the nationalistic tendencies of the Neo-Confucian movement to their ultimate limit. Kaibara, through his popular writings, perhaps more than any other Japanese, brought Confucian ethics into the homes of the average Japanese. He did not limit himself to humanistic studies, but also carried out extensive biological research. While not a modern scientific thinker like the "Dutch" scholars of eighteenth century Japan, Kaibara's belief that man cannot be understood without understanding nature was a significant step toward broadening Confucian studies beyond the literary classics.

While the Confucian school of learning had prominence and official backing well into the nineteenth century, certain important dissenting schools also existed. Those of major prominence were the Wang-Yangming (Oyomei) School, the Kogaku-ha or Classical School, and the Setchu Gakuha or Eclectic School. The Wang-Yangming School was devoted to the teachings of the Chinese philosopher from whom it received its name. The Classical School set itself to the task of purifying Confucian learning by cleansing it of Buddhist influences. Thus, this school was often at odds with the Chu Hsi School of Sung Confucianism. The Eclectic School, as its name implies, sought to establish a perfect system by incorporating campatable elements from all philosophic schools.

The Wang-Yangming School in particular, with its emphasis on the unity of knowledge and action, supplied several pioneers of change and leaders of the new movement toward modernization and westernization. This school held that self-knowledge was the highest goal of learning and rejected the intellectualism and, indeed, the authority of the standard Confucian works and urged instead introspection and self study. The Wang-Yangming School, which emphasized deeds over words, represented a sharp break with traditionalism and, as might be expected, drew to it and nourished some of the more vigorous Japanese minds; often men with reforming, if not revolutionary, ideas were to be found within its ranks.

The latter part of the Tokugawa period saw many significant economic, social, and ideological changes. The top-heavy social structure with an increasing number of families in the leisure, or semileisured, classes put inordinate pressures on the farmer. Taxes increased to the level where the farmer was unable to even profit from a good harvest. Merchants through manipulation of rice prices increased the likelihood of the farmer starting down the one-way path of indebtedness. The daimyo, for his part, contracted further financial obligations to the merchants and in turn sought to wring an even greater output from the farmers. The inevitable result from this continued pressure led to several bloody peasant uprisings in the late eighteenth century. The government's reaction to the worsening economic situation was to urge thrift and frugality on all classes. The government did not limit itself to exhortation, however, and encouraged the opening of new rice fields, the cultivation of new crops, and even provided professional advice to the farmer. The samurai and daimyo, although generally respecting the call to frugality, at times had to move outside the exclusive agricultural economy to support themselves. Some fiefs began to establish small textile and wine industries. But half measures were not enough, and whereas seventeenth century Japan had been relatively prosperous, eighteenth century Japan became increasingly beset with economic difficulties.

Prestige resided with the daimyo and their samurai, but with the purse strings being held by the merchants, and human nature being what it is, certain compromises were made. Envious of the townsman, some samurai forgot their knightly oaths and emulated entrepreneurial pursuits and the carefree ways of the merchant class. The commoners, for their part, aspired to samurai titles and privileges, and were not above paying for them. Further, the habit, so popular in much of western history, of exchanging the daughter of a wealthy family for a titled but penniless son-in-law became common.

The increased impoverishment of the samurai made them beholden to the merchant class, and increased the actual and potential power of the merchants. Yet, as has been mentioned, the merchants were not the most important leaders of the change that ushered in the

Meiji era, although it might be argued that they were influential in modifying the common attitudes toward entrepreneurial activities. It was not until the Meiji period, however, that the merchants received wide recognition for their role as a vital means for promoting national goals.

It should be added that some of the Tokugawa Shoguns understood the political expedience of assisting in every way possible the establishment of the samurai as responsible members of the emerging society. By the end of the Tokugawa period, the once functionless samurai had become active in the government and police and had formed the core of a newly emergent business class.

VARIABLES CONTRIBUTING TO CHANGE

What is frequently overlooked or played down in generalized statements regarding Tokugawa Japan, is that several distinct traditions existed throughout the entire period. Each class in the highly stratified society had its own well defined and religiously prescribed tastes and customs. But there are ways of classifying the cultural traditions other than by social class. Since cultural preferences varied not only on the basis of class origin, but also were related to the degree of urbanism of the family, it has been suggested that three separate traditions pertinent to the development of Japan can be identified. These are: (1) the village tradition, (2) the elite tradition, and (3) the townsman tradition.[6]

It was in the village tradition that conservatism and traditionalism were most pronounced. The patriarchal family system, the paternalistic nature of the village power structure, and the deep seated superstitions were all characteristic of this tradition. The elite urban tradition is identified mainly by its contributions to the classic Japanese arts—the Noh, tea ceremony, and certain cultured literary forms. It has been argued, however, that contemporary Japan owes little to either of these traditions, but rather, to a substantial degree, is the product of the townsman's culture.[7]

The townsman tradition was born among the commoners of the great cities of Yedo (Tokyo), Osaka, and Kyoto, but later gathered followers in all classes. The townsman rejected the simple ways of the village folk and parodied the classical arts of the urban elites. The term *bourgeois* has even been used in the description of this way of life, for unlike the samurai who practiced rigorous "unostentatiousness," the townsman loved to make and spend money. However, during the latter part of the Tokugawa period, the pervasiveness of Neo-Confucian morality caused even the townsman to show public con-

tempt for the value of money. The materialistic tastes and entrepreneurial spirit incorporated in the townsman tradition spurred
rapid economic advancement under Meiji rule. But whether these
characteristics played an important role in the downfall of the Shogunate and led to the establishment of the Meiji government is highly
controversial. As Bellah [8] successfully argues, the revolution of 1868
was not entirely or even primarily a bourgeois revolution.

Not only was the townsman tradition an exception to the static
image usually painted of the Tokugawan culture but other exceptions
have also been discovered. Even among the landlords, a class historically noted for its resistance to social and economic change, and in
Japan associated with the conservative elements of the samurai tradition, significant steps were taken to stimulate economic growth and
industrial expansion. The village landlord valued education—as evidenced later by the large percentage of business leaders in the twentieth
century whose parents and grandparents belonged to the landlord
class—respected work, and sought personal and family achievement.[9]

The landlords were often guided by samurai ideals and even affected
many of the knightly tastes and discipline. Yet, it has been suggested
by a minority of students of Japanese history that all of the ideals
of the samurai were not necessarily antithetical to economic progress.
The emphasis on hard work, the purifying nature of frugality, and
the sense of duty to parents, emperor, and nation bear resemblance
to the "Protestant Ethic" frequently discussed as a significant motivat-
ing force for industrial development in the West.

One of the most unique hypotheses concerning the ingredients fostering development in Japan has been proposed by Levy [10] in a comparison of the conditions of modernization in China and Japan. Levy
defines individualism as "the manner and basis on which a person
makes and/or is expected to make decisions affecting his future and
the future of others with whom he interacts." [11] Individualism is present, ". . . insofar as the person himself is the major referent of that
decision." [12] And since the achievement or maintenance of modernization involves an increasing number of complex decisions, individualism has a positive contribution to make.

There are, however, two types of individualism according to Levy
. . . "individualism by ideal" and "individualism by default." The
former implies that individualism is at least somewhat institutionalized for various activities and for persons in various social categories.
Rarely is individualism by ideal widespread throughout a society;
however, in certain of the highly developed societies (according to

Max Weber, those imbued with the Protestant Ethic) such a quality of independence may be expected. Individualism by default implies that the individual must make choices on the basis of his own criteria due to the absence of generalized criteria for judgment. Both types of individualism tend "to increase if not maximize the probability and/or the possibility of heterodox decisions." [13] However, only those societies where individualism by ideal is widespread "have made social change a central virtue. . . ." [14]

In contrasting the conditions in nineteenth century China with those of Japan during the same period, Levy notes the prevalence in the former of *individualism by default*. The Chinese merchants in particular, because of the social stigma attached to their occupation, were forced to accept a degree of self-reliance—at least within moral limitations of family codes and the technical limitations of bureaucratic laws. When, under the impact of new occupations and new individual freedoms, the traditional family structure began to break down, a new impetus to individualism by default was forthcoming. Without the security or stability of family values and standards, fleeting public support was given first to one radical cause, and then another.

According to Levy, the keys to the change in the early stages of Japan's modernization were the merchants and samurai. Although the merchants ideally occupied a socially marginal role as they did in China, the presence of individualism by default was less apparent in Japan. Merchants in Japan, for example, could not hope for quick profit through land speculation since the Shogunate prohibited the sale of lands. Furthermore, in contrast to the situation in China, the Japanese merchants in actuality had important ties with other elements of the national power structure. With the daimyo, who controlled the fief where he lived, the Japanese merchant owed certain allegiance and thus indirectly had responsibilities to the people as a whole. Also, the samurai and merchants found a mutual need for each other's strengths in fulfillment of their respective goals of efficiency and profit. Moreover, the merchant, because of his financial role, probably was at times used by the Shogunate as a buffer to the ambitions of the daimyo.

It may seem somewhat unusual to stress any kind of individualism in a discussion of Japan's development, or in China's development either; however, Levy's argument has merit. To the extent that individualism by ideal is related to the individual internalization of achievement goals, then such an ingredient was amply visible in

Tokugawa Japan. Yet, individualism presumably implies that an individual might readily follow his own goals even if these were in conflict with family or class goals. Such was not the typical case in Japan. While class and national goals could, and often did, supersede family goals, the type of rugged individualism associated with the American frontier, or even the politically organized and ideologically cohesive dissenter groups of eighteenth century England, were not characteristic of Tokugawa Japan.

E. E. Hagen [15] has suggested that five laws are operative in the process of change: (1) law of group subordination, (2) law of rejection of values, (3) law of social blockage, (4) law of group protection, and (5) law of nonalien leadership. All of those laws were found operative in late Tokugawa Japan. The groups subordinated were: Tozama hans (politically), samurai (economically), wealthy peasants (locally in social and political power), and merchants (socially). These groups rejected the status quo values of the Shogunate by seeking education—even "Dutch studies"—or in the case of the merchants, by seeking to rise above their assigned class. As an example of the third "law," merchants were prevented, by statutory law, from owning land and people could not change occupations. In Japan the subordinated groups sought to protect their own members. The whole society will only follow the deviant group if this group's values and practices are not too alien.

Hagen's fifth law suggests that the whole society will only follow the deviant group if this group's values are not too alien. Probably more attention needs to be given to the role of values in Japan's modernization. Some observers argue that if Japan had not been challenged by the West it would not have modernized; nevertheless, Japan harbored values which seemed to bulwark the process of change. The human-divine hierarchy in Japanese society is well known. The relationship between family (through ancestor worship), village (through local deities), and the whole nation (through the Emperor) to imperial ancestors is a matter of history. Individual existence resulted from the blessings of spirits and ancestors. To repay these blessings the individual had an obligation to work and, if necessary, to sacrifice himself for the group. The submergence of the individual to the group did not necessarily obstruct the diffusion of modern ideas.

First of all, because of its stress [stress of value patterns] on group coherence and group discipline it provided a relatively well organized, disciplined social structure on which a modern state could be erected rather rapidly and that modern state then was able to direct and control the energy of the society in the direction of, at least in some spheres, very rapid modernization. And, secondly, I think the structure of values provided the energy for work necessary in a modern economy by gearing the obligation of individuals to work for the group into the structure of economic life.[16]

Moreover, even the hierarchical nature of society aided development in making it possible to "exercise intense discipline and motivate a high labor output." [17] Perhaps the elements of transcendence also had historical importance in providing a backdrop for modernization. The presence of such elements "often ended up not in breaking through the traditional pattern of values but in rationalizing it, codifying it and creating the ideological basis for the famous Meiji absolutism." [18]

Probably more attention should also be given population shifts and their influence on development. It is generally recognized that a certain level of urbanization is necessary to provide for the needs of industrialization and, as Lerner [19] has demonstrated, the interrelation between literacy, urbanization, mass media, and modern styles of living. Modern society is "participant"—hence the need for literacy programs and the use of mass media. However, Lerner hypothesizes that these ingredients go hand in hand with urbanization and argues that only when 7 to 17 per cent of the population resides in cities of over 50,000 inhabitants, can literacy rates begin to rise significantly.

Detailed data on the Japanese population and the degree of urbanization is not available. No census was taken between the beginning of the Tokugawa era and 1721. Although demographers estimate that the population growth under the Tokugawas was slight (from approximately 18 million to 25 million) there is evidence that the seventeenth century and the first part of the eighteenth century saw considerable population shift from rural to urban areas. At least by the early Meiji period Japanese urbanization had reached the 7 per cent level.[20]

But this is a two-way street. Not only is a degree of urbanization needed to assist the spread of literacy, but literacy is a multiplier of knowledge, new ideas, new skills—development. Throughout the Japanese empire, for example, the number of post offices grew from 172 in 1872 to 6,563 in 1907; telephone communication between Tokyo and other Japanese cities was begun in 1888; by 1907 there were 75,229 telephone subscribers in Japan. The first newspaper appeared in Japan in 1861; by the early 1900's, 54 newspapers were published in Tokyo alone and 375 throughout the country. The total number of books published grew from 5,441 in 1877, to 27,905 in 1905.[21] This data implies an increasingly participant society and, therefore, one which exchanged "traditional" for "modern" styles of living.

EDUCATION AND SOCIO-ECONOMIC PROGRESS

Analyses of personality change, identification of entrepreneurial activities, enumeration of values supportive of change, or even parallel educational trends, and structural changes in society do not provide an adequate framework in which a fruitful examination of formal education can take place. The authors would like to utilize one theoretical model of social structure in examining the contributions of programs for formal education in preparing the way for basic changes in Japanese society and in the early stages of modernization. The authors believe that one approach to the study of modernization which appears to offer a useful scheme in which education can be fitted is associated with the name of Talcott Parsons.[22] The organizing idea behind the Parsonian approach is that every society has *system,* otherwise it would fail to hold together in the form it presently has.

According to Parsons, the first imperative for a social system is that the actors who make it up have a system of underlying values which are consistent with the fulfilling of other social imperatives. Basic commitment to societal ways must be inculcated and reinforced (when under personality strains or change in belief systems). What this means, in more pedestrian language, is that people must feel at least a minimal amount of duty to do or not do certain things, and a sense of justification in so doing or not doing. Parsons and Smelser label this imperative, "latent pattern maintenance and tension management." It is latent because it underlies the other social needs, and its existence is implied in the very fact that other imperatives of the social system are accomplished.

The second imperative for a social system is that the system evolve ways of achieving a certain degree of favorable relations to situations external to the social system. These "favorable" relations to situations are external to the social system and are goals for the social system in that society seeks to organize its relation to external factors in such a way that the stability of the social system is maximized. Put more simply, the "collectivity" must react to the resources, the geography, and other social systems in such a way that its own integrity is sustained. This need of the social system is called "goal gratification"; the social system must achieve gratification in its efforts to attain stability in terms of its relations with external factors. To accomplish gratification in its goals, internal processes within the social system must be controlled or directed. In the absence of such direction, the imperative of goal gratification for the system would be unsatisfied.

The third of the crucial needs of a social system which must be met, is the requirement of "means" which the social system can adapt in pursuing essential goals in its relations with the external situation. Thus, the production of adequate means is an imperative for the survival of any social system. To use a simple example, the social system may have to maintain its own stability by reacting to another social system in war, but only if adequate "means" war material are available, can the system attain the goal of maintaining its own stability. The goal may be to attain further resources for the social system from the external world; the capital already available to it may act as "means" which it can adapt to the aim of obtaining yet more resources. This third imperative of the social system is entitled "adaption," meaning that the social system must engender certain adaptive processes which create adequate "means" if all the other functional needs are to be met.

Fourth, in any social system, the actors and institutions which perform primarily in the fulfillment of one or another of the imperatives already mentioned, must not act in such an uncoordinated manner that internal friction within the social system becomes destructive of it. The activities of all units must be integrated so that a certain solidarity appears in their interaction. This fourth functional imperative of any social system is called "integration." It simply indicates that no social system can survive unless there is a continuous adjustment in the activities of people and organizations, in terms of one another. Too much working at "cross-purposes" will make the survival of the social system untenable.

Any specific organization of people or clusters of these organizations can be considered as having a definite relationship to each of the four social systems' imperatives. Still, in most contemporary social systems there seems to be a distinct tie between institutions and organizations and certain of the fundamental needs. In other words, some concrete organizations are almost completely oriented to one of the social imperatives and only slightly involved in the others. For example, the complex of business and industrial organizations, sometimes called "the economy," is more involved in the "adaptive" aspects of a social system than in others, such as the "goal gratification" concern.

Where does the school fit into this picture? Toward which of the functional imperatives of a social system is it most strongly oriented? Many textbooks emphasize the role of the school in inculcating values and in reinforcing them in developing personalities. Certainly this role places the school most directly in the "latent pattern maintenance and tension management" aspect of a social system. But other writers speak of educational institutions primarily in terms of their training aspect, particularly in relation to the fulfillment of economic roles. Comments are constantly made regarding the higher earnings of those who complete more schooling with the implication that they are more productive actors in the social system. This emphasis sees the role of the school located more in the "adaptive" processes of a social system. The school is, in this last view, related to the functional imperative of creating generalized "means" which allow the social system to adequately pursue the other social imperatives. Still other commentators are insistent on the school's role in creating imaginative administrators and organizers for the social system. This role would underline the school's place in the integrative needs of a social system.

The difficulty in settling on a meaningful description of the role of education in a social system is perhaps similar to the problem of placing banks as institutions in an analysis of the social matrix. The truth is that there are banks and there are banks. Small savings banks certainly belong more in the adaptive sphere of a social system, in a word, in the economy. But large central banks are probably more properly located in the goal gratification processes of a society; so, too, with schools. *Elementary schools* in most societies belong primarily in the value inculcating and tension management phase of the social system, even though they have secondary relationships with the other social imperatives. *Higher education* is more clearly associated with the integrative needs of society, and at times with the goal gratification needs, while *high schools and vocational schools* obviously have prime concerns in the field of the adaptive needs of the social system. More so than with other institutions, the schools have meaningful roles to play in all four of the social imperatives, but observation reveals that even schools relate more to one social need than to others depending on the exact kind of school one is specifying.

As a society moves toward "development" certain further assumptions may be made. One characteristic of the so-called developed countries is the clear differentiation of the fields of social action which are oriented toward fulfilling the four societal imperatives. The adaptive or economic organizations become clearly distinct from the goal gratification of "political" aspects of society. The inculcating of basic values becomes more specifically located in the family and the lower school, and these institutions have only residual direct concern in the other key functional areas. This is not to say that the values inculcated are more rigid or more fully internalized in the less developed country.

In a situation where the functional imperatives become associated with very specific and separated groups of actors, what particular peculiarities might characterize the type of underlying values which the family and lower school have a prime role in forming and supporting? Certainly the value that accepts the distribution of rewards on the basis of achievement, rather than ascription, is thought by many to be a necessary value on the part of a significant number of people in the social system. Further, dynamic change in the adaptive sphere of the social system must have a positive acceptance in the values of the society. Economic change must be accepted as a part of what is considered the "normal" and right way of things in economic production. *Such a pattern of inculcated values tends to grow to fruition in a social system where the institutions primarily associated with the goal gratification imperative make demands on the adaptive institutions which cannot be met in any adequate manner.* In such a situation the role of integration to readjust the component parts to some degree of coordination becomes particularly significant. The organizing ability of entrepreneurs, both to fit the adaptive system more to the changed demands of the policy, for more productivity in a generalized sense, and to the changed image of the consumers and workers in the pattern maintenance sphere, comes to have a determining influence on social change in the direction of a new state of social equilibrium. The innovations which the entrepreneurs undertake, if successful in recreating some degree of social equilibrium, are then made to appear virtuous, and innovation itself comes to have a positive connotation in the value system inculcated in those institutions mainly concerned with pattern maintenance.

How does formal education fit into this picture of change in the direction of economic development? Again, it is necessary to distinguish between various levels and types of formal education. The elementary school generally *will have a much more important role in the pattern maintenance aspect of a social system after the strains which create social change in the direction of economic development have created the innovations which transform the adaptive sphere of society and its relations to other social imperatives. The role of the elementary school in societies with little differentiation among institutions, in terms of the imperatives of the social system, is usually limited to mild reinforcement of the values inculcated by the family, along with some small exposure to the values of other cultures either explicitly or implicitly.* But formal education at the higher levels may have a very important role in initiating social change. Higher educational institutions generally can be considered more oriented to the social imperative of integrative need, but they also have an important role to play in the goal gratification aspects of society. The inculcating of political sensitivity and awareness of general system goals in those persons who will have prime responsibility in this regard may devolve, for a variety of reasons, on institutions of higher education.

The authors identify the period between 1850–1875 as the time of basic change in Japanese society. Accepting the assumptions made above, particular attention, then, needs to be given to the role of elementary and higher schooling during the middle or later part of the Tokugawa period (immediately prior to the time when Japanese society began to undergo basic changes), and at the end of the Tokugawa and in the early Meiji periods (the period of basic societal change).

During the Tokugawa period, many alterations in the social fabric of Japan were occurring, which were to set the stage for the basic structural changes, and which definitely began to move Japan away from its traditional social order in the period from 1850 to 1875. From 1700 to 1868, elementary schooling became increasingly prevalent, and by the end of this Tokugawa period, nearly every fief had its own fief school. However, the fief schools, devoting their full energies to memorization of elementary Confucian classics, did not, for the most part, reflect the forces which were preparing for a major shift in Japanese society. It is necessary, then, to look beyond the elementary school for any significant contributions to the preconditions of Japan's development.

One truly difficult question concerning a society in the process of modernization is to determine the degree and the manner in which education contributes to the beginnings of social change. It was argued in our earlier theoretical discussion that if dissatisfaction with old system goals occurs, and if the adaptive sphere is particularly unsuited to any alteration to new system goals, that a strain may be set up which becomes conducive to inducing a long run cycle of change to a modern equilibrium. In Japan, it is clear that among certain powerful groups there was a great deal of dissatisfaction with the old system goals by the late Tokugawa period. By way of example, Takano Choei (1804–1850), who became a learned scholar of the Dutch language and Western learning, led a group of Western oriented scholars in condemning the policy of the Shogunate in resisting the introduction of Western knowledge. One of the group of scholars associated with Takano was Katsu Rintaro, who later wrote a memorial highly critical of Japanese military organization, and proposed schools for the training of Japan's military men and diplomats in Western arts and political procedures. In his student days Katsu was under the patronage of the powerful lord of Fukuoka whose clan, like the powerful Satsuma clan, was interested in the fostering of Western learning. Western or "Dutch" learning had been seeping into Japan through Nagasaki, its only opening to the outside world since the early Tokugawa period. In 1838 a school for the study of the Dutch language was founded and the following year a school of medicine opened. By 1875 an estimated eighty physicians trained in Western medicine were practicing in Tokyo. In 1855, the "Institute for the Study of Barbarian Writings" was established to translate Western documents. This institute in the Meiji period became incorporated into Tokyo University, which has remained as the apex of the Japanese educational system down to the present day.

What role did education play in the creation of this dissatisfaction, and what aspect of education, if any, was involved? We have already pointed out the influence of Western learning on such men as Takano and Katsu. But what of the existing educational institutions? Since the turn of the eighteenth century, the only significant institution which might be identified with higher learning had been the *Shoheiko* (School of Prosperous Peace), a center of orthodox Confucian scholarship located in Tokyo, controlled completely by the Tokugawa clan, and limited to members of the clan. This institution was run in such a way that no true dissatisfaction with social system goals was communicated to the participants. To satisfy their own needs and in reaction to the monopoly of the Shoheiko, a number of feudal clans began their own higher schools. By 1850, there were two hundred and fifty such clan schools dedicated to what can be loosely called higher learning. These schools competed with the Shoheiko for the services of the most distinguished scholars and some of these schools, such as the Mito and Satsuma, emphasized, much more strongly than did the Shoheiko, Japanese history and literature. The approach to these topics stressed the role of the emperor and national destiny in opposition to the Shoheiko, which remained a center for the study of Confucian classics and was not interested in the national movements which threatened Tokugawa rule. People who attended these clan schools became progressively more discontented with the political posture of Japanese society and at the same time became more sensitive to the military and material advantages of the West. Lombard points out:

That there were men ready to lead in the restoration was due in large measure to the influence of certain schools, notably that of Mito; and that there were men ready to welcome foreign association was also due to the work of certain independent teachers whose efforts kindled the foregleams of the second great awakening.[23]

Yet another thread in the role of education in preparing the way for change is to be found in certain subtle changes which occurred in the integrative subsystem of Japanese society during the century preceding the restoration. The older pattern of integrative symbols relating to social stratification called for the relegation of merchants to the least honored position of all; obedience, poverty, and self-efface-ment were thought to be proper for merchants. By 1800, many lecture halls were filled by people listening to a new system of philosophy which, while accepting the moral and ethical principles found in Con-fucian writings, also taught that knowledge was of little use divorced from action. In addition, this philosophy rationalized a more respect-able role for the merchants in Japanese society. For these, it argued, were absolutely necessary to the economic welfare of the people and were working for the good of all. Moreover, while urging frugality and economy in personal living, this philosophy defended the right of merchants to make profit, teaching that this was as morally proper as the stipend of the samurai. This philosophy in Japanese history is known as the Shingaku movement, and was first developed by a Ishida Baigan in the early part of the eighteenth century. Thus it is generally to be argued that Japanese educational patterns in the higher levels of learning actually influenced social processes in a way that induced strain between the polity and other institutions in Japa-nese society; this strain became acute by the 1850's.

Once a basic disequilibrium in the Japanese social structure had set in, the role of the elementary school system in reinforcing trends making for further change and societal differentiation became very important. Note, for example, the following facts about Japanese ele-mentary education during the decades following the beginnings of basic social change in Japan.

1. Even the fief schools which were still in existence in the 1860's had by this time begun to offer instruction in Western scholarship for the young. (Instructors were frequently Western missionaries.)

2. During the fifth year of Meiji (1872) a proclamation was issued dividing schooling into three levels (primary, middle, and higher) and defining a scheme for compulsory education (by 1875, 35 per cent of primary-age children were in school).

3. By early Meiji the Western approach to arithmetic, hygiene, and science was becoming entrenched in the primary school curriculum.

4. Particularly in the early Meiji period Japan copied the American approach to the training of teachers, emphasizing techniques common to American normal schools (Pestalozzian progressive methods, object lessons, etc.).

5. Drawing so much from American pedagogical practices and American educational advisers, the Japanese primary schools looked very much like those in America. As one contemporary Japanese scholar disclosed:

And even the courses of study and school supplies, not to mention desks, seats, and blackboards, were imported from America. The primary school reader published by the Department of Education which was the only text-book used in our primary schools for a period of ten years was a translation of Marcus Wilson's reader.[24]

That the Japanese government expected the primary schools to play a reinforcing and diffusing role with respect to new national goals can be seen from the following:

1. One article of the Imperial Oath of Five Articles (1868) stated: "Knowledge shall be sought for throughout the world, so that the welfare of the Empire may be promoted." [25]

2. The Education Law issued by the Department of Education in 1871 stated in its preamble: "Every man only after learning diligently each according to his capacity will be able to increase his property and prosper in his business. Hence knowledge may be regarded as the capital for raising one's self; who then can do without learning? . . . It is intended that henceforth universally (without any distinction of class or sex) in a village there shall be no house without learning, and in a house no individual without learning." [26]

There is little doubt then that the Japanese leaders expected and received from the elementary schools a performance which helped internalize values among the young not inconsistent with the now rapidly changing Japanese society. A case in point was the great stress which these schools put on the importance of loyalty to the emperor, who in Japan by this time was a symbol of the new and the changing, rather than the old and the static; both school curriculum and, particularly, school ritual stressed this point. Although Japan's elementary education during this period definitely emphasized the new, the changing, and the modern, it, probably more than other modernizing societies, also insisted on symbolizing in the schools ancient and strict family discipline and tradition.

It appears that the always difficult social necessity of managing personality tensions, which becomes particularly exacerbated in times of social differentiation and modernization, was handled in Japan during this time by a rather unique ability to utilize the schools. It appears that the always difficult social necessity of managing personality tensions, which becomes particularly exacerbated in times of social differentiation and modernization, was handled in Japan during this time by a rather unique ability to utilize the schools. They both extolled the new, and at the same time taught an extraordinary amount of precepts successfully aimed at family discipline and stability. The Japanese family was certainly a rather successful moderator of personality tensions during most of the century after the restoration. Indicative of the government's view of morality, the influential 1890 Imperial Rescript on Education and earlier less famous proclamations demanded that all citizens show reverence for ancestors and filial piety. This sacred document was read daily in schools throughout Japan and stories are told of teachers losing their lives in attempting to rescue the Rescript from burning school buildings.

One part of the elementary school's role in supporting the modernization of Japanese society was the increased emphasis put on the achievement of status as an approved value, as the Meiji period wore on. Parsons has argued that the American school system today has as a prime function: the taking of a great mass of children, who in the family by the very nature of family life are generally accorded only ascribed status based on age or sex, and instilling in them the virtues and possibilities of achievement of status. This role of the American schools can be considered as absolutely necessary for the continuity of a modern society consistent with high institutional differentiation and a dynamic economic sphere. The Japanese school in the centuries before the restoration, with only a tiny proportion of the children attending, and these few chosen on the basis of ascription (usually those born to samurai estate), narrowly circumscribed even the small range of achievement which they imbued—only certain items of martial prowess and excellence in living up to parts of a code of chivalry were thought to be important to acquire. However, by the end of the nineteenth century all this had changed completely. For example, by 1900 over 90 per cent of beginning school age children were entering school, and the whole conception of the role of achievement had widened markedly. One official document directed to school personnel in the 1890's illustrates the vastly altered nature and range of the importance of achievement by this time.

The only way in which an individual can raise himself, manage his property and prosper in his business and so accomplish his career, is by cultivating his morals, improving his intellect, and becoming proficient in the arts;

the cultivation of morals and improvement of intellect and proficiency in arts cannot be attained except through learning.[27]

But what was the pattern in higher schooling during this crucial period? A number of important trends and turning points occurred in Japanese higher schooling in the decades after 1850. First, the increasing institutional differentiation in Japan during this period in which institutions became more specifically located in the various functional subsystems of society was paralleled by a great amount of qualitative differentiation within higher schooling. Vocational and technical schools tied almost completely to the economy developed in considerable numbers between 1860 and 1880. Courses of study largely prepared by foreign advisers were established to provide the new skills needed in engineering, mining, railways, shipbuilding, lighthouse operation, and new manufacturing industries. Opportunity began to be available for the education of girls at the secondary level in both general and vocational courses.

It has been suggested that the "transformation of an underdeveloped society into a developed one entails transformation of the contents of the minds of the elite who direct and of the men who man such underdeveloped society." [28] The new government—whose slogan was "the rapid promotion of industry, civilization, and enlightenment"—was very conscious of the need to develop modern institutions of higher education. In 1869 the government combined the *Shoheiko,* the *Kaiseijo* (Institute of Western Learning), and the *Igakusho* (Institute of Western Medicine). In 1877, this became the University of Tokyo which remained the only fullfledged university in Japan until 1897.

Between 1885 and 1890 faculties of engineering and agriculture were added to the existing faculties of medicine, science, literature, and law. The nature of the courses of study, the entrance requirements, and the social backgrounds of the student body all indicate the leadership role expected of Tokyo University. By 1873 the student entering this institution was required to demonstrate some competence in a modern language (usually English), and some knowledge about the modern (Western) world. During his studies at the university the student was expected to extend his learning in both of these areas.

A rather remarkable amount of attention was given to the sciences and mathematics in the new university. The study of Western medicine being well entrenched, courses in physiology, biology, and chemistry found a natural place in the curriculum. Other natural sciences and mathematics also came to form a significant part of the curriculum at the University of Tokyo. As a further indication of the scholarly interest in mathematics and the sciences, academic societies were formed to promote their study. The applied sciences were not overlooked. Courses in civil and mechanical engineering, veterinary science, mining, metallurgy, forestry, and "practical astronomy" were offered. Scientific agriculture became so respected that in 1890 a college of agriculture was added to the University of Tokyo.

In the humanities and social sciences it should be noted that during the first few decades after the restoration American, English, French, and German instructors could be found both at the university and middle school levels. Resulting from the avid interest in the West and the presence of Western instructors, there developed among young intellectuals great interest in Western literature and philosophy, Western novels, Spencerian philosophy and, later, Hegelian philosophy. In the early Meiji period the Japanese intellectual and political leaders were much taken with British empiricism, classical economics, and Spencerian utilitarianism, for in these they foresaw practical solutions to their political and economic problems.

The government Edict for Education in 1872 gave all Japanese people equal opportunity for education. Moreover, the opportunity for advanced education for all those who completed elementary schooling was officially open on the basis of academic qualifications. The following table shows the rapidity of the "democratizing" of the student body at the University of Tokyo between 1878 and 1884.[29]

Year	Peers	Ex-Warriors *	Commoners
1878	0.6	73.9	25.5
1880	0.9	73.6	25.5
1882	0.1	49.1	50.8
1884	0.2	50.2	49.6

* (Quite obviously in 1884 the ex-samurai class was still represented out of proportion to its size. One reason for this situation appears to be the greater desire for education on the part of samurai families.)

It should not be concluded that all aspects of Japanese education made a positive contribution to Japan's development. There was a continued use of a formal, literary variant of the complex Japanese language, traditional teaching techniques which frequently fostered memorization rather than analysis, and a university curriculum which gave an exceedingly large proportion of time to the study of the arts. The aim of this paper, however, is not a full accounting of the many ramifications of premodern and early modern Japanese education; it is rather to commence explorations into some of the educational stimulants to Japan's modernization and, further, to fit education into a schema or model for viewing social change.

NOTES

1. E. E. Hagen, *On the Theory of Social Change* (Homewood, Ill.: The Dorsey Press, 1962), p. 254.

2. Marion J. Levy, "Contrasting Factors in the Modernization of China and Japan," *Economic Growth: Brazil, India, Japan,* edited by Simon Kuznets, Wilbert E. Moore and Joseph J. Spengler (Durham, N.C.: Duke University Press, 1955).

3. Count Shigenobu Okuma, *Fifty Years of New Japan,* Vol. II (New York: Dutton, 1909), p. 125.

4. *Ibid.,* p. 126.

5. Frank A. Lombard, *Pre-Meiji Education in Japan* (Tokyo: Kyo Bun Kwan, 1913), p. 216; Robert Bellah, *Tokugawa Religion* (Glencoe, Ill.: The Free Press, 1957), pp. 104–105; Hugh Borton (ed.), *Japan* (Ithaca, N.Y.: Cornell University Press, 1951), pp. 272–273.

6. Robert J. Smith, "Pre-Industrial Urbanism in Japan: A Consideration of Multiple Traditions in a Feudal Society," *Economic Development and Cultural Change,* Vol. IX (October 1960), pp. 241–254.

7. *Ibid.,* p. 242.

8. Bellah, *op. cit.,* pp. 104–105.

9. Thomas C. Smith, "Landlords' Sons in the Business Elite," *Economic Development and Cultural Change,* Vol. IX (October 1960), p. 107.

10. Marion J. Levy, "Some Aspects of Individualism and the Problem of Modernization in China and Japan," *Economic Development and Cultural Change,* Vol. X (April 1962), pp. 226–240.

11. *Ibid.,* p. 226.

12. *Ibid.,* p. 227.

13. *Ibid.*

14. *Ibid.*

15. E. E. Hagen, "How Economic Growth Begins: A General Theory Applied to Japan," *Public Opinion Quarterly,* Vol. XXII (Fall 1958), pp. 373–390.

16. Robert N. Bellah, "Values of Social Change in Modern Japan," *Asian Cultural Studies,* Vol. III (October 1962), p. 33.

17. *Ibid.,* p. 41.

18. *Ibid.,* p. 40.

19. Daniel Lerner, *The Passing of Traditional Society* (Glencoe, Ill.: The Free Press, 1962).

20. Irene B. Taeuber, "Urbanization and Population Change in the Development of Japan," *Economic Development and Cultural Change,* Vol. IX (October 1960), pp. 1–28.

21. *Ibid.*

22. Talcott Parsons and Neil J. Smelser, *Economy and Society* (London: Routledge and Kegan Paul, 1956); also Talcott Parsons, *The Social System* (Glencoe, Ill.: The Free Press, 1951).

23. Lombard, *op. cit.*, p. 90.

24. Inazo Nitobe et al., *Western Influences in Modern Japan* (Chicago: University of Chicago Press, 1931), p. 36.

25. Dairoku Kikuchi, *Japanese Education* (London: J. Murray, 1909), p. 45.

26. *Ibid.*, pp. 68–69.

27. *Ibid.*, p. 68.

28. Joseph J. Spengler, "Tradition, Values and Socio-Economic Development," in *Economic Growth: Brazil, India, Japan, op. cit.*, p. 5.

29. *Japan's Growth and Education* (Tokyo, Japan: Ministry of Education, 1963), p. 34.

Government Policy and International Education: A Selected and Partially Annotated Bibliography

Compiled by **FRANKLIN PARKER**

The movement toward a world view has a long history, moving inexorably in our time through such formative efforts as the League of Nations, the United Nations, and many other international organizations. America, originally a nation of borrowers, has in recent years become an exporter in this movement of aiding the uplift of the majority of mankind. The Marshall Plan, Point Four, and the Agency for International Development are a few high American moments in this sweep toward a better future.

It was symbolically and significantly a conservative American, Wendell Willkie, whose *One World* theme marked the growing up to international maturity of most modern Americans. Why did the then-reading public flock to his book? I think it was because like him they came to see after two bitter intercontinental wars that the world is

---

Sectional co-compilers include Jack C. Willers, University of Illinois (India, U.S.A., Communist bloc, West Germany); Paul A. McWilliams, University of Connecticut (France, Turkey, Canada, Japan, Korea, Latin America); Richard R. Renner, University of Florida (Ecuador and Chile); and Josef Mestenhauser (Communist bloc). Although major bibliographic verification was done by A. Stan Rescoe, George Peabody College for Teachers, Library School, some incomplete and unverified references, particularly of foreign sources, are included for their possible value to scholars.

interdependent and organic. They came to see that the world was changing and that it must change for the better.

Part of this change is seen in irrevocable involvement by Americans in international and intercultural affairs. The international flow of students studying and traveling abroad has reached mammoth proportions. Educational missions abound. Technical aid flourishes. Cultural exchanges are common. The Peace Corps has inspired hosts of imitators. Few countries are now without long-range economic and educational improvement plans. Ordinary citizens are seeing more of the world than ever before, realizing its marvelous variety, and poignantly sensing its deeper needs. American involvement, when seen in the large, must surely be to transfer something of the benefits and practices of an open society to the broader arena of an Open World.

The bibliography that follows is concerned with the stated or implied policies, influences, and effects arising from such intercultural contacts as (1) exchanges of teachers, artists, musicians, writers, scientists, and others; (2) students studying in countries other than their own; (3) educational missions from one country to another; (4) technical and educational aid from agencies of one government to another; and (5) observations of an educational or cultural nature of private citizens traveling abroad. Some helpful items of national education and comparative education are included.

This bibliography is the composite work of several teaching and research scholars and is based mainly on periodical and other indexes. It is the voluntary labor of college and university professors wanting to share with youth and their colleagues intercultural and international educational concerns. Their reward is the hope that students and other scholars will be led to do further research on these topics, and that inevitable error, bane of bibliographers, if noted, will be forgiven.

The entries within each section of the Bibliography are set in chronological order.

UNITED STATES

Books and Pamphlets

1. Kandel, Isaac Leon. *United States Activities in Interculture Relations.* Washington: American Council on Education, Series 1, no. 23, 1945.

2. *Handbook for Counselors of Students from Abroad.* Experiment Edition. New York: The National Association of Foreign Student Advisors, 1949.

> This handbook is principally a discussion of the "why," "what," and "how" of meeting the needs and solving the problems of foreign students. It contains a directory of organizations in the U.S. concerned with these students.

3. American Council on Education. Theodore C. Blegen, Chairman. *Counseling Foreign Students.* Washington, D.C.: American Council on Education, Student Series 6, no. 15, XIV, 1950.

This publication discusses the significance, desirable direction of development, and the unresolved problems of caring for foreign students in U.S. colleges.

4. Cherrington, Ben Mark. "Why Educational Exchange?" *Report of the Conference on International Education Exchanges,* 1951, pp. 11–15.

5. Crawford, William Rex, and Margaret Van B. Cole. "Survey of Exchange of Persons: The Present Situation." New York: Social Science Research Council, January, 1952. Mimeographed.

Goals of various types of exchange programs and the patterns of administration are summarized. Some operational problems are discussed. Materials available for research and studies in progress are surveyed.

6. UNESCO. *Agreement on the Importation of Educational, Scientific and Cultural Materials; A Guide to Its Operation.* New York: Columbia University Press, 1952.

7. Committee on Friendly Relations Among Foreign Students. *The Unofficial Ambassadors.* New York: The Committee, 1953.

The annual census of students from abroad in colleges and universities of the U.S. is included.

8. Institute of International Education. *The Goals of Student Exchange.* An analysis of goals of programs for foreign students. New York: Committee on Educational Interchange Policy, 1955, 15 pp.

9. Collingwood, Charles C. "Education and American Foreign Policy." *American Association of School Administrators Official Report,* 1956, pp. 118–132.

10. "Open Doors: A Report on Five Surveys: Foreign Students; Foreign Doctors; Foreign Faculty Members in the U.S.; U.S. Students; U.S. Faculty Members Abroad, 1955–56." Institute of International Education, 1956.

11. National Association of Foreign Student Advisors. *United States and International Educational Exchanges.* National Association of Foreign Student Advisors, 1956.

12. Institute of International Education. Committee on Educational Interchange Policy. *Expanding University Enrollments and the Foreign Student.* A case for foreign students at U.S. colleges and universities. New York: The Institute, 1957, 10 pp.

13. Institute of International Education. Committee on Educational Exchange Policy. *The Foreign Student: Exchangee or Immigrant?* A discussion of the foreign student who takes up permanent residence in the United States. New York: The Institute, 1958, 17 pp.

14. Institute of International Education. Committee on Educational Interchange Policy. *Twenty Years of United States Government Programs in Cultural Relations.* New York: The Institute, 1959, 30 pp.

15. Institute of International Education. Committee on Educational Exchange Policy. *African Students in the United States.* A guide for sponsors

of student exchange programs with Africa. New York: The Institute, 1960, 30 pp.

16. Institute of International Education. Committee on Educational Interchange Policy. *College and University Program of Academic Exchange.* Suggestions for the study of exchanges of students, faculty, and short-term visitors. New York: The Institute, 1960, 36 pp.

17. U.S. Exchange Mission to the U.S.S.R. Engineers Joint Council. *The Training, Placement, and Utilization of Engineers and Technicians in the Soviet Union.* New York: The Council, 1961, 101 pp.

This report, based on visit of the Council's Exchange Mission to the U.S.S.R. in July, 1960, discusses secondary (technicum) and higher engineering education; planning of manpower requirements and placement of graduates; and continuing education and utilization of engineers and technicians. A technicum curriculum for "tool production" technician-technologist is included.

18. Weidner, Edward W. *The World Role of Universities.* New York: McGraw-Hill, 1962, 306 pp.

International programs of American universities have lacked direction. In such programs as student-abroad, student and professor exchange and research, and technical assistance and training, the author notes problems, disappointments, and weaknesses. But university participation is necessary and may become more effective through a basic change in philosophy and operation, for which he offers recommendations.

19. Committee on Educational Interchange Policy. *A Foreign Student Program for the Developing Countries During the Coming Decade.* New York: Committee on Educational Interchange Policy, 1962, 29 pp.

20. Hunnicutt, Clarence W. (ed.). *America's Emerging Role in Overseas Education.* Syracuse: Syracuse University School of Education, 1962.

21. Southern Association of Colleges and Schools. *Improving International Understanding through Binational Education.* Atlanta: Southern Association of Colleges and Schools, 1962.

22. Parsons, Algene. *International Education; A Classified Annotated List of Recent Books, Pamphlets, and Periodical Articles.* Student Personnel Methods Bulletin: Reading Guide, The Institute, 1962, 20 pp.

23. Allen, Herman R. *Open Door to Learning; The Land-Grant System Enters Its Second Century.* Urbana: University of Illinois Press, 1963, 193 pp.

Chapters on: International Affairs; University Projects Overseas; The Foreign Student, Scholar, and Trainee in the U.S.; Education of Americans for Service Overseas; Recommendations on International Affairs.

24. U.S. Advisory Commission on International Educational and Cultural Affairs. *A Beacon of Hope—The Exchange-of-Persons Program.* Washington: U.S. Advisory Commission on International Educational and Cultural Affairs, April 1963, 65 pp.

25. Brickman, William W. *Foreign Students in the United States; A Selected and Annotated Bibliography.* Princeton, New Jersey: College Entrance Examination Board, 1963, 24 pp.

26. Institute of International Education. Committee on Educational Interchange Policy. *Foreign Professors and Research Scholars at U.S. Colleges and Universities.* New York: Committee on Educational Interchange Policy, Institute of International Education, CEIP Statement, no. 17, 1963, 28 pp.

27. Institute of International Education. *IIE Services to Colleges and Universities.* New York: Institute of International Education, 1963, 19 pp.

28. Johnson, Walter. *American Studies Abroad; Progress and Difficulties in Selected Countries.* Washington: U.S. Advisory Commission on International Education and Cultural Affairs, July 1963, 66 pp.

29. International Schools Services. *New Links for Overseas Schools.* International Schools Service, III, no. 2, December 1963.

30. Gardner, John W. *A.I.D. and the Universities; Report to the Administrator of the Agency for International Development.* Washington: Agency for International Development, April 1964, 51 pp.

31. *Research in International Education; Research in Progress and Research Recently Completed, 1963–64 Survey.* New York: National Association of Foreign Student Advisors and the Institute of International Education, April 1964, 65 pp. Mimeographed.

32. Gatheru, R. Mugo. *Child of Two Worlds: A Kikuyu's Story.* New York: Frederick A. Praeger, 1964, 230 pp.

Author, an African, came to the United States to further his education. He writes an intensely moving portrait of a foreigner's involvement in a strange, new culture. His purpose was "to wrest from the white man's world the magic of higher education and to use it in order to gain independence, mental as well as political, for himself and his people." *The Manchester Guardian.*

33. Larsen, Roy E. and James M. Davis. *Report on the East-West Center, Hawaii, by the United States Advisory Commission on International Educational and Cultural Affairs.* Washington: The Commission, May 7, 1964, 43 pp. Mimeographed.

34. *Military Assistance Training Programs of the U.S. Government.* New York: Committee on Educational Interchange Policy, Institute of International Education, CEIP Statement, no. 18, 1964, 28 pp.

35. Brickman, William W. "Selected Bibliography of the History of International Relations in Higher Education." Philadelphia: University of Pennsylvania, July, 1964, 13 pp. Mimeographed.

36. *Proceedings of the Conference on International Rural Development.* Jointly Sponsored by Agency for International Development, U.S. Department of Agriculture, Association of State Universities and Land-Grant Colleges, Washington, D.C., July 27–28, 1964, 185 pp.

37. Sochor, Eugene, Rapporteur. *Teacher and Curriculum.* Report of the Conference on "American Education in a Revolutionary World" held under the Joint Sponsorship of the U.S. National Commission for UNESCO and the New York State Education Department, Washington, D.C.: U.S. National Commission for UNESCO, 1964, 76 pp.

38. Committee on the College and World Affairs. *The College and World*

Affairs. New York: The Committee on the College and World Affairs, 1964, 74 pp.

39. Bennett, John Williams, and others. *In Search of Identity; the Japanese Overseas Scholar in America and Japan.* Social Science Research Council. Committee on Cross-Cultural Education, 369 pp.

40. Johnstone, W. C., Jr. "Government Programs that Call for Cooperation with Higher Education," *Role of Colleges and Universities in International Understanding.* pp. 675–683.

41. White, G. C. "Responsibility of Education for a Workable Foreign Policy," *Postwar Problems in Business, Education and Government.* Nashville, Tenn.: Vanderbilt University, 1944. pp. 107–116.

Government Documents

42. U.S. Advisory Commission on Educational Exchange. "International Educational Exchange; United States Advisory Commission and the Program of the Department of State," *U.S. Department of State Publication* no. 3313, 1948.

43. U.S. Department of State. "Educational Exchanges Under the Fulbright Act." Publication no. 3657; International Information and Cultural Series no. 9, 1948, 14 pp.

44. "Expanded Educational Program Asked by U.S. Advisory Commission," *U.S. Department of State Bulletin,* XX (Feb. 27, 1949), 263–265.

45. U.S. Department of State. "Developing International Understanding," *U.S. Department of State Bulletin,* XX (April 10, 1949), 439–442.

46. Williams, M. H. "Our Educational and Ideological Task in Today's World," *U.S. Department of State Bulletin,* XXI (Oct. 24, 1949), 609–611.

47. Johnstone, W. C., Jr. "Exchange Programs in American Foreign Relations," *U.S. Department of State Bulletin,* XXI (Dec. 19, 1949), 925–929.

48. "United States and Iraq Sign Educational Exchange Agreement," *U.S. Department of State Bulletin,* XXV (Aug. 27, 1951), 336.

49. *Exchange Teaching Abroad Under Public Law 534, 79th Congress, Fulbright Act.* [U.S. Superintendent of Documents, Catalog no. FS 5.2: Ex 2/3.], 1953, 18 pp.

50. Riley, R. L. "Increasing International Understanding Through Educational Exchange," *U.S. Department of State Bulletin,* XXX (Feb. 1, 1954), 162–165.

51. Dulles, John Foster. Office of Information and Educational Exchange. "International Educational Exchange Program," *U.S. Department of State Bulletin,* XXX (April 5, 1954), 499–507.

In this twelfth semi-annual report of the Secretary of State to the Congress, March 22, 1954, on the International Educational Exchange Program, purposes, scope, and results of the U.S. exchange program are noted. Over 100 countries of the free world participated. Fundamental purpose of the U.S. program is to build up a receptive climate overseas as an antidote for anti-American forces.

52. Quattlebaum, Charles A. "A Report on Educational Exchange Under the Fulbright Act in 1953," *U.S. Department of State Bulletin,* XXX (June 7, 1954), 889–894.

This report on the Fulbright program discussed the status of executive agreements, the program's activities and accomplishments and a summary of the evaluation of the program. The administration was described in detail.

53. Key, D. M. "Role of Our Government in International Education Exchange," *U.S. Department of State Bulletin,* XXXII (March 7, 1955), 381–385.

54. Kalijarvi, T. V. "Teacher and Foreign Policy," *U.S. Department of State Bulletin,* XXXII (June 27, 1955), 1040–1047. Same: *Vital Speeches,* XXI (October 1, 1955), 1531–1535.

The Deputy Assistant Secretary for Foreign Affairs, speaking at State Teachers College, Fitchburg, Mass., commencement, stressed the need for more concern for international relations in the classroom. Government failure in the international exchange program and foreign relations area would stem from failure to maintain an enlightened public.

55. "Educational Exchange Under the Fulbright Act in 1954," *U.S. Department of State Bulletin,* XXXIII (Aug. 8, 1955), 232–243.

This is the eighth annual report to Congress by the Under Secretary of State, April 22, 1955, on the operation of the Department of State under Public Law 584.

Some 3,882 foreign nationals from 76 countries studied in the United States in 1954; 1,938 Americans participated abroad. Cost to U.S. Government amounted to $7,652,074 in foreign currency. Ten thousand private American citizens contributed to the program in 1954; grants from foundations, colleges, hospitals, civic and community groups totaled $4,742,000. Similar groups abroad gave $1,400,000.

56. *The International Educational Exchange Program, 1955.* [U.S. Superintendent of Documents, Catalog no. S 1.67: 46.], 1955, 56 pp.

57. U.S. Department of State, Office of Information and Educational Exchange. "How the International Educational Exchange Program Contributes to U.S. Foreign-Relations Objectives," *Education Digest,* XXIII (December 1956), 52–54.

To meet the increased need for international understanding, the U.S. Department of State cooperates with other nations in interchange of persons, knowledge, and skills; technical services; and the interchange of developments in the fields of education, the arts, and the sciences. The U.S. conducts negotiations with other countries regarding policy and procedures of exchange programs, and shares with private organizations the cost of certain exchange activities.

58. *Teaching About the United Nations in United States Educational Institutions: January 1, 1932–December 31, 1955, Report by the United States under ECOSOC Resolution 446.* XIV [U.S. Superintendent of Documents, Catalog no. FS 5.3: 955/8.], 1956, 40 pp.

59. U.S. Office of Education. Bodenman, Paul S. (Division of International Education. Office of Education). "American Cooperation with Higher Edu-

cation Abroad; a Survey of Current Programs," *U.S. Office of Education Bulletin* no. 8 (1957), 207–211.

This bulletin surveys nongovernmental programs of educational institutions and various foundations along with U.S. Government programs dealing with international educational exchange. It outlines some of the supporting congressional legislation and the program operations. Institutions in the U.S. and abroad which participate in exchange programs are listed and the type of contract under which each university works is indicated.

60. *International Educational Exchange Program: 1948–1958.* Department of State Publication no. 6710; International Information and Cultural Series no. 60, 1958.

61. *Citizen's Role in Cultural Relations, an Account of Public-Private Cooperation in the International Educational Exchange Program.* [U.S. Superintendent of Documents, Catalog no. S 1.67: 69.], 1959, 36 pp.

62. U.S. Congress, House. Committee on Government Operations. *Government Programs in International Education* (Survey and Handbook); 42nd Report by the Committee on Government Operations. House Report no. 2712, 85th Congress, 2nd Session, X, 1959, 251 pp.

63. U.S. International Cooperation Administration. "Technical Cooperation: The Dramatic Story of Helping Others to Help Themselves." Department of State Publication no. 6815; Economic Cooperation Series no. 52, 1959.

64. U.S. International Educational Exchange Service. "The Citizens' Role in Cultural Relations; An Account of Public-Private Cooperation in the International Educational Exchange Program of the Department of State." Publication no. 6854; International Information and Cultural Series no. 69, 1959, 35 pp.

65. U.S. International Educational Exchange Service. "Educational Exchange Grants." Publication no. 6789; International Information and Cultural Series no. 64, Revised Edition, 1959, 26 pp.

66. *Educational and Cultural Diplomacy.* [U.S. Superintendent of Documents, Catalog no. S 1.67: 82.], 1961, 69 pp.

67. *International Educational Exchange, a Selected Bibliography.* [U.S. Superintendent of Documents, Catalog no. FS 5.214: 14066.], 1961.

68. *Toward a National Effort in International Educational and Cultural Affairs.* [U.S. Superintendent of Documents, Catalog no. S 1.67: 78.], 1961, 82 pp.

69. *Center for Cultural and Technical Interchange Between East and West (East-West Center).* Report by Special Mission from Subcommittee on State Department Organization and Foreign Operations of Committee on Foreign Affairs Pursuant to House Resolution 60; July 30, 1962.

70. *Educational and Cultural Diplomacy.* [U.S. Superintendent of Documents, Catalog no. S 1.67: 85.], 1962, 93 pp.

71. U.S. Congress, House. Committee on Foreign Affairs. *Center for Cultural and Technical Interchange Between East and West (East-West Center).* Hearings before Subcommittee on State Department Organization and Foreign Operations, 87th Congress, Dec. 13, 1961 to Jan. 8, 1962, 364 pp.

72. U.S. Department of Health, Education, and Welfare; Office of Education. *Education for Freedom and World Understanding.* Washington: U.S. Government Printing Office, 1962, 62 pp.

A report of the working committees of the Conference on the Ideals of American Freedom and the International Dimensions of Education, March 26–28, 1962. Conference addresses: "Education for Freedom in a Free Society," by Sterling M. McMurrin; "The International Dimensions of United States Education," by Philip H. Coombs; and "America and a Free World," by Abraham Ribicoff.

73. *Communist International Youth and Student Apparatus and a Monograph Prepared for the Subcommittee to Investigate the Administration of the Internal Security Act and Other Internal Security Laws of the Committee on the Judiciary, Senate.* [U.S. Superintendent of Documents, Catalog no. Y 4.J 39/2: C 73/44.], 1963, 83 pp.

74. *Educational and Cultural Exchange Opportunities.* [U.S. Superintendent of Documents, Catalog no. S 1.67: 83.], Rev. 1963, 27 pp.

75. *Women in Educational Exchange with the Developing Countries.* New York: Committee on Educational Interchange Policy, Institute of International Education, CEIP Statement no. 16, 1963, 27 pp.

76. U.S. Bureau of Educational and Cultural Affairs. *Foreign Visitor Programs, Foreign Leader Program, Foreign Specialist Program, Educational Travel Program, Voluntary Visitor Program.* [U.S. Superintendent of Documents, Catalog no. S 1.67: 86.]. Department of State Publication no. 7631, 1964, 11 pp.

77. Foreign Affairs Committee, House of Representatives. *Winning The Cold War: The U.S. Ideological Offensive.* Hearings before the Subcommittee on International Organizations and Movements, 88th Congress, January, 1964. Washington: U.S. Government Printing Office, 1964.

78. *Planning to Study in the United States: A Guide to Prospective Students from Other Countries.* [U.S. Superintendent of Documents, Catalog no. FS 5.214: 14040.], Rev. 1964, 32 pp.

79. *The Foreign Assistance Program: Annual Report to the Congress for Fiscal Year 1963.* U.S. Superintendent of Documents, 1964, 88 pp.

This report focuses mainly on Agency for International Development programs, including educational assistance, around the world. Brief mention is made of educational assistant programs up through 1963.

80. *"Welcome Stranger!", Suggestions for Schools and Communities When Receiving Visiting Educators from Abroad.* [U.S. Superintendent of Documents, Catalog no. FS 5.214: 14097.], 1964, 8 pp.

Magazines

81. Duggan, S. P. H. "American Activities in International Education," *Political Quarterly,* XV (October 1944), 317–329.

82. "Bill for the Exchange of Students," *Higher Education,* II (Jan. 15, 1946), 5.

This bill, introduced to the Senate by Senator Fulbright, provided for the sale of surplus properties abroad for the promotion of good will by making use of the credits established to finance the exchange of students in various fields. This was to be done only as long as the goods sold would accrue to the interest of the United States.

83. McMurry, R. M. "Division of International Exchange of Persons of the Department of State," *Institute of International Education News Bulletin,* XXI (May 1946), 15–17.

This division is responsible for facilitating the exchange of advanced university students and industrial trainees, visiting professors and specialists. Grants are given for research, study, lectureships, and for consultative or advisory services in connection with projects which will further cultural relations between the U.S. and the foreign country concerned.

84. Benton, William. "Fulbright Bill Promotes International Understanding," *American Teacher,* XXXI (December 1946), 4.

85. Haygood, V. "Government Aid to Foreign Students in the U.S.," *Institute of International Education News Bulletin,* XXII (May 1947), 17–19.

86. Duggan, S. P. H. "Private Versus Official Supervision of Student Exchange," *School and Society,* LXVII (April 17, 1948), 291–292.

87. Clarke, Eric T. "Colleges' and Military Government's Program for Cultural Exchange," *Association of American Colleges Bulletin,* XXXV (March 1949), 82–87.

88. Johnstone, W. C., Jr. "American Government's Program for International Educational and Technological Cooperation," *American Association of University Professors Bulletin,* XXXV (March 1949), 29–37.

89. Todd, L. P. "America's Foreign Commitments: Their Implications for Education," *Social Education,* XIII (April 1949), 149–150.

90. "Educational Exchange Act Grants," *Institute of International Education News Bulletin,* XXV (January 1950), 31–33.

The Department of State has two student exchange programs under the Educational Exchange Act:

(1) The Travel and Maintenance—grants awarded to foreign students in the form of travel and/or maintenance, depending upon student's financial needs.

(2) Inter-American Fellowships—sponsored by Inter-American Cultural Relations—the annual exchange of two graduate students between each of the participating countries.

91. "Office of Education, Its Services and Staff," *School Life,* XXXII (April 1950), 101+.

This article describes the personnel and programs of the U.S. Office of Education, Division of International Education Relations.

92. Odegaard, C. E. "Fulbright Exchange Program in Operation," *National Association of Secondary School Principals Bulletin,* XXXIV (October 1950), 143–154.

A detailed report on the procedures of administration of the Fulbright Program and of its difficulties and limitations.

93. Wodlinger, D. E. "Fulbright Program; Recent Developments," *Institute of International Education News Bulletin,* XXVI (October 1950), 24–26.

94. "American Foreign Policy and American Education: Comments from Readers," *Progressive Education*, XXVIII (January 1951), 83–88.

95. "Department of State Programs," *Higher Education*, VII (Jan. 1, 1951), 103.

State Department programs were established to allow U.S. citizens to study abroad and foreign students to study in the United States. No restrictions were placed upon subject field studied. Grants were given only to graduate students for not longer than one year.

96. Harrington, F. H. "Role of the United States in Foreign Affairs," *Social Education*, XV (February 1951), 53–55.

97. Green, A. G. "Marshall Plan for Education," *School Executive*, LXX (March 1951), 66–67.

98. Carter, M. R. T. "Our Foreign Policy," *National Education Association Journal*, XL (May 1951), 329–331.

99. Holland, Kenneth. "Educational Exchange with Foreign Countries," *Educational Forum*, XV (May 1951), 413–418.

A study of the activities of the Institute of International Education—along with the total number of students studying abroad and here in the United States.

100. "Educational Exchange Agreements," *United States Department of State Bulletin*, XXV (Sept. 10, 1951), 432–433.

101. Cherrington, Ben Mark. "Clear and Consistent Policy," *Institute of International Education News Bulletin*, XXVII (December 1951), 5–6.

The policy of the State Department of the U.S. was stated to be:

The encouragement and strengthening of cultural relations and intellectual cooperation between the U.S. and other countries by use of cultural exchange which must be reciprocal and reflect a partnership between the government and the private institutions of the land.

102. Gardner, John W. "The Foreign Student in America," *Foreign Affairs*, XXX (July 1952), 637–650.

Suggestions are made regarding the objective of student exchange as well as the selection, orientation, housing, kind of training, education in a democracy and follow-up studies suitable for foreign students.

103. Moore, Forrest G. "Student Interchange; a Government and Voluntary Agency Partnership," *School and Society*, LXXV (Feb. 9, 1952), 84–87.

This article discussed the different motivations behind student exchange programs, including the objectives and aims of the exchange program. What the government and voluntary agencies expect to accomplish was listed along with some suggestions about future programs.

104. Bond, M. "State Department Program," *California Journal of Secondary Education*, XXVII (April 1952), 200–201.

105. Chevalier, W. T. "United States and International Education," *National Business Education Quarterly*, XXI (October 1952), 74–78.

106. Caldwell, Oliver J. "New Horizon in Education: Activities of Government Agencies," *Education Record*, XXXIII (October 1952), 528–541.

107. Stevenson, Adlai E., and Dwight D. Eisenhower. "Exchange of Persons," *Institute of International Education News Bulletin,* XXVIII (November 1952), 2–3.

These are statements of the 1952 presidential candidates on exchange of persons.

From my own experience in the Department of State and the United Nations I know that one of the most effective ways to convey the real cultural values of one society to the people of another is an actual exchange of persons. . . . I find it heartening that the peoples of the free world are binding themselves together not only through diplomatic and military cooperation, but also through joint educational and cultural undertakings. . . . (A. E. Stevenson).

I firmly believe that educational exchange programs are an important step toward world peace. Because of failures in human relationships my generation has suffered through two world wars, the threat of another will not be removed until the peoples of the world come to know each other better, until they understand each other's problems and needs and hopes. Exchange-of-persons programs can contribute immeasurably to such understanding. (D. D. Eisenhower).

108. Bodenman, Paul S. "Educational Cooperation with Foreign Countries," *Higher Education,* IX, no. 13 (March 1, 1953), 145–150.

This article summarizes some of the major programs for which the Government has direct responsibility. The main objectives of these programs are briefly stated.

109. Gibson, R. C. "Point IV Missions in Education," *Higher Education,* IX (March 1, 1953), 158–159.

110. Miller, H. A. "U.S. Government Programs of International Exchange," *Education Record,* XXXIV (October 1953), 313–326.

A brief history of international education introduces the article. A compilation of statistical and financial information not previously published concerning U.S. Government exchange programs for July 1, 1951, to June 30, 1952, as well as data concerning the Information Center Service Program, U.S. Department of State, and the efforts of institutions of higher learning are included.

111. Caldwell, Oliver J. "Education Provides a New Approach to Diplomacy," *Nation's Schools,* LIV (February 1954), 43–47.

Several programs were briefly summarized to illustrate their efforts for education and understanding.

112. Niefeld, S. J., and H. Mendelsohn. "How Effective Is Our Student-Exchange Program?" *Educational Research Bulletin,* XXXIII (February 1954), 29–37.

The program of the Educational Exchange Service was evaluated by educators from their personal experiences and observations.

A summary was presented of the findings of 1952–1953 survey taken by the Advisory Commission on Educational Exchange to evaluate the Educational Exchange Service of the Department of State. The overwhelming endorsement given to the program by college administrators surveyed

(90% affirmative) is tempered by recognition of the indirect nature of the survey. For future assessments, direct empirical methods are recommended as means of determining actual effectiveness of the program.

113. Morrill, J. L. "International Educational Exchange Program of the U.S. Government; Evolution of an American Idea," *Institute of International Education News Bulletin,* XXIX (April 1954), 12–17.

114. Cieslak, Edward Charnwood. "Bibliography; Selected and Annotated," *Phi Delta Kappan,* XXXV (December 1953), 349–356.

This annotated bibliography prepared by the Admission Counselor at Wayne University, Detroit, includes several annotations relevant to government policy and international education.

115. Roseman, A. "Inter-University Contracts in the U.S. Foreign Aid Program," *Higher Education,* XI (September 1954), 1–5.

116. Colligan, F. J. "U.S. Government Exchange Programs with the Other American Republics," *Institute of International Education News Bulletin,* XXX (April 1955), 2–8.

117. Caldwell, Oliver J. "International Education Activities of the Office of Education," *Higher Education,* XII (September 1955), 4–6.

The Assistant Commissioner for International Education, Office of Education, notes two functions of the United States in international education activities: (1) to help people to learn about each other and to create a basis for better understanding; and (2) to help people gain knowledge and skills which enable them to raise their standards of living.

Sixteen laws and many appropriation acts since 1938 have provided funds to move people to and from the U.S. for the purpose of sharing ideas and skills. The government fosters valuable interaction by giving and receiving instruction, both in and out of the classroom, and through observation tours.

Activities of the Office of Education in international education are in two areas: (1) Statutory responsibilities financed by Congressional appropriation, including comparative educational practices and situations, evaluation of foreign academic credentials, consultation on curriculum changes and recommendation on educational policies. (2) Transferred responsibilities received from other federal agencies, including veteran education abroad, clearing house of information for educational exchange programs, educational materials laboratory, educators for technical assistance, teachers for foreign assignment, teacher exchanges, and training for visiting teachers.

118. Fraser, Mowat G. "Educational Progress in Korea," *Institute of International Education News Bulletin,* XXXI (January 1956), 13–16.

119. Mendelsohn, H., and F. E. Orenstein. "Survey of Fulbright Award Recipients; Cross-Cultural Education and Its Impacts," *Public Opinion Quarterly,* XIX (Winter 1955–56), 401–407.

120. Exton, E. "Viewing Washington's International Role," *American School Board Journal,* CXXXIII (December 1956), 43–44.

121. "Ten Years of the Educational Exchange Programs," *Social Review,* XXX (December 1956), 458–459.

122. "International Exchanges of Trainees," *International Labour Review,* LXXV (March 1957), 230–245.

123. Cotner, Thomas E. "International Exchange and Training Programs Administered by the Office of Education, 1939–57," *Higher Education,* XIII (May 1957), 171–172.

The Director, Educational Exchange and Training Branch, Division of International Education, Office of Education, gives a summary report of international exchange and training programs carried on by the Office of Education. Different programs are explained briefly, and statistical figures of participating individuals and nations are noted which indicate an increase in participation throughout most of the programs.

Included are a summary of various programs administered and the number of grantees involved since the Office of Education became engaged in 1949 in International Educational Exchange Aid Training Programs and also statistical information of the number of students and teachers involved from 1939 to 1957.

124. Holland, Kenneth. "Opportunities to Study or Teach Abroad," *Educational Forum,* XXII (November 1957), 13–20.

125. Brickman, William W. "Decade of International Educational Exchange," *School and Society,* LXXXVI (April 26, 1958), 199.

126. Rowson, Richard C. "U.S. Foreign Policy Today," *Institute of International Education News Bulletin,* XXXIV (September 1958), 40–47.

The Executive Assistant to the President of the Foreign Policy Association gives a surface view of the fundamental objectives of American foreign policy, tracing its history from Washington's warning against entangling alliances through the Neutrality Acts of 1936. Foreign policy changes since 1936 and their causes are explained.

127. Flack, Michael Julius. "Sources of Information on International Educational Activities; an Exploratory Survey Prepared for the Committee on Education and International Affairs," *American Council on Education* (1958), 114 pp.

128. James, H. T., and L. W. Downey. "Intergovernmental Relations to Education," *Review of Educational Research,* XXVIII (October 1958), 277–296.

129. "The Development of Inter-American Exchange and the Institute of International Education (IIE)," *Institute of International Education News Bulletin,* XXXIV, no. 2 (October 1958), 10–15.

This was a chronological study of the development of the programs of Inter-American Exchange and the Institute of International Education.

130. Fraser, Mowat G. "Blind Spot in Our Foreign Policy," *Educational Forum,* XXIII (January 1959), 151–153.

A plea was made for increased educational aid to supplement the economic and military aid given by the United States to underdeveloped nations. Three reasons are given for U.S. failure to provide such aid: U.S.

reluctance to "meddle" in internal affairs of other countries, cost (which is mistakenly considered prohibitive), and simple tradition.

131. Riepe, D. "Fulbright in Retrospect," *Institute of International Education News Bulletin,* XXXIV (April 1959), 55–58.

132. Stoke, H. W. "National Necessity and Educational Policy; with Reply by P. H. Phenix," *Phi Delta Kappan,* XL (April 1959), 266–271.

133. Tewksbury, Donald G. "American Education and the International Scene," *Teachers College Record,* LX (April 1959), 357–368.

134. American Society for Engineering Education. "Final Report: ASEE Engineering Education Exchange Mission to the Soviet Union, November, 1958," *Journal of Engineering Education,* XLIX, no. 9 (May 1959), 839–911.

Information is included on the administration of Soviet higher education, administration and faculty of engineering education institutions, students, curricula, facilities, undergraduate and graduate studies, and research.

135. Quattlebaum, Charles A. "Government Programs in International Education," *Education Record,* XL (July 1959), 249–255.

The article summarizes a 251-page report of the Committee on Government Operations, U.S. House of Representatives. Included in the article are:

1. a history of international education;
2. the developments in international education since 1939;
3. the principal programs of the U.S. Government:
    a. educational exchange program of the Department of State (includes some favorable and unfortunate effects of this program),
    b. technical cooperation program of the International Cooperation Administration (includes the effects on higher education of the ICA program),
    c. overseas information program of the U.S. Information Agency;
4. the differences between the programs of the International Educational Exchange Service and of the International Cooperation Administration;
5. the educational activities of other U.S. Government agencies;
6. the programs of international agencies, especially the United Nations;
7. the programs of other countries, especially Russia;
8. summary observations respecting U.S. programs.

136. Caldwell, Oliver J. "Education, an Instrument of International Policy," *Higher Education,* XVI, no. 8 (April 1960), 13–14.

Education and its role in international policy were reviewed.

137. Hubbert, Erin. "Evaluation of the Fulbright Program," *Institute of International Education News Bulletin,* XXV (April 1960), 39–45.

Three methods of evaluating the program are described: survey research, operations research, and case histories.

Chief of the Program Evaluations Staff of the Bureau of International Cultural Relations states that a synthesis of these evaluation studies clearly indicates a "net gain in the efficacy of total American diplomacy."

138. Ruffner, R. W. "Technical Cooperation in Education Through the

International Cooperation Administration," *Higher Education,* XVI (April 1960), 7–12.

This article is concerned with the U.S. Government and International Education, and the Office of Education services. Governmental programs, giving the departments that were responsible for each, were discussed.

139. Storey, Robert G. "Fulbright Program Faces the Future," *Institute of International Education News Bulletin,* XXXV (April 1960), 2–7.

This discusses the principal source of funds and the general operation of the Fulbright program. The author gave an evaluation of the outlook of the Fulbright program.

140. Kennedy, John F., and Richard M. Nixon. "Two Statements on International Exchange," *Institute of International Education News Bulletin,* XXXVI (October 1960), 2–3.

Vice President Nixon describes the student exchange program as providing new generations in underdeveloped and newly emerging nations opportunities to "see for themselves the superiority of democracy."

Senator Kennedy, on the other hand, though he also emphasizes the need for educational experiences to promote democratic interests, would create a foundation for International Educational Development which would have the creative responsibility of building new educational institutions within the developing nations.

141. Tead, Ordway. "What Are America's Purposes?" *Educational Forum,* XXV (March 1961), 317–323.

The author presses for a revival and strong reaffirmation of personal commitment to our democratic ideals throughout our education system in order that we may take a more positive and effective stance in promoting democracy all over the world. Education too long has failed—only partially teaching patriotism, and now more than ever will fail the world if we fail ourselves.

142. Brooks, J. J. "Overseas School: A New International Resource," *School and Society,* LXXXIX (April 8, 1961), 189–190.

143. Davis, James M. "Federal Aid for International Student Exchange," *School and Society,* LXXXIX (April 8, 1961), 169–170.

Essentially this is a plea for awareness by the government of its responsibility to foreign students:

1. not to allow the foreign student to be squeezed out, even if enrollments in higher education do increase to the extent predicted;

2. to continue and increase financial support of foreign students on the grounds that higher education is a valuable way for the government to extend technical assistance to many less developed parts of the world.

144. Brooks, J. J. "Overseas Schools: Crucibles of International Education," *Teachers College Record,* LXIII (October 1961), 14–18.

145. Schmidt, Liselotte. "Study Abroad: A Bibliography," *Comparative Education Review,* V, no. 2 (October 1961), 142–155.

There are 106 annotations of useful selections.

146. "Exchange Act Expanded," *School Life,* XLIV (November 1961), 3–4.

147. Rogers, V. R. "Intra-American Exchange Program," *Phi Delta Kappan*, XLIII (January 1962), 170.

148. Beck, Robert Holmes. "The Professional Training in Education of Foreign Students in the U.S.," *Journal of Teacher Education*, XIII (June 1962), 140–143.

Challenge of world illiteracy is being met by the programs for training foreign nationals in education. Some general statistics of the number of foreign students studying in the various subjects in the U.S. during 1959–1960 were given in the article. This article also discussed the reasons these students came to the U.S. to study.

149. "The Effectiveness of the Educational and Cultural Exchange Program of the U.S. Department of State," *Overseas*, II (April 1963), 22–25.

Committee findings were based on detailed studies of four grantees, visits by Commission members to Europe, Latin America, and Africa, and interviews with all levels of individuals acquainted with the program, both at home and abroad.

150. Evans, Luther H. "United States Educational Activities Overseas," *Overseas*, III (November 1963), 10–13.

The Director of International and Legal Collection at Columbia University, formerly Director-General of UNESCO and Librarian of Congress, claims that the U.S. Government and the American people do not realize the importance of our role in education abroad. Underdeveloped nations need education and appreciation of science and technology. While vocational education is of immediate importance, education at all levels and in all areas must be carried on at the same time. Control and guidance must be centralized due to weaknesses of local control at this time. Allowances must be made for the development of national unity and common purpose.

151. "Fulbright-Hays Agreements: Afghanistan and Argentina with the United States," *Overseas*, III (November 1963), 32.

PEACE CORPS

Books and Pamphlets

152. Albertson, Maurice L., Andrew E. Rice, and Pauline Birkey. *New Frontiers on American Youth: Perspective on the Peace Corps.* Washington, D.C.: Public Affairs Press, 1961, 212 pp.

153. Hayes, Samuel Perkins. *An International Peace Corps: The Promise and Problems.* Washington, D.C.: Public Affairs Institute, 1961, 96 pp.

154. Hoopes, Roy. *The Complete Peace Corps Guide.* New York: The Dial Press, 1961, 180 pp.

155. Rogers, David. *The Peace Corps Girls.* Chicago: The Dramatic Publishing Company, 1962.

A play in three acts suitable for high school production about Peace Corps volunteer teachers who help form a PTA and a blouse export industry in a town in the Philippines.

156. Kittler, Glenn D. *The Peace Corps.* New York: Paperback Library, 1963, 127 pp.

157. Spencer, Sharon. *Breaking the Bonds: A Novel About the Peace Corps.* New York: (Tempo Books) Grosset and Dunlap, 1963, 184 pp.
A teenager's novel about Anne Elliott and Bob Byers, Peace Corps volunteer teachers in Nigeria.

158. Wingenbach, Charles E. *The Peace Corps: Who, How and Where.* New York: John Day Co., revised edition, 1963, 188 pp.

159. Madow, Pauline (ed.). *The Peace Corps.* New York: The H. W. Wilson Co., The Reference Shelf, XXXVI, no. 2, 1964, 172 pp.
Descriptions and evaluations of the Corps, its origins, operations, and accomplishments, set forth by Government officials, observers of world affairs and others.

Government Documents

160. Kennedy, John F. "Peace Corps Created on Pilot Basis; President Seeks Permanent Legislation," *Department of State Bulletin,* XLIV (March 20, 1961), 400–403.

161. Cleveland, Harlan. "Internationalizing the Concept of the Peace Corps," *Department of State Bulletin,* XLIV (April 17, 1961), 551–552.

162. "President Kennedy Names Members of Peace Advisory Council," *Department of State Bulletin,* XLIV (April 24, 1961), 583.

163. Kennedy, John F. "President Proposes Legislation for Establishing Peace Corps," *Department of State Bulletin,* XLIV (June 19, 1961), 980.
A letter to Senate President Lyndon B. Johnson spelling out the initial request for $40 million to establish the Peace Corps. Describes the President's concept of what the Corps would do and its relationship to the country development assistance plans already in effect.

164. Rusk, Dean. "Plan for International Development," *Department of State Bulletin,* XLIV (June 26, 1961), 1005–1006.

165. Kennedy, John F. "Peace Corps Legislation Signed Into Law By President Kennedy," *Department of State Bulletin,* XLV (October 9, 1961), 603.

166. ――― to L. B. Johnson. "President Recommends Expansion of Peace Corps," *Department of State Bulletin,* XLIX (July 29, 1963), 170–172.
A letter from President Kennedy to the President of the Senate L. B. Johnson recommending an increase in funds for Peace Corps expansion. An excellent account of the broad accomplishments of the Peace Corps and of the precedent set for other countries who are in turn developing similar peace corps.

167. "President Nyerere of Tanganyika Visits Washington," *Department of State Bulletin,* XLIX (August 5, 1963), 198–199.
An account of the first visit of President Nyerere to the U.S. since Tanganyika's independence. It includes an announcement of another group of Peace Corps volunteers being sent to Tanganyika, with a short description of the work completed there thus far by the two previous groups.

Magazines

168. "Peace Corps Plan," *Commonweal,* LXXIII (January 6, 1961), 377.

169. Samuels, G. "Force of Youth as a Force of Peace," *New York Times Magazine* (February 5, 1961), 26.

170. "Go Everywhere Young Man," *Time,* LXXVII (February 24, 1961), 59.

171. "Role for Youth," *Science,* CXXXIII (March 10, 1961), 690.

172. "Peace Corps Shapes Up," *America,* CIV (March 11, 1961), 746.

173. "Personal Business," *Business World* (March 11, 1961), 125.

174. "What the Peace Corps Can Do," *Business Week* (March 11, 1961), 144.

175. "ABC of Kennedy's Peace Corps," *U.S. News and World Report,* L (March 13, 1961), 44–45.

176. "Answering the Call," *Newsweek,* LVII (March 13, 1961), 19–20.

177. "Peace Corps," *New Republic,* CXLIV (March 13, 1961), 3–4.
A criticism of the value of the Peace Corps to newly developing countries as well as underdeveloped countries. The need for capital rather than youth is most vital to these countries; it is inferred that the good will accrues to the American through his personal experience in the country in which he serves.

178. "Not for Propaganda But for Peace," *Christian Century,* LXXVIII (March 15, 1961), 317.

179. Kennedy, John F. "Peace Corps; Message to Congress," *Vital Speeches,* XXXVII (March 15, 1961), 325–327.

180. "Reveille for the Peace Corps," *Senior Scholastic,* LXXVIII (March 15, 1961), 18.

181. Shriver, Sargent. "Peace Corps Catches Fire in Colleges," *Life,* L (March 17, 1961), 34–41.

182. "Peace Corps Plan; Pilot Model," *Commonweal,* LXXIII (March 17, 1961), 625.

183. McGory, M. "Accent on Youth," *America,* CIV (March 18, 1961), 776.

184. Canavan, F. P. "Catholic Campuses View the Peace Corps Plan," *America,* CIV (March 18, 1961), 789–790.

185. "Peace Corps," *Nation,* CXCII (March 18, 1961), 225.

186. "Newest Frontier," *Time,* LXXVII (March 10, 1961), 81.

187. Lindley, Ernest K. "Peace Corps," *Newsweek,* LVII (March 20, 1961), 30.

188. "Peace Corps at Home," *New Republic,* CXLIV (March 20, 1961), 9.
A criticism of the individual Americans who comprise the Peace Corps and a vote for Eleanor Roosevelt's suggestion of a Peace Corps at home. A slap at the "American" personality.

189. "Peace Corps; Old Story to U.S. Missionaries," *U.S. News and World Report,* L (March 20, 1961), 58.

190. "Ah Yes, the Peace Corps," *National Review,* X (March 25, 1961), 171–172.

191. Brickman, William W. "Peace Corps and Educational Competence," *School and Society,* LXXXIX (March 25, 1961), 135.

192. Penniman, H. "Peace Corps Requirements," *America,* CIV (March 25, 1961), 808.

193. "Peace Corps Set Up," *Science News Letter,* LXXIX (March 25, 1961), 183.

194. DuShane, G. "Idealism for Export," *Science,* CXXXIII (March 31, 1961), 977.

195. "New Peace Corps," *Bulletin of Atomic Scientists,* XVII (April 1961), 169–171.

196. Shriver, R. Sargent. "Peace Corps: Its Director Tells What to Expect," *U.S. News and World Report,* L (April 3, 1961), 90.

197. "How About Urdu?," *Time,* LXXVII (April 7, 1961), 24–25.
The inception of the Peace Corps and the many questions presented to Sargent Shriver and his National Advisory Council for the Peace Corps. The majority of the questions came from potential volunteers.

198. "No Children's Crusade," Summary of interviews; African and Asian personnel at U.N., *America,* CV (April 8, 1961), 49–50.

199. Barlow, R. M. "Paying the Price for Peace," *America,* CV (April 8, 1961), 72–73.

200. Moats, A. L. "Peace, It's Wonderful," *National Review,* X (April 8, 1961), 211–212.

201. Stokerker, C. F. "Peace Corps in Perspective; Questions and Answers," *Christian Century,* LXXVIII (April 12, 1961), 450–452.

202. "Kibbutz and Peace Corps," *America,* CV (April 15, 1961), 144.

203. Staggers, H. O. "Peace Corps Idea Address," *Vital Speeches,* XXVII (April 15, 1961), 395–397.

204. "Peace Corps: Outward Bound," *Newsweek,* LVII (April 17, 1963), 31–32.
The Peace Corps critics and the reactions to some of their most damaging criticism. A short article highlighting the Corps' mission.

205. "What Teachers Should Know About the Peace Corps," *NEA Journal,* L (May, 1961), 26.

206. "Tanganyika Lo," *Newsweek,* LVII (May 1, 1961), 35–36.
The Peace Corps gets off the ground and Tanganyika with its steaming jungles is its first mission. Basic information concerning the Peace Corps' first marching orders.

207. "Teens Sound Off on Foreign Aid," *Senior Scholastic,* LXXVIII (May 3, 1961), 11–12.

208. Humphrey, Hubert H. "Peace Corps on Trial," *P.T.A. Magazine,* LV (May 1961), 4–6.

209. "Peace Corpsman," *Time,* LXXVII (May 12, 1961), 10–11.
Sargent Shriver's visit to India and his efforts to explain the purpose and objectives of the new Peace Corps met with success in New Delhi where Prime Minister Nehru annnounced himself strongly for the Corps.

210. McNaspy, C. J. "How We Look To Others," *America,* CV (May 13, 1961), 274–275.

211. Kimble, George H. T. "Challenges to the Peace Corps," *New York Times Magazine* (May 14, 1961), 9.

212. O'Hara, J. "Daughters of the American What," *Commonweal*, LXXIV (May 19, 1961), 198.

213. "Clicks and Thumps," *Newsweek*, LVII (May 22, 1961), 23–24.
A short glimpse into the problems faced by the Peace Corps staff very early in the Corps' development. Discusses briefly the idea of regional college conferences and why they were started.

214. "Peace Corps Test of Aspirants," *Life*, L (June 2, 1961), 62–63.

215. Sokolsky, George E. "Can the Peace Corps Do the Job?" *Saturday Review*, XLIV (June 17, 1961), 17–19. Discussion, XLIV (July 8, 1961), 2–7.

216. "Peace Corpsman," *Time*, LXXVII (June 23, 1961), 10–11.
Short biographical sketches of a few of the first group of Peace Corps volunteers being sent abroad.

217. "Peace Corps; Questions and Answers," *Seventeen*, XX (July 1961), 20+.

218. "Peace Corps and Churches and American Catholics," *America*, CV (July 1, 1961), 477.

219. "Better Way," *Newsweek*, LVIII (July 10, 1961), 43.
The Peace Corps' first contingent of volunteers undergoing training at Rutgers University with a glimpse into the personalities that made up what was considered the cream of the crop in the early days of the Corps.

220. "Keep Peace Corps and Missions Separate," *Christian Century*, LXXVIII (July 12, 1961), 845–846.

221. "Peace Corps Is Born," *New Republic*, CXLIV (June 12, 1961), 4–5.

222. Shriver, R. Sargent. "Peace Corps Needs Farm Men and Women," *Successful Farming*, LIX (July 1961), 17.

223. "Truth About the Peace Corps," *U.S. News and World Report*, LI (July 24, 1961), 40–42.

224. Hanson, D. "Across the Editor's Desk," *Successful Farming*, LIX (August 1961), 22.

225. "Peace Corps Boot Camps," *Time*, LXXVIII (August 11, 1961), 30–31.

226. "Opportunities for Service in the Peace Corps," *Occupational Outlook Quarterly*, V (September 1961), 15.

227. DeMott, B. "Peace Corps Secret Mission," *Harper*, CCXXIII (September 1961), 638.

228. "Eye of the Storm," *Newsweek*, LVIII (Sept. 4, 1961), 20.
A view of Sargent Shriver's personality as presented in the Kamen case; one of the first Peace Corps volunteers to have national publicity because of his actions prior to joining the Corps.

229. "And Away They Go," *Time*, LXXVIII (Sept. 8, 1961), 22–23.

230. Quigley, T. E. "Open Letter to Newman Clubs," *America*, CV (Sept. 9, 1961), 706–707.

231. "Peace Corps on Campus; Training in Puerto Rico," *New York Times Magazine* (Sept. 10, 1961), 28–29.

232. "Peace Corps Takes the Field," *Life*, LI (Sept. 16, 1961), 63–66.

233. Rowe, D. N. "Peace Corps in Reverse?" *National Review,* XI (Sept. 23, 1961), 195.

234. Linebarr, W. "Peace Corps: Ready, Set, Go!" *Senior Scholastic,* LXXIX (Sept. 27, 1961), 14–16.

235. "Much Ado About a Post Card," *Life,* LI (Oct. 27, 1961), 84.

236. "She Had No Idea," *Time,* LXXIV, no. 28 (Oct. 27, 1961), 24.
A report on the "Michelmore Post Card" incident in Nigeria. One of the first tests of the Peace Corps organization in foreign relations. It came off well for the Corps.

237. "Postcard Gone Astray," *America,* CVI (Oct. 28, 1961), 109.

238. "Borrioboola-Gha," *New Republic,* CXLII (Oct. 30, 1961), 4–5.

239. "Peace Corps Suffers Some Growing Pains," *U.S. News and World Report,* LI (Oct. 30, 1961), 4.

240. "Story of a Postcard," *Newsweek,* LVIII (Oct. 30, 1961), 28.

241. "Peace Corps: Negroes Play Vital Role," *Ebony,* XVII (November 1961), 30–40.

242. "Card That Strayed," *Senior Scholastic,* LXXIX (Nov. 1, 1961), 30.

243. Pitt, M. "Madge Shipp and the Peace Corps," *Negro Historical Bulletin,* XXV (November 1961), 32.

244. O'Gara, James. "Innocence Abroad," *Commonweal,* LXXV (Nov. 3, 1961), 142.

245. "Postcard Postscript with Questions and Answers," *Life,* LI (Nov. 3, 1961), 115–116.

246. Conklin, P. "Questions of Black or White," *New Republic,* CXLV (Nov. 6, 1961), 8–9.

247. Knebel, F. "On Trial Sargent Shriver and the Peace Corps," *Look,* XXV (Nov. 7, 1961), 34–37.

248. "Corpsman in Ghana," *Time,* LXXVIII (Nov. 17, 1961), 20–21.
The Peace Corps in Ghana and the first real field test of the Corps. Reactions are good from both the volunteers and the people of Ghana. A good report of Americans in Africa.

249. "On Duty in Ghana," *New York Times Magazine* (Nov. 21, 1961), 29.

250. "Peace Corps Report; Inspection Tour of Latin America," *America,* CVI (Dec. 2, 1961), 318.

251. "On the Job With the Peace Corps in Africa and South America," *U.S. News and World Report,* LI (Dec. 4, 1961), 68–70.

252. Braestrup, P. "Peace Corpsman No. 1; a Progress Report," *New York Times Magazine* (Dec. 17, 1961), 11.

253. "Peace Corps on Christmas Eve," *Newsweek,* LVIII (Dec. 25, 1961), 13–16.

254. "Report on the Peace Corps," *Time,* LXXVIII (Dec. 29, 1961), 10–11.
An interesting report on the Peace Corps mission in various parts of the world with comments by the corpsmen as to their reception, work loads, and social life abroad.

255. "Up Front with the Peace Corps," *Life,* LII (Jan. 5, 1962), 18–25.

256. "Peace Corps Problems Akin to Those of Missions," *Christian Century,* LXXIX (Jan. 24, 1962), 101.

257. Nugent, J. P. "Peace Corps Comes to Tanganyika," *Reporter,* XXVI (Feb. 1, 1962), 35–36.

258. "Peace Corps Project, Tunisia II" (Peace Corps Training Program syllabus), Oklahoma University Extension Division, Norman, Oklahoma (Feb. 18 to May 3, 1962).

259. "Help Wanted," *Senior Scholastic,* LXXX (March 14, 1962), 16.

260. Shriver, R. Sargent. "Mango for the Peace Corps Teacher," *NEA Journal,* LI (April 1962), 48–49.

261. ———. "Job Was Tough," Address before 17th National Conference on Higher Education, Chicago, *Vital Speeches of the Day* (March 6, 1962), 407–411.

262. Ellickson, Jean. "Librarian in the Peace Corps," *Wilson Library Bulletin,* XXXVI (June 1962), 833–834.

263. "Youths Potential," *America,* CVII (July 7, 1962), 453.

264. Ottenad, T. W. "Peace Corps Wins Its Way," *Progressive,* XXVI (August 1962), 19–22.

265. Kroon, George, and N. A. Haverstock. "Profile of a Peace Corpsman," *Saturday Evening Post,* CCXXXV (Sept. 8, 1962), 77–81.

266. "Vogue's Eye View of a Loving Sign," *Vogue,* CXLI (Feb. 1, 1963), 91.

267. Shriver, R. Sargent. "When Peace Corps Teachers Return," *NEA Journal,* LII (March 1963), 13–14.

268. Davis, W. "Peace Corps Volunteer: An American Image," *Science News,* LXXXIII (March 16, 1963), 165.

269. Boegli, J. C. "My Life as a Peace Corps Girl," *Good Housekeeping,* CLVI (April 1963), 84–85.

270. "Teachers Wanted," *Senior Scholastic,* LXXXII (April 17, 1963), 11+.

271. Walsh, J. "Peace Corps: Agency Flourishes As Congress Smiles, Numbers Still Grow But Full Results Are Not Yet In," *Science,* CXL (April 26, 1963), 371–372.

272. "Forty-four Countries Call," *Scholastic Life,* XLV (April 1963), 27.

273. "Inside the Peace Corps," *Seventeen,* XXII (May 1963), 152–153.

274. Burdick, Eugene, and Lederer, W. "Ugly American Revisited," *Saturday Evening Post,* CCXXXVI (May 4, 1963), 78–81.

275. "Hundreds of Senior Citizens Wanted," *Christian Century,* LXXX (May 29, 1963), 701.

276. Kubic, M. J. "Colombia Senor Ron," *Newsweek,* LXI (June 3, 1963), 48.

277. Callaway, H. L. "Doers, Not Do-Gooders, the Peace Corps in Nigeria," *Mademoiselle,* LVII (June 1963), 126–129.

278. Shriver, R. Sargent. "I Have the Best Job in Washington," *New York Times Magazine* (June 9, 1963), 34.

279. Barnett, David. "Volunteers Resent 'Here' Role; Researcher Tells Findings," *Peace Corps Volunteer,* I (July 1963), 2.

280. "Additional Career Opportunities for Volunteers Who Are Completing Two Years of Service," *Peace Corps Volunteer,* I (July 1963), 22–23.

281. "It Is Almost As Good As Its Intentions," *Time,* LXXXII (July 5, 1963), 18–22.

282. Shriver, R. Sargent. "Peace Corps: Frontier for Youth," *Parents Magazine,* XXXVIII (July 1963), 46–47.

283. Edwards, M. "Teachers in the Peace Corps," *Saturday Review,* XLVI (July 20, 1963), 42–44.

284. Shriver, R. Sargent. "Two Years of the Peace Corps," *Foreign Affairs,* XLI (July 1963), 694–707.

285. Shapian, R. "Reporter at Large; Peace Corps in the Philippines," *New Yorker,* XXXIX (September 28, 1963), 50–52.

286. "Here's How They See It Now," *Peace Corps Volunteer,* I (October 1963), 2–3.

287. "Broad Horizons," *Recreation,* LVI (October 1963), 356–358.

288. Prank, Ginna. " 'Vacation' Is Teachers' Plight," *Peace Corps Volunteer,* II (November 1963), 6–7.

289. "Peace Corps Needs 9,000 in 1964," *Library Journal,* LXXXVIII (Nov. 15, 1963), 4448.

290. "Peace Corps Placing Kennedy Libraries Abroad," *Public Weekly,* CLXXXIV (Dec. 16, 1963), 22.

291. "Exam; Conducted by Civil Service Commission," *New Yorker,* XXXIX (Dec. 21, 1963), 22–23.

292. Hardberger, P. "Peace Corps Volunteers Praise P. E. Project," *Popular Electronics,* XX (Jan., 1964), 54–55.

293. Shriver, R. Sargent. "Close Look at the Peace Corps and Its Volunteers," *U.S. News and World Report,* LVI (Jan. 6, 1964), 38–41.

294. "Kennedy Libraries Drive Collects Over 4,000 Books," *Public Weekly,* CLXXXV (Jan. 6, 1964), 57.

295. "Peace Corps Needs Librarians for University of Brasilia," *Library Journal,* LXXXIX (Jan. 15, 1964), 209.

296. Pearson, David. "The Peace Corps Volunteer Returns," *Saturday Review,* XLVII, no. 42 (Oct. 17, 1964), 54–64.

Return adjustment problems examined through completion of Service Conferences, reported by the Peace Corps deputy information director.

297. Fairfield, Roy P. "Peace Corps Training at Ohio University," *School and Society,* XCII, no. 2249 (Nov. 14, 1964), 339–341.

NEW YORK TIMES

1950

298. January 27, p. 46, c. 1.

Bishop Kiwanuka seeks funds from U.S. to send African to the U.S.

299. September 5, p. 19, c. 5.

Fifty-one students sponsored by International Educational Institute and U.S. due in U.S. from Austria.

1951

300. January 30, p. 22, c. 3.
Six Japanese teachers study in U.S. under auspices of MacArthur staff unit.
301. February 15, p. 24, c. 2.
Two German students tour U.S. under U.S. State Department and International Educational Institute auspices.
302. September 23, p. 11, c. 3, 4.
John H. Whitney Foundation offers six foreign scholars fellowships to teach in U.S. colleges; 190 U.S. scholars to study in France under government program.
303. December 19, p. 43, c. 1.
Japanese and U.S. students win Everglaze exchange fellowships.

1952

304. January 10, p. 31, c. 8.
U.S. Senator Kefauver urges more funds for world student exchange programs.
305. January 13, p. 111, c. 2.
Comr. Rosenfield urges exchanges between U.S. and students exiled from Eastern Europe.
306. January 18, p. 7, c. 4.
Indian cultural leaders return to Bombay from Communist China and U.S.S.R. and are impressed by cultural gains.
307. January 28, p. 7, c. 2.
Twenty Belgian workers in U.S. for work-study program under MSA.
308. February 1, p. 5, c. 1.
Some USSR moves consolidating cultural holds in East Austria.
309. February 3, p. 9.
International Educational Institute offers U.S. college students eighty grants for study and teaching in France; France offers thirty-five graduate fellowships.
310. February 13, p. 36, c. 1.
New York Educational Board and Greek Embassy offer teachers course on Greece.
311. February 17, p. 8, c. 5.
Assistant Professor W. W. Culver (U.S.) calls dropping of American House Program, West Germany, a loss to U.S.-German relations.
312. February 20, p. 7, c. 3.
Seven artists, members of International Educational Institutional Arts Program under Ford and Rockefeller Foundations' auspices, arrive in the U.S.
313. February 24, p. 58, c. 7.
New York Herald Tribune and some overseas airlines sponsor U.S. tour by twenty from abroad.
314. March 5, p. 3, c. 1.
U.S.S.R. continues program in India.

1952 (Cont.)

315. March 16, p. 34, c. 4.
Four named sponsors of Jewish Agency for Palestine work-study tour in Israel for U.S. students and teachers.

316. March 19, p. 12, c. 3.
World Communists mark Victor Hugo's 150th birth anniversary; plan to fete Leonardo daVinci and others to show backing of free interchange among peoples.

317. March 19, p. 14, c. 6.
Dr. Conant urges greater exchange between Britain and U.S. universities.

318. March 23, p. 3, c. 1.
F. Kortner plans U.S. tour with German and Austrian actors under West German Government auspices.

319. March 26, p. 11, c. 2.
International Educational Institute reports rise in exchanges between U.S. and other countries during 1951.

320. April 7, p. 23, c. 3.
Ford Foundation unit plans quarterly *Perspectives USA* showing cultural life to nations abroad.

321. April 8, p. 31, c. 4.
Premier Erlander urges free exchange of ideas.

322. April 16, p. 24, c. 1.
Kenneth Holland sees 70,000 specialists and students in exchange programs between U.S. and other countries.

323. April 20, p. 11, c. 3.
International Educational Institute names eight to Foreign Artists Program under Ford and Rockefeller Foundations' auspices.

324. April 27, p. 19, c. 1.
UNESCO drafts plan to aid potential missions from soft-currency countries.

325. May 18, p. 17, c. 3, 4.
UNESCO issues supplement to survey on summer study abroad; New York University Education School offers a summer study program, Israel.

326. July 11, p. 2, c. 3.
Seventy-seven U.S. and Pakistani students and teachers in exchange program under auspices of U.S. Education Foundation in Pakistan.

327. July 20, p. 9, c. 2.
Forty-seven German students are first of 1,000 to arrive in the U.S. under U.S. Government and International Educational Institute auspices.

328. August 29, p. 21, c. 3.
Dewey urges student exchanges between U.S. and others.

329. September 13, p. 9, c. 6.
Eight hundred Iranians to study in the U.S. under government pact.

330. November 24, p. 1, c. 4.
New York Times survey finds exchange programs between U.S. and other countries effective.

1952 (Cont.)

331. December 10, p. 23, c. 5.
R. Harris cites role of U.S. State Department division in exchange of 7,200 from seventy-two countries during 1951.

1953

332. July 21, p. 16, c. 6.
First of 670 foreign students arrive in U.S. for year's study under U.S. Government-sponsored program.

1954

333. March 17, p. 27, c. 3.
Britain and USSR students plan summer exchange program.
334. March 22, p. 15, c. 6.
UNESCO reports that the U.S. with 33,693 foreign students replaces France as student "mecca."
335. August 6, p. 9, c. 2.
U.S. and British teachers to exchange posts under U.S. State Department program.
336. September 5, p. 7, c. 3.
U.S. high school teachers sought for posts under State Department program for France and West Germany.

1955

337. January 22, p. 13, c. 3.
American-Scandinavian Council offers program in Scandinavia to U.S. students.
338. May 1, p. 9, c. 3.
International Educational Institute supervised 2,800 foreign students in U.S. in 1954.
339. June 8, p. 60, c. 2.
Israel offers first fellowship to U.S. students.
340. June 13, p. 4, c. 3.
Four hundred Chinese from Singapore, Malaya, and Indonesia to study in Communist China at government invitation.
341. June 25, p. 16, c. 1.
Fifty-one New York City high school students plan study tour in Israel and Europe under Jewish Education Committee auspices.
342. June 26, p. 9, c. 3.
International Educational Institute issues publication, *Summer Study Abroad,* for U.S. students.
343. July 24, p. 9, c. 3, 4.
English-language assistants sought in the U.S. for posts in West German high school under State Department program. International Educational Institute issues publication on aims of world exchange program.

1955 (Cont.)

344. August 4, p. 27, c. 4.
British teachers exchange posts under State Department auspices.
345. August 23, p. 19, c. 6.
Three hundred foreign high school students in U.S. for year under American
Field Service auspices.
346. September 11, p. 19, c. 1.
President Eisenhower and Ambassador Melas hail U.S.-Greek student ex-
changes.

1956

347. January 17, p. 13, c. 3.
President Eisenhower's budget message asks more funds for State Department
international exchange program.
348. February 7, p. 20, c. 6.
Adlai E. Stevenson aids fund to bring more exchange students to U.S.
349. February 8, p. 7, c. 3.
British Council announces accordance in principle on Great Britain-U.S.S.R.
exchanges.
350. February 19, p. 79, c. 3.
International Educational Institute reports Italy and three Italian universities offer grants to U.S. graduate students.
351. February 23, p. 29, c. 8.
Six New York City high school students of three major religious faiths to
visit Israel in exchange with Israel high school pupils; program instituted at
invitation of Israeli school system; New York City Education Board presents
Silver's comments.
352. April 2, p. 3, c. 3.
Moscow University invitation to Harvard to exchange professors and students, 1956–57, is part of U.S.S.R. drive for exchanges with U.S. Tass reports
students at five U.S. institutions favor exchanges. U.S. Government officials
are skeptical.
353. May 5, p. 3, c. 6.
U.S. and Peru sign three-year student exchange accord.
354. May 20, p. 2, c. 5.
France and U.S.S.R. agree to student exchanges; communiqué on Moscow
talks.
355. June 18, p. 14, c. 3.
Some U.S. students and teachers to tour India under World University Service auspices.
356. August 4, p. 17, c. 7.
Two hundred U.S. and British teachers exchange posts under U.S. State Department auspices; U.S. teachers briefed in New York City; 225 others to
teach in Europe and elsewhere, some in exchange for foreign teachers; record number of U.S. teachers abroad.

1956 (Cont.)

357. August 5, p. 19, c. 1.
Thirty-two U.S. students plan year in Israel.
358. August 15, p. 21, c. 1.
One hundred British teachers in the U.S.
359. September 18, p. 37, c. 2.
Oxford University and Moscow University agree on professor and student exchange to start this summer.
360. November 6, p. 32, c. 3.
U.S. and Argentina sign pact for exchange program; U.S. will use funds acquired under Surplus Agriculture Commodities Agreement.

1957

361. January 20, p. 11, c. 3.
U.S. graduate students offered study and teaching grants by France.
362. March 17, p. 51, c. 1.
Forty scholars from Middle East and Asia to study at four U.S. universities in next five years; Chicago University coordinates program; Ford Foundation gives $300,000.

1958

363. September 17, p. 41, c. 2.
U.S. State Department reports three U.S. professors will lecture abroad under international exchange program.

1959

364. January 8, p. 4, c. 7.
Ford Foundation gives International Educational Institute $130,000 for program for twenty Yugoslav Government leaders and scholars studying and traveling in U.S. during 1959–1960.
365. November 5, p. 14, c. 4.
Ford Foundation gives $290,000 to International Schools Foundation to expand program for Americans abroad; Fr. Brooks and G. MacKenzie to survey needs.

1960

366. February 24, p. 1, c. 8.
U.S.S.R. plans University of Friendship of Peoples in Moscow offering specialized tuition-free training to Asians, Africans, and Latin Americans.
367. March 30, p. 17, c. 2.
State Department to increase exchanges with Africa.
368. June 8, p. 6, c. 4.
French Government withdraws $17,000 subsidy for Students' National Union because of political activity against Algerian war.
369. June 26, p. 46, c. 5.

1960 (Cont.)

Forty from U.S. to study abroad under international fellowship exchange program.
370. July 24, p. 9, c. 1.
Canada and U.S.S.R. plan teacher exchange.
371. November 3, p. 32.
Excerpts from John F. Kennedy's speech urging U.S. "Peace Corps."

1961

372. May 29, p. 1, c. 7.
U.S. plans scholarship program for Africans at 150 leading institutions.
373. October 17, p. 1, c. 4.
U.S., Canada, and seventeen European nations hold policy conference on economic growth and investment in education.

1962

374. January 25, p. 3, c. 5.
Ghana and U.S. sign accordance to exchange students and university personnel.

1963

375. March 6, p. 8.
"Shriver's Peace Corps and the New Frontier," by James Reston.
376. September 8, p. 65, c. 3.
Twenty-three Africans from seven countries in U.S. under first graduate fellowship program sponsored by U.S., African governments, and U.S. universities.

LATIN AMERICA

Books and Pamphlets

377. Jardim, Germano. *Methodology in Statistics of Education and Culture in the American Nations.* Rio de Janeiro: Servico Grafico do Institute Brasileiro de Geografia e Estatistica, 1949, 86 pp.
Chapter III, "Administration of Education," contains a brief description of the administrative structure of official agencies in charge of education in each of the American republics.
378. Neal, Marian. "United Nations Programs in Haiti." *Carnegie Endowment for International Peace,* International Conciliation, no. 468, February, 1951, pp. 81–118. In Frank, Peter G., *Implementation of Technical Assistance.*
Subchapter, "The UNESCO Fundamental Education Pilot Project in Marbial" (pp. 102–111), is an evaluation of the problems and achievements of the project.
379. Fleming, Philip B. *Letter to the President.* Washington Institute of Inter-American Affairs, 1952, 3 pp. Mimeographed.

Reprint of a letter to the President of the U.S. from the then U.S. Ambassador to Costa Rica, describing the activities of Costa Rica's 4-S program, initiated by the Cooperative Education Program following the example of the 4-H Club.

380. Carles, Ruben Dario. *Panama and the Institute of Inter-American Affairs; Vocational Education 1952.* Washington: Institute of Inter-American Affairs, n. d., 12 pp. Mimeographed.

Report by the Minister of Education of Panama to the Institute of Inter-American Affairs on the operation of the Point Four program in vocational education during that year.

381. Gibson, R. C. "Institute of Inter-American Affairs Education Program in Latin America." *Yearbook of Education,* 1954, pp. 572–580.

382. Hanson, Earl Parker, and Charlotte Leeper Hanson (eds.). *Change Through Interchange: Developing Our Human and Natural Resources Through Inter-American Exchange.* (The report of the Conference sponsored by the Institute of International Education and the Pan American Union in cooperation with the Department of State of the Commonwealth of Puerto Rico.) New York: Institute of International Education, 1958, 33 pp.

383. Adams, Richard N., and Charles C. Cumberland. *United States University Cooperation in Latin America.* East Lansing, Michigan: Michigan State University, Institute of Research on Overseas Programs, 1960, 264 pp.

384. Carley, Verna A. *Report of Progress in Teacher Education: Technical Cooperation in Forty Developing Countries.* Washington, D.C.: International Cooperation Administration, 1960, 101 pp.

385. Institute of International Education. *Annual Report 1960.* New York: The Institute, 1960. Unpaged.

386. Regional Conference of Directors of American Schools (Inter-American Schools Service). *A List of United States Sponsored Schools in Latin America.* Washington, D.C., 1960.

387. Mauck, Willfred. *Inter-American Cooperation in Education.* Washington: Institute of Inter-American Affairs, n. d., 14 pp. Mimeographed.

The story of the first few years of cooperative education programs sponsored jointly by the governments of the U.S. (through the Institute of Inter-American Affairs) and of the host Latin American nations, under the Point Four program.

Government Documents

388. International Labour Office. *Vocational Training in Latin America.* Geneva: International Labour Office, 1951, 319 pp. (Studies and Reports, no. 28).

Report on industrial, agricultural, and commercial training on the basis of information collected on the spot. Appendix I, "Notes on Various Countries," contains surveys on the current status of vocational education in Argentina, Bolivia, Brazil, Chile, Colombia, Costa Rica, Cuba, Ecuador, Guatemala, Mexico, Peru, Uruguay, and Venezuela. Appendix II, "Reso-

lutions Adopted by Conferences of American States Members of the I.L.O."
389. Iverson, Kenneth R. *Ten Years of Point Four in Latin America.*
Washington: Institute of Inter-American Affairs, 1952, 7 pp. (Reprinted from
Export Trade and Shipper, Jan. 7, and Jan. 28, 1952, and issued as the Institute's *Building a Better Hemisphere* series, no. 2).
General article summarizing achievements of Point Four programs, including educational programs in Latin America.
390. Gibson, R. C. *Rural Schools of Peru, Peruvian-North American Cooperative Program in Rural Education.* Washington: U.S. Department of
Health, Education, and Welfare, Office of Education, 1955, 23 pp. (Studies in
Comparative Education).
Concerned largely with cooperative programs in Peru. Subheading, "Peru
and Bolivia Develop a New Rural School Program" (pp. 4–5), gives an
account of the 1945 Warisata Conference where the foundations were laid
for the cooperative programs in both Bolivia and Peru.
391. Ageton, Arthur A. "Good Partnership in Paraguay," *Department of
State Bulletin,* XXXV (November 1956), 847–854.
392. "Educational Exchange Agreement with Argentina," *Department of
State Bulletin,* XXXV (Nov. 26, 1956), 861–862.
393. Freeburger, Adela R. *Guide for the Evaluation of Academic Credentials from the Latin American Republics.* Washington: U.S. Department of
Health, Education, and Welfare, Office of Education, 1957, 55 pp. (Studies
in Comparative Education).
Contains general remarks on evaluating education in Latin America, followed by résumés of the organization of education by country and has a
glossary of common educational terminology in use in Latin America.
394. Pan American Union. *The Pan American Union's International Exchange Program of Students and Professors.* Washington: Pan American
Union, 1958. (Information Series Bulletin 1958, no. 2).
395. U.S. International Cooperation Administration. *Fact Sheet, Mutual
Security in Action. International Cooperation Administration.* U.S. Department of State Publication no. 6843, Inter-American Series no. 56, September
1959, 11 pp.
396. ———. *Fact Sheet, Mutual Security in Action, Brazil.* U.S. Department
of State Publication no. 6951, Inter-American Series no. 57, March 1960.
397. U.S. Department of State. "Alianza Para Progreso." Address by President John F. Kennedy, March 13, 1961. U.S. Department of State Publication no. 7164, Inter-American Series no. 65. Washington 25, D.C.: U.S. Department of State, Office of Public Services, 1961, 14 pp.

Magazines

398. Houle, Cyril O. "Some Significant Experiments in Latin American
Education; American School in Puebla," *Elementary School Journal,* XLIX,
no. 2 (October 1948), 61–66.
Brief description of the development of U.S. sponsored schools in Latin
America, in general, and the Colegio Americano in Puebla, in particular.

399. Duckles, Edwin. "Friends in Mexico," *Impetus* (March–April 1950), 4–6.

Twenty-five or thirty young men and women from five different countries selected by the American Friends Service Committee to work as volunteers side by side with the Mexican staff members of the Ensayo Piloto, Mexico's pilot project in fundamental education.

400. O'Hara, Hazel. "Puppets Can Teach," *Americas*, II, no. 12 (December 1950), 20–21.

On the use of puppet shows to bring health education to rural areas in El Salvador. Reply from T. H. Butterworth, U.S. Public Health Service, with editorial rejoinder, in *Americas*, III, no. 2 (February 1951), 48.

401. Stevenson, Gordon K. "Nucleos Escolares Rurales," *Phi Delta Kappan*, XXXII, no. 5 (January 1951), 209–211.

Origin of the Nucleos Escolares Rurales in Bolivia and the adaptation of the idea by the Guatemalan Government in cooperation with the Institute of Inter-American Affairs.

402. Newell, Gladys E. "Cuban Fortnight," *New York State Education*, XXXVIII, no. 6 (March 1951), 419–421.

Account of the author's visit to Cuba as one of a group of U.S. teachers invited by Cuban Government in celebration of 50th anniversary of Cuba's school system. Brief general comments on Cuban education.

403. Benjamin, G. K. "Community Goes to School in Guatemala," *Educational Outlook*, XXVI, no. 3 (March 1952), 91–101.

Survey of developments in literacy and adult education in Guatemala since World War II; roles of Guatemala and U.S. Governments and of international organizations such as UNESCO.

404. Laguerre, Enrique. "The International Project at Patzcuaro," *International House Quarterly*, XVI, no. 3 (Summer, 1952), 158–162.

On UNESCO's Latin American fundamental education center in Patzcuaro, Mexico.

405. Wirth, A. F. "Secondary Education in Ecuador," *School and Society*, LXXVI, no. 1979 (Nov. 22, 1952), 325–328.

Describes briefly some principal characteristics and problems of Ecuadorian secondary education and tentative proposals for change emerging from recent cooperative work between Ecuadorian Government and Point Four international mission.

406. Barley, Bernadine. "Mexico; Laboratory of the Future," *United Nations World*, VI, no. 12 (December 1952), 47–50.

Brief article on Crefal, UNESCO's Latin American fundamental education center in Patzcuaro, Mexico, for teachers from Latin American countries.

407. Hayman, Lee R. "Yankee College in Mexico," *Americas*, V, no. 5 (May 1953), 21–23, 27.

Article on Mexico City College, U.S. style liberal arts college founded by the U.S. citizens and organizations in Mexico City.

408. Mahiman, J. "Point Four in Paraguay," *American Vocational Journal*, XXVIII, no. 5 (May 1953), 24–25.
Point Four efforts in vocational education in Paraguay.

409. Wiggin, Gladys A. "What Should Be Communicated?" *School and Society*, LXXVII, no. 2009 (June 20, 1953), 385–390.
An experiment in international education with educators from Bolivia, Ecuador, and Peru during a ten-month workshop at the Center for Educational Leadership, University of Maryland.

410. Betancur-Majia, Gabriel. "Columbia's Institute for Advanced Training Abroad," *Institute of International Education News Bulletin*, XXVIII (June 1953), 20–21.

411. Hall, G. L. "Educational Cooperation with Paraguay," *Journal of Teacher Education*, V (September 1954), 203–204.

412. Colligan, Francis J. "U.S. Government Exchange Programs with the Other American Republics," *Institute of International Education News Bulletin*, XXX, no. 7 (April 1955), 2–8.

413. Wilhelm, Rolf. "A Voluntary Team in the El Salvador Rural Settlement Project," *Fundamental and Adult Education*, VII, no. 2 (April 1955), 65–70.
Describes the fundamental and adult education project operated by the Institute de Colonizacion Rural of El Salvador and the American Friends Service Committee at El Sitie del Nino, El Salvador.

414. "Industrial Education for Guatemala," *U.S. National Commission for UNESCO, Newsletter*, II, no. 6 (April 29, 1955), 2.
Brief note on the establishment of an advisory commission to plan industrial education for training badly needed Guatemalan skilled workers.

415. Crane, Robert E. L. "Educational Workshop for Latin Americans," *Institute of International Education News Bulletin*, XXX, no. 7 (April 1955), 19–23.

416. Bellegard, Dantes. "Mass Education in Latin America," *Institute of International Education News Bulletin*, XXX, no. 7 (April 1955), 19–23, 67.
Overview of Haitian education, with particular reference to the principles expressed by the Charter of the Organization of American States.

417. Rose, T. E. "Teacher-Student to Brazil," *Institute of International Education News Bulletin*, XXX, no. 7 (April 1955), 50–53.

418. Jensen, A., and P. H. Jensen. "American School in Mexico," *The Educational Record*, XXXVI (July 1955), 250–255.
On a typical U.S.-sponsored school in Latin America: the American School of Torrean, Coahuila, Mexico.

419. Vezanni, Almando. "Skilled Hands for Industry," *Mexican-American Review*, XXIII, no. 9 (September 1955), 16–17, 27–29.
On the Centro de Adiestramiento para Operadores set up by the Mexican Government, Mexican Highway Association, and U.S. International Cooperation Administration to train workers to handle and service highway construction equipment and agricultural machinery.

420. Bosemberg, H. W. "Teachers of Teachers: OAS Training Center in Venezuela Sets Off Educational Chain Reaction," *Americas,* VIII, no. 3 (March 1956), 14–18.

On the Inter-American Rural Normal School (now known as the Inter-American Rural Education Center), established at Rubio, Venezuela, under the OAS Technical Cooperation Program to train rural normal school teachers and administrators from Latin American countries.

421. "Teacher-Training School: Experimental College Paraguay-Brazil, Asuncion," *Architectural Record,* CXIX, no. 4 (April 1956), 247–252.

Photographs and architectural plans of two modern Latin American school buildings: the Paraguay-Brazil Experimental College in Asuncion, Paraguay, and a secondary school in Rio de Janeiro, Brazil.

422. Landau, Georges D. "ITA Keeps Them Flying: Brazil's Modern Aeronautical Institute," *Americas,* VIII (June 1956), 12–17.

423. Klemer, Elizabeth J. "Experiences with Public Education in Peru," *Education,* XXX (June 1956), 623–629.

424. Landau, Georges D. "School for Public Servants: A New Departure in Brazilian Education," *Americas,* VIII (November 1956), 12–15.

425. Venezuela, Ministerio de Educacion, *Revista Para el Magisterio,* LXXXIV (December 1956), 2–151.

426. Tully, G. Emerson. "Guidance in the Federal Industrial and Technical Schools of Brazil," *School and Society,* LXXXV (Jan. 5, 1957), 7–10.

427. Holmberg, Allen R. "Education Intervention in Peru," *Journal of Education,* LXXXIX, no. 1058 (September 1957), 381–384.

Report of the Director of the Cornell-Peru Project in Vicos, Peru, on the role of formal and informal education in this action-research program in community development among Andean Indians.

428. Fitzgerald, Dean T. "The Significance of American Schools in Latin America," *Comparative Education Review,* I, no. 2 (October 1957), 19–22.

Discusses the role and significance of these bilingual, bicultural schools to Latin American students, to U.S. students-members of families residing in Latin America, to the Latin American teaching profession, and to inter-American relations in general.

429. Inter-American Issue. *Institute of International Education News Bulletin,* XXXIV, no. 2 (October 1958), 1–48.

430. Pan American Union. *Teaching Opportunities in Latin America for U.S. Citizens.* Washington: Pan American Union (1958), 6. (Information Series Bulletin, 1958, no. 4).

431. Simonpietri, Andre C. "Some Developments in Scientific Relations with Latin America," *National Academy of Sciences and National Research Council News Report,* XV (January–February 1960), 5+.

432. Cohen, Herman J. "The Fulbright Program in Latin America," *Institute of International Education News Bulletin,* XXXV, no. 8 (April 1960), 8–17.

A review of the development of the Fulbright program in Latin America.

433. Rippy, J. Fred. "Vague Plans and Huge Expenditures for the Solu-

tion of Hemispheric Problems?" *Inter-American Economic Affairs*, XIV (Autumn, 1960), 55–70.

434. Simon, S. Fanny. "Teachers Against Illiteracy," *The American Teacher Magazine*, XLV (December 1960), 9–10, 22.

435. Holland, Kenneth, "CHEAR," *Institute of International Education News Bulletin*, XXXVI (May 1961), 3–9.

436. Crane, Robert E. L. "Educational Workshop for Latin Americans: University of Puerto Rico," *School Life*, XLIV (July 1962), 5–7.

437. Schroeder, R. C. "Soul for the Alliance: Third Inter-American Education Ministers Meeting, Bogotá, Colombia," *Americas*, XV (October 1963), 2–6.

438. U.S. National Student Association. "The Rise of Latin American Left," Political Background Project, USNSA, Philadelphia, 51 pp. Mimeographed.

439. Keating, L. C. "American Aid to Education in Peru," *School and Society*, XCII (May 2, 1964), 206–208.

ECUADOR

Books and Pamphlets

440. Washburne, Carleton. "La educación en Colombia y Ecuador," *Nueva Era* (Quito), XII (1962), 239–248.

441. Romo Dávila, Carlos. *El proyecto educativo en el Ecuador y en Latinoamérica*. Quito: Casa de la Cultura Ecuatoriana, 1956, 68 pp.

Sees a need for a new practical orientation to problems of educational reform in Latin America. The formation of an Inter-American Union of Educators is proposed to encourage professional solidarity and facilitate cooperative programs on a hemispheric basis.

442. Rubio Orbe, Gonzalo. *Promociones indígenas en América*. Quito: Casa de la Cultura Ecuatoriana, 1957, 403 pp.

Studies the problem of educating and raising the standard of living of indigenous populations in Latin America. Based on the author's wide experience in Mexico, Bolivia, Peru, and Ecuador. Pages 303–401 deal with problems of Indian education in Ecuador.

443. Larrea, Julio. *La educación en los Estados Unidos*. Quito: Editorial Universitaria, 1960, 222 pp.

444. ———. *La educación nueva: significados, fines, organización, métodos, la formación del maestro, la educación para la comprensión internacional, la educación latinoamericana en la brecha*. Quito: Casa de la Cultura Ecuatoriana, 1960 (second edition), 370 pp.

Includes educational theories of Montessori, Dalton, Decroly, Dewey, Cousinet, etc., and twentieth-century educational systems. Comparative data are drawn mainly from England, Germany, France, Netherlands, Italy, and the United States. The systems are examined from the point of view of objectives, organization, teaching methods, inspection and supervision, education for international understanding, and educational tendencies in Latin America.

Magazines

445. Taylor, Jessie E. "Point Four in Quito," *Minnesota Journal of Education*, XXXI (April 1951), 24–25.

446. Uzcátegui, Emilio. "A Comparison Between Education in the State of California and in the Republic of Ecuador," *Filosofía, Letras y Ciencias de la Educación* (Quito), V, no. 16 (October–December 1952).

447. Chavez, Ligdano. "Formación de profesores en algunos paises de América: Uruguay, Brasil, Puerto Rico y México. Nuevas orientaciones en el Ecuador," *Revista Ecuatoriana de Educación*, VI, no. 25 (January–April 1953), 288.

Entire issue is devoted to a comparative examination of teacher preparation in the countries mentioned. Most of the data were gathered while the author was on a UNESCO fellowship in 1951–1952.

448. García, Zebedeo. "Algunos aspectos del programa de educación que llevan a cabo el Ecuador y en los Estados Unidos," *Nueva Era* (Quito), XXIII (1955), 49–50.

449. Guerra, E. L. "Interpreting the Civilization and Culture of the United States in Ecuador," *Journal of Educational Sociology*, XXXI (January 1958), 138–140.

A New York professional educator who served at the universities at Guayaquil and Quito relates briefly his experiences as a professor there and his activities in explaining the United States way of life.

450. "Group from Ecuador Visits," *New York Times* (February 23, 1962), p. 9, c. 8.

Forty-two Ecuadorian high school students visit Miami, Florida, families for two weeks sponsored by the *Miami Herald*, Dade County School Board, and several Latin American agencies. A month earlier, a Peruvian group participated in "Operation Amigo."

451. Academy of Sciences. *Ecuador*. Moscow: Academy of Sciences (1963). The entire work is in Russian, with chapters prepared by various authors. Pages 169–186 deal with education, particularly university student activities. The principal source for this chapter is the periodical, *Mundo Estudiantil*.

452. Boegli, J. C. "My Life as a Peace Corps Girl," *Good Housekeeping*, CLVI (April 1963), 84–85. (Same as no. 269.)

453. Brooks, R., and E. Brooks. "Ecuador: Peace Corps Volunteers," *National Geographic Magazine*, CXXVI (September 1964), 338–345.

CHILE

Books and Pamphlets

454. Amunátegui y Solar, Domingo. *El sistema Lancáster en Chile y en otros países sud americanos*. Santiago: Imprenta Cervantes, 1895, 371 pp.

455. Samper, Armando. *Technical Cooperation in Latin America: A Case Study of Cooperation in Secondary Education in Chile*. Washington: National Planning Association, 1957, 83 pp.

A history and an analysis of secondary education in Chile as well as an account and appraisal of the program of technical cooperation with Chile in this field from 1945 to 1948. Conclusions and recommendations based on this report are drawn for cooperative education programs in Latin America.

Government Documents

456. Fernández, P., and W. Howe. "United States Replies to Chilean Students' Letter to President Eisenhower," *U.S. Department of State Bulletin*, XLII (April 25, 1960), 648–658.
Contains texts of letters.

Magazines

457. Gaw, Esther Allen. "Education in Chile," *Institute of International Education News Bulletin*, XIV (Jan. 1, 1939), 5–7; same, *Elementary School Journal*, XXXIX (March 1939), 487–489.
Dean of Women at Ohio State who spent a summer session at the University of Chile describes the system and its problems, largely on the basis of data from Amanda Labarca Hubertson and Wilhelm Mann.

458. Hall, Robert King. "Federal Control of Education in Argentina, Brazil and Chile," *School Review*, L (November 1942), 651–660.
This comparative study of federal control concludes that systems are too inflexible to be functional. Even minor local reform calls for legislation. Relative ease of legal change blinds authorities to need for actual change. Secondary schools seen as agents for much federal propaganda.

459. Fuentes Vega, Salvador. "A educacão pública no Chile," *Revista Brasiliera de Estudos Pedagögicos* (Río) (November 1945), 232–242.

460. González Ríos, Rubén. "Educacão secundaria no Chile," *Revista Brasiliera de Estudos Pedagögicos* (Río) (December 1946), 432–437.

461. "University of Chile Offers Summer Session Scholarships," *School and Society*, LXXIV (Oct. 20, 1951), 250.
Room, board, and tuition scholarships for citizens of American nations, including two for the U.S.

462. Spears, H. "Point Four Precursor, How Educational Aid Program Worked in Chile," *School Executive*, LXXI (November 1951), 84–85.

463. Salas, Irma. "Education in Chile," *International House Quarterly* (Spring, 1952), 68–75.
The basic educational principles and practices in Chile compared with other countries. Developments from 1875 to 1945. Girls' and women's education. Experimental secondary schools.

464. Dulanto, Reynaldo. "La educación secundaria en Chile," *Educación* (Organo de la Facultad de Educación, Lima), VIII, no. 17 (1953), 60–72.

465. Palacín Iglesias, Gregorio. *La educación en los Estados Unidos y en Latinoamérica*. Mexico: La Impresora Azteca, 1955, 265–279.

466. Labarca Hubertson, Amanda. "Influencias norteamericanas en la educación chilena," *La Nueva Democracia* (New York), XLI, no. 1 (January 1961), 78–89.

467. Jobet Burquez, Julio C. "El problema educacional en Chile," *Politics* (Caracas), XVII (August–September 1961), 79–102.

468. "British Schools in Chile: Support from British Council," *Times Educational Supplement,* no. 1902 (Oct. 12, 1961), 793.

469. Smith, George E. "International Understanding and the Peace Corps in Chile," *Hispania,* XLV (May 1962), 301–302.

470. Marotz, R. "With the Peace Corps," *Journal of Home Economics,* LV (April 1963), 277–278.

FRANCE

Books and Pamphlets

471. Society for American Scholarships in French Universities. *Science and Learning in France.* Chicago: R. R. Donnelley, 1917, 454 pp.
A survey of opportunities for American students in French universities; an appreciation by American scholars.

472. International Institute of Intellectual Co-operation. *University Exchanges in Europe.* Paris: The League of Nations Institute of Intellectual Co-operation, 1928.
Handbook of the institutions and measures in all the European countries to facilitate the work of professors, students, and teachers abroad.

473. Harley, John Eugene. *International Understanding; Agencies of Education for a New World.* London: Oxford University Press, 1931, 604 pp.

474. *Fundamental Education, Common Ground for All Peoples; Report of a Special Committee to the Preparatory Commission of the U.N.'s Educational, Scientific and Cultural Organization.* Paris: UNESCO, 1946.

475. Miles, Donald W. *Recent Reforms in French Secondary Education, with Implications for French and American Education.* New York: Bureau of Publications, Teachers College, Columbia University, 1953, 163 pp.

476. Parsons, James Russell. *French Schools Through American Eyes.* New York: C. W. Bardeen, n. d.
A report of the New York State Department of Public Instruction.

477. Bodenman, Paul S. *American Cooperation With Higher Education Abroad: A Survey of Current Programs.* Washington, D.C.: U.S. Office of Education, Bulletin no. 8, 1957.

478. Institute of International Education. *Handbook on International Study.* New York: Institute of International Education, 1955, 350 pp.
A guide for foreign students on study in the U.S. and for U.S. students on study abroad.

479. French Cultural Services in the United States. *On the Granting of Credits for the French Baccalaureat.* New York: The Cultural Services, June 1956, 14 pp.
This study written by a committee of professors in the U.S. presents facts concerning the French baccalaureat and their evaluation of it in terms of American education.

480. Flack, Michael J. *Sources of Information on International Educational Activities.* Washington: American Council on Education, 1958, 114 pp.

An exploratory survey prepared for the Commission on Education and International Affairs of the American Council on Education.

481. UNESCO. *Education for International Understanding; Examples and Suggestions for Classroom Use.* Paris: UNESCO, 1959, 116 pp.

482. Hollingshead, Byron S. "Some Differences Between American and European Education," *Third Workshop of Educational Organizations (Condensed Report), April 28–30, 1959.* Washington, D.C.: U.S. Department of Health, Education and Welfare, Office of Education, 1959, 8 pp.

Using French education as the chief example, a comparison is made with education in the U.S. Included are some of the basic factors behind recent reforms in French education.

483. Cotner, Thomas Ewing. *International Education Exchange; a Selected Bibliography.* Washington, D.C.: U.S. Department of Health, Education and Welfare, 1961.

484. Kinkead, Katherine T. *Walk Together, Talk Together; the American Field Service Students' Exchange Program.* New York: Norton, 1962.

485. Barker, H. Kenneth (ed.). *AACTE Handbook of International Education Programs.* Washington, D.C.: American Association of Colleges for Teacher Education, 1963.

486. *Study Abroad, International Handbook; Fellowships, Scholarships, Educational Exchange.* Paris: UNESCO, yearly.

Government Documents

487. France, Ministry of National Education. *Education in France During the School-Year 1955–1956.* Paris: Centre National de Documentation Pedagogique, 1956, 12 pp.

This brochure deals with the administration of education, organization and reform, curriculums and methods, teaching staff, the French Union Overseas, and relations with foreign countries during 1955–1956.

Magazines

488. "France: Education at Mid-Century," *Current History,* XXXV (August 1958), 65–118.

489. "Continental Approaches; Franco-German Systems Discussed," *Times Educational Supplement* (May 19, 1961), 1039.

490. Maurois, Andre. "Frenchmen Appraise U.S. Schools," *Overseas,* I (September 1961), 14–16.

491. Houser, R. A. "Pedagogy or Popcorn," *Overseas,* II (October 1962), 16–20. Discussion, II (December 1962), 27–28.

492. des Closets, J. P. Cosnard. "American Students in France: Summer of Learning and Travel," *Overseas,* II (March 1963), 17–20.

493. Guterman, S. L. "Church-School Question in England and France," *Comparative Education Review,* VII (June 1963), 28–35.

494. Capelle, G. "Teaching English in Europe: France," *English Language Teaching,* XVIII (October 1963), 3–9.

WEST GERMANY

Magazines

495. "Resumption of Cultural Relations with Germany and Austria," *Institute of International Education News Bulletin*, XXII (May 1, 1947), 7–8. The policy to resume cultural relations with Germany is intended to further the reorientation of the German people toward peace and democracy. Selection based upon ability and those who have demonstrated their opposition to Nazism and their belief in democratic principles.

A similar policy was announced at the same time for Austria. Because of the overcrowded conditions of educational institutions in Germany and Austria it will be impossible for American students to study in those countries for the time being.

496. Ziemer, G. A. "Should We Trade Teachers with Germany?" *Saturday Evening Post*, CCXX (April 17, 1948), 10, 28.

497. von Becherath, H. "Cultural Cooperation with German Universities," *High School Journal*, XXXII (May 1949), 130–133.

498. Spielvogel, Robert F. "German Meets America; German Student Studying in U.S. Under IIE Auspices," *Institute of International Education News Bulletin*, XXV (April 1950), 32–33.

A plea for an increased exchange program on the grounds that one can study the institutional structure of a country, but yet not get an understanding of the country. Proposes that international relations can be promoted by increased personal contact among people of different nations.

499. Kline, James D. "German Exchanges, Before and After Fulbright," *Institute of International Education News Bulletin*, XXVIII (February 1953), 23–27.

This article explains German organization for educational exchanges and the ways the German government is meeting the challenge of increasing numbers of visiting students.

500. Gariss, P. J., and H. Ott. "American-German Teacher Exchange," *German Quarterly*, XXVII (March 1954), 104–109.

The authors were among the first (1952–1953) American high school teachers to teach in West Germany and West Berlin as regular members of a secondary school staff. They collected pertinent information from all nineteen American exchangees and summarized their experiences. Despite difficulties and disappointments, the exchange program with Germany was unanimously endorsed by all American participants.

501. Wodlinger, D. "Scholarship Programs in Germany, Austria, and Switzerland," *German Quarterly*, XXXI (January 1958), 33–37.

A review of the contributions of the Institute of International Education from its small beginnings in 1919, through its acceptance in 1949, of the U.S. Government's request to administer international educational programs, to its present position as the largest private agency in its field.

502. "Foreign Students: West Germany's Welcome," *Times Educational Supplement*, MCCCIX (October 30, 1959), 509.

503. Neuse, W. "Why Do We Send Our Undergraduates to Germany?" *German Quarterly*, XXXIV (May 1961), 215–217. Discussion: XXXV (January 1962), 98–99.

504. "Annual Report of the German Academic Exchange Service," *School and Society*, XC (Nov. 17, 1962), 394.

505. Green, W. "German Exchange Students in the United States—A Case Study," *Human Organization*, XIII (Fall, 1964), 16–22.

FINLAND

506. Broms, B. "Scholarship Programs Linking the United States and Finland," *American Scandinavian Review*, II (March 1961), 15–19.

U.S.S.R.

Books and Pamphlets

507. Counts, George S. *The Challenge of Soviet Education.* New York: McGraw-Hill, 1957, 330 pp.

508. Barghoorn, Frederick C. *The Soviet Cultural Offensive: The Role of Cultural Diplomacy in Soviet Foreign Policy.* Princeton: Princeton University Press, 1960, 353 pp.

Information on foreign student exchanges, visits to the Soviet Union by U.S. educators, scientists, physicians, "area specialists," and other groups. Deals with youth festivals, teaching of humanities and foreign languages in the U.S.S.R., libraries in the U.S.S.R., and other related subjects.

509. Bereday, George Z. F., and J. Pennar (eds.). *Politics of Soviet Education.* New York: Praeger, 1960, 217 pp.

510. Bereday, George Z. F., William W. Brickman, and Gerald Read (eds.). *The Changing Soviet School.* Boston: Houghton Mifflin, 1960, 514 pp.

511. Bronfenbrenner, Urie. "Some Problems in Communicating with Americans About the Soviet Union." n. d. Mimeographed.

512. *Comparative Education Tour to the USSR, 1960.* London/Oxford: University of London Institute of Education, University of Oxford, Department of Education, 1961, 56 pp.

Describes all levels of education in the U.S.S.R. and includes information on specific schools visited.

513. YMCA Exchange Group (Johns, Ray, and others). "Education in the USSR," *Thirty Days in the USSR: A Summary Report of the YMCA Exchange Group Which Visited the USSR May 15 to June 13, 1960.* 1960, 53, 13 pp.

Outlines some characteristics of education in the U.S.S.R. and lists some observations made by the delegation.

514. Amar, Andrew Richard. *A Student in Moscow.* London: Ampersand, Ltd., 1961, 64 pp.

515. Pipes, Richard (ed.). *The Russian Intelligentsia.* New York: Columbia University Press, 1961, 234 pp.

516. Burg, David. "The Peoples' Friendship University," *Problems of Communism*, X, no. 6 (November–December 1961), 50–54.

Points up some of the reasons why the university may have been established, and discusses difficulties facing it on completion of the first academic year.

517. Bird, Christopher. "Scholarship and Propaganda," *Problems of Communism*, XI, no. 2 (March–April 1962), 32–37.

Based on author's research in his study of Russo-African relations, article describes Africanist training and research centers in the Soviet Union, Soviet approach to African history, publishing activity, and organs of popular agitation which give increasing attention to African reporting.

518. London, College of Preceptors. *Education in the Soviet Union* (ed. by J. Vincent Chapman). London: The College of Preceptors, 1962, 111 pp.

This report, based on a visit to the U.S.S.R. by a delegation from the College, contains information on some of the institutions visited, summarizes the views of the delegates, and points out differences between the English and Soviet educational systems.

519. Rosen, Seymour M. *The Peoples' Friendship University in the USSR.* (Studies in Comparative Education, OE-14073). Washington, D.C.: U.S. Department of Health, Education and Welfare, Office of Education, April, 1962, 13 pp.

The following subjects are covered: scope of Soviet programs in international education; preparatory faculties of Moscow and Kiev universities; establishment of, admission to, and program of Friendship University— its problems and advantages.

520. Forschungsstelle Der Friedrich-Ebert-Stiftung. *The Soviet Bloc and the Developing Countries.* Hanover: Verlag fur Literatur und Zeitgeschehen, 1962, 39 pp.

Includes information on research and scientific institutes and higher schools in the Soviet Union, the Peoples' Friendship University, training at works enterprises, and Soviet schools in the developing countries.

521. *John Dewey's Impressions of Soviet Russia and the Revolutionary World: Mexico-China-Turkey 1929.* Introduction and notes by William W. Brickman. New York: Teachers College, Columbia University, 1964, 178 pp.

The six chapters on Soviet Russia are: "Leningrad Gives the Clue," "A Country in a State of Flux," "A New World in the Making," "What Are the Russian Schools Doing?," "New Schools for a New Era," and "The Great Experiment and the Future."

522. U.S. Department of State. *A Summary Report on the United States Exchanges Program with the Soviet Union.* Washington, D.C.: Department of State, Soviet and Eastern European Exchanges Staff, April 18, 1964, 11 pp. Mimeographed.

523. Webbink, Jane B. *African Students at Soviet Universities.* Cambridge, Massachusetts: Harvard University, 1964, 26 pp. Lithographed.

524. Azrael, Jeremy K. "The Educational System as an Agency of Political Socialization in the USSR," *Education and Political Development* (ed. by James A. Coleman). Princeton, New Jersey: Princeton University Press, 1965.

Government Documents

525. U.S. Office of Education. Division of International Education. "Education in the USSR," *Bulletin,* no. 14, 1957, Division of International Education, 226 pp.

526. U.S. Office of Education. "Soviet Commitment to Education," *Bulletin,* no. 16, OE-14062, 1959, Report of the First Official U.S. Education Mission to the U.S.S.R. 135 pp.

527. U.S. Department of Health, Education and Welfare. "Teaching in the Social Sciences and the Humanities in the U.S.S.R.," OE-14025, December 1959, 47 pp.

528. Rokitiansky, Nicholas, and William Medlin. "Bibliography of Published Materials on Russian and Soviet Education," OE-14033, February 1960, U.S. Department of Health, Education and Welfare, 70 pp.

529. Medlin, William, Clarence Lindquist, and Marshall Schmitt. "Soviet Education Programs," *Bulletin,* no. 17, OE-14037, 1960, U.S. Department of Health, Education and Welfare, 281 pp.

530. Rosen, Seymour M. *The Preparation and Education of Foreign Students in the USSR* (Information on Education Around the World). U.S. Department of Health, Education and Welfare, Office of Education, OE-14034–44, July, 1960, 8 pp.

  Tables list foreign students by field of study in the U.S. and U.S.S.R.; number of students from non-Communist countries of Asia, Africa, and Latin America in the U.S. and the U.S.S.R.; and total enrollment of foreign students in the U.S. and U.S.S.R. for the years 1950–1953.

531. U.S. Office of Education. Division of International Education. "The Preparation and Education of Foreign Students in the USSR," Washington, 1960 (Information on Education Around the World, no. 44), 8 pp.

532. Caldwell, Oliver J., and Loren R. Graham. *Moscow in May 1963; Education and Cybernetics; An Interchange of Soviet and American Ideas Concerning Education, Programmed Learning, Cybernetics, and the Human Mind.* U.S. Department of Health, Education and Welfare, Office of Education Bulletin, no. 38, OE-14106, 1964, 49 pp.

533. Rosen, Seymour M. *Soviet Training Programs for Africa.* U.S. Department of Health, Education and Welfare, Office of Education Bulletin, no. 9, OE-14079, 1963, 13 pp.

  Information on the training of Africans in the U.S.S.R., Soviet study and research in U.S.S.R. on Africa, and training programs in Africa connected with Soviet developmental projects. Appendix A includes a six-year curriculum in Eastern languages attached to Moscow State University, and Appendix B includes excerpts from an account by the Africa Institute in Moscow of the Soviet training programs in Africa.

534. ———. "Higher Education in the USSR," *Bulletin,* no. 16, OE-14088,

1963, U.S. Department of Health, Education and Welfare, Office of Education, 195 pp.

535. U.S. Joint Publications Research Service. *Soviet News Reports Tension between Komsomol Youth and Foreign Students.* Washington, 1963, 11 pp. (Joint Publications Research Service no. 19, 106).

536. Apanasewicz, Nellie, and Seymour M. Rosen. *Soviet Education: A Bibliography of English-Language Materials.* Washington, D.C.: U.S. Department of Health, Education and Welfare, Office of Education Bulletin, no. 29, OE-14101, 1964.

537. Rudman, Herbert C. "Structure and Decision-Making in Soviet Education," *Bulletin,* no. 2, OE-14094, 1964, U.S. Department of Health, Education and Welfare, 64 pp.

538. U.S. Department of State. "Report on Exchanges with the Soviet Union and Eastern Europe," *Report no. 22,* January 1, 1964, 71 pp.

539. U.S. Department of State. "The Education of Students from Developing Countries in the Sino-Soviet Bloc," n. d., 8 pp. Mimeographed.

Magazines

540. Woody, Thomas. "Faults and Futures in American-Soviet Cultural Relations," *School and Society,* LXIV (Sept. 28, 1946), 209–213.

541. Benne, Kenneth D. "American Teaching Profession, World Peace and American-Soviet Relations," *Progressive Education,* XXVIII (October 1950), 1–3.

542. "Soviet Students Arrive: Value of International Exchange," *Times Educational Supplement,* no. 1974 (Feb. 27, 1953), 186.

543. "Soviet Educational Structure," *Times Educational Supplement,* no. 2012 (Nov. 20, 1953), 918.

544. Hamburg, C. H. "Ideology and Foreign Policy," *Social Education,* XVIII (January 1954), 25–28.

545. Soth, L. K. "Exchanges in Perspective," *Institute of International Education News Bulletin,* XXXI (November 1955), 2–5.

546. "Soviet-American Cultural Exchanges: A Review Since 1917," *Institute of International Education News Bulletin,* XXXII (October 1956), 16–22.

1917–24: No formal programs in cultural exchange.

1925: All Union Society for Cultural Relations with Foreign Countries exchanged books, art, and organized tours for performers and professional groups.

1926: American Society for Cultural Relations with U.S.S.R. originated.

1929–31: (First Five Year Plan)—U.S. companies had ⅓ of Soviet contracts for assistance; Dneiper Dam built under Hugh L. Cooper and Co.

1934–39: American students study in Russia until outbreak of war.

1941–45: Military equipment and trainees sent to U.S.S.R.

1945–47: Person-to-Person exchanges.

1947: Russia's "States Secrets Act" forbids informal relations with other nations.

1947: Russia accepted nationals from Balkans and Korea in colleges "too crowded" for Americans.

1950: New strategy of U.S.S.R. to picture itself as the seat of true culture as compared to decadent materialism in U.S.

1952: New activities of exchange with Asian countries, including India.

1950–55: Increase in U.S.S.R. cultural and technical person-to-person exchanges and in Russian delegations abroad.

1955: Agricultural group visits U.S. from Russia.

547. Childs, John L. "Education and Politics in the Soviet Union," *Teachers College Record*, LVIII (April 1957), 351–354.

548. Holland, Kenneth. "Soviet Union and Exchange of Persons," *Institute of International Education News Bulletin*, XXXII (November 1957), 2–5. Author, who is President of the Institute of International Education, determined that the Minister of Higher Education in Moscow favored two-way exchanges of specialists and students in summer visits to cultural and educational institutions, in one-to-three year periods of study to deepen knowledge in one field, and by providing exchangee's entire higher education.

At this time more than 100 U.S. schools have asked for Russian students. Both countries need to learn about each other and to compare experiences. While Soviets can learn production methods of U.S. factories, Americans can use team methods of teaching science and advanced technology.

U.S. and Soviet Union began negotiations on October 28, 1957, directed toward the development of this exchange program.

549. Institute of International Education. Committee on Educational Interchange Policy. *Academic Exchanges with the Soviet Union.* New York: Institute of International Education, 1958, 28 pp.

550. Brickman, William W. "Educational Exchanges with Soviet Russia," *School and Society*, LXXXVI (Feb. 1, 1958), 67.

551. Medalie, R. J. "Observations on East-West Exchange," *Institute of International Education News Bulletin*, XXXIV (November 1958), 2–11. The author visited the Soviet Union in the summer of 1958, as a member of the first U.S.-U.S.S.R. student exchange group. In relating experiences of the group, the author notes various attitudes of Russian students toward the U.S. Values which justify the exchange program are given.

552. "Contact with Soviet Bloc: I—Full-Time Students," *Times Educational Supplement*, no. 2288 (March 27, 1959), 532. International cultural and educational contacts with the Communist bloc are described as greater than generally imagined. Numbers of exchange students between Communist and non-Communist nations are given, with indications of the degree of emphasis on science and technology. The general pattern is for students from the underdeveloped countries to go to the Communist bloc, while technicians from the bloc go to projects in the underdeveloped countries. Thus, few Soviet students are abroad.

553. "Contact with Soviet Bloc: II—Tourists, Books, Films, Radio," *Times Educational Supplement*, no. 2289 (April 3, 1959), 566.

The interchange of full-time students and research workers between the Communist and non-Communist world is described as inhibiting contacts with non-Communist opinion. While exchanges and tourists are encouraged for monetary reasons, large areas behind the iron curtain are barred to exchange persons.

554. Veiksham, V. A. "The Moscow Center in Comparative Education," *Comparative Education Review,* III, no. 1 (June 1959), 4–5.

555. Holland, Kenneth. "Future of U.S.-USSR Exchanges," *Institute of International Education News Bulletin,* XXXV (September 1959), 2–9.

556. "Lunik Plus I: Russians in Devon," *Times Educational Supplement,* no. 2313 (Sept. 18, 1959), 239.

Report of the first exchange visits of Soviet teachers of English to Devonshire. Twenty-five Soviet visitors were exposed to lectures, tutorials, and discussions. The summer program emphasized the learning and teaching of the English language.

557. "Exchange Agreement Between Moscow and Columbia," *School and Society,* LXXXVIII (Jan. 16, 1960), 26, 28.

An experimental agreement to exchange not more than five professors from each institution during 1960 was instituted. The agreement included the assurance of mobility, adequate facilities, and academic freedom with the stipulation that all requests are relevant to the area of study of the visiting professor. This exchange seemed to be based upon a similar successful exchange of students.

558. "Soviet Schools," *Senior Scholastic,* LXXVI (March 2, 1960), 6T.

559. Okullo, S. O. "Negro's Life in Russia: Beatings, Insults, Segregation; Interview," *U.S. News and World Report,* XLIX (August 1, 1960), 59–60.

560. "New-Type University for the Developing Countries," *Times Educational Supplement,* no. 2367 (Sept. 30, 1960), 386.

The University of Friendship in Moscow opened September 28, 1960, for the purpose of promoting cultural relations with developing countries.

561. Kahan, Arcadius. "The Economics of Vocational Training in the USSR," *Comparative Education Review,* IV, no. 2 (October 1960), 75–83.

562. "Three Who Went to Moscow: African Students," *Time,* LXXVI (Oct. 3, 1960), 27–28.

563. "African Students in USSR Denounce Discrimination, Deceit, Brutality," *AFL-CIO Free Trade Union News,* XV (December 1960), 4–6.

564. "Eastern Europe and the Soviet Union," *Institute of International Education News Bulletin,* XXXVI (December 1960), 46–51.

U.S.S.R. and Eastern European cultural and educational exchange policy is classified into three areas: (1) exchanges betwen East Europe and the U.S.S.R., (2) exchanges with non-Communist countries, and (3) exchanges with anti-Communist countries (usually characterized by formal government agreement).

In 1960, the U.S.S.R. opened the Peoples Friendship University for students from Asia, Africa, and Latin America. Only limited educational exchange has occurred, however, between the U.S. and the U.S.S.R. Concentration is in the graduate area, a result of the 1958 Lacey-Zoroubin Agreement.

565. "Free Ride in Moscow: Friendship University," *Time*, LXXVII (Jan. 6, 1961), 38+.

566. Cox, R. "Segregation in Moscow: An African's Story," *U.S. News and World Report*, L (March 6, 1961), 94.

567. Juviler, Peter H. "Communist Morality and Soviet Youth," *Problems of Communism*, X, no. 3 (May–June 1961), 16–24.

568. Mulehezi, I. "I Was a Student at Moscow State," *Reader's Digest*, LXXIX (July 1961), 99–104.

569. "Soviets Announce Educational Goals," *Overview*, II (September 1961), 87.

570. Burasevich, I. E. "Forming the Dialectical Materialist World Outlook of Students," *Soviet Education*, IV (November 1961), 28–31.

The objective of the general education polytechnical school is the establishment of a dialectical materialist world outlook in the student. The study of physics and labor relations provides opportunities for achievement of this objective. Emphasis is placed on a love for labor for the common good and the role of the Soviet Union in the conquest of space and other scientific areas.

571. Weintal, Edward. "Our Link to Moscow," *Overseas*, I (November 1961), 12–16.

572. Elyutin, V. P. "Higher School at a New Stage: the Higher School's Foreign Ties," *Soviet Education*, IV (January 1962), 35–38.

The Minister of Higher and Specialized Secondary Education of the U.S.S.R. notes the expanding cultural and scientific ties of Russia with all countries of the world, especially the Communist nations and the countries which have liberated themselves from colonialism. Twelve hundred foreign students and graduates from sixty-five nations are attending Soviet higher schools.

Influenced by the cultural and scientific achievements, and attracted by the democratic essence of Soviet education, an even greater number are seeking to enter.

The Minister pledged that the personnel of the higher schools would do everything possible to graduate highly educated specialists who are completely devoted to the ideas of Marxism-Leninism and are prepared to serve their socialist countries selflessly in order to attain the great goal of the complete victory of Communism.

573. Korolev, F. F. "Rounded Development of the Human Personality: The Paramount Task of Communist Construction," *Soviet Education*, IV, no. 3 (January 1962), 3–19. (Trans. from *Sovietskaia Pedagogika*, 1961).

574. Bronfenbrenner, Urie. "Soviet Methods of Character Education: Some Implications for Research," *Cornell Soviet Studies Reprint No. 5*, Cornell University, Ithaca. Reprinted from *American Psychologist*, XVII, no. 8 (April 1962), 550–564.

575. ———. "Soviet Studies of Personality Development and Socialization," *Cornell Soviet Studies Reprint No. 6,* Cornell University, Ithaca. Reprinted from *Some Views on Soviet Psychology,* American Psychological Association (1962), 63–86.

576. ———. "Secrecy: A Basic Tenet of the Soviets," *New York Times Magazine* (April 22, 1962), 7+.

577. Kahan, Arcadius. "Entrepreneurship in the Early Development of Iron Manufacturing in Russia," *Economic Development and Cultural Change,* X, no. 4 (July 1962), 395–422.

578. Prybla, Jan S. "Soviet Aid to Foreign Students," *Queen's Quarterly,* LXVIII (Winter, 1962), 641–650.

579. "U.S. Students in Russia," *Time,* LXXX (Nov. 30, 1962), 66.

580. Kairov, I. A. "The New CPSU Program and the Tasks of Pedagogical Science," *Soviet Education,* V, no. 3 (January 1963), 3–16. (Trans. from *Sovietskaia Pedagogika,* no. 9, 1962).

581. McCarry, C. "African Students Who Quit the Soviet Union," *American Federationist,* LXX (January 1963), 18–21.

582. "Troubles in the Big Red Schoolhouse," *Senior Scholastic,* LXXXII, no. 6 (March 6, 1963), 6+.

583. Kennedy, J. C. "African Students in Russia," *Commonweal,* LXXVIII (May 3, 1963), 161–163.

584. Malkova, Z. "Pragmatism and Pedagogy," *Soviet Education,* V, no. 7 (May 1963), 42–45. (Trans. from *Uchitel'skaia Gazeta,* May 9, 1963).

585. Vulfson, B. "The Crisis of Bourgeois Pedagogy," *Soviet Education,* V, no. 7 (May 1963), 40–42. (Trans. from *Uchitel'skaia Gazeta,* May 7, 1963).

586. ———. "Existentialism and Pedagogy," *Soviet Education,* V, no. 7 (May 1963), 45–47. (Trans. from *Uchitel'skaia Gazeta,* May 11, 1963).

587. Shabad, S. "Amerikanets in a Moscow School," *New York Times Magazine* (June 9, 1963), 44+.

588. "Africans in Russia: Le Rouge et Le Noir," *Economist* (Dec. 21, 1963), 1247–1248.

589. "We, Too, Are People: African Students vs. Soviet Policy," *Time,* LXXXII (Dec. 27, 1963), 20–21.

590. "Red and Black: African Demonstration in Moscow," *Newsweek,* LXII (Dec. 30, 1963), 28.

591. "Now, Race Riots in Moscow," *U.S. News and World Report,* LV (Dec. 30, 1963), 5.

592. Pfeifer, G. "Red and the Black: Racism in Moscow," *Reporter,* XXX (Jan. 2, 1964), 27–28.

593. "African Lesson for the Russians," *Life,* LVI (Jan. 3, 1964), 4.

594. "Anger in Red Square: Demonstration Protesting Racial Discrimination by African Nations," *Senior Scholastic,* LXXXIII (Jan. 10, 1964), 17.

595. "Good-by Lumumba U; African Students Leave Russia," *Newsweek,* LXIII (Feb. 10, 1964), 80+.

596. Afanasenka, E. I. "The Decisions of the June Plenary Meeting of the CPSU Central Committee and the Tasks of Public Education Bodies," *Soviet Education*, VI, no. 5 (March 1964). (Trans. from *Uchitel'skaia Gazeta*, August 17, 1963).

597. Dunbar, E. "African Revolt in Russia," *Look*, XXVIII (May 5, 1964), 31–35; reprinted in *Reader's Digest*, LXXXV (August 1964), 71–74.

598. Soviet Press. "Rules on Foreign Students and Their Organizations: Regulations on Foreign Citizens Studying in Higher and Specialized Secondary Educational Institutions of the USSR," *Current Digest of the Soviet Press*, XVI (May 13, 1964), 24–25.

599. Hans, Nicholas. "The Soviet Approach to Comparative Education," *Comparative Education Review*, VIII, no. 1 (June 1964), 90–94.

600. Hammer, Darrell P. "Among Students in Moscow: An Outsider's Report," *Problems of Communism*, XIII, no. 4 (July–August 1964), 11–18.

601. Bronfenbrenner, Urie. "The Mirror Image in Soviet-American Relations: A Social Psychologist's Report," *Cornell Soviet Studies Reprint No. 4,* Cornell University, Ithaca. Reprinted from the *Journal of Social Issues*, XVII, no. 3 (1961), pp. 45–56.

POLAND

Books and Pamphlets

602. Zalewska-Trafiszowa, Halina. *Foreign Students in Poland*. Warsaw: Polonia Publishing House, 1962, 151 pp.

603. ———. *Educational Opportunities for Foreigners in Poland*. Warsaw: Polonia Publishing House, 1963, 55 pp.

Government Documents

604. Apanasewicz, Nellie, and William Medlin (compilers). *Selected Bibliography of Materials on Education in Poland*. Washington, D.C.: U.S. Office of Education. International Educational Division, February 1960. OE-14030. iv, 64 pp.

Magazines

605. "New Directions in Poland," *Times Educational Supplement*, no. 1804 (Nov. 25, 1949), 820; no. 1805 (Dec. 2, 1949), 841.

606. Addams, Jane. "Polish Change and Exchange," *Institute of International Education News Bulletin*, XXXIII (April 1958), 2–7.

Author is director of the Polish Exchange Program for the Institute of International Education. The Program was established in 1957 as a result of social upheaval in Poland.

The first Polish exchangees concentrated on social sciences and have lifted cultural aspirations and achievements. Social and cultural change includes broadening of the freedom of expression, including teaching.

Polish universities have been expanding since 1956, opening new areas of study and emphasizing sociology and psychology in an effort to make up for lost time and to re-establish cultural relations with other nations.

Exchange students in the U.S. have sought to make up Polish deficiencies, especially in linguistics, sociology, architecture, city planning, and international law.

Changes in Poland and the exchange of scholars are closely allied, and it is hoped that this freedom of expression will continue to grow.

607. ———. "Polish Exchange: Touchstone for Understanding," *Institute of International Education News Bulletin*, XXXV (September 1959), 16–23.

608. "Information on Application Procedure for Admission to Institutions of Higher Education in Poland Affecting Foreign Candidates," *People's Republic of Poland*. Warsaw: Ministry of Higher Education, 1962.

609. "Cold War Thaw; Exchange of Students Between the United States and Poland," *Overseas*, III (November 1963), 31.

Six graduate students, five from Stanford University and one from the University of California, are studying at the University of Warsaw, while four Polish graduate students are at Stanford University.

E. Howard Brooks, Associate Dean of the Stanford University Graduate Division, reports that the American students are studying mathematical logic, Slavic languages, and history and political philosophy.

For the past two years U.S. students have been doing research in Russia under an agreement between the Academy of Sciences and the American Council of Learned Societies.

610. Lottich, Kenneth V. *Poland, Champion of Latin Christianity*. Zurich: Institute of Arts and Letters, 1963, 81 pp.

611. Ministry of Education. *Institutions of Higher Education in Poland*. Information and Statistic Bulletin, Ministry of Higher Education, Warsaw (1963), 59.

612. Rosen, Seymour, and Nellie Apanasewicz. "Higher Education in Poland," Part I, *Bulletin*, no. 19, OE-14082. U.S. Office of Education, 1963, 37 pp.

EAST GERMANY

Magazines

613. "Foreign Students in East Germany," *Times Educational Supplement*, no. 2331 (Jan. 22, 1960), 114.

East German authorities do not publish figures on visiting foreign students. Their numbers are determined by political arrangement at embassy level with each country concerned. The regions supplying most of the exchange students to East Germany are in this order: Africa, South America, Asia, the Middle East, Albania, Bulgaria, Finland, Greece, Iceland, Poland, Rumania, Hungary, and the Soviet Union. The care of foreign students is a prime obligation of the State Secretary for Universities.

614. Lottich, Kenneth V. "Extra-curricular Indoctrination in East Germany," *Comparative Education Review*, VI, no. 3 (February 1963), 209–211.

YUGOSLAVIA

Government Documents

615. Tomich, Vera. "Education in Yugoslavia and the New Reform," *Bulletin*, no. 20, OE-14089. U.S. Office of Education, 1963, 146 pp.

Magazines

616. Elliot, A. J. A. "School Reform in Yugoslavia: How UNESCO Helped," *Institute of International Education News Bulletin*, XXXIV (December 1958), 19–21.

Director of the Clearing House and Advisory Service Section of UNESCO's Exchange of Persons Service relates the means by which UNESCO aided the Yugoslavs in learning more about modern trends in education. Although other countries do not necessarily have educational problems identical to those of Yugoslavia, much can be learned from the imaginative and constructive use which Yugoslavia has made of UNESCO's technical and educational assistance.

RUMANIA

Books and Pamphlets

617. Ministry of Education. *Development of Education in the Rumanian People's Republic in the 1962–1963 School Year.* Report submitted to the 26th International Conference on Public Education, Geneva (July 1963). Bucharest: Rumanian People's Republic, Ministry of Education, 1963, 87 pp.

618. National Commission. *Education, Work, Recreation of Youth in Rumania.* Bucharest: National Commission of the Rumanian People's Republic for UNESCO, 1963.

619. *Foreign Students in the Rumanian People's Republic.* Bucharest: Meridiane Publishing House, 1963, 45 pp.

Government Documents

620. Haase, Harta, and Seymour Rosen. "Education in Rumania," *Bulletin*, OE-14050 (July 1960), U.S. Office of Education, 1960, 26 pp.

621. Braham, Randolph L. "Education in the Rumanian People's Republic," *Bulletin*, no. 1, OE-14087 (1964), U.S. Office of Education, 1964, 229 pp.

Magazines

622. Sims, Albert G. "Education in Rumania," *Institute of International Education News Bulletin*, XXXIII (May 1958), pp. 2–7.

The Vice President for Operations of the Institute of International Education, having visited Rumania, found its educational system to have, in comparison with that of the United States, more rigid discipline, more intense indoctrination of knowledge, and a higher level of subject matter achievement in mathematics, languages, and the sciences.

Only 6 per cent of those who start school go to grades 8 through 11. Institute quotas for each academic field are filled with little regard for personal choice. Strong emphasis is placed on academic achievement which determines future success. Night schools are open for every educational level; one-third of those in institutes are obtaining degrees in this way.

The Director General of Higher Education in Rumania expressed desire at this time to exchange graduate students in selected fields.

623. Braham, Randolph L. "The Rumanian Schools of General Education," *Journal of Central European Affairs,* XXI, no. 3 (October 1961), 319–349.

CZECHOSLOVAKIA

Government Documents

624. Apanasewicz, Nellie, and Seymour Rosen. "Selected Bibliography of Materials on Education in Czechoslovakia," *Bulletin,* OE-14053 (August 1960), U.S. Office of Education, 1960, 37 pp.

625. ———. "Education in Czechoslovakia," *Bulletin,* no. 27, OE-14090 (January 1963), U.S. Office of Education, 1963, 40 pp.

Magazines

626. Kubat, Daniel. "Patterns of Leadership in a Communist State: Czechoslovakia, 1946–1958," *Journal of Central European Affairs,* XXI, no. 3 (October 1961), 305–318.

AUSTRIA

Government Documents

627. "Austria Signs Fulbright Agreement; Educational Opportunities for 1951 Announced," *U.S. Department of State Bulletin,* XXIII (July 31, 1950), 192–193.

Magazines

628. Graham, Carolyn. "Exchange Acorn Sprouts Again," *Institute of International Education News Bulletin,* XXVI (January 1951), 26–27.

COMMUNIST BLOC (AND MISCELLANEOUS)

Books and Pamphlets

629. King, Edmund James (ed.). *Communist Education.* Indianapolis: The Bobbs-Merrill Co., 1963, viii, 309 pp.

630. Hungarian News and Information Service. "Two-Year Cultural Pact Signed with Britain," *New Hungary* (London), no. 103 (April 1964).

Government Documents

631. U.S. Information Agency. "The Image of America Among Vietnamese University Students," *Research and Reference Service,* December 1959, 35 pp. Mimeographed.

632. U.S. Department of State, Bureau of Education and Cultural Affairs. "Changing Roles of Youth in the Developing Nations," 39 pp. Mimeographed.

Magazines

633. Gullahorn, John Taylor, and J. E. Gullahorn. "Role of the Academic Man as a Cross-Cultural Mediator," *American Sociological Review,* XXV (June 1960), 414–417.

634. Caldwell, Oliver J. "What Others Are Doing," *Annals of the American Academy of Political and Social Science,* CCCXXXV (May 1961), 112–121.

635. Vakar, Nicholas. "Creeds and Communist," *East Europe,* X, no. 12 (December 1961), 6–14.

636. Shapiro, Leonard. "The Party's New Rules," *Problems of Communism,* XI, no. 1 (January and February 1962), 28–42.

637. Bird, Christopher. "Scholarships and Propaganda," *Problems of Communism,* XI, no. 2 (March–April 1962), 32–37.

638. McClintock, Charles G. and Henry Turner. "The Impact of College Upon Political Knowledge, Participation and Values," *Human Relations,* XV, no. 2 (May 1962), 163–177.

639. "Segregation in Sofia," *Newsweek,* LXI (Feb. 25, 1963), 42.

640. Fisher, J. "Universities and the Political Process in S.E. Asia," *Pacific Affairs,* XXXVI (Spring, 1963), 3–15.

641. Robin, S. S., and F. Story. "Ideological Consistency of College Students," *Sociological and Social Research,* XLVIII (January 1964), 187–196.

642. Burks, Richard V. "Perspectives for Eastern Europe," *Problems of Communism,* XIII, no. 2 (March–April 1964), 73–81.

643. "Be Nice to the Foreign Students," *Kulturni Tvorba* (Prague), Nov. 14, 1963. (Trans. in *East Europe* (May 1964), 23–24.)

CHINA

Books and Pamphlets

644. Hevi, Emmanuel John. *An African Student in China.* New York: Praeger, 1963 (c. 1962), 220 pp.
    "Nothing that we Westerners can say about the Communist Chinese can match the bitterness and anger of this young African," wrote John Barkham in the *Saturday Review Syndicate,* who traveled to Communist China in quest for an education. "His burning book is a warning to African new nations not to take on China's chains."

Magazines

645. Thomas, S. B. "Recent Educational Policy in China," *Pacific Affairs,* XXIII (March 1950), 21–33.
    The government's determined policy of opposition to "American imperialism" is creating a general atmosphere in which the schools are placing Western oriented culture and educational forces on the defensive. Concurrently, in accordance with the Peking government's stated policy of

supporting the Soviet bloc in world affairs, there has been a corresponding emphasis on Russian literature, arts, and language. General encouragement is being given to the study and emulation of Soviet cultural and educational practices.

646. "Trends in Chinese Education," *World Today*, VII (November 1951), 480–488.

647. "Exchange Through the Ages," *Institute of International Education News Bulletin*, XXXI (January 1956), 37–38.

648. Lauwerys, Joseph A. "China's Educational Expansion: Major Issues of Policy," *Times Educational Supplement*, no. 2196 (June 21, 1957), 895.

649. "Educational Lessons from Red China," *School and Society*, LXXXVII (March 28, 1959), 157.

650. Liu Shui Sheng. "Life in a Chinese University," *Institute of International Education News Bulletin*, XXXVI (February 1961), 20–26.

TURKEY

Magazines

651. Tompkins, E. E. "Turkey and the United States—Educational Partners," *School Life*, XXXVI (February 1954), 79–80.

652. Gould, Harry G. "The Land Grant College Experiment in Turkey," *Institute of International Education News Bulletin*, III (May 1956), 26–29.

653. Ozinonu, Lamia, and Kemal Ozinonu. "Visit to a Turkish High School," *The Clearing House*, XXXI (September 1956), 11–14.

654. Warren, Fletcher. "Contributions of Turkish American Cultural Relations to the Economic Development of Turkey," U.S. *Department of State Bulletin*, XXXVI (Feb. 11, 1957), 214–216.

655. U.S. Information Agency. "Attitudes of Turkish Students toward the U.S. Military and Indications of the Present and Future Standing of the U.S.," *Research and Reference Service* (October 1958), 21 pp. Mimeographed.

656. Baker, Eric. "New Endeavor in Greece and Turkey," *Christian Century*, LXXVI (July 22, 1959), 849–850.

657. Baymar, F. "Concern for Children Is World Wide in Turkey," *Children's Education*, XXXVI (December 1959), 179–180.

658. "Technology for Turkey," *Time*, LXXVI, no. 2 (July 11, 1960), 87–89.

659. Leubke, Paul T. "I Could Write Only Two Words," *NEA Journal*, L, no. 5 (May 1961), 29–30.

660. "Midwesternizing Turkey," *Time*, LXXX, no. 3 (July 20, 1962), 53–54.

661. Borton, N., and J. W. Borton. "Turkey; Peace Corps Volunteers," *National Geographic*, CXXVI (September 1964), 330–333.

IRAN

Magazines

662. Baldwin, G. B. "Foreign-Educated Iranians, a Profile," *Middle East Journal*, XVII (Summer, 1963), 264–278.

AFRICA

Books and Pamphlets

663. Bane, M. J. "African Problem in America." *National Catholic Educational Association Proceedings* (1950), 279–281.

664. Conference Board of the Associated Research Councils. Committee on International Exchange of Persons. "Educational Exchanges; Aspects of the American Experience; Report of a Conference Sponsored by the Committee, Princeton, New Jersey, Dec. 2–4, 1954," *National Research Council* (1955), 71–72.

665. Carr-Saunders, A. M. *Staffing African Universities.* London: The Overseas Development Institute, 1963, 26 pp.

666. Curle, Adam. *Educational Strategy for Developing Societies; Study of Educational and Social Factors in Relation to Economic Growth.* London: Tavistock Publications, 1963, 180 pp.

Author suggests that economic planning is likely to be successful only to the extent that it is related to social and particularly to educational criteria. Among many intercultural educational influences given is that of English education in British West Africa.

Government Documents

667. *Ayo Visits the U.S.A.* [U.S. Superintendent of Documents, Catalog no. IA 1.2: Ay 6], 1953, 116 pp.

A story about the things an African woman named Ayo sees and does while on a visit to America. Essentially a reader written for students at the intermediate level who are studying English as a foreign language. Includes teaching suggestions, exercises, and a glossary.

Magazines

668. Sloan, Ruth C. "Educational Exchanges with Africa: Fallacies of Generalization," *Institute of International Education News Bulletin,* XXV (November 1949), 23–26.

669. ———. "Students from Africa," *Institute of International Education News Bulletin,* XXV (May 1950), 29–30.

670. ———. "African Students in the United States," *Institute of International Education News Bulletin,* XXIX (March 1954), 38–40.

671. Pifer, Alan. "What Africa Has to Offer American Students and Researchers," *Institute of International Education News Bulletin,* XXIX (March 1954), 9–15.

672. "Pilgrims in Africa," *Economist,* CXCVI (July 30, 1960), 474.

673. Henry, David D. "The 1960 Nigerian-American Scholarship Program," *Institute of International Education News Bulletin,* XXXVI (November 1960), 17–25.

This article discusses the problems of selecting and financing African candidates for degree programs in American universities and suggests some solutions to the situation.

674. Murphy, E. Jefferson. "African Exchange Problems," *Institute of International Education News Bulletin*, XXXVI, no. 3 (November 1960), 11–16.

An evaluation of the problems encountered in the African Exchange Program, dealing with selection and placement of the foreign student.

675. Smythe, Hugh H., and Mabel Smythe. "African Student Selection Programs," *Institute of International Education News Bulletin*, XXXVI, no. 3 (November 1960), 34–40.

Observations on the evaluation, selection, and placement of Africans to American universities by various organizations.

676. Smyke, Raymond J. "African Assignments for American Teachers," *NEA Journal*, L (May 1961), 27–28.

677. "Special Fund for African Students," *Higher Education*, XVII, no. 9 (July 1961), 12.

About a special grant by the State Department given to the African students now in the U.S.

678. "Rioting Between African and Bulgarian Students," *African Diary*, II (Sept. 15–21, 1962), 761–762.

679. "Americans for Africa," *Times Educational Supplement*, no. 2420 (Oct. 6, 1961), 427.

680. Caldwell, Oliver J. "Africa and American Education," *American Association of Colleges for Teacher Education, Yearbook*, XVI, no. 2 (1963), 102–112.

This article describes African educational needs as an urgent challenge for American education. The author describes current African education problems and what America should do about it.

681. Moritz, Paul R. "Africa: Learning by Involvement," *Overseas*, I (March 1962), 17–20.

682. Trent, W. J., Jr. "United Negro College Fund's African Scholarship Program," *The Journal of Negro Education*, XXXI, no. 2 (Spring, 1962), 205–209.

On the selection, financing, orientation, placement, and the program in 1961–62.

683. Evans, P. C. C. "American Teachers for East Africa," *Comparative Education Review*, VI, no. 1 (June 1962), 69–77.

Discusses the reasons why American teachers are needed for Africa. Tells of the State Department requesting Teachers College, Columbia University, to recruit, select, and train teachers for secondary schools of East Africa and also tells some of the things that some educators who are enthusiastic endorsers of this program have said about it.

684. Cotner, Thomas E. "Teacher Education and U.S. Training Programs with African Countries," *American Association of Colleges for Teacher Education, Yearbook*, no. 1 (1962), 78–83.

A brief summary is given in an attempt to delineate the activities of agencies of the U.S. Government in supplying teachers and teacher training in Africa and to Africans in the U.S.: (1) Student Exchange (Institute of International Education; Department of State), (2) Teacher Exchange (U.S. Office of Education; Department of State), (3) International Teacher Development Program (U.S. Office of Education; Department of State), (4) Professors and Research Scholars (Conference Board of Associated Research Councils; Department of State), (5) Technical Assistance Program in Education (U.S. Office of Education; AID), (6) U.S. Information Agency's English Teaching Program, (7) Teachers Under the Peace Corps, and (8) United Nations Educational, Scientific, and Cultural Organization.

685. "Bulgaria—African Students Leave after Clash," *East Europe*, XII (March 1963), 36–37.

686. "Ethiopian Student Tells of Disillusionment," *East Europe*, XII (March 1963), 40–41.

687. Dillon, Wilton. "Wandering African Intellectuals," *New Republic*, CXLVIII (March 9, 1963), 17–19.

688. "U.S. Exploring Ways to Help African Students," *U.S. Department of State Bulletin*, no. 48 (March 11, 1963), 375.

689. Bonfanta, Jordan. "African Students at Iron Curtain Schools Flee a Hateful Epithet 'Cherni Maimuno,'" *Life*, LIV (March 15, 1963), 19.

690. "AID Extends Contract for Guinean Training Program," *Higher Education*, XX, no. 6 (April 1963), 12.

Describes a $1,092,776 contract amendment awarded the African-American Institute by the Agency for International Development to continue its services in administering an academic and vocational training program for students from Guinea.

691. Greig, E. E. "History Students Exchange Tapes with African Youths: Intercultural Exchange Promotes Understanding," *Chicago Schools Journal*, XLIV (May 1963), 368–370.

692. Morgan, G. D. "Exploratory Study of Problems of Academic Adjustment of Nigerian Students in America," *The Journal of Negro Education*, XXXII (Summer, 1963), 208–217.

693. "Africans Study in U.S.," *Higher Education*, XX (September 1963), 17.

694. Carroll, D. R., and P. Edwards. "Teaching English Literature to West African Students," *English Language Teaching*, XVIII (October 1963), 38–44.

695. Hagberg, P. "American Student in Africa," *Overseas*, III (October 1963), 18–22.

696. Luke, K. D. "U.S. Influence on East African Education," *Overseas*, III (October 1963), 4–9.

697. Bigelow, Karl W. "Teachers for Africa," *Overseas*, III (November 1963), 18–22.

698. ———. "Africa, Teacher Education, and the United States: the Fourth Charles W. Hunt Lecture," *American Association of Colleges for Teacher Education, Yearbook*, XVI, no. 2 (1963), 102–112.

This article describes why the challenge of African education to American education is one of the great emergent challenges of our day. We should receive more African students and we must ourselves go to Africa to serve its expanding universities and teachers colleges.

699. "Joint Anglo-American T.E.A.: Teachers for East Africa," *Times Educational Supplement,* no. 2543 (Feb. 4, 1964), 364.

700. Sammartino, P. "Some Thoughts on Education in West Africa," *Liberal Education,* L (March 1964), 43–48.

701. "Teachers for East Africa: 1964," *Higher Education,* XX (March 1964), 15.

INDIA

Government Documents

702. "Fulbright Agreement for Educational Exchange with India Signed," *U.S. Department of State Bulletin,* XXII (Feb. 13, 1950), 243.

Magazines

703. Desai, F. "Fellowship Through Education," *New Era,* XXX (July 1949), 157–159.

704. Hingorani, D. K. "Educational Partners: India and America," *School Life,* XXXVII (December 1954), 33–34.

705. Lambert, R. D., and M. Bressler. "An American Education for Students from India," *Journal of Higher Education,* XXVI (March 1955), 23–33. Nineteen Indian students at the University of Pennsylvania attained "average" academic performance. Those in the Arts and Sciences in general were superior in academic achievement to those in the School of Business and Finance, in that Indian students excel when there are continuities in methodological and substantive emphasis between past and present training, and when academic success in the U.S. is related to future status advancement in India. Indian students most admired the presence of "democracy in the method of instruction," but disliked the "climate of fear" induced by congressional investigations.

706. Kenney, N. J. "On Being an Exchange Student in India," *Institute of International Education News Bulletin,* XXXI (February 1956), 9–11.

707. George, J. C. "To the U.S. and Back Home," *Institute of International Education News Bulletin,* XXXI (April 1956), 57–59.

708. Riepe, Dale. "Fulbright in Retrospect," *Institute of International Education News Bulletin,* XXXIV (April 1959), 55–58. The author, head of the Philosophy Department at the University of North Dakota, was a Fulbright student in India and a Fulbright lecturer in Japan. "The Fulbright program has enriched the lives not only of the grantees and their families, but also of thousands of other people throughout the world. . . . It has encouraged the best in ourselves and in our foreign friends on every continent."

709. Marshall, M. W. "Company of Scholars," *Journal of Higher Education,* XXXII (October 1961), 395–398. The author, faculty member at Brooklyn College, indicates that the major concern of the Indian Minister of Education is not merely the extension of formal education in India, but also the harnessing of knowledge already possessed in the areas of agriculture and religion. Educational advancements can be based, it is claimed, by cultivating the precepts of the *Gita* and the rich Indian heritage of myth and folklore.

710. Clark, K. "Fulbright to India," *Texas Outlook*, XLVI (July 1962), 11+.

711. Johnson, Edward W. "Indian Foreign Policy: Neutralism and Geopolitics," *Social Studies*, LIII (December 1962), 243–248.

Description of six factors influencing Indian foreign policy: location, size and shape, climate, population, natural resources and industrial capacity, and political and social organization.

712. "Internationalism in India; UNESCO's Associated Schools Project," *Overseas*, III (January 1964), 32.

JAPAN

Books and Pamphlets

713. Broderick, James. *Saint Francis Xavier (1506–1552)*. New York: Farrar, Straus & Young, 1952.

Biography of Xavier and history of Christian missionary influence on Japan and the East. The Japanese period in Xavier's career is well described.

714. Schwantes, Robert S. *Japanese and Americans: A Century of Cultural Relations*. New York: Harper and Brothers, 1955, 380 pp.

A pioneer study of cultural interchange between the U.S. and Japan. Appraises the impact of American ideas, institutions, education, technology, and religion upon Japan. Invaluable bibliographical essay.

715. Bennett, John W., Herbert Passin, and Robert McKnight. *In Search of Identity: The Japanese Overseas Scholar in America and Japan*. Minneapolis: University of Minnesota Press, 1958, 369 pp.

716. Japanese National Commission for UNESCO. *School Textbooks in Japan 1957: A Report of a Survey from the Standpoint of Education for International Understanding and Cooperation*. Tokyo: The Commission, 1958, 203 pp.

717. Cosenza, Mario E. (ed.). *The Complete Journal of Townsend Harris, First American Consul and Minister to Japan*. Revised edition. Rutland, Vermont: Charles E. Tuttle, 1959.

This classic in American-Japanese relations, long out of print, has been republished with the cooperation of the Japan Society. Skillfully edited and provided with an invaluable introduction and notes.

Magazines

718. Russell, J. D. "Survey of Educational Exchange with Japan," *Higher Education*, VI (Dec. 1, 1949), 73–75.

This survey was instigated at the request of General Douglas MacArthur who was, at the time, Supreme Commander for the Allied Powers in Japan. The Japanese leaders viewed an educational exchange program as an important instrument for assisting in the rapid democratization of their country. It is noted in the article that Japanese universities were not well prepared to receive students from the U.S. The exchange encouraged graduate students and, when possible, teachers.

719. ———. "Report on Educational Exchange with Japan," *College and University*, XXV (April 1950), 381–386.

720. Scarangello, Anthony. "Public Schools in Japan," *NEA Journal*, XLV (February 1956), 87–89.

721. Bowles, Jane T. "Japan: A Challenge to the Foreign Student," *Institute of International Education News Bulletin*, XXXI (April 1956), 14–16.

722. Hidaka, Daishiro. "The Aftermath of Educational Reform," *Annals of the American Academy of Political and Social Science*, CCCVIII (November 1956), 140–155.

723. Morito, Tatsuo. "Educational Reform and Its Problems in Postwar Japan," *Teachers College Record*, LX (April 1959), 385–391.

Problems arising out of the postwar educational reforms, and suggestions for their solution by a former Minister of Education. Covers finance, administration, moral education, teacher training, and teachers' organizations.

724. "Cultural and Educational Exchange to Be Discussed by U.S. and Japan," *U.S. Department of State Bulletin*, XLVI (Jan. 15, 1962), 99.

725. Bennett, J. W. "Innovative Potential of American-Educated Japanese," *Human Organization*, XXI (Winter, 1962–1963), 246–251.

726. Duke, Ben C. "American Education Reforms in Japan Twelve Years Later," *Harvard Educational Review*, XXXIV, no. 4 (Fall, 1964), 525–535.

KOREA

Government Documents

727. "United States Educational Commission in Korea: Agreement Between the United States of America and Korea, Signed at Seoul, April 28, 1950; Entered into Force, April 28, 1950." Publication no. 3866, *Treaties and Other International Acts*. Serial no. 2059, 1950.

Pamphlet

728. Koenig, Clara H. *The Republic of Korea: A Guide to the Academic Placement of Students from the Republic of Korea in United States Educational Institutions.* American Association of Collegiate Registrars and Admissions Officers. Committee on Evaluation of Foreign Student Credentials, 1958, 80 pp.

Available from Chairman, Committee on Special Publications, AACRAO, Office of the Registrar, Ohio University, Athens, Ohio.

Magazines

729. "South Korea Develops Vocational Centres," *Times Educational Supplement*, no. 2250 (July 4, 1958), 1105.

This brief item reports on three recently completed school projects financed under the United Nations Korean Reconstruction Agency's 11½ million dollar educational program. Most of the details concern training offered at a modernized fisheries school.

730. Douglas, W. A. "Korean Students and Politics," *Asian Studies*, III (December 1963), 584–595.

731. Kim, C. I. Eugene, and Ke-Soo Kim. "April, 1960, Korean Student Movement," *Western Political Quarterly*, XVII (March 1964), 83–92.

UNESCO

Books and Pamphlets

732. Laves, Walter H. C., and Charles A. Thomson. *UNESCO: Purposes, Progress, Prospects*. Bloomington: Indiana University Press, 1957, 469 pp.

733. Pillsbury, Kent. *UNESCO Education in Action: A Field Study of the UNESCO Department of Education*. Kappa Delta Pi International Educational Monographs no. 4. Columbus: Ohio State University Press, 1963, 106 pp.

734. Shuster, George N. *UNESCO: Assessment and Promise*. New York: Published for the Council on Foreign Relations by Harper and Row, 1963, 130 pp.

735. Sathyamurthy, T. V. *The Politics of International Cooperation; Contrasting Conceptions of UNESCO*. Geneva: Librairie Droz, 1964, 314 pp.

736. *School and Community in Education for International Understanding*. Paris: UNESCO, 1964, 86 pp.

Carole Methven, Child Care Officer of the London County Council, has edited for the UNESCO Institute for Education in Hamburg a report on recommendations of a seminar held in Belgium, July, 1963. Twenty-three countries were represented by specialists who discussed the ways schools and communities can promote mutual understanding among different members and different civilizations.

Government Documents

737. UNESCO. *The American Interest in UNESCO*. [U.S. Superintendent of Documents, Catalog no. S 5.48:Am3/2], 1963, 35 pp.

Magazines

738. Parker, Franklin. "UNESCO at 15: Young Adam in Troubled Eden," *School and Society*, LXXXIX, no. 2201 (Dec. 16, 1961), 431–433.

739. Sathyamurthy, T. V. "Changing Concepts of Intellectual Co-Operation," *International Review of Education*, IX, no. 4 (1963–1964), 385–395.

740. Benton, William. "Progress Report on UNESCO," *Saturday Review*, XLVII, no. 10 (March 7, 1964), 16–18, 28–30.

741. Parker, Franklin. "UNESCO in Perspective," *International Review of Education*, X, no. 3 (1964), 326–331.

New York Times

1960

742. July 7, p. 2, c. 6.
UNESCO sponsors International Conference on Public Education.
743. November 11, p. 14, c. 4.
UNESCO executive board approves plan to recruit 500 French-speaking teachers for the Congo.
744. November 14, p. 8, c. 6.
UNESCO holds general conference to weigh U.S. aid plan to Africa.

1961

745. March 1, p. 10, c. 4.
UNESCO assigns 28 Haitian high school teachers to the Congo.
746. March 15, p. 4, c. 4.
UNESCO plans educational aid program to 31 African nations of $15 million.
747. May 16, p. 43, c. 6.
UNESCO holds conference on developing education in Africa.
748. August 20, Sec. IV, p. 10, c. 3.
UNESCO holds international conference on production of textbooks. Sixteen countries are participating.
749. September 18, p. 22, c. 3.
UNESCO-sponsored teacher training course for Africans opens.
750. October 15, Sec. IV, p. 7, c. 3.
Journalism teachers from six Asian countries attend UNESCO seminar in Manila.

1962

751. February 18, Sec. IV, p. 7, c. 6.
UNESCO issues 13th edition of *Study Abroad;* 200,000 students abroad in 1961.
752. May 5, p. 28, c. 1.
Six West Germans are in U.S. test study of educational methods.
753. June 8, p. 13, c. 2.
Reactions of West Germans to U.S.
754. July 7, p. 3, c. 6.
UNESCO sets program to teach 350 million to read and write in ten years.
755. September 9, Sec. IV, p. 11, c. 6.
UNESCO-sponsored conference of experts from fifteen Arab countries reviews rise in secondary school enrollment.
756. September 9, p. 21, c. 2.
UNESCO executive board allots educational aid funds to Burundi.
757. September 9, p. 21, c. 2.
UNESCO executive board allots education aid funds to Rwanda.
758. September 9, p. 21, c. 1.

1962 *(Cont.)*

UNESCO allots Algeria $200,000 for sixty teachers.
759. October 21, Sec. IV, p. 7, c. 3.
UNESCO-sponsored conference of textbook publishers from twenty-two countries proposes international association.
760. November 4, Sec. IV, p. 7, c. 6.
UNESCO to lend Algeria $200,000 to hire sixty French-speaking teachers.

1963

761. April 14, Sec. IV, p. 7, c. 4.
Ford Foundation gives $200,000 to UNESCO for establishment of International Institute for Education Planning.
762. April 28, Sec. IV, p. 9, c. 3.
UNESCO urges recasting of African and Far Eastern educational systems with stress on secondary schools.
763. June 2, p. 18, c. 1 & 2.
UNESCO makes report to U.N. asking for world-wide anti-illiteracy drive involving 700 million people.
764. June 9, Sec. IV, p. 11, c. 5.
UNESCO aided twenty-six countries in education in 1962. Director notes lack of experts hampers projects.

1964

765. March 8, Sec. IV, p. 7, c. 5.
UNESCO publication *Study Abroad* shows 250,000 students study abroad.
766. April 27, p. 54, c. 8.
U.S. research ship arrives in Calcutta on expedition sponsored by UNESCO.

INTERNATIONAL

Books and Pamphlets

767. Hughes, Emmet John (ed.). *Education in World Perspective: The Vassar International Conference on World Education Problems.* New York: Harper and Row, 1962, 201 pp.
768. *Educational Exchange in the Economic Development of Nations.* New York: Committee on Educational Interchange Policy, 1961, 25 pp.
769. Selltiz, Claire, June R. Christ, Joan Havel, and Stuart W. Cook. *Attitudes and Social Relations of Foreign Students in the United States.* Sponsored by the former Committee on Cross-Cultural Education. Minneapolis: University of Minnesota Press, 1963, 434 pp.

Government Documents

770. U.S. Information Agency. "Arab Student Attitudes Toward the U.S. Versus the U.S.S.R.," *Research and Reference Service,* June 1958, 19 pp. Mimeographed.

771. ———. "The Comparative Image of the U.S. vs. the Communist Powers Among Philippine University Students," *Research and Reference Service,* May 1960, 27 pp. Mimeographed.

772. Research and Information Commission. "Problems of Overseas Students in Europe," 1962–1964. Submitted to the 11th International Student Conference, New Zealand, June 22–July 1, 1964, 95 pp.

Magazines

773. Britt, W. H. "Educational Relations of United States with Europe," *Baltimore Bulletin of Education,* XXIX (September 1951), 11–14.

774. Anderson, C. Arnold. "World Patterns of Education," *Comparative Education Review,* IV, no. 2 (October 1960), 68–69.

775. Troester, Carl A., Jr. "Our Growing International Relations Programs," *Journal of Health, Physical Education, and Recreation,* XXXI (December 1960), 10.

776. "East-West Race to Teach Afro-Asians," *The Times* (London) (July 27, 1961), 11.

777. Rusk, Dean. "Education: Key to International Development," *Overseas,* I (September 1961), 6–7.

778. Clark, H. "Daddy's Little Girl," *Newsweek,* LIX (Jan. 8, 1962), 40.

779. Bowles, Chester. "Education for World Responsibility," *U.S. Department of State Bulletin,* XLVI (Feb. 5, 1962), 206–210.

780. Viederman, S. "Academic Exchange, a Narrow Bridge," *Bulletin of the Atomic Scientists,* XVIII (February 1962), 17–21.

781. Punke, Harold H. "Education and Leadership by Western Democracies," *Social Studies,* LIV (January 1963), 17–21.

782. Wilson, Howard E., and Miller R. Collings. "Education for International Understanding," *National Elementary Principal,* XLII (May 1963), 11–17.

783. "Trouble in Paradise," *New Statesman,* LXVI (Dec. 27, 1963), 931.

784. "Soviet Union: Girl Trouble," *New Republic,* CL (Jan. 11, 1964), 9.

DOCTORAL DISSERTATIONS

(Alphabetically by Author)

785. Abejo, Andres Z. "An Evaluation of the Scholarship Program of the Philippine Board of Scholarship for Southeast Asia." Michigan State University, 1959. 153 pp. Micro. no. 60-1707. Source: *Diss. Abst.* XX, no. 12 (1960), 4570–4571.

Evaluation of scholarship program financed by the Asian Foundation, San Francisco. Recipients were from twelve Asian countries. Questionnaires were used by both students and professors indicating that the program was successful in promoting cultural exchanges.

786. Akhun, Ilban Iswail. "Turkish Engineering Students Studying in the United States." University of Missouri, 1961. 174 pp. Ed.D. Micro. no. 61-6028. Source: *Diss. Abst.* XXII, no. 8 (1962), 2726.

Author determined through questionnaire that most students had prior college experience before coming to the United States. Finances and problems with language were the most serious difficulties faced by the students. Students held generally favorable opinions of U.S. education.

787. Allaway, William Harris. "Development of International Understanding in Foreign Students at the University of Kansas." University of Denver, 1957. 466 pp. Source: Eells, p. 216.*

788. Allbee, Lewis. "Education as an Implement of U.S. Foreign Policy, 1938–1948," Yale University, 1948. Source: *Doctoral Dissertations Accepted by American Universities, 1947–1948,* p. 98; Eells, p. 1.

789. Amstuty, J. B. "The Indonesian Youth Movement, 1908–1955." Ph.D., Fletcher School of Law and Diplomacy, Tufts University, 1958.

790. Arjona, Adoracion Quijano. "An Experimental Study of the Adjustment Problems of a Group of Foreign Graduate Students and a Group of American Graduate Students at Indiana University." Indiana University, 1956. 164 pp. Ed.D. Micro. no. 17-757. Source: *Diss. Abst.* XVI, no. 9 (1956), 1838.

The Mooney Problem Checklist and a questionnaire were mailed to sixty-two foreign students and sixty-two American students. Findings were that foreign students have more problems, but that there was no significant difference of serious concern.

791. Barager, Joseph R. "Sarmiento and the United States." University of Pennsylvania, 1951. 301 pp.

European and particularly U.S. influences on the life and educational work of D. F. Sarmiento in Chile and Argentina.

792. Bardis, Panes Demetrium. "Dating Attitudes and Patterns Among Foreign Students at Purdue University," Purdue University, 1955.

793. Barnes, Eugene Burdette, Jr. "The International Exchange of Knowledge in Western Europe, 1680–1689." University of Chicago, 1947. 151 pp.

794. Bassiouny, Mahmoud Youssef. "World Unity and Child Education with Special Reference to the Function of the Schema." Ohio State University, 1949. 500 pp. Source: Ohio State University, *Abstracts of Dissertations* (Autumn and Winter, 1949–1950), 21–26; Eells, p. 20.

795. Bateman, Kenneth Arden. "A Casebook Recording the Cooperative Effort of Educators of Germany and the United States in Establishing an Experimental School in Hessen, Germany." Wayne State University, 1962. 750 pp. Ed.D. Micro. no. 62-903. Source: *Diss. Abst.* XXI, no. 10 (1962), 3466.

From various sources, author studies the organizational programs of the school and the attitude of the Germans about the school. Implications are made concerning similar endeavors.

796. Bennett, Alvin LeRoy. "The Development of Intellectual Cooperation under the League of Nations and the United Nations." University of

---

* Walter Crosby Eells, *American Dissertations on Foreign Education* (Washington, D.C.: Committee on International Relations, National Education Association of the United States, 1959). 300 pp.

Illinois, 1950. 299 pp. Univ. Micro. no. 2,211. Source: *Microfilm Abstracts* XI, no. 2 (1951), 154–155.

797. Bjork, Richard Emil. "The Changing Roles of American Universities in International Relations: A Study of Certain Perceptions of Universities' International Activities and the Impacts of Such Activities on Universities' Participation in International Relations." Michigan State University, 1961. 342 pp. Univ. Micro. no. 61-2677. Source: *Diss. Abst.* XXII, no. 2 (August 1961), 622–623.

To gauge their views of the universities' roles in international relations, 423 persons related to international higher education programs (including 303 university, 87 government, and 23 foundation staff members) were interviewed. In contrast to the position of many government personnel that university programs should include political acts to support foreign policy objectives, university people saw their goal as primarily educational. Universities want independence in their operations and have been reorganizing to develop new forms for conducting international programs.

798. Bohn, Ralph Carl. "An Evaluation of the Educational Program for Students from Foreign Countries: With Emphasis Upon Orientation Procedures, Individual Problems, and Psychological Variables." Wayne State University, 1957. 361 pp. Ed.D. Micro. no. 58-1174. Source: *Diss. Abst.* XVIII, no. 4 (1958), 1344.

The study investigated the effectiveness of the program directed by the Technical Training Section of the U.S. Office of Education. Teachers and administrators from Asia, Africa, and South America revealed that major adjustment problems were encountered. Over one-third indicated that the educational program failed to fulfill their objectives.

799. Cajoleas, Louis Peter. "The Academic Record, Professional Development, and Return Adjustment of Doctoral Students from Other Lands: A Study of Teachers College Alumni, 1946–1955." Columbia University, 1958. 295 pp. Micro. no. 58-2611. Source: *Diss. Abst.* XIX, no. 2 (1958), 250–251.

From data secured from Teachers College and from questionnaires returned by alumni, a study was made of the academic record, professional development, and return adjustment of 156 doctoral students from thirty countries. Study revealed lower academic record than a control U.S. group. Upon return to their countries, there was no professional employment or return adjustment problems.

800. Canary, Peyton Henry, Jr. "The Scriptural Teachings of the World's Living Religions on International Understanding and Goodwill." Indiana University, 1933. 356 pp. Source: *Selected Graduate Theses in Religious Education* (1934), 9–10.

801. Chou, Frank Hau-Tsin. "A Study of the Foreign Student Program at the University of Georgia, 1948–1949 through 1958–1959." University of Georgia, 1960. 209 pp. Ed.D. Micro. no. 60-4650. Source: *Diss. Abst.* XXI, no. 8 (1961), 2158.

Data were compiled through admission records and personal interviews to establish adjustment and attitudes toward the U.S. of foreign students.

Findings revealed a mixed reaction to the U.S. Study also reveals U.S. students are race conscious toward nonwhite foreign students.

802. Chow, John Yu-Ching. "Factors Related to the Establishment of the Position, 'Foreign Student Advisor.' " University of Tennessee, 1963. 130 pp. Ed.D. Micro. no. 64-7853. Source: *Diss. Abst.* XXV, no. 1 (1964), 218.

Through questionnaire author sought educational background, status, administrative duties, and responsibilities of fifty-three foreign student advisors in institutions of up to 3,000 foreign students. He found varied background factors and wide service functions among the advisors.

803. Chu, Jennings Pink-Wei. "Chinese Students in America: Qualities Associated with Their Success." Columbia University, 1922, 55 pp.

804. Cieslak, Edward Charnwood. "A Study of the Administrative and Guidance Practices for Students from Abroad in Representative Collegiate Institutions of the United States." Wayne State University, 1953. 391 pp. Ed.D. Micro. no. 8-167. Source: *Diss. Abst.* XIV, no. 5 (1954), 944.

The survey was designed to ascertain the problems of collegiate institutions with regard to foreign student programs. Questionnaires were submitted to 200 institutions and 800 students. The survey recommends a clarification of the objectives of exchange programs and more uniformity in evaluations of foreign school credentials.

805. Clark, Violet Esther Wuerfel. "Ghanaian Students in the United States, 1959–60." University of Michigan, 1963. 180 pp. Micro. no. 64-799. Source: *Diss. Abst.* XXIV, no. 6 (December 1963), 2321.

Findings of questionnaires sent to 144 Ghanaian students and to institutions of higher education they attended uncovered that there were higher academic achievement and satisfaction among those who: (1) had received secondary certificates after the 5th or 6th Form than those received after the 4th Form, (2) held government grants than those who did not, (3) were over thirty years of age, (4) were married than were single, (5) were in the U.S. less than two years than those more than two years, (6) expected to be in the U.S. less than three years than those who expected to remain longer.

806. Cragg, Edith Marion Catherine. "A Study of the Content of Literature Textbooks for English-Speaking Students in Canadian High Schools in Relation to International Understanding Between the United States and Canada and Canadian Unity." Northwestern University, 1950. 253 pp. Source: *Summaries of Doctoral Dissertations,* XVIII (1950), 235–241.

807. Crum, Clyde Eugene. "A Study of the Development and Underlying Principles of International Educational Organizations." University of Colorado, 1950. Source: University of Colorado, *Abstracts of Theses* (1951–1952), 56–58.

808. Davidsen, Oluf Mejer. "Visiting Scandinavian Students at the University of Wisconsin, 1952–54: A Study in Cross Cultural Education." University of Wisconsin, 1956. 263 pp. Ph.D. Micro. no. 17-305. Source: *Diss. Abst.* XVI, no. 12 (1956), 2381.

Through personal interview, author studied forty Scandinavian students to determine academic and social adjustments and impressions of the U.S. The students' academic and social adjustments were good. Their impressions of the U.S. were highly differentiated but generally favorable.

809. DeSousa, Rev. Herman Joseph. "The Adjustment Problems of Indian Graduate Students in American Universities." Fordham University, 1956, 380 pp.

810. Enea, Norma. "American and French Public Secondary Education: An Analysis of Current Criticisms and Reforms with Observations and Recommendations of Exchange Teachers, 1948–1959." The University of Buffalo, 1961. 295 pp. Ed.D. Micro. no. 61-4658. Source: *Diss. Abst.* XXII, no. 7 (1962), 2248.

Author used the Franco-American Exchange Teaching Program to analyze secondary education in France and the U.S. Data were collected in the form of a questionnaire sent to exchange teachers. Study upholds exchange teaching as a legitimate source of information for comparative education.

811. Feldman, Edwin. "UNESCO and American Schools: 1946–1957." Stanford University, 1960. 313 pp. Micro. no. 60-6704. Source: *Diss. Abst.* XXI, no. 10 (1961), 2942–2943.

Through literature, correspondence, interviews, and questionnaire, author illustrated UNESCO organizations and their significance for schools in the U.S. Study revealed extensive potential assistance.

812. Feng, Yen-Tsai. "An Analysis of the Impact of the Several Different Concepts of International Cultural Cooperation upon the Establishment and the Development of the United Nations Educational, Scientific, and Cultural Organization during Its First Six Years." University of Denver, 1953. 469 pp.

813. Fitzgerald, Dean T. "American Schools in Latin America." University of Tulsa, 1954. 201 pp.

814. Foo, Thoong-Sien. "Method in Moral Judgment—An Intercultural Analysis." Columbia University, 1950. 153 pp. Univ. Micro. no. 1,848. Source: *Microfilm Abstracts,* X, no. 3 (1950), 69–70.

815. Fuoss, Donald Eugene. "An Analysis of the Incidents of the Olympic Games for 1924 to 1948 with Reference to the Contribution of the Games to International Good Will and Understanding." Columbia University, 1952. 297 pp.

816. Gagliotti, Arthur F. "An Analysis of United States Government Educational Aid to Underdeveloped Countries in Relation to the Educational Needs of Such Countries." Ph.D. New York University, 1962. 366 pp. Order no. 62-3279. Source: *Diss. Abst.* XXIII (1962), 884–885.

Through publications of various governments, author explored such educational needs of seventy-two underdeveloped countries as (1) availability of vocational and higher education, (2) primary and secondary school places, (3) literacy, (4) teacher supply, and (5) school construction. Author then analyzed various U.S. and UNESCO educational aid programs and their order of priorities.

817. Gephart, Mary Louise. "A Study of the Professional Needs of Students from Other Lands Who Have Studied Home Economics in College and Universities in the United States and Who Have Returned Home." Columbia University, 1954. 269 pp.

818. Gezi, Khalil Ismail. "The Acculturation of Middle Eastern Arab Students in Selected American Colleges and Universities." Stanford University, 1959. 260 pp. Micro. no. 59-3701. Source: *Diss. Abst.* XX, no. 5 (1959), 1641–1642.

Open-end interview schedules submitted to students and foreign student advisors revealed social, economic, linguistic problems were major adjustment areas. Recommendations to participating countries are given.

819. Gilbert, William Ralph. "A Study of an Interchange of Teacher Programs on the Local, National, and International Levels with Emphasis on the Seattle, Washington, Public School Exchange Program." University of Washington, 1955. 350 pp. Univ. Micro. no. 12,984. Source: *Diss. Abst.* XV (September 1955), 1560.

Questionnaire to teachers and administrators in Seattle and six other cities explored exchange program benefits and suggested improvements to U.S. and foreign exchange program administrators.

820. Gillett, Margaret. "The Colombo Plan and Australia's Role in Its International Education Program." Columbia University, 1961. 193 pp. Ed.D. Micro. no. 62-3550. Source: *Diss. Abst.* XXIII, no. 4 (1962), 1232.

Author did research in published reports of the Colombo Plan Council and member governments. The Colombo Plan was originated by Australia, and study reveals Australia's program makes all resources of education and government available for Colombo Plan trainees with favorable results.

821. Graham, Grace. "Foreign Students in an American University." Stanford University, 1952. 269 pp.

822. Green, Eleanor Kuhlman. "A Study of the Structure and Interaction of a Group of Turkish Students at the University of Florida, October, 1952, to June, 1953." University of Florida, 1956. 664 pp. Ed.D. Micro. no. 17,551. Source: *Diss. Abst.* XVI, no. 11 (1956), 2096.

The author collected data from the University of Florida and held personal interviews with a group of Turkish students. Study indicated that interaction of the group changed as the group adjusted to a new environment.

823. Hansome, Marius. "World Workers' Educational Movements: Their Social Significance." Columbia University, 1931. 596 pp.

824. Hao, Peter Te Yuan. "An Analysis of Certain Learning Difficulties of Chinese Students in New York City." New York University, 1955. Micro. no. 12,218. 373 pp. Source: *Doctoral Dissertations Accepted by American Universities, 1954–1955,* p. 204.

Linguistic, vocabulary, and reading difficulties rather than quantitative difficulties affected the learning abilities of 113 China-born students at Columbia, Fordham, and New York universities, and were significantly related to their length of residence in the U.S., length of study in the U.S., and their extracurricular successes.

825. Harper, Heber Reece. "What European and American Students Think on International Problems: A Comparative Study of the Worldmindedness of University Students." Columbia University, 1931. 255 pp.

826. Hassan, Abi el-bassit Mohammed Awad. "Social Interactions Between Foreign Students and Americans in a Mid-Western Community." Purdue University, 1961. 215 pp. Ph.D. Micro. no. 61-5726. Source: *Diss. Abst.* XXII, no. 7 (1962), 2492.

Study investigated social interaction between foreign students and U.S. students. Through questionnaire, author verified that students' interaction was significantly related to political relations between their country and the U.S., social class position, and occupational prestige. Students' favorable or unfavorable reaction corresponded to adjustment.

827. Hauch, Arthur Andrew. "Some Educational Factors Affecting the Relation between Canada and the United States." Columbia University, 1932. 100 pp.

828. High, Sidney Cooke, Jr. "The Joint Philippine-American Project for Explaining and Improving Vocational Industrial Education in the Philippines, 1951–1956." Stanford University, 1960. 924 pp. Ed.D. Source: *Diss. Abst.* XXI, no. 9 (1961), 2553–2554.

Study revealed the project to aid the underdeveloped vocational education in the Philippines was highly successful. Guide lines for future work in underdeveloped countries and lists of specific suggestions for future study are given.

829. Hintz, Carl William Edmund. "Internationalism and Scholarship: A Comparative Study of the Research Literature Used by American, British, French, and German Botanists." University of Chicago, 1952. 175 pp.

830. Ho, Genevieve Po-Ai. "Factors Affecting Adaptation to American Dietary Pattern by Students from Oriental Countries." The Pennsylvania State University, 1961. 114 pp. Ph.D. Micro. no. 62-1719. Source: *Diss. Abst.* XXII, no. 11 (1962), 3977.

The author purposed to provide an estimate of dietary changes between countries and evaluate factors involved. Students were interviewed and results showed that there was significant relationship between nationality and adaption to food. Adjustment was in accord with overall adjustment.

831. Ho, Perry Yewton. "A Comparative Study of the Ingenuity of American and Chinese Students." University of Southern California, 1926. 58 pp.

832. Hoben, Katherine Hunter. "The Out-of-Country Experience of Costa Ricans Sponsored By the U.S. Technical Cooperation Agencies 1952–1956: A Study of Technical Cooperation Training." The American University, 1961. 410 pp. Ph.D. Micro. no. 61-3712. Source: *Diss. Abst.* XXII, no. 4 (1961), 1236.

Author established the success of the mission through personal interviews and records of the U.S. Operation Mission. Better planning at the Washington level and more financial help are recommended.

833. Hountras, Panos Timothy. "Factors Associated with the Academic

Achievement of Foreign Graduate Students at the University of Michigan from 1947 to 1949." University of Michigan, 1955. 147 pp. Ph.D. Micro. no. 11,297. Source: *Diss. Abst.* XV, no. 5 (1955), 762–763.

The purpose of the study was to discover factors associated with the academic achievement of foreign graduate students. Data collected from university records indicated that factors were varied.

834. Hutchins, Brahna Chalefman. "Counseling Programs as Related to Foreign Students in Ten Institutions of Higher Education in New York: An Exploratory Survey." Columbia University, 1955. Source: Eells, p. 216.

835. Hyer, June. "Trends in International Education from World War I through World War II." University of Texas, 1947. 337 pp.

836. Iyengar, N. Singammal. "Workers' Education: A Functional Approach." Northwestern University, 1955. 235 pp. Univ. Micro. no. 15,137. Source: *Diss. Abst.* XV (December 1955), 2424–2425.

837. Kiell, Norman Tenese. "A Study of Attitudes of Indian and Pakistani Students: A Study of Attitudes of Indian and Pakistani Students in the United States toward America and American Democracy and the Responsibility of American Educational Institutions toward Exchange Students." Columbia University, 1949. 189 pp.

838. Knudson, Emma R. "Folk Music as a Tool in Inter-Cultural Education." Northwestern University, 1946. 390 pp. Northwestern University, *Summaries of Doctoral Dissertations,* XIV (1946), 133–138.

839. Koo, May. "American Students Contact With and Attitudes Toward Foreign Students." Michigan State University, 1962. 129 pp. Micro. no. 63-3727. Source: *Diss. Abst.* XXIII, no. 12 (1964), 4605–4606.

Through questionnaire, author determined that American students sought opportunities to know foreign students and had no preferences between European and other foreign students.

840. Lathrop, John Clarke. "Promotion of International Understanding through the Exchange of High School Students: A Project of the Metropolitan School Study Council Providing Exchange Visits between American, Latin-American, and Scandinavian Students." Columbia University, 1943. 107 pp.

841. Levai, Blaise. "A Study of Group Discussions among Indian Students on a Controversial Subject." University of Michigan, 1952. 87 pp. Univ. Micro. no. 3,586. Source: *Diss. Abst.* XII, no. 3 (1952).

842. Lougheed, Virgil Robert. "A Study of Administrative, Counseling, and Social Practices Affecting Foreign Students at an Urban University." Wayne State University, 1956. 287 pp. Micro. no. 17,161. Source: *Diss. Abst.* XVI (September 1956), 1625, Eells, p. 216.

843. Maberly, Norman Charles. "The Validity of the Graduate Record Examinations as Used with English-Speaking Foreign Students." University of Southern California, 1962. 218 pp. Ed.D. Micro. no. 62-6071. Source: *Diss. Abst.* XXIII, no. 7 (1963), 2424–2425.

The study sought to find the extent and validity of the GRE with relation to foreign students. Study indicated the GRE is widely used and reported unfavorably on the validity.

844. MacKay, Vera Alma. "Intercultural Education: An Historical Narrative and the Role of Indiana University." Source: Indiana University, *Studies in Education,* 1954, pp. 103–107.

845. Mierzwa, Dorothy Rise. "A Study of Some of the Problems of Adjustment Experienced in the Non-Academic Areas by International Students in Teachers College." Columbia University, 1953. 133 pp.

846. Mitchell, Joy Ann Hayes. "The Foreign Student in the Graduate School at George Peabody College for Teachers, 1956–1962." George Peabody College for Teachers, 1962. 165 pp. Ph.D. Micro. no. 63-1886. Source: *Diss. Abst.* XXIII, no. 10 (1963), 3691–3692.

Through questionnaire, author studied student needs and problems. Recommendations for change in policy and practice of the institution were made in the following areas: admission, orientation, programming policies, language development, and instructional practices.

847. Mottershead, Noel Francis. "A Comparative Study of World Movements in Adult Education." University of California, Berkeley, 1949. 436 pp.

848. Murase, Kenneth. "International Students in Education for Social Work: An Assessment of the Educational Experience by International Graduates of Schools of Social Work in North America, 1948–1957." Columbia University, 1961. 371 pp. D.S.W. Micro. no. 61-1083. Source: *Diss. Abst.* XXII, no. 2 (1961), 673–674.

The study seeks to determine whether social work education is relevant to the needs of an underdeveloped country. Questionnaires were returned from 225 students with a favorable reply.

849. Myers, Noel Thomas. "Characteristics of Most and Least Effective International Cooperation Administration Educators Serving Overseas." Indiana University, 1961. 175 pp. Ed.D. Micro. no. 61-3218. Source: *Diss. Abst.* XXII, no. 4 (1961), 1071–1072.

The author obtained data from field supervisors of the characteristics of successful and unsuccessful personnel. Findings revealed success or failure depended very much on personal characteristics. Long experience in teaching and advanced degrees were not factors in determining success or failure.

850. Nash, Sister Mary Louise. "A Study of Adjustment Problems of Sister Students from Kerala, India, Attending Liberal Arts Colleges in the United States." The Catholic University of America, 1963. 133 pp. Ph.D. Micro. no. 64-399. Source: *Diss. Abst.* XXIV, no. 6 (1963), 2364.

Author, through personal interviews and questionnaire, determined that students had great difficulty in adapting to Western spiritual ideas.

851. Orellana, Marina. "Possible Contributions of Educational Thought and Practice in America to Vocational Education in Chile." Smith College, 1942. 148 pp.

852. Orr, Paul G. "Binational Education and United States Related Schools in Latin America." Michigan State University, 1963. Source: *Diss. Abst.* XXIV, no. 13 (1963–1964), 60.

853. Patterson, Charles J. "A Comparison of Performances of Mexican and American Children in a Bicultural Setting on Measures of Ability, Achievement and Adjustment." Michigan State University, 1960. Source: *Diss. Abst. Index* XX, no. 13 (1959–1960), 65.

854. Pavri, Dina Mehervanji. "A Study of the Scholastic Achievement and Related Problems of Foreign Graduate Students at the University of Virginia from 1957–1961." University of Virginia, 1963. 134 pp. Ed.D. Micro. no. 64-688. Source: *Diss. Abst.* XXIV, no. 6 (1963), 2327–2328.

Through records of the university and submission of questionnaire to the students, author described academic achievement of students and factors related to success or failure.

855. Porter, John Wilson. "The Development of an Inventory to Determine the Problems of Foreign Students." Michigan State University, 1962. 271 pp. Micro. no. 63-1749. Source: *Diss. Abst.* XXIII, no. 10 (1963), 3783.

Foreign and American students completed the Michigan International Student Problem Inventory with the result that the inventory was verified to be able to differentiate between foreign and U.S. students, and that the inventory can be used to help foreign students.

856. Porter, Robert Dickey. "A Personnel Survey of 1,105 Foreign Students at the University of Washington." University of Washington, 1962. 234 pp. Ph.D. Micro. no. 63-4437. Source: *Diss. Abst.* XXIV, no. 1 (1963), 164.

Author used grade point, earning of a degree, and freedom from academic warnings to establish academic success of foreign students. The study supported the conclusion that foreign students generally had higher academic levels than American students.

857. Rempel, Averno Milton. "Studies of the Role of the State University of Iowa in World Affairs: I. Foreign Students Relationships; II. Certain Variables Involved in the Development of International Understanding." State University of Iowa, 1954. 405 pp. Univ. Micro. no. 7,012. Source: *Diss. Abst.* XV (April 1955), 519–520.

858. Salas Díaz, Darío Enrique. "A Comparative Study of the Normal Schools of the United States and Chile." New York University, 1907. 88 pp.

A Chilean educator compares these institutions in terms of admission pattern, academic training, professional courses in Education, preparation and effectiveness of normal school staffs, student life, organization and administration, and teachers' salaries. Concludes with comments on what Chile can learn from U.S. normal schools.

859. Santos, Antusa Perez. "A Study of the Problems Faced by Foreign Students at Indiana University with Implications for Action." Indiana University, 1959. 205 pp. Ed.D. Micro. no. 59-6587. Source: *Diss. Abst.* XX, no. 9 (1960), 3580–3581.

Data were collected from both questionnaire and personal interview. Indiana University personal services approximate those available in other universities. Study revealed financial, social, and academic problems are the most frequent problems, while personal and religious problems are the least frequent. Recommended more complete advisory service and better facilities for teaching English.

860. Schuiteman, Robert Allen. "A Study of Colombian Nationals Who Attended Collegiate Institutions in the United States." Ph.D. University of Michigan, 1957. 279 pp. Univ. Micro. no. 53-986. Source: *Diss. Abst.* XVIII (1958), 1308–1309.

The purpose of the study was to assess opinions of 116 Colombian alumni of U.S. colleges about their experiences in America and their readjustment to Colombian life. Findings revealed a generally favorable reaction to living and studying in the U.S. although racial prejudice and discrimination made a bad impression. Those questioned had readjusted well and attained a higher professional status in Colombia. Their attitudes will contribute positively to feelings toward the U.S. and international good will.

861. Seguel, Leopoldo F. "Proposals for the Foundations of a State Program of Instructional Improvement in the Elementary Schools of Chile." Teachers College, Columbia University, 1942. 78 pp.

Chapters on social and educational trends in Chile, analysis of an important curriculum program in Virginia (c. 1930) as it might aid Chile, and instructional leadership in the state department of elementary education in Chile.

862. Semmes, Sister Catherine. "The Teaching of English to Foreign-Born Students." Fordham University, 1931. Source: Eells, p. 216.

863. Skinner, Maynard Clyde. "The Foreign Student Advisors' Office: Practices, Problems, and Procedures in Selected Colleges and Universities." University of Colorado, 1963. 245 pp. Ed.D. Micro. no. 64-1944. Source: *Diss. Abst.* XXIV, no. 9 (1964), 3597.

Traces earliest foreign student advisor to 1907. Evaluates effectiveness of the foreign student advisor. Attempts to gain insights into foreign student problems and policies in American higher education.

864. Smith, Hayden Richard. "The Effectiveness of Two Instructional Procedures in Comparative Education." University of Michigan, 1957. 157 pp. Univ. Micro. no. 58-996. Source: *Diss. Abst.* XVIII (April 1958), 1309–1310.

At the University of Michigan this study was conducted to discover the relative effectiveness of two teaching methods in producing desirable changes in attitudes toward a UNESCO fundamental education project. While the control group received no special instruction, one experimental group had a lecture and discussion on the Fundamental Education Center in Patzcuaro, Mexico; the other experimental group had a film and discussion about the same UNESCO center. Attitudes were tested by the Remmers Generalized Attitude Scale before and after instruction and again two and a half months later. Statistically significant attitude changes which persisted were found in the film group. No significant changes resulted in the total lecture group.

865. Stevens, Thomas Carl. "The Construction of a Questionnaire for International Alumni Follow-up." Indiana University, 1963. 69 pp. Micro. no. 64-5143. Source: *Diss. Abst.* XXIV, no. 12 (1964), 5151-5152.

Author completed a questionnaire to establish the framework of a formal program of continuing relations with returned foreign students.

866. Stidham, Kathryn Healey. "The Foreign Student in an American Metropolis." University of Chicago, 1929. 127 pp.

867. Stine, Dorothy Pearce. "The Role of the United States in International Educational Exchange of Teachers and Students." University of Houston, 1954. 379 pp. Univ. Micro. no. 9,676. Source: *Diss. Abst.* XIV, no. 10 (1954), 1609-1610.

868. Stoker, Spencer Longshore. "A Study of International Education." Stanford University, 1931. 243 pp. Source: Stanford University, *Abstracts of Dissertations* (1930-1931), 60-65.

869. Stout, Kenneth Deane. "International Teacher Exchange Programs Under the Fulbright Act." University of Tennessee, 1956. 187 pp.

870. Sudhalter, David Lewis. "The Political and Psychological Indoctrination of School Children in the U.S.S.R." Boston University, 1962. Source: *Index to American Doctoral Dissertations,* p. 179.

871. Tappert, Esther Elizabeth. "International Intellectual and Cultural Cooperation between Two Wars: A Study of the Development of the Concept and Its Propagation under the Auspices of the League of Nations." Yale University, 1946. 316 pp.

872. Terman, Earle Luther. "The Development and Application of National Educational Survey Techniques with Special Emphasis on Criteria for Measuring Intelligence Internationally." New York University, 1930. 83 pp.

873. Vaswani, Hari Valiran. "A Study of the Problems of Foreign Students at the Berkeley Campus of the University of California." University of California, Berkeley, 1950. 165 pp.

Questionnaires from 448 foreign students elicited these recommendations: (1) proper placement in desired fields of study; (2) practical training after completion of academic studies; (3) housing in organized living groups or if possible in American homes; (4) help in language, reading, study, and financial problems.

874. Weary, Bettina. "Occupational Differentials in the Perceptions and Opinions of Foreign Students." The American University, 1960. 161 pp. Ph.D. Micro. no. 60-2477. Source: *Diss. Abst.* XXI, no. 1 (1960), 259-260.

Through questionnaire study attempted to prove that difference in attitudes toward Americans was the result of occupational differences rather than differences of national background. Studies of students from four political areas and four occupational fields revealed differences to be of occupational origin.

875. Wee, Joo Liat. "A Study of Students from Other Lands Who Received Master's Degrees in Educational Administration from Teachers College, Columbia University, 1950-1962." Columbia University, 1963. 224 pp. Ed.D. Micro. no. 64-7212. Source: *Diss. Abst.* XXV, no. 1 (1964), 259-260.

Author studied the academic records of foreign students to determine success of services offered by the institution. He recommended financial help and provision of advisors to discover reasons for lack of achievement and to provide help.

876. Westmeyer, Troy Rudolf. "Administration of the New York University–Ankara Project: A Case Study in Technical Assistance." New York University, 1963. 384 pp. Ph.D. Micro. no. 64-1788. Source: *Diss. Abst.* XXIV, no. 9 (1963), 3830.

877. Wolf, Frank Edward. "The Cultural Surrogate in International Relations: A Case Study of the Role of a Fulbright Teacher of Science Education from the United States in Bassein, Burma, for a One-Year Program." New York University, 1956. 223 pp. Univ. Micro. no. 20,007. Source: *Diss. Abst.* XVII, no. 12 (December 1957), 2889–2890.

878. Yieh, Tsung-Kao. "The Adjustment Problems of Chinese Graduate Students in American Universities." University of Chicago, 1934. ii, 127 pp.

879. Young, George Patrick, Jr. "A Study of the Potential for the Achievement of Better Inter-American Relationships Through North American Schools in Latin America." University of Illinois, 1960. 154 pp. Ed.D. Micro. no. 61-222. Source: *Diss. Abst.* XXI, no. 10 (1961), 3153.

The author gathered information through questionnaire, from thirty-seven schools in Latin America, about the objectives of the schools. Replies indicated the objectives to be promoting friendship, knowledge and respect for participating countries, cultures; and demonstration of U.S. methods of instruction. The study concluded that the schools are not fulfilling these objectives.

MASTER'S THESES

(Alphabetically by Author)

880. Addison, Winford Dewey. "The Educational Activities of Kiwanis International." University of Chicago, 1930. 200 pp.

881. Athearn, Clarence Royalty. "A World Educational Association to Promote International Good Will." Boston University, 1924.

882. Blair, Ruth Margaret. "The System of Education in Germany for the American Exchange Teacher." Oregon State College, 1954. 98 pp.

883. Cull, Alan Clive Kenyon. "A History and Exposition of a Student International Exchange Project between Central School, Yankton, South Dakota, and Caversham Secondary Modern School, Reading, England." University of South Dakota, 1955. 270 pp.

884. Dankers, Marion E. "A Study of the Development of Inter-American Understanding: An Educational Challenge." Claremont Graduate School, 1943. 94 pp.

885. Dolliver, Edith Nicholson. "The Treatment of International Ethics in Some Recent Textbooks on Ethics." Boston University, 1930. 196 pp.

886. Dunson, Charles Edward. "An Investigation of Teacher Adjustment to Exchange Positions between the United States and Great Britain." University of Southern California, 1951. 118 pp.

887. Edelman, Nathan. "A Translation of J. L. Claparede's 'The Teaching of History and the International Spirit,' with a Translator's Introduction on the Bearing of the International Spirit on History Instruction." College of the City of New York, 1934. 140 pp. Source: *Abstracts of Theses (1923–1939)*, p. 75.

888. Endres, Mildred Swaney. "World Citizenship and the Role of the School in Its Development." Allegheny College, 1951. 60 pp.

889. Fenn, William P. "The Use of Schools for American Children in the Far East for Education in Internationalism." New York University, 1928. 90 pp.

890. Folsom, Morrill Gabriel. "Cultural Interrelations of India, Japan, and the West." University of Denver, 1947. 97 pp.

891. Hawkins, Effie Izah. "Recent Progress in Educational Reorganization in Selected World States." Stanford University, 1923. 107 pp.

892. Hensel, Joan Elizabeth. "Inter-American Intellectual Cooperation." Clark University, 1940. 194 pp. Source: *Abstracts of Dissertations and Theses* (1940), pp. 39–91.

893. Hess, Lelah Christina. "Intellectual Cooperation between the United States and Latin America." Ohio State University, 1938. 94 pp.

894. Ho, Thomas C. K. "An Analysis of Current Concepts and Activities in International Education." Catholic University of America, 1950. 56 pp.

895. Klavon, Sister Mary Viola. "An Analysis of the Leiter International Performance Scale." Catholic University of America, 1943. 41 pp.

896. Lambie, Margaret. "International Treaties, Conventions, and Agreements Affecting the Practice of the Teaching Professions by Aliens." American University, 1928. 130 pp.

897. Latshaw, Mary Lewers. "Interchange of Teachers." George Washington University, 1938. 122 pp.

898. Lit, Mark David. "International Organizations with an Educational Program for World Peace." University of Southern California, 1950. 89 pp.

899. Lloyd, Everett T. "The Place of International Student Correspondence in Modern Language Teaching." College of the City of New York, 1937. 128 pp. Source: *Abstracts of Theses (1923–1939)*, p. 100.

900. McClimans, Grace Bell. "The Program of the United States Government for the Interchange of Students." Stanford University, 1949. 67 pp.

901. McGrath, Ellen Marie. "Why International Organization for Education?" Boston University, 1949. 142 pp.

902. Negi, Lakshmi Singh. "Teaching for International Understanding between India and the United States." University of Southern California, 1952. 77 pp.

903. Nettings, Dena. "Projects That May Contribute to Christian Internationalism in High Schools under the Board of Foreign Missions of the Presbyterian Church in the United States of America." Presbyterian College of Christian Education, 1938. 144 pp.

904. Nutt, Merle Caro. "Education for International Understanding through Rotary International." State University of Iowa, 1954. 266 pp.

905. Philleo, Helen Isabelle. "The Work of the Fourth, Fifth, Sixth, and Seventh Pan-American Conferences in the Economic, Social, and Intellectual Fields." University of Wisconsin, 1938. 245 pp.

906. Pickett, Douglas Robinson. "Some Selected Principles of Understanding Human Behavior and Their Application to Program Development in Foreign Cultures." Cornell University, 1958. 62 pp.

907. Rollins, William Bert, Jr. "The Exchange of Teachers Between the United States and Great Britain, 1946–47." University of California, Los Angeles, 1949. 86 pp.

908. Schrader, Arthur F. "The International Institute as an Intercultural Educational Agency." University of Buffalo, 1957. 115 pp.

909. Sheldon, Albert Bradley. "The Development of International Education." Columbia University, 1914. 37 pp.

910. Takayama, William Kiyoshi. "Some Fundamental Factors and Principles Underlying Education in Nationalism and Internationalism in Japan." Columbia University, 1918. 62 pp.

911. Vangsnes, Johannes. "The United National Appeal for Children: An Experiment in International Organization." Columbia University, 1949. 138 pp.

912. Ward, Phyllis Anne. "The International Exchange of Students as a Project to Promote International Understanding." Stanford University, 1947. 114 pp.

913. Weiner, Merveyn M. "Leaves of Absence for Overseas Teaching." San Francisco State College, 1958.

914. White, William Berry. "A Student Travel Plan to Promote International Good Will." Stanford University, 1947. 75 pp.

915. Young, Beula Lavon. "Building International Friendships through the Study of Intercultural Relationships." New Jersey State College, Newark, 1958. 85 pp.